The Guide to SQL Server

The Guide to SQL Server

ALOKE NATH

Addison-Wesley Publishing Company, Inc.
Reading, Massachusetts Menlo Park, California New York
Don Mills, Ontario Wokingham, England Amsterdam Bonn
Sydney Singapore Tokyo Madrid San Juan

Library of Congress Cataloging-in-Publication Data

Nath, Aloke.
The guide to SQL Server / Aloke Nath.
p. cm.
Includes bibliographical references and index.
ISBN 0-201-52336-1
1. Data base management. 2. SQL server. I. Title.
QA76.9.D3N384 1990
005.75'6–dc20 90-46499
CIP

Set in 11-point Century Schoolbook by Impressions Publishing Services

ABCDEFGHIJ-MW-943210

First Printing, December 1990

To my parents

Contents

Appendixes

Foreword

The age of client/server computing on microcomputer-based systems is here! The rapid growth of computing power on the desktop and the availability of sophisticated multi-user operating systems have brought mainframe relational database power to the PC. *The Guide to SQL Server* introduces SYBASE SQL Server, a high performance, multi-user relational database management system. Based on experience with the Microsoft SQL Server, the book shows how SQL Server's sophisticated client/server architecture can enable your PC to run your entire business. Microsoft SQL Server currently supports DOS, Windows, and OS/2 client workstations.

The Guide to SQL Server helps the user meet the challenges posed by this powerful new technology. PC users who are unfamiliar with client/server technology and relational databases are exposed to these concepts and their underlying theory. Users are also introduced to SQL Server's features, operation, and administration so they can use it effectively.

After an introduction to local area networks and client/server computing, *The Guide to SQL Server* details SQL Server database management—including data definition, manipulation, and administration. The book serves as a comprehensive introduction that shows how SQL Server's rich feature set can provide a platform for mission-critical application development.

This is the first commercially available guide that focuses exclusively on SQL Server. The book therefore also acts as a reference for users already familiar with the SYBASE SQL Server on other platforms. The Sybase products for OS/2 are 100% compatible with the SYBASE system on VAX, Sun, and other platforms. This means that our customers can develop their applications on any of several hardware platforms and then scale those applications, without any additional programming, to other hardware platforms we support.

The Guide to SQL Server discusses TRANSACT-SQL, the Sybase enhanced version of standard SQL, and covers system administration and performance tuning aspects of the Server. Since the Server spans a wide range of platforms, it provides an enterprise-wise, comprehensive data management solution. Thus, everyone from PC workgroups to mini and mainframe users can learn how to use this new and powerful DBMS effectively.

Like the high performance SQL Server, *The Guide to SQL Server* can save you time. In addition to explaining the basic concepts, it carefully distills information that spans several volumes of manuals, and often provides valuable insights into the architecture and inner workings of SQL Server. The book uses the same example database that is shipped with the Server, so that users can try the examples provided. And you'll find a summary of TRANSACT-SQL syntax and a glossary of common terms.

For a handy guide to new users, and as a comprehensive backup reference for more advanced users, follow *The Guide to SQL Server.*

Robert S. Epstein
Executive Vice President
Sybase, Inc.

Preface

In the world of hardware and software every so often there comes a product that sparks the interest of the user community. Often this is because the product is based on revolutionary or significantly enhanced technology. However, often these products are of interest simply because they represent a level of functionality hitherto unknown for that type of product. Eventually some of these products have gone on to become extremely successful, and in many cases they have become the de facto standard by which all products in that category are judged. Lotus in the spreadsheet market, UNIX in the OS area, and the Macintosh for graphical user interfaces are just a few examples.

In the world of relational database management systems, SQL Server is such a product. Although it is far from dominant in the industry at the present time, it is already receiving a lot of attention from corporate users and the press. It is not "just another relational DBMS"; its architecture, features, and implementation really do set SQL Server apart from its competitors.

What then is SQL Server? It is a high performance, SQL-based, relational database server developed specifically for distributed transaction processing environments. It was developed originally for the Unix and VMS environments on minicomputers by Sybase, Inc., in 1986. Since then it has been ported selectively to a wide variety of minicomputer and mainframe environments, including Stratus, Sun, and SEQUENT computers, and is now available on several different platforms. Today the SYBASE SQL Server is acknowledged as the leading RDBMS vendor for transaction processing applications. However, until recently, SQL Server was largely excluded from microcomputer environments, primarily because of hardware restrictions, memory limits, and the lack of Operating System capabilities to support such sophisticated software needs.

With the release of powerful new 386 and 486 personal computer machines, the proliferation of PC local area networks, and the introduction of Microsoft's multitasking operating system OS/2, all that changed. In April 1989, with the help of microcomputer heavyweights like Microsoft and Ashton-Tate, SQL Server was ported to the OS/2 environment and, for the first time, the power and features of SQL Server became available to PC LAN users. This book discusses the functionality of the microsoft SQL Server as implemented in Version 1.0.

I for one am excited to be associated with this product and have decided to do my best to express in writing its capabilities, features, and principles for the benefit of the user community. Who are the users who would benefit from this knowledge? First there are PC users who have been exposed to LANs for the purpose of sharing devices and files. SQL Server brought them a level of sophistication and capability heretofore found only in mini and mainframe environments. Even SQL, as a language, surfaced in the microcomputer world only a few years ago. There is, clearly, a large knowledge gap to be filled.

Second are users who are already familiar with the technology, or with the other SQL-based Servers that have surfaced in the last few years. For them the specifics of SQL Server are still interesting—if not for any other reason than SQL Server's special features that set it apart—user-defined types, triggers, and stored procedures are just a few. Understanding the inner workings of SQL Server—how and why it works the way it does—is another reason the curious user may want to learn more about SQL Server.

Third are users in other environments who may be interested in learning about SQL Server in the PC LAN environment.

Although such details as installation and network environment differ on different platforms, the SQL Server product is essentially the same in all environments. With multivendor, heterogenous solutions becoming more and more common, it is quite possible that a variety of front-end clients, running DOS, OS/2, UNIX, or Macintosh, will be accessing different back-end SQL Servers (running under OS/2, UNIX, VMS, and so on). Intellectual curiosity about SQL Server could well turn into practical advantage.

This book hopes to address the issues outlined. It is aimed at a wide range of users, including consultants, administrators, developers, and managers who have varying degrees of exposure to relational database servers. It includes users of workstation DBMSs such as dBASE and Paradox and users who may have knowledge of the SYBASE SQL Server on other platforms. In light of this potential audience, deciding what topics to include in and omit from the book was no easy task. The basic assumption I have made about the readers is that they have had some level of exposure to databases and LANs, but not necessarily relational systems or database server technology.

In addition, even though SQL Server has been available in the minicomputer arena for some time, there has been no book published about it (to the best of my knowledge). Since the Server specifics are the same, users of the SYBASE SQL Server on other platforms can use the book to gain some understanding of what SQL Server is all about.

The book is not, and does not intend to be, a language reference guide, in the sense that it does not cover every nuance of each TRANSACT-SQL command. Rather, it covers the material in depth sufficient to clarify the concepts and usage of the feature or command being explained. It is not an SQL language book; in fact, there are some excellent books on the subject listed in the bibliography. Finally, although the programming interface (DB-LIBRARY) and some operational aspects are covered, the book does not serve as a programmer's or administrator's guide.

Structure and Overview

The chapters of the book fall into three general areas. Chapter 1 and Chapter 2 cover concepts and basics of relational databases, networks, and database servers. For more advanced users, these chapters can easily be skipped. Chapters 3 through 9 discuss architecture, language implementation, and features of SQL Server. These are of particular interest to the end users, database designers and consultants. Finally, Chapters 10 through 12 discuss the operational aspects of the Server—installation, administration, and troubleshooting. These chapters are for administrators especially, although other users may find them interesting. In addition, the book provides related appendixes and a glossary of terms.

Throughout the book, when new terms are introduced, they are in bold type and are defined for the reader's benefit (for example, **interprocess communication**). In many cases, although the term may be a common one, it is defined to ensure that my usage of the term within the book is understood by the reader. These terms can also be found in the glossary. When SQL statements are discussed, the syntax and semantics of the statement are provided within the text. This is what a sample of syntax looks like:

Syntax

```
sp_bindrule <rule>, <object> [,FUTUREONLY]
```

Examples that the user can try out are provided from the sample *pubs* database that comes with the SQL Server package. For more advanced features, several examples are provided, which help to explain the concept or usage. The appendices provide the complete SQL syntax and the structure and content of the *pubs* database. This is what an example looks like:

Example 9-8

```
use empdb
<exec>
sp_adduser jackm, jack
<exec>

use pubs
<exec>
sp_adduser jackm, jack
<exec>
```

```
OUTPUT:

New user added.
New user added.
```

With examples, the user must be in the right database to execute the statements. This is accomplished by issuing the appropriate USE statement as shown above. In most cases the USE statement is not indicated explicitly; it is assumed that the user is in the correct database. Often several statements must be entered in sequence to accomplish a task. Sometimes they can be executed together; at other times they must be executed separately. Execution of one or more statements is indicated by using the ⟨exec⟩ notation as in the example above. Depending on the client application used the exact command needed to execute the query could vary. The exact commands are discussed in Chapter 3. If a single statement is to be executed the ⟨exec⟩ is assumed and omitted for clarity.

In general, lowercase is used for the names of database objects (columns, tables, databases, and so on), aliases, data types, filenames, group names, login IDs, database options, and passwords. If the server is installed as a case-sensitive server, the items will be case-sensitive.

The following is an overview of the book by chapter.

Chapter 1: Concepts and Basics. This chapter discusses the basics of relational database management systems and relational database languages.

Chapter 2: Local Area Networks, Client/Server Computing, and Database Servers. Chapter 2 provides background information on local area networks and client/server computing.

Chapter 3: Architectural Overview. Chapter 3 provides a high-level architectural overview of SQL Server, its salient features, and its client components. It discusses TRANSACT-SQL (the Server's version of SQL) and the various enhancements it provides over standard SQL.

Chapter 4: Data Definition. Chapter 4 discusses the Server environment and the creation, destruction, and alteration of the basic database objects within SQL Server.

Chapter 5: Data Retrieval. This chapter discusses data retrieval using the SELECT statement. It discusses the various optional clauses on the SELECT statement and advanced queries using joins and subqueries.

Chapter 6: Data Modification. This chapter discusses data modification statements. The concepts of implicit and explicit transactions are presented. Finally, control-of-flow language statements in TRANSACT-SQL are discussed.

Chapter 7: Views and Procedures. Chapter 7 examines two database objects, procedures and views, in depth.

Chapter 8: Integrity Features. This chapter describes the rationale of Server-based integrity and explains the integrity features of the Server, many of which are unique. These include user-defined types, rules, defaults, and triggers.

Chapter 9: Security. Chapter 9 talks about SQL Server's security features. The chapter discusses the various user authentication schemes and the user hierarchy. It discusses the two kinds of permissions that can be assigned and how to assign or revoke them within TRANSACT-SQL. Finally, it discusses how views and stored procedures can be used as security mechanisms.

Chapter 10: Installation and Storage Management. This chapter talks about installation and maintenance of the storage on the Server. It also talks about transferring large amounts of data in and out of the system.

Chapter 11: Data Consistency and Recovery. Chapter 11 discusses the importance of data consistency in light of concurrent transactions and system failures, and how it is achieved. The concept of distributed transactions is introduced, and recovery from media failures is discussed. Finally, the Database Consistency Checker is discussed.

Chapter 12: Tuning the Server. The final chapter talks about tuning and troubleshooting the Server. Tuning can be achieved at the levels of the individual query, the database, or the entire Server. Some common Server problems, their causes, and solutions are outlined.

Appendix A: This appendix is a fact sheet on SQL Server. It discusses minimum hardware and software requirements, software versions, and various database limits (such as maximum table size, maximum number of tables that can be joined, and so on).

Appendix B: This appendix presents the complete syntax for all the TRANSACT-SQL statements and system procedures.

Appendix C: This appendix gives the structure and contents of the sample pubs database that is used throughout the book in the examples. The script to create the database is also included.

Appendix D: Appendix D presents the structure of the system tables, in both the master and other databases.

A glossary and a bibliography are also included.

Acknowledgments

I would like to thank everyone who has contributed to making this book possible. In particular, I would like to thank Tony Lima and Robert Persinger for reviewing the text and offering suggestions for improving the book; Sandy Emerson and the Server Development Group at Sybase for keeping me honest; Julie Stillman and Elizabeth Grose at Addison-Wesley for keeping the pressure on and being understanding when unusual circumstances arose; and last but not least, I would like to thank my family for all the moral support and encouragement they have provided.

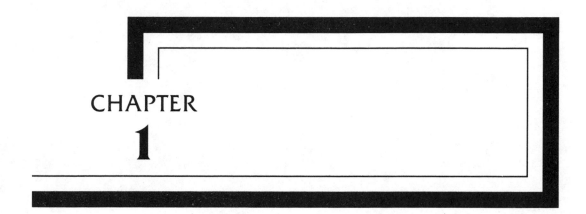

CHAPTER 1

Concepts and Basics

Introduction

With any product it is necessary to understand the theoretical and conceptual foundation on which it is based in order to appreciate its capabilities. This is certainly true with Structured Query Language (SQL) Server. SQL Server represents a new class of product—it is a relational database server that encompasses many different technologies that are still evolving: relational database management systems, local area networks, and client-server computing. The primary focus of this chapter is a discussion of the relevant concepts behind these technologies. This chapter (and the next) lays the foundation for understanding the subject of this book. It is for readers who have little or no familiarity with these concepts. Readers who are already familiar with the material presented here can go on to Chapter 2 or Chapter 3 without losing continuity.

What is SQL Server and what are the concepts and technologies relevant to it? The first part of the question has already been answered in the introduction. It is, very simply, an SQL-based, relational database server intended for transaction processing environments. SQL Server is based on client/server architecture which divides processing into two components—a front-end, or client component, and a back-end, or server component. SQL Server itself constitutes the back-end database server, with which many different front-end client applications communicate, typically over a local area network (LAN).

The second part of the question has an answer that is based on the answer to the first part. A database server means a database management system (DBMS) based on the client/server model and intended primarily for use in local area network environments. A relational DBMS is one that conforms to the relational data model and provides a set-oriented database language. SQL is such a language, and in fact, the predominant database language used in relational systems today. At the very least then, the concepts and technologies to be covered are relational DBMSs, SQL, LANs, and the client/server architecture.

It was stated earlier that the focus of the book is SQL Server in the microcomputer environment. The discussions in the first two chapters will be skewed toward that focus. Some theoretical concepts are introduced, but this is kept to a minimum. In most cases, the concepts behind the theory are explained in simple terms. The correlation between theoretical and commonly used terms is made, when necessary.

Data, Databases, and Database Management Systems

At the risk of being too elementary, this section begins by discussing some simple concepts—data, databases, and database management systems. This will at least ensure that we have the same understanding of terms used in the book.

Data

Data, simply defined, are nothing more than facts about entities. **Entities** are very general and represent any object or thing that is identifiable. You can capture facts about entities—they are places, individuals, corporations, events, and so on. For example, the fact that Mary's height is sixty-seven inches is a piece of data. The fact (height = 67″) is datum about an entity (the person Mary). If we say that the cost of an automobile is $20,000, we are using automobile as an entity.

A way to understand these concepts is to examine a simple example. Let us take a book, *Frank's Long Journey Home*, ISBN 0-200-00000-9, written by Bill Smith in 1989, which is 687 pages long and published by Addison-Wesley. The book itself (the thing) is an entity, about which there are certain facts—*Frank's Long Journey Home* (its title), 0-200-00000-9 (ISBN), Bill Smith (its author), 1989 (its year of publication), 687 pages (length), and Addison-Wesley (its publisher). Each of these facts about the entity describes certain **attributes** of the entity, such as title, ISBN, author, year of publication, length, and publisher. That is, books may be described in terms of these attributes, and this particular book is described in terms of these particular facts about it. Figure 1-1 illustrates the concepts of entity and attribute.

An entity can be associated with one or more entities. Such associations are termed **relationships**. For example, the book

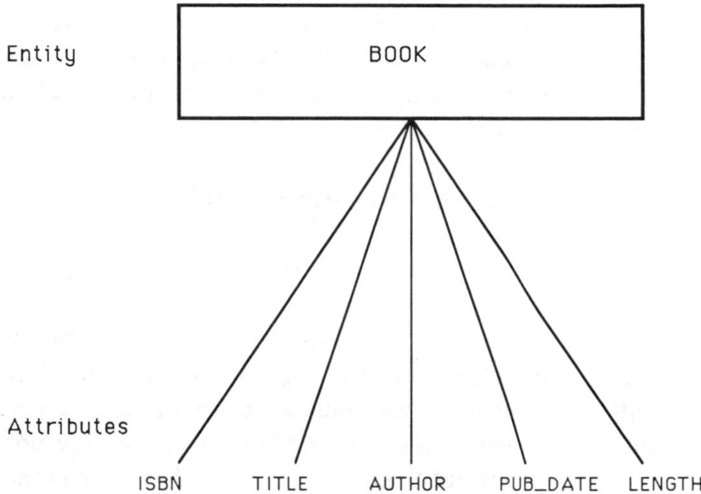

FIGURE 1-1 Entities and Attributes

entity may be related to the store entity through the relationship "sold by." In this case only two entities are related; this is said to be a binary relationship. The classification of entities, attributes, and relationships is somewhat subjective–there is no hard and fast rule for deciding what is one or the other. For example, author was just used as an attribute of the book entity, but author can be considered an entity with attributes such as name, address, and phone. In this case book is related to author through the relationship "is authored by."

Entities are related to other entities in a variety of ways. For example, a book can have only one publisher, but a publisher can publish several books. This is termed the **cardinality** of the relationship "publishes." The different kinds of relationships possible are:

- One-to-one: There is no example of this kind of relationship between the entities discussed.
- One-to-many: Each publisher publishes many books; however, each book is published by only one publisher. The relationship "publishes" between publisher and book is one-to-many.

- Many-to-many: An author may have authored several books, and a book may have many authors. The relationship "authors" between author and book is many-to-many.

Figure 1-2 illustrates the kinds of relationships that exist between these entities.

Certain attributes serve as unique identifiers of an entity. For example, a social security number is unique to an individual; an ISBN is unique to a book. These are called **key attributes.** While it is helpful in locating a book to know that it is 687 pages long, this piece of data does not uniquely identify a book. Nor does the title uniquely identify a book; it is entirely possible—although unlikely—for more than one book to share the same title. However, a book's ISBN number sufficiently identifies it, because each ISBN number is unique. A book's ISBN attribute is a key attribute.

Databases

Databases serve two primary purposes. One is to capture data about entities and relationships. The other purpose is to provide information to users of the database. A **database**, more formally defined, is a shared, integrated collection, or repository, of data. The two words that should be stressed in the definition of a database

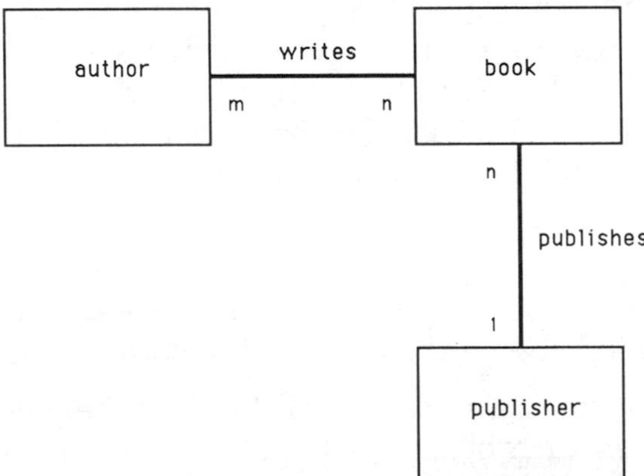

FIGURE 1-2 Relationships

are shared and integrated. Shared means that several users can access the data within the database concurrently. Integrated means the partial or complete removal of redundancy (the same information recorded more than once). In terms of this definition, the employee phone and location directory stored in a file on your PC is, strictly speaking, not a database—it is not shared and may, in fact, exist on several other PCs. When this same information is stored centrally on a corporate computer that is accessible to many employees, it constitutes a database.

Database Management Systems

Now that you understand what data and databases are, let us talk about database management systems. A DBMS is the software that manages the storage of and access to the data in databases. It is really an automated computer-based information management system. The word management encompasses several functions that include security, concurrency, and recovery. Users and programs access and store data by interacting with the DBMS, as is shown in Figure 1-3.

Most DBMS has some internal way of physically storing the data on storage devices. How the data are physically organized on the disks, how they are accessed, and so on are dealt with at the **internal level** of the database. The DBMS is responsible for insulating the application or user (to varying degrees) from the intricacies of the internal level and presenting a simple, logical view

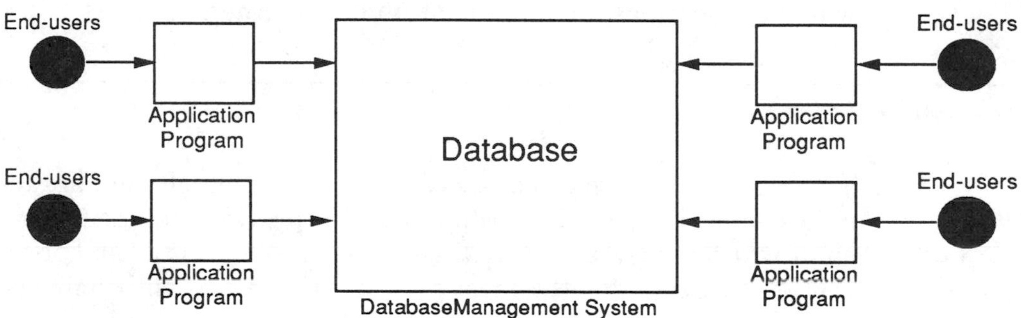

FIGURE 1-3 A simplified view of a DBMS

of the data. The **conceptual level** is where the logical or conceptual view is presented. A major goal of most DBMSs is to provide **physical data independence**. The underlying changes in the storage and access mechanisms at the internal level do not affect the applications that use the data.

To reiterate, DBMSs have at least two views of the data—the conceptual view, which is the logical view for the users, and the internal view, which is closest to the physical organization of the data. The DBMS is responsible for mapping a user request at the conceptual level to a request to get data at the physical level. Often, there is a third level, termed the **external level**, which is where a logical view of the data is presented an individual user.

The terms used here—external, conceptual, physical—are by no means universal. Several other terms are used to describe the same concepts—user view, logical structure, physical structure; subschema, schema, physical schema; and so on. In the following discussion I will try to equate comparable terms.

Every DBMS has a **data dictionary** (also called a catalog), which is used to record information about its databases and database objects. The dictionary is actually a database itself—it contains data about the actual data. This information is referred to as **metadata**, and the dictionary is sometimes referred to as a **metadatabase**. The dictionary contains information about the objects, the various levels in the DBMS, and the mappings between them. In many cases, this information is also maintained in some processed or compiled form for efficiency. A comprehensive data dictionary may also include information about the usage of the data, for example, which programs refer to which tables or columns, or which applications are dependent on one another.

Data Models

The first section discussed the elements about which data are recorded—entities and relationships. DBMSs provide two distinct levels at which to view and store these data—the conceptual and physical levels. Users, for the most part, are concerned with only the logical or conceptual view of the data, since it is at this level that they interact with the DBMS.

The conceptual view of the data, which is the user view, is based on a model, the **database model**. The database model defines the way in which entities, attributes, and relationships can logically be structured. Mapping from the conceptual level to the physical level is the responsibility of the DBMS; it provides physical data independence. Normally, the same data model is used for the external view as for the conceptual view, except that the view the individual user sees may be a subset of the entire conceptual view.

Three data models—the hierarchical, network, and relational models—have been used by various DBMSs in the past few decades. The next section will briefly explain the basic ideas behind the hierarchic and network models. The relational model, on which SQL Server is is based, will then be examined more closely.

Hierarchical and Network Models

The **hierarchical model** is based on the idea of a hierarchy, a concept we encounter every day. For example, the organization of most corporations is hierarchical: corporation, divisions, departments, and employees. In the hierarchical model, entities and relationships must be modeled in the form of a tree. For example, the publisher, book, and author entities can be organized in a hierarchy as shown in Figure 1-4.

The hierarchical model has some restrictions. First, because of the superior and subordinate nature of entities, it is not possible to record information about a book, without first recording its publisher information. That is, the book only exists in the context of the publisher. Second, a child entity can only be related to one parent entity, a restriction imposed by the tree structure. For example, it is not possible to define a stores entity at the publishers level, even though it is related to books in the same way publishers is. The third restriction, which follows from the first, prevents any subordinate entity from being related to an entity more than one level up the hierarchy. For example, an author cannot be related to publishers.

Hierarchical systems model one-to-one and one-to-many relationships naturally, in that each instance of a superior entity can be related to zero or more subordinate entity instances. However, many-to-many relationships are difficult to represent directly.

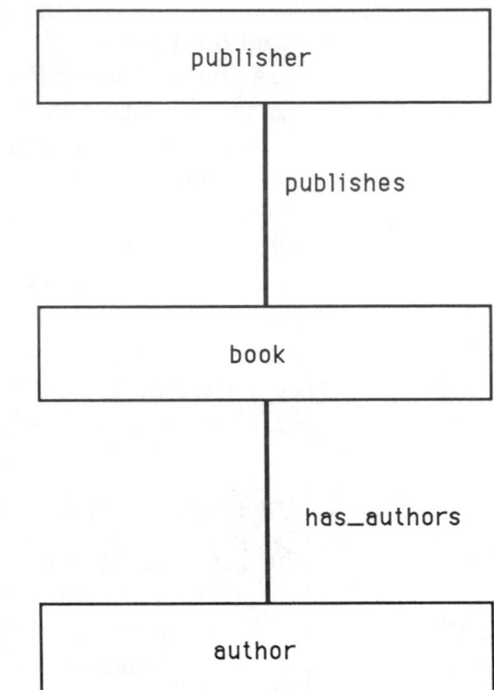

FIGURE 1-4
A hierarchical view of the *pubs* database

For example, the relationship between books and authors is really many-to-many, not the one-to-many relationship demanded by the tree structure. Despite these limitations, many successful hierarchical systems have been built, of which the most notable is probably IBM's Information Management System (IMS).

The network data model relaxes some of the restrictions imposed by the hierarchical model. In the network model an entity can be related to more than one parent entity, and subordinate entities can be related to superior entities. It allows entities to be related in the form of a network or graph. For example, the network model allows an affiliation relationship between publishers and authors. The network model still has the problem of modeling many-to-many relationships directly and of certain entity instances existing only in the context of other entity instances, but it is definitely more general than the hierarchical model.

In 1971, the CODASYL Database Task Group (DBTG) published a report proposing a standard architecture for systems based on the network model. Three languages were proposed: a subschema data definition language (the external level), a schema data definition language (the conceptual level), and a data manipulation language. This proposal came to be widely adopted as network-based systems grew in popularity in the seventies and eighties. The most popular network-based DBMS is Cullinet's IDMS.

Both network and hierarchic systems, though efficient from the viewpoint of database access, have one primary drawback. Relationships between entities are represented by means of pointers embedded in actual physical records that represent these entities. That, in itself, is not all bad. What is bad is the trickiness of navigating these pointers to follow the relationships between entity instances. For example, if you want to find all the books published by John Wiley, you first retrieve the publishers instance for John Wiley, then follow the pointers representing the publishes relationship to find all the books published by that publisher. This puts a severe limitation on physical data independence–when relationships change, the application program is affected.

The primary reason for the tremendous acceptance of the relational model is that it provides a high degree of physical data independence–it insulates users from the intricacies of the underlying storage structures. At the same time, it is simple and has a firm theoretical foundation, based on the mathematical concept of sets. The next section explores the relational model in detail.

The Relational Model

From the viewpoint of this book, the relational model is of particular importance because SQL Server is a relational database server. This warrants an examination of the relational model in more depth than that of the hierarchical and network models. The basic precepts of the relational model will be described in common terms with brief references to the underlying theoretical and mathematical terms–just to make the reader aware of them.

The relational data model was first proposed by E. F. Codd in 1970 in a landmark paper entitled "A relational model of data for large shared data banks." Codd's insight was that if data are constrained to fit the mathematical concept of relations (which is based on sets), then there are precise relational operations that can be carried out on the data, yielding well-defined and predictable results. Codd also defined a **data sublanguage** for use within programming languages (based on first order predicate calculus) that can be used with relations.

In Codd's relational model, all data are viewed as sets of **tables** (formally, relations) and nothing but tables. Each table has a fixed number of **columns** (formally, attributes) and a variable number of **rows** (formally, tuples). This view is deceivingly simple; the concept of a table is simple and well understood. For example, the database on books, publishers, and authors can be represented as in Figure 1-5.

Each column has values that are drawn from an underlying domain (a set of values). A row, then, is an ordered set of column values, with the values drawn from underlying domains. There is

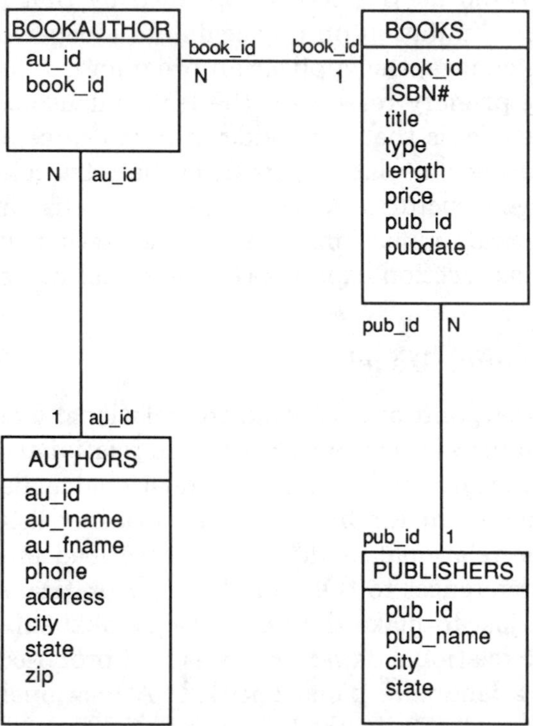

FIGURE 1-5 A relational view of tables for books, authors, and publishers

no informal term that is exactly equivalent to domains, but data type approximates it. The commonly used vocabulary for these formal terms is:

Formal term	**Informal term**
relation	table
tuple	row
attribute	column
domain	data type

There are additional properties of tables in Codd's model worth noting:

1. There are no duplicate rows.
2. There is no implied ordering of rows.
3. There is no implied ordering of columns, because each column value is drawn from an underlying domain.

Two other concepts are part of the relational model—**primary** and **foreign keys**. A primary key is any column or set of columns whose values uniquely identify the rows in the table. The concept of primary keys is similar to key attributes (discussed earlier in the chapter) that uniquely identify an entity; however, entities do not exactly map one-to-one to tables. Based on property 1 in the preceding list, the primary key is always guaranteed to exist. In the worst case, all of the columns in the table together constitute the primary key. For example, in a table of books, the ISBN column can be a primary key since it uniquely identifies all the rows of the table. A foreign key is a column or set of columns whose values match the primary key values of another table. For example, the publisher ID column in the books table is a foreign key, since its values correspond to the publisher ID primary key of the publishers table.

The way in which relationships are represented in the relational model really sets it apart from the hierarchical and network models. In the relational model, all relationships are represented by foreign to primary key mappings. In other words, the association (or instance of the relationship) in the different tables is represented strictly in terms of data values and not by explicit pointers as it is in the other models. For example, the relationship published by between a book and its publisher can be represented by the foreign key publisher ID in the book table, which maps to the publisher ID primary key in the publishers table.

There are two rules that follow from the definition of the relational model. First, a primary key value cannot be partially or wholly null. A **null** value is an unknown or inapplicable value. This follows from the fact that the primary key must uniquely identify the rows in the table. If unknown values were allowed, two rows with null values for the primary key would not be distinguishable. This is known as the **entity integrity** rule.

The second rule states that no foreign key value may reference a primary key value that does not exist. This rule makes perfect sense. After all, foreign key values that match primary key values represent associations between the rows. A nonmatching value is like saying that a book is published by a nonexistent publisher. Of course, the publisher may not be known, hence foreign key values can be null. This is known as the **referential integrity** rule.

Codd also defined a new set of operators in addition to the standard set-theoretic operators (union, intersection, and difference) for use with relations. These are the select, project, product, join, and divide operators, which form the basis for an algebra for relations, which is known as **relational algebra.** These operators will be covered in more detail later in the chapter.

In summary, the relational model provides some key benefits that have led to its tremendous acceptance. The first, of course, is its simplicity. It presents a simple view of the data—the familiar notion of a table with rows and columns. Second, it provides a high degree of physical data independence—the user does not need to be aware of any access paths or storage structure details in order to access the data. Third, it has a firm theoretical foundation that is based on the mathematical concept of relations. Finally, and probably the most overlooked, is the symmetry of the relational model. In a hierarchic or network model, some questions are easier to answer than others. For example, in the hierarchic structure shown in Figure 1-4 it is easier to find all the authors of a particular book, rather than find all the books authored by a particular author.

Database Languages

The two primary views of data within a DBMS are the conceptual, or logical, view and the internal, or physical, view. The next thing you need is a **database language** at the conceptual level (and possibly at the external level) for defining and manipulating the database objects. The data definition aspect of the language allows you to define the logical structure of the database; the manipulation aspect allows you to retrieve or update the data within the databases. The task of mapping this to internal storage structures and access mechanisms is left to the DBMS. This language ideally should provide both one-time (or ad-hoc) access to the database and more controlled, repetitive, programmatic access.

Most DBMSs provide such a language, which usually includes both data definition and data manipulation capabilities. When it is a stand-alone language for interacting with the database, it is termed a **query language** (a misnomer, since it really does much more than querying). In addition, the DBMS also provides a set of language constructs that can be used within a programming language for database access. These constructs are more formally termed a **data sublanguage**. The language is not really a complete language; rather it is a language subset intended for use within a programming language to develop database applications. Quite often the two languages overlap greatly or are identical. Hence, the term database language will be used generically to mean both the data sublanguage and query language.

Language Components

Database languages, then, are primarily concerned with the definition of database objects and the manipulation of the data within these objects. In general, they are not concerned with application aspects—for example, presenting data or specifying the logic of a program. A database language has two major components—the **data**

definition language (DDL) and the **data manipulation language** (DML). It may have other, minor components for data control or data administration.

The DDL allows the user to define the logical structure of the database—the ability to create, modify, and remove databases and database objects. Database objects are tables, views, indexes, rules, and so on. These objects are normally created and known within the context of a database. The creation of a database object specifies the structure of the object. For example, when you create a table, you specify its columns and their associated data types. When you create an index, you specify (among other things) which table it is defined on and which columns make up the index. You can also modify or alter the structure of the object and remove or delete an object (and any associated objects and data within them).

The DML, on the other hand, allows the addition, deletion, and modification of the actual data contained in the database objects. In a relational database, tables are the basic object for storing data. Data manipulation therefore implies adding or deleting rows from tables, or modifying the data in the columns within a row. Other database objects such as indexes and rules are defined for allowing fast access to row data or for constraining column values to a specified range. These other objects do not contain data that are directly manipulated through the DML.

Relational Database Languages

Relational database languages, too, have a DDL and a DML component. They may also include other statements for data control and data administration. Most relational languages are based on operators that are more powerful than the traditional record-oriented languages of nonrelational systems. Several classes of relational database languages have been proposed over the years. Three important ones are discussed here. Two were proposed in Codd's original paper—relational calculus, based on first order predicate calculus, and relational algebra, based on the set of operators for relations. The third is a mapping-oriented language, based on the concept of mapping.

Relational Algebra Relational algebra is based on the collection of operators that includes the traditional set operators (union, intersection, and difference) and special relational operators (projection, restriction, join, product, and division). These operators deal with whole relations and always produce new relations as the result. This is known as the property of **closure** in mathematics.

The following paragraphs explain the relational operators. The projection operator returns only the specified columns of a table and eliminates the others. For example, if you project the book table on ISBN and title, you get a result table with all the rows of the book table, but only two columns—ISBN and title. The restriction operator is complementary to the projection operator. It returns all the columns of a table, but the subset of only the rows that satisfy a specified condition. For example, if you want only the voluminous books, you can restrict the book table on the condition pages $>$ 500.

The join operator is the hallmark of the relational model. It represents the way in which relationships are materialized in the model. The join operator compares column values in two tables and includes in the result table all rows that satisfy the comparison. The most common comparison is based on equality ($=$ operator). This is known as an **equijoin**. For example, if you want to find the titles and author names of all books, you can join the books table and the authors table on the author ID columns in the two tables. (It is not necessary for the two column names to be the same.)

The other two operators, product and division, are less commonly used in algebraic languages. The product (also called **cartesian product**) of two tables just concatenates every row in one table with every row in the other table. Thus the if the first table has m rows and the second n rows, the product has $m \times n$ rows. Division can be expressed in terms of the other operators. The idea behind the division operator is shown in Figure 1-6.

There are few commercial languages that have been based on relational algebra per se. However, languages such as SQL do implement some of the algebra operators. Relational algebra also serves as a basis for evaluating other languages (this is discussed later) and for query optimization.

Relational Calculus Relational calculus is based on having a predicate calculus for use with relations. This idea and a

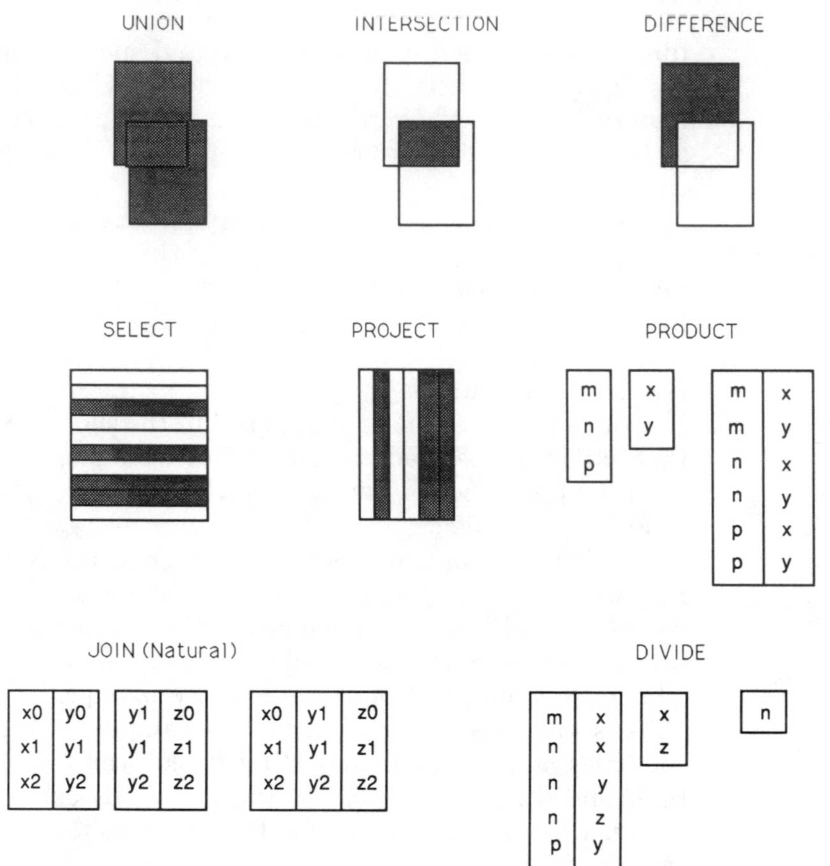

FIGURE 1-6 The relational algebra operators

language based on relational calculus, called ALPHA, was first proposed by Codd in 1971. The basic construct in relational calculus is a **query variable**—a variable that ranges over the rows of a table. A query in a calculus-based language involves a **target**, which specifies the columns to be returned, and a **qualification**, which selects rows from the target table based on an expression involving the query variable. For example, the following query in a calculus-based language called QUEL retrieves all books that are over 500 pages in length.

Example 1-1

```
RANGE OF B IS BOOKS
RETRIEVE (B.ISBN, B.TITLE) WHERE B.LENGTH > 500
```

Here the query variable is B, and the target is ISBN, title. The qualification is (B.LENGTH > 500). The language QUEL is implemented in the INGRES system. In addition, IBM's Query By Example (QBE) and SQL both have some constructs based on relational calculus.

Mapping-Oriented Languages The third class of languages, mapping-oriented languages, was proposed by Boyce in 1974. It was targeted at high-level users, who were not necessarily familiar with concepts such as query variables. The basic construct in such languages is mapping, which extracts a subset of the columns and rows within a table. For example, if you want to retrieve the list of books that are longer than 500 pages, you can write the query in Example 1-2.

Example 1-2

```
SELECT ISBN, TITLE
FROM BOOKS
WHERE LENGTH > 500
```

Of course, this is equivalent to an algebraic restrict (the WHERE clause) followed by an algebraic project (the SELECT clause). The result of a mapping can also be nested inside another mapping, allowing more powerful queries. The most popular of these languages is SQL; another is the one introduced by Boyce called SQUARE.

Relational Completeness When Codd first proposed relational calculus, he defined a relational database language to be **relationally complete** if it is powerful enough to express any query that can be expressed in relational calculus. Often, this definition is extended to include the additional constraint that the information be retrievable in a single statement. In other words, if the information can be derived from the tables of the database, a query to retrieve this information can be formulated using the language constructs. Codd showed that relational algebra is relationally complete. Most of the other languages mentioned, including SQL and QUEL, are relationally complete, too.

As relational systems emerged, the question of whether a system was truly relational or not was posed. It is generally now accepted that a true relational system is one which is based on "relational principles" and supports a database language that is relationally complete. Codd defined several rules (thirteen in all, although they are referred to as Codd's 12 Rules) to assess the degree of conformance of a database system to the relational model.

Rule 0
A relational DBMS must be able to manage databases entirely through its relational capabilities.

Rule 1 - The Information Rule
All information in a relational database (including table and column names) is represented explicitly as values in tables.

Rule 2 - Guaranteed Access
Every value in a relational database is guaranteed to be accessible by using a combination of the table name, primary key value and column name.

Rule 3 - Systematic Null Value Support
The DBMS provides systematic support for the treatment of null values (unknown or inapplicable data), distinct from default values, and independent of any domain.

Rule 4 - Active, On-line Relational Catalog
The description of the database and its contents is represented at the logical level as tables, and can therefore be queried using the database language.

Rule 5 - Comprehensive Data Sublanguage
There must be at least one language supported that has a well-defined syntax and is comprehensive, in that it supports data definition, manipulation, integrity rules, authorization and transactions.

Rule 6 - View Updating Rule
All views that are theoretically updatable can be updated through the system.

Rule 7 - Set-level Insertion, Update and Deletion
The DBMS supports not only set-level retrievals, but also set-level inserts, updates and deletes.

Rule 8 - Physical Data Independence
Application programs and ad-hoc programs are logically unaffected when physical access methods or storage structures are altered.

Rule 9 - Logical Data Independence
Application programs and ad-hoc programs are logically unaffected, to the extent possible, when changes are made to the table structures.

Rule 10 - Integrity Independence
The database language must be capable of defining integrity rules, they must be stored in the on-line catalog, and they cannot be bypassed.

Rule 11 - Distribution Independence
Application programs and ad-hoc requests are logically unaffected when data is first distributed, or when it is redistributed.

Rule 12 - Non-Subversion
It must not be possible to bypass the integrity rules defined through the database language by using lower level languages.

Structured Query Language

Structured Query Language (or SQL) is a high-level, set-oriented, nonprocedural database language for relational database systems. It is high-level because the language is similar to English. That it is set-oriented means that SQL deals with sets of data, unlike languages that provide only record-at-a-time capability. The set orientation is very similar to—in some cases exactly the same as—the algebraic manipulations discussed previously. That it is nonprocedural means that in SQL you specify what it is you want to retrieve, not how you want to retrieve it. The job of figuring out how the data can best be retrieved is left to the DBMS.

Although the Q in SQL stands for query, SQL is really much more than a query language; it provides all the data definition and update capabilities that are needed in any database language. SQL is a powerful language that has been shown to be relationally complete. In addition, many commercial SQL implementations include facilities for controlling access to the data and for database administration.

SQL was developed originally in the late seventies at IBM San Jose Research Laboratories as part of the experimental System R Project. Since then there have been many commercial implementations of SQL—first at the mini and mainframe level, in such products as ORACLE and DB2, and later at the microcomputer level in products such as dBASE, IBM's Extended Edition, and SQL Server. SQL is now the de facto standard for relational database languages.

Although many other relational database languages have been developed, SQL has become important for two reasons. First, it is important if portability is a concern. An application using SQL on the minicomputer can now be ported easily to a PC or PC LAN, assuming, of course, that a suitable relational environment exists at that level. Second, SQL is important from the viewpoint of connectivity between heterogeneous platforms. If a DBMS on the PC LAN wants to get some data off the corporate mainframe, it is much easier when they both speak the same language. More and more, vendors are realizing the importance of SQL and moving to incorporate it into their DBMS products.

Although the many SQL implementations differ slightly, they are essentially similar with respect to the key constructs in the language. Two primary standards have emerged for SQL—the ANSI SQL standard (X3.135-86) and the IBM SAA SQL standard. The ANSI standard defines compliance at two levels—level 1 and level 2. Level 1 is a subset of level 2 and defines the minimum subset needed for any reasonable SQL implementation. ANSI is working on a second standard, the ANSI SQL2 standard, which extends the first standard in several areas, such as data integrity. IBM's SAA standard, on the other hand, is an attempt to unify the SQL implementations on their different platforms to achieve cross-platform portability. Most vendors claim compatibility with at least one or the other of the SQL standards.

Host Languages

The nature and benefits of SQL as a language have been explored. This section turns to some of the other languages used for application development. The natural question that arises is why we need a language other than SQL for developing applications. The following paragraphs explain the answer to that question.

SQL, as explained earlier, is the standard database language for relational systems. However, database languages in general and SQL in particular are concerned primarily with the definition and manipulation of database objects. It is therefore not a complete language and normally has to be supplemented by a "fuller" language to develop useful applications.

These fuller languages normally provide the constructs that fall outside data definition and manipulation (for example, conditional execution or screen manipulation) that are necessary for developing any application. SQL itself is used from within the application to perform all functions related to the database. Several ways of providing this database interface are discussed in the next section.

There are several application development languages to choose from. They range from traditional programming languages like COBOL, C, or PL/1 to fourth-generation languages like dBASE and INFORMIX 4GL. These languages are referred to as host languages, because they traditionally were run on host (mainframe) computers. The interface is called a **host language interface**, (HLI). In the microcomputer world, this interface is more commonly referred to as an **applications programming interface** (API).

Host Language Interfaces The previous section discussed the need to provide a host language interface (or applications programming interface) to the database system. There are two primary approaches to providing such an interface, the embedded approach and the library approach. In the following sections the two approaches are described and compared and their advantages and disadvantages are discussed.

Embedded Approach Many DBMSs provide an HLI using the **embedded approach**. In this approach, any statements required for database access are embedded directly in the appropriate place in the source code and usually denoted by some special character (such as $). The database language statements are processed along with the source code through an external precompiler. The precompiler calls the precompiler DBMS interface to parse and compile the database language statements. It replaces the SQL statements in the source program with appropriate calls, in the source language, to the run-time DBMS interface. A modified source program is thereby generated. The modified source program then goes through the process of normal compilation and linking to produce an executable program. The entire process is diagrammed in Figure 1-7.

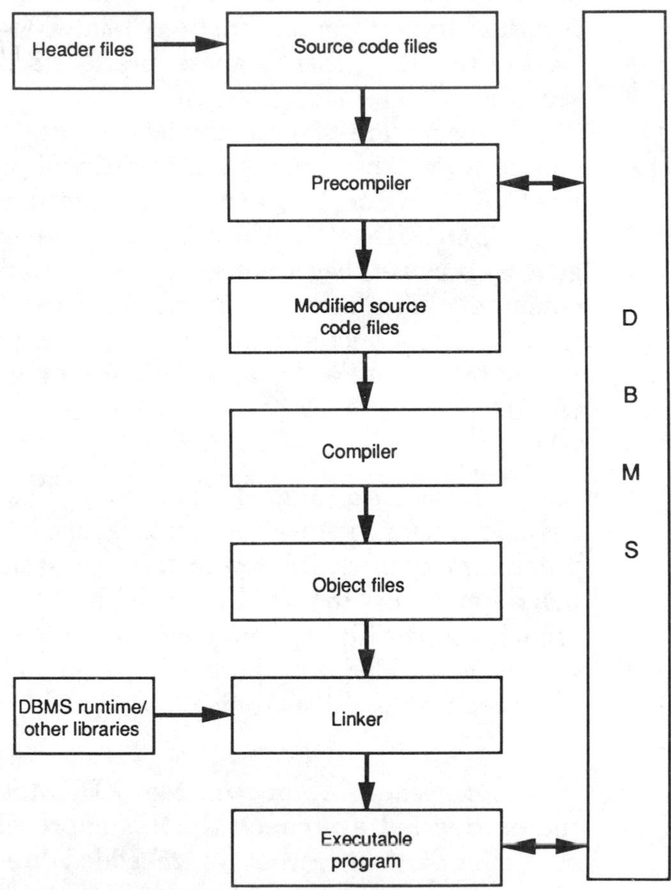

FIGURE 1-7 Embedded SQL approach

Library Approach The other approach to providing a host language interface is known as the **library** or **call-level approach**. The database interface is provided through a library of function calls (or procedures). These functions form the standard interface to the database. Since they are just like regular external function calls, they are linked with the source program in the same way that other library functions are.

In this approach, the source program contains the appropriate DBMS interface function calls. The function calls vary depending on the DBMS interface; however, they usually allow the application to establish a connection (sometimes termed a session) with the DBMS, compile a statement, execute it, retrieve result rows, and terminate a connection. In addition, there are functions that return status or schema information. The source program is then compiled normally and linked with the database library (along with any other required libraries) during the link phase. The process is no different from that of compiling and linking any other program. The library approach is illustrated in Figure 1-8.

The Approaches Compared Since both of the approaches have been used by DBMS vendors to provide an HLI, the natural question is, what advantages and disadvantages does each approach provide. This section attempts to throw some light on this question. It is assumed that SQL is the database language in the following discussion.

The embedded approach provides several advantages. First, the SQL specified by the user within the source program is exactly the same as the SQL that is used from an ad-hoc interface. This means that a query already used (and debugged) from an ad-hoc interface is guaranteed to work within the program.

Second, embedded SQL provides a major advantage in its ability to port across many different hardware platforms, all supporting SQL DBMSs. As long as an appropriate precompiler is available for the platform in question, the task of porting applications to it is very easy—it is simply a matter of running the program through the precompiler and then compiling the application for that platform.

The major disadvantage of the precompiler approach is the two-step process—precompilation and then compilation—required

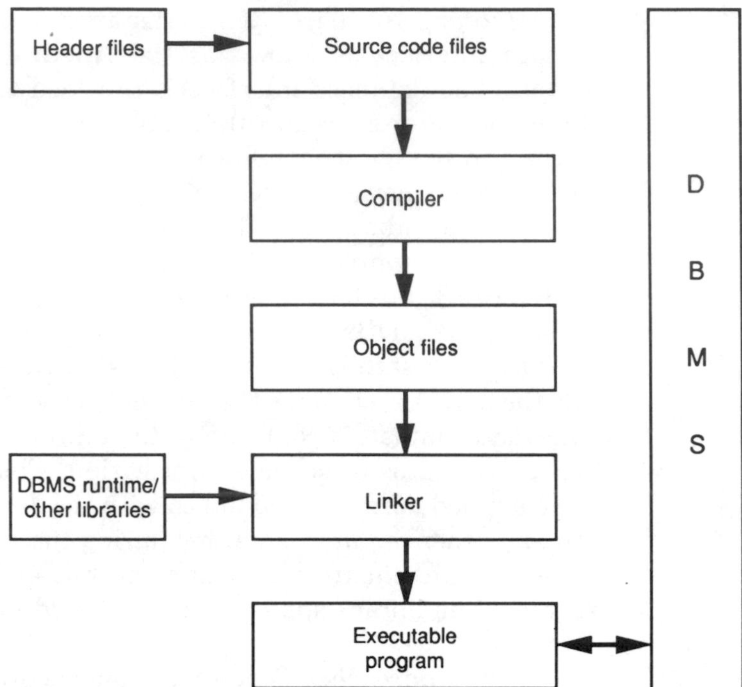

FIGURE 1-8 The library approach

to produce an application. This two-step process is cumbersome and requires the developer to be familiar with another piece of software (the precompiler). Also, since the original source code is modified by the precompiler, most debugging tools available with compilers provide references to lines in the modified source program only, not the original source program.

Another disadvantage of embedded SQL is that it requires additional constructs (in both SQL and the programming language) to support database access. Since SQL is a set-oriented language and since most applications require row-at-a-time (or record-at-a-time) access, constructs such as **cursors** need to be supported in embedded SQL. A cursor defines a current row position in a set of result rows returned by an SQL query. Once a cursor is opened (activated), then operations such as fetch next row or fetch previous row can be performed on that cursor. Cursors can be deactivated or reused when they complete an operation.

The library or call-level approach is generally much more closely tied to a particular DBMS and hence does not provide the same degree of portability across different DBMSs on multiple hardware platforms. However, an application written for a particular DBMS call-level API on one platform can easily be ported to another platform on which the same DBMS (and hence the same API) is supported.

A major advantage of the library approach is that it avoids the two-step process used by the embedded SQL approach. By using ordinary programming language function calls, the process of developing an application is greatly simplified. The call-level interface thus provides a higher degree of application integration with the DBMS.

In summary, the need for an HLI is clear. Most DBMSs provide one or the other of the interfaces, and they provide an equivalent level of functionality. The embedded approach has definite portability benefits, whereas the call-level approach is simpler for development and more flexible. It should also be noted that one interface does not preclude the other; a DBMS can provide both, if the need exists.

Summary

This chapter went through the basic foundations of database theory. It examined various data models, including the relational model, and its advantages over the other models. Relational database languages in general and SQL in particular were explored. In summary, the theoretical and conceptual underpinnings of SQL Server from a database perspective, were covered.

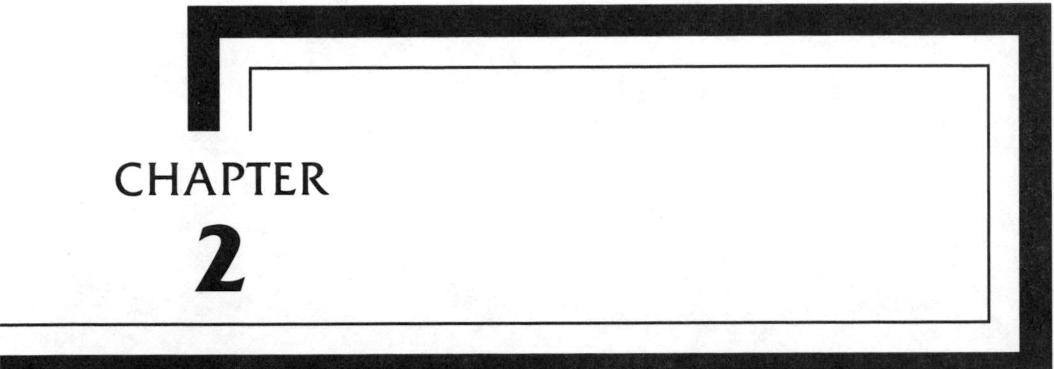

CHAPTER 2

Local Area Networks, Client/Server Computing, and Database Servers

Introduction

Chapter 1 talked about DBMSs in general and then focused more specifically on relational systems. This chapter focuses on the other core component that plays a significant role in the database server environment—the local area network (LAN). Database server technology really represents the evolution of two significant trends in the past decade—the move to relational database systems and the move to various forms of distributed processing, with the LAN as the enabling technology.

A discussion of local area networks must begin with a definition of what it is and then provide a framework for it. A **local area network** is a communications network that enables data communication between devices within a small geographic area. The term device is generic and encompasses a wide variety of devices including computers, printers, telephones, modems, faxes, peripheral devices, and so on. However, this discussion is mostly concerned with communication between computers and peripheral devices. A small geographic area entails distances that are within a few thousand meters, typically within a building or a few buildings. LANs are different from **wide area networks** (WANs) in that WANs make communication possible over much larger distances—across cities and countries, even around the globe.

The most common framework for discussing networks is the seven-layer **Open Systems Interconnect** (OSI) model for data communication developed by the **International Standards Organization** (ISO) in the early seventies. ISO is an international body, based in Paris, which develops standards for data communication. The aim of OSI is to define what kinds of functions are to be provided at each layer and thereby facilitate communication among heterogenous equipment from different vendors. Figure 2-1 shows the various layers of the OSI model.

Each layer in the OSI model builds on the layer immediately below it, providing additional functionality as it progresses up the seven layers. For example, the network layer is responsible for routing packets of data from source to destination node across possibly different paths in the network. The transport layer, on the other hand, guarantees that the packets are received in the right format

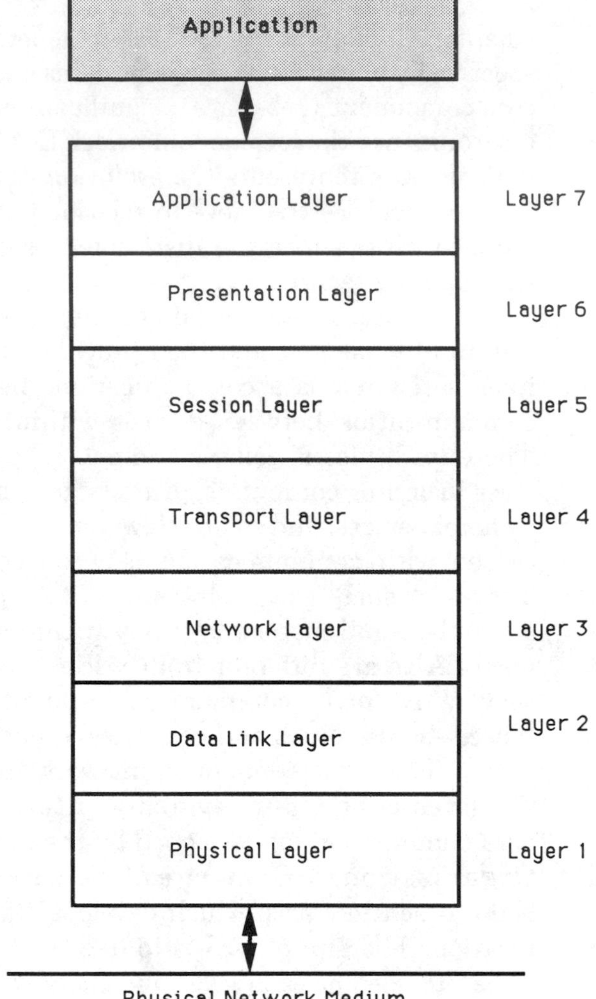

FIGURE 2-1 The layers of the OSI model

and right order at the destination node. The layered approach also serves to isolate the higher layers from the details of the lower layers. If, for example, you decide to use a new network medium such as optic fiber instead of coaxial cable—a physical layer concern—it should theoretically be possible to do so without affecting the higher layers.

The physical layer is the lowest layer in the OSI model. It deals with the actual, physical wiring or cables, electrical connections, and signals that make data communication possible. All other layers are dependent on it. The most common standard at this layer is RS-232C, which defines the meaning of various pins and signals on a physical connector. Other standards are RS-449 and X.21, which is used in Europe.

The data link layer is concerned with forming data messages, managing the flow of data into and out of a node, and adding the appropriate addresses of the source and destination nodes. Common protocols include High-Level Data Link Control (HDLC) and Bisynchronous. In microcomputer-based LANs, it is at this layer that protocols like Token Ring, Ethernet and Arcnet are implemented. Often, data link functions are performed by special hardware in the network adapter cards that are installed in the workstations.

The network layer resolves any addressing conflicts and decides how data packets (messages, split into fixed-size chunks) are routed through the network based on various network conditions. Since all nodes communicate with other nodes in a LAN, no intermediate routing is necessary. In WANs, the network layer software usually resides on special switching nodes that are part of the network. The network layer software is responsible for intermediate routing. For LAN communication, the network layer is not of primary significance, except to provide remote or internet communication between different networks.

The transport layer is typically responsible for ensuring that properly addressed messages are assembled and disassembled into or from packets before they are passed to the higher layers. It is typically also the layer that guarantees reliable, error-free delivery of the messages. Thus, if a particular network route fails, the transport layer finds an alternate route. The common protocols that exist at the transport layer are Transmission Control Program/Internet Program (TCP/IP) and ISO Transport Class 4 (TP4).

The session layer is responsible for establishing connections (or sessions) between computers on the network in order to enable applications to communicate. The functions handled at this level are name recognition, logging, security, administration, and so on. The session layer is commonly the programmer's interface to the network. NetBIOS Extended User Interface (NETBEUI) and Advanced Program to Program Communications (APPC) are both session layer interfaces.

The presentation layer is concerned with the formatting of data for presentation to such devices as printers and terminals. It is also capable of encoding data in a variety of ways, including encryption and file formatting. In order for communication to occur, both computers must be using the same presentation protocol. If they speak different protocols, the appropriate conversions take place in this layer. Terminal emulation is performed at this level.

The application layer has functions that are mainly user specified. At this level you find such functions as database management, electronic mail, OS prompts, and services for file/printer servers.

It is important to note that, although the OSI model segments the functions into distinct layers, in practice the layers are not so clear-cut. The model serves as a framework for implementation; however, many vendor network offerings have protocol layers that span multiple OSI layers, do not conform to the OSI model, or do not fit neatly into any of the layers. The are several reasons for this. Many products are developed for proprietary environments, where standards are thought not to be critical. Other products were developed before ISO proposed its model. However, there is definitely a push toward open standards and protocols that conform to the OSI model. Presently, ISO and The Corporation for Open Systems are in the process of certifying vendors who write to the specific interfaces for the OSI layers as defined in the OSI specification.

The OSI reference model is a framework on which to base the discussions that follow. The next section addresses LAN topologies and associated protocols and explains how they fit within that framework.

Network Topologies

LANs are mainly categorized on the basis of the topologies and the transmission media they employ. The **topology** describes the configuration in which the communicating devices are connected.

Often, a distinction is made between **physical topology**, which is how the actual wires and cables are connected, and **logical topology**, which describes how the messages flow within the LAN. This chapter refers mostly to the physical topology. Common LAN topologies include star, bus, and ring. The transmission medium is the actual cable or wiring used to carry the data. The three media appropriate for LANs are twisted pair wire, coaxial cable, and optical fiber.

Star Networks

Star is one of the oldest and most commonly used topologies. The easiest analogy to a star network is our telephone system—all calls from one telephone to another telephone are handled by a central switching exchange. In star LANs, communication from one computer to another is handled in a similar manner, through a central computer. The data from the source node are sent to the central computer, which then forwards it to the destination node. AT&T's STARLAN is a product that is based on the star topology. Figure 2-2 illustrates the star topology.

There are several advantages inherent in the star topology. The foremost is that it is easy to add additional nodes to the network. All network administration and maintenance can be performed centrally. Problem diagnostics are greatly simplified, as are setting different security mechanisms. The disadvantages of this

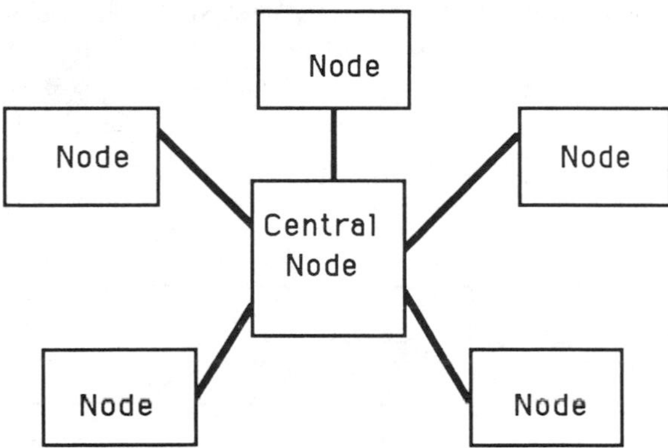

FIGURE 2-2 Star topology

topology are that the central computer may be a bottleneck for the LAN or, even worse, that, if the central computer experiences a system failure, the entire LAN will fail. This problem is addressed by other types of LANs.

Bus Networks

A bus network is one in which all nodes share a single transmission medium, but only one node can transmit at a time. An analogy might be a street on which there are several houses, but the street is only wide enough to accommodate a single car. In order to deliver anything from one house to another, the sender first needs to make sure the road is clear before getting on it. Figure 2-3 illustrates the bus topology.

When a node needs to communicate with another node, it first checks to see if there is any traffic on the network. If not, it transmits the data (with the appropriate source and destination addresses) through the bus. Each node monitors the bus and copies data addressed to itself. Gateway Communication's G-Net is an example of a network that uses the bus topology.

A major advantage of the bus topology is that the failure of any one node does not cause the entire LAN to fail, which is possible in star networks. The disadvantages are that is it difficult to run LAN-wide diagnostics and it is fairly easy to compromise the security of bus networks.

Ring Networks

The ring topology combines features of both the star and bus topologies. It consists of several computers joined together in a the

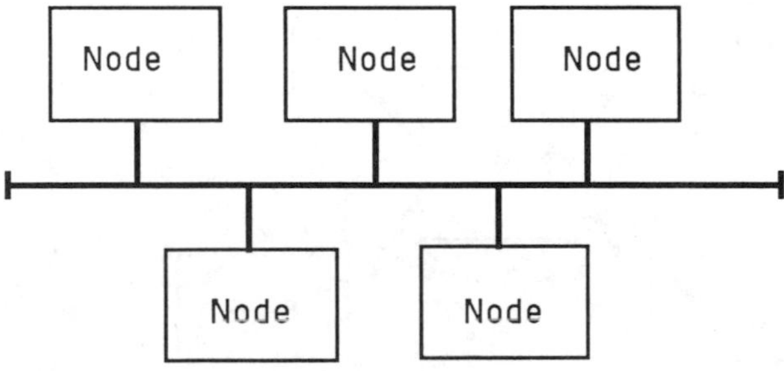

FIGURE 2-3 Bus topology

form of a closed loop, or ring. In this topology, the sending node waits its turn and then puts the data on the ring (with source and destination addresses). The data circulate from node to node in one direction on the ring, until the receiving node receives it. The recipient node copies the data, and then returns the data to the sender. This acts as an acknowledgment that the data got to the destination node. Figure 2-4 illustrates the ring topology.

One of the most important considerations in a ring network is how to ensure that all nodes on a network have equal access to the network. On an IBM ring network, a token, which circulates around the ring is used to regulate access to the network. When delivery is successful, only the token is returned to the sending node, not the entire message. This makes the LAN more efficient. IBM LANs are referred to as token-ring networks.

There are many advantages to this type of topology including ease of LAN-wide diagnostics, the fact that if one node fails, the entire LAN doesn't (providing that appropriate bypass software exists), and the ease with which various ring networks can be bridged together. Use of such bridges makes it easier to connect a variety of LANs together to form extremely powerful workgroup environments.

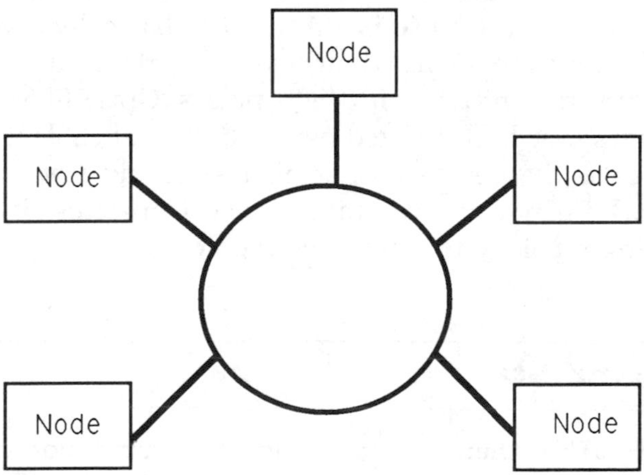

FIGURE 2-4 Ring topology

Transmission Media

A few words about transmission media will be helpful before discussing LAN protocols. Twisted pair wiring is one of the most common media used in LANs today. It consists of two twisted wires (with about 6 turns per inch). It is popular because it is the same as some forms of telephone wiring, which is normally preinstalled in office buildings. The advantage of the twisted pair medium is that it is economical; the disadvantages are that it suffers from noise interference and has a maximum data transmission rate of approximately 10Mbits per second.

Coaxial cable is a transmission medium that has an inner copper conductor surrounded by plastic insulation and then by some kind of shielding. There are at least two different types of coaxial cables in use—thin and thick—and two different transmission methods—baseband and broadband. The major difference between the transmission methods is that baseband accommodates only a single channel and broadband accommodates multiple channels. The advantages of coaxial cables are that they allow higher transmission rates and can span larger distances than twisted pair wiring. In addition, they provide shielding from noise interference. However, they are more expensive, and rarely are they preinstalled in office buildings.

Optic fiber is a new transmission medium that is getting much attention for use in LANs. It is basically a very fine (about the thickness of a single hair) extruded glass cable, through which data are transmitted using light pulses. Optic fiber has several advantages over both twisted pair and coaxial cable including higher data rates, lighter weight, smaller size, and lower noise susceptibility. Its major disadvantage is cost. Optic fiber is more suited to the ring topology than the bus topology.

LAN Protocols and Standards

In all LANs, there is some kind of transmission channel that is shared among several communicating devices. To allow orderly communication between any two nodes, there must be some method, or **protocol**, that is used to regulate access and contention to the media in a LAN. These methods are known as media access control (MAC) protocols. For LANs, MAC protocols can be categorized as either **random access** or **controlled access**. In random access protocols, nodes attempt to access the medium randomly, whenever needed. Controlled access protocols, on the other hand, use some algorithm to determine the sequence and time a node will have access to the medium. The most commonly used random access protocol is **carrier sense multiple access with collision detect (CSMA/CD)**. The common controlled access protocols are the **token bus** and **token ring**.

CSMA/CD and token bus protocols dominate bus LANs. Token ring is most common on ring networks. From the viewpoint of the OSI model, MAC protocols form the lower part of the data link layer since they control access to the physical transmission medium. Generally, MAC protocols are encoded into a chip, or chip set, on LAN adaptor boards used to connect the devices to the LAN. For this reason, they are sometimes referred to as hardware protocols.

Before CSMA/CD is discussed, the CSMA protocol without collision detect should be understood. In CSMA, nodes listen for an ongoing transmission on the LAN; if there is none, they transmit their message. If a transmission is in progress, the node waits for some time period (determined by an algorithm) before trying again. This is similar to the way operators communicate on a CB radio channel. If all the operators on the channel to speak at once, none of their messages is received reliably. So each CB operator waits until the channel is clear and then transmits his or her message. Each operator is using "carrier sense" by waiting for a clear channel before talking.

On a LAN, transmitted messages are sent as streams of bits. Each node has sophisticated sensing and transmission circuitry. When a node wishing to transmit senses there is no transmission in progress, it broadcasts the message across the LAN. While the node is transmitting, all of the other nodes on the LAN know enough to listen and to refrain from broadcasting. When the node is through transmitting, it broadcasts a "message finished" message across the LAN, and other nodes are free to broadcast.

With CSMA a problem can occur, known as **collision**. A node, sensing that the medium is clear, might begin transmitting before a previously transmitted message has reached its destination node (assuming a finite delay from transmission of data to their arrival at the destination node). This results in the two messages colliding; consequently neither message is delivered reliably. It is possible to add collision detection to the CMSA protocol. It allows one workstation to listen while it transmits (also known as listen while talking). The node is able to transmit bits of data on the line and compare them as they go out. Should the node notice strange voltage levels on the line, it senses that there has been a collision and turns off transmission at once. The transmission is retried after a random time period based on some algorithm.

The CSMA/CD protocol has proved to be an effective way to provide efficient error-free communication. However, since it can't prevent collisions, the major disadvantage is that under heavy loads there will be a lot of collisions, which significantly reduces performance. CSMA/CD is the foundation of the Ethernet LAN standard. It has been implemented by such companies as 3Com, Ungermann-Bass, and Interlan.

As effective as the CSMA/CD protocol is, there is still a problem: Communication is carried out in a random, unstructured environment. One attempt to deal with this is the token-passing bus protocol. In this scheme, all the nodes on the bus form a logical ring based on a position number. Each node knows of a preceding node and a succeeding node. A control packet is then passed around the bus, based on the logical order established. The control packet determines which node has access to the medium and for how long. The node that has the control packet is able to transmit or receive messages. When the node is done or its allotted time is over, it relinquishes control of the bus by passing the control packet to the next node in the logical sequence.

All of this complex logic is coded into an integrated chip and is carried out at the hardware level. The most important advantage of token bus is its fair and regulated access, guaranteeing a limited worst-case wait time for access to the bus. However, the complexity and the overhead involved are its principal disadvantages; a node still has to wait its turn even if the other nodes have nothing to transmit. The most common token bus protocol implementation is known as ARCNET, available from such vendors as Thomas Conrad.

For ring networks, the most common MAC protocol used is the token-passing ring scheme. The token-passing scheme is basically a variation of the token bus scheme. It uses a small packet that travels around the ring and controls access to it. When no node is transmitting, the packet is marked free. When a node wishes to transmit, it marks the packet busy when it passes by, and immediately transmits its data packets. No other nodes can transmit while the token packet is in the busy state. The destination node copies data addressed to it as they pass on the ring. The token packet eventually travels around the ring and returns to the source node. The sending node resets the token packet to free when it receives the token packet and when it has finished transmission. The next node down the ring can then seize control of the ring and transmit.

The main advantage of token ring is regulated access to the ring. The token packet allows for an easy acknowledgement scheme, since it is returned to the sender. Additionally, nodes can have different transmission priorities based on data transmission needs. The major disadvantage is the complexity of monitoring the token to avoid error situations such as a token packet being busy forever or the loss of the token packet. Proteon's proNET and IBM's Token Ring are examples of products that use the token ring scheme.

The IEEE Standards

The Institute for Electronic and Electrical Engineers (IEEE) used the OSI reference model as a foundation on which to base a set of standards for LANs. The committee structure of IEEE follows a numbering system like the Dewey decimal system. The general committee working on network standards is 802, and the various subcommittees are numbered 802.1, 802.2, and so on. Hence, these standards are known as the IEEE 802.X standards, which comprise the three areas: logical link control (LLC), media access control (MAC) and physical. They encompass the data link layer and the physical layer of the OSI.

The LLC layer (802.2) is a common layer for all MAC protocols. It defines standards for formats and exchange of data (error control, acknowledgments, and so on) between nodes. It provides two types of services, virtual circuit and datagram. A virtual circuit is a connection-oriented exchange (like a telephone call) in which you first set up the logical connection between sender and receiver. A datagram service is connectionless (like the post office); you just address packets to the destination, and they get routed appropriately. The MAC layer defines three standards for different topologies and access methods: the CSMA/CD bus (802.3) standard, the token bus (802.4) standard, and the token ring (802.5) standard.

When the 802 committees first met, the standard for bus networks was Xerox Ethernet. In 1980 both Intel and DEC announced that their products would all be Ethernet compatible. Standard 802.3 is an attempt by the IEEE to provide an Ethernet-compatible standard without being vendor specific. The standard allows several wiring options at the physical level, including twisted pair and coaxial cable.

The 802.4 token bus standard was developed for networks in which it is essential to avoid data collision. By synchronizing signals across the LAN, collision problems can be avoided. This standard also allows for several wiring options. However, it has lost its significance to the 802.3 for bus networks and is much less used today.

The 802.5 standard defines the no-collision standard for LANs that are based on a ring topology. It employs the active token-passing scheme. The standard has received much attention from IBM, and an increasing number of vendors now have token-ring interface cards for mini and mainframe computers.

Higher-Layer Protocols (Software Protocols)

The previous section discussed various topology, media, and protocol alternatives that were concerned with the two lowest layers of the OSI model. The LAN standards that exist at this level were also discussed—the Ethernet (CSMA/CD) and the token ring standards. That is, however, only part of the picture. Enabling applications (both client and server) to communicate across the LAN requires higher-layer OSI protocols. These are discussed next.

The layers of **protocol software**, the protocol stacks, are what enable applications to communicate. This software resides on each node of the network and is responsible for translating application information across the network–from application information into messages, from messages into packets, from packets into bits that are then appropriately routed to the destination addresses where they are then translated back up the stack to be understood by the destination application.

For most network-based applications or services, the presentation layer is the logical interface for communication or access to network resources, since this is where the network operating system (NOS) software resides. This software offers both a wide range of network services and independence from lower-level details. In practice though, many applications may need to, or may choose to, use session or transport layer interfaces for greater control of the network resources than is possible with the higher-level interfaces.

The common transport level stacks in use include:

- Transmission Control Program/Internet Program (TCP/IP). A transport protocol stack commonly used in the UNIX environment by vendors such as Sun, AT&T, and Apollo, but gaining popularity in other environments.
- Xerox Network System (XNS). Xerox and 3Com use XNS protocols.
- Sequenced Packet Exchange/Internet Packet Exchange (SPX/IPX). Novell's subset implementation of XNS protocols.
- NetBIOS Extended User Interface (NetBEUI). This is really a session layer protocol developed jointly by IBM and Sytek. Many vendors today provide either the NetBIOS version or a NetBIOS emulator.

Each protocol stack that is used to connect distributed applications consists of layers comparable to those in OSI model. For example, the interface to the NetBEUI protocol stack is a session layer interface because is allows such processing as call setup, hang up, send, or receive.

In addition to the network interfaces provided by the protocol stacks, other network services are needed to ensure a stable network environment. Such services include security, resource management, name service, remote and internetwork process communication services, and distributed file management. This software commonly resides on one or more nodes that are known as Servers. It is commonly referred to as the **network operating system** (NOS). In addition, there are programmatic interfaces for manipulating these services. Vendors often supply such interfaces, which are dependent on the operating system.

These interfaces provide the functions and data structures for using NOS system services and enabling communication between network nodes. One such interface is the Server Message Block (SMB) developed by Microsoft. It is a protocol used with DOS and OS/2 file systems. Another is Network File System (NFS), developed by Sun; it is commonly used in the UNIX and TCP/IP environments. A third is File and Terminal Access Methods (FTAM), which is the OSI standard for distributed file system services (also known as X.400).

Depending on the network OS, these services can also be extended in the application domain to include electronic mail service, print services, accounting functions, database management, as well as network administration and diagnostic tools.

Another important component of the programmatic interfaces provided within the network operating systems are the functions that allow applications to interact with the various layers of information, messages, or bits that have been described. In addition, these interfaces enable access to more generic network resources. Applications that interact with the network transport software utilize these interfaces. Some common interfaces include the named MS redirector and NetBIOS; others will be described later in this chapter.

Bridges and Gateways

In many situations it is necessary to move data into and from the LAN—either to other LANs or to host machines. This is accomplished with **bridges** or **gateways**. A bridge simply switches data from one LAN to another without carrying out protocol conversions. This enables the user of one LAN to access the resources of another. Bridges usually operate at the network layer or the data link layer and may or may not be media dependent. Usually bridges that operate at the network layer are MAC protocol and media independent. Such bridges, for example, can connect an Ethernet coaxial LAN to a token-ring twisted pair LAN. On the other hand, bridges that operate at the data link layer are media dependent; they can only connect token ring LANs to other token ring LANs, for example. Gateways, on the other hand, allow networks or computers running dissimilar protocols to communicate. They actually perform protocol translation—up one network's protocol stack and down the other network's stack. Gateways typically run on the OSI session layer interface. Figure 2-5 illustrates the concepts of gateways and bridges.

In PC-based LANs, gateways are especially important for PC-to-mainframe or PC-to-minicomputer communication, because PC LANs and mini/mainframes use very different protocol stacks. In connecting two PC LANs you need to provide exactly the same

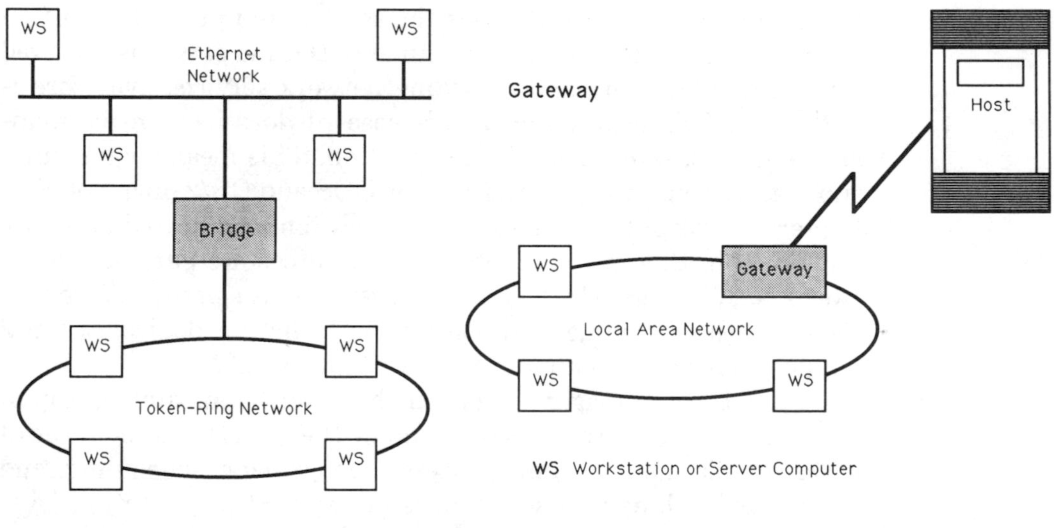

FIGURE 2-5 Gateways and Bridges

type of gateway if the two LANs are using different protocols. However, if the two LANs are using the same session layer (NetBIOS, for example), there is no need for a gateway, a bridge is sufficient.

PC Local Area Networks

Since the focus of this book is on SQL Server in microcomputer environments, this section focuses on PC LANs more specifically. In the PC LAN environment there are basically two network operating systems that dominate: Novell's NetWare and Microsoft's LAN Manager. Both NetWare and LAN Manager provide support for DOS and OS/2 workstations, but only LAN Manager servers run on the OS/2 operating system.

LAN Manager and NetWare

The difference between the two NOSs lies in their architecture. Novell uses a proprietary implementation of Xerox Network System (XNS) called SPX/IPX as the underlying transport protocol. On top of that it provides NetWare Core Protocol (NCP) for access to network services. NCP spans the session and presentation OSI layers. Hence in NetWare environments the file server is reserved for running NetWare and providing network services. NetWare is both the NOS and the OS in this case–it does its own file management, task scheduling, I/O, and so on. This means you cannot run standard applications written for DOS and OS/2 on a NetWare file server, except by using something called nondedicated NetWare for OS/2. In this mode, the server's resources are partitioned between NetWare and OS/2. This however can pose performance bottlenecks; the recommended solution is to have a dedicated OS/2 application server computer on the NetWare LAN.

A LAN Manager server, on the other hand, runs on top of OS/2. The NOS in this case uses all of the underlying facilities of OS/2 for file management, process management, scheduling, and so on. LAN Manager itself resides at the OSI presentation layer and is implemented on top of the NetBIOS session protocol stack, an interface defined by IBM. This insulates it from underlying transport protocols and hardware considerations. Therefore, other transport stacks, such as TCP/IP, or other access protocols, such as token-ring, can be substituted without affecting any LAN Manager services.

This discussion will not delve deeper into the architectural differences between the two network operating systems. Both NOSs are moving in the direction of providing transport protocol and hardware independence, while retaining control of the network operating system and its features.

In the case of LAN Manager, for example, this means the adherence to two standards: (1) Each transport must provide a NetBIOS interface at the session layer; (2) each transport is written to conform to a specific interface based on the network driver interface specifications (NDIS) at the data link layer. In this way, different transport stacks and network drivers (for network adapter cards) can be substituted, without affecting functionality. For example, LAN Manager intends to support the TCP/IP and ISO TP4 transport stacks, while there are already network drivers for all of the popular access protocols and hardware. Figure 2-6 illustrates the LAN Manager protocol architecture.

In the case of NetWare, too, there are similar interfaces defined with the objective of providing transport and hardware independence. The open link interface (OLI) defines how higher-level protocol stacks communicate with network drivers, so that a single driver works with multiple transport stacks and vice-versa. At the other end, Novell's NetWare has a standard interface that defines how the higher layers should interact with the transport stack. This interface provides for connection-oriented communications with other workstations and servers. The NetWare Core Protocols, which provide client/server capabilities, use this interface. Figure 2-7 illustrates the NetWare protocol architecture.

Interprocess Communication

The NOS provides an additional capability that is crucial to implementing client/server applications–**interprocess communication** (IPC). Interprocess communication in its most elementary form is simply the ability of two processes on the same machine to communicate–a facility provided by OS/2 and many other operating systems. However, IPC (or remote IPC, as it is sometimes

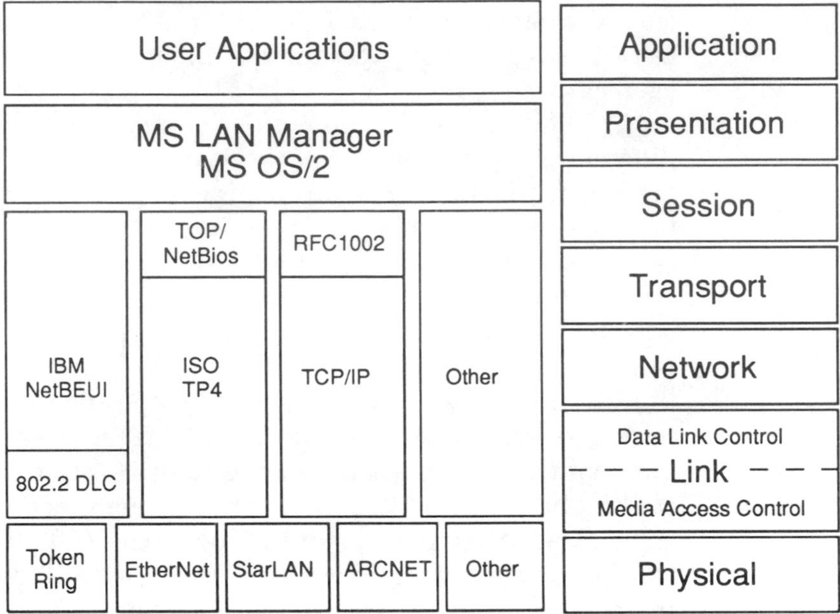

FIGURE 2-6 LAN Manager protocol architecture

termed) is generally taken to mean the ability of two different processes, such as applications, on different computers to communicate. Both NetWare and LAN Manger provide different forms of interprocess communication.

In the case of client/server-based applications, it is readily apparent why the IPC is needed. The client application running on the workstation must be able to communicate with the server application running on the server machine. Server applications comprise a variety of things—mail servers, database servers, communication servers, and so on.

IPC is implemented at various levels—at the presentation, session, and even the transport layers. Obviously, the higher-level interfaces hide much of the underlying complexity, whereas the lower-level interfaces provide more control and flexibility. Also, IPC is implemented in a number of ways, depending on whether it is local or remote. These ways include the use of shared memory, flags, semaphores, pipes, and queues. Shared memory is just common memory that is accessible by both processes and hence can be used

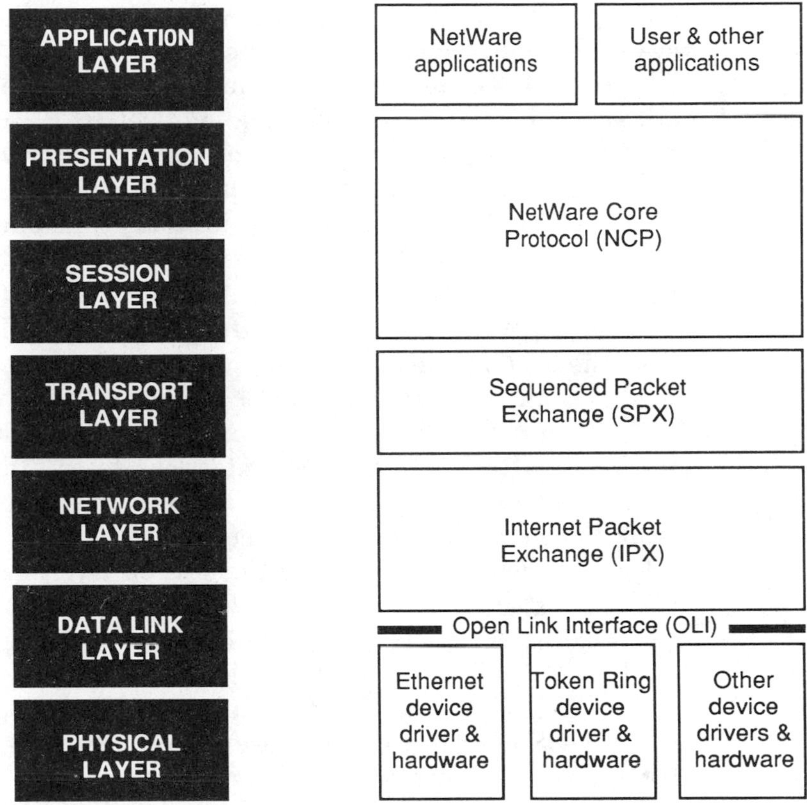

FIGURE 2-7 NetWare protocol architecture

for IPC. Flags and semaphores alert the other process that some event has occurred; they usually are a signal to perform a predefined operation. Semaphores are like flags except that they also synchronize communication. Pipes and queues are similar in that both provide the actual channel for communication between processes. There are many different standards for providing IPC in PC LAN environments. IBM's NetBIOS and Microsoft's named pipes are two that will be discussed further.

NetBIOS NetBIOS, as mentioned earlier, is a standard session layer protocol developed by IBM that allows peer-to-peer communication across the network and provides independence from underlying transport protocols and hardware. NetBIOS is the most popular protocol used for LANs today, and is used by most available applications.

NetBIOS is a lower-level interface to the network that requires a fair amount of programming. NetBIOS calls are written to the smallest possible "pieces" of network interprocess communication that are handled by the network basic input/output system. NetBIOS encompasses the network, transport, and session layers of the OSI model. At the presentation level of the OSI model, the NOS is loaded and it decides, when a call is made by the application, whether to send the request out to the LAN or to give it to the local operating system.

Both LAN Manager and NetWare support a NetBIOS interface. In LAN Manager, the one currently available transport stack is IBM's NetBIOS Extended User Interface (NetBEUI/DLC), which presents a NetBIOS interface at the session level. In fact, all transport stacks supported by LAN Manager must present this same interface at the session layer. With a TCP/IP transport stack, for example, the RFC 1002 session layer protocol (see Figure 2-6) provides the mapping from NetBIOS at the session level to TCP/IP at the transport level.

In the NetWare environment, too, IPC is supported through a NetBIOS emulator at the session level that runs on top of the SPX/IPX transport layer. NetWare also supports other levels of IPC including its own native NetWare (SPX/IPX) and IBM's LU6.2.

Named Pipes It was mentioned that there are different levels of IPC interfaces. Pipes and queues are an important part of the IPC mechanism of OS/2. Pipes allow for serial, two-way communication of variable amounts of data (messages) between two related processes. Queues are like named pipes except that the data exchange is not serial—instead, messages are stacked or queued-up for the receiving process. The receiving process can handle the data in any order it wants.

Named pipes are nothing more than an extension of pipes that enables communication between processes distributed across the network. By adding a name to the pipe, it can be directed across the network. When a named pipe is established between two processes, the network OS statically links a name (a file handle) to each end of the pipe. From that point on, reliable two-way communication is established between the processes through the pipe. Access to the named pipe can also be controlled through regular security mechanisms. Figure 2-8 illustrates how named pipes work.

The named pipes protocol is a high-level IPC interface, especially when compared to NetBIOS. For example, a single call at the named pipes level can translate into several NetBIOS calls. The network handles such details as session management, authorization, and so on. Also, the pipe naming is done automatically by the NOS (according to a convention), independent of programmatic control. The named pipes interface is the same for both local and remote IPC. (NetBIOS provides only for remote IPC.) Using named pipes, the application developer is free to concentrate on providing the core functionality of the distributed application, without worrying about network details.

The named pipes protocol is, of course, native to LAN Manager and is used by SQL Server. Named pipes support has been

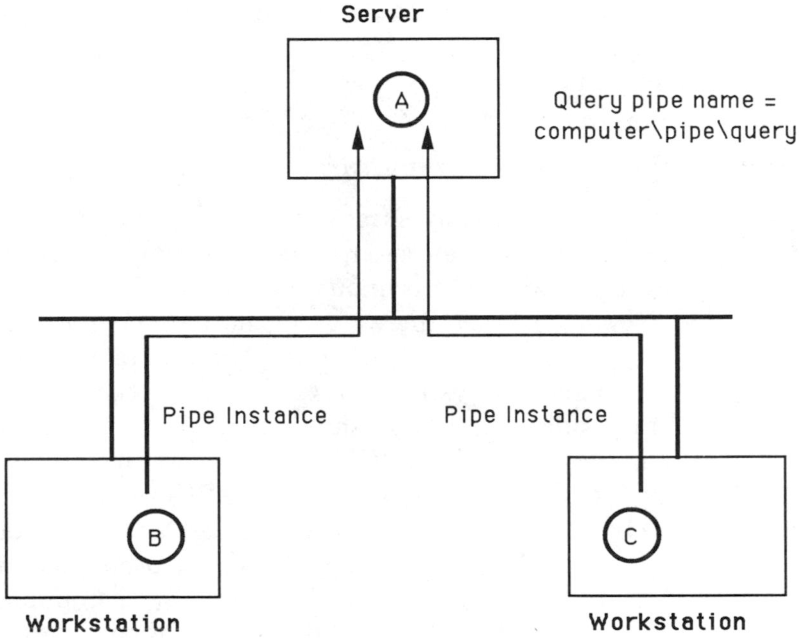

FIGURE 2-8 Named pipes protocol

extended to DOS-based workstations in LAN Manager, and thus serves both DOS and OS/2 clients.

Novell also provides named pipes in the form of an OS/2 requester for workstations running OS/2 on a NetWare LAN. This is implemented on top of the SPX/IPX stack. Thus an OS/2 workstation can provide named pipes support and act as either a workstation or server, depending on configuration parameters. (Currently, named pipes support does not exist for DOS workstations; however, Novell will provide it in the future.) In this way, SQL Server can be run on a NetWare LAN, with both DOS and OS/2 workstations.

Distributed Computing

Distributed computing is made possible by the LANs. This section describes two forms of distributed processing, client-based and client/server, and discusses the differences between them. How the two forms evolved and their relative benefits will be addressed. In order to understand this, you need to know something about more traditional forms of computing that use single and shared processor systems.

Traditional Computing

There are, broadly speaking, three classes of computer systems—according to size, power, and cost—that are prevalent today: microcomputers, minicomputers, and mainframes. Lately, the dividing lines between these systems have become blurred; however, this is still a valid classification. Another, more conceptual way to classify computer systems does not concern their size or cost. Instead it considers the relationship between the users and the central processing unit or units (CPUs) in the overall computer system.

For instance, a dedicated CPU for each user (the case with PCs), has certain advantages or disadvantages. On the other hand, one central CPU that supports many users has a different set of benefits and drawbacks. Traditionally, computer systems have either been shared processing systems or single processing systems. The shared processing systems—the minis and mainframes—run proprietary hardware vendor multiuser operating systems or operating systems such as UNIX. Single processing systems—microcomputers—run single user operating systems such as DOS. These forms of computing are examined in further detail next.

Single Processing Systems Single processing systems dedicate one CPU to each user. These are typically PC-based systems, in which the PC has a single CPU running DOS, supporting a single user. In these systems there can be only one application active at a time. Figure 2-9 illustrates the single processor system.

There are obvious advantages to this type of arrangement. Each PC offers all of its processing power to the user (the user does not have to share his or her CPU cycles with anyone). Each user can customize the computer to suit his or her individual needs, likes, or desires. It is this individual orientation that prompted the development of user-friendly, customizable applications for PCs. Since each user controls the PC, it became apparent that productivity was directly related to the comfort the individual user feels with the application environment. Therefore, unlike large mainframe systems where applications serve the needs (as best as possible) of the user community at large, PC applications are easy to use and highly customizable to suit individual needs.

But there are also disadvantages to single processing systems. They cannot share data with other users or applications in any convenient way. (There's always the so-called sneaker net—hand carrying your data on a floppy disk to another user—but that

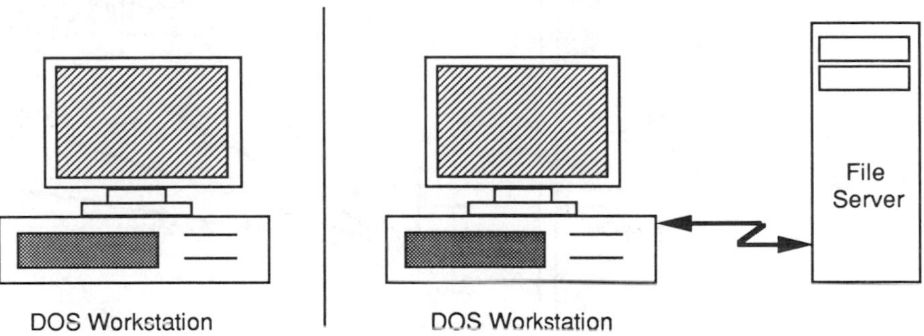

FIGURE 2-9 Single processing systems

quickly gets cumbersome if the amount of data is large, or if there are several versions of it). Thus, there is no practical way data can be used cooperatively; it is impossible for more than one user to be working on the same data at the same time. This can severely limit the overall productivity of a group of users.

Shared Processing Systems More common than single processing systems are **shared processing** systems. In these systems, many users share the processing capabilities of a single CPU (or, in the case of multiprocessor systems, several CPUs). This CPU supports all the users with both applications and data. (Another commonly used term for shared processing is host processing.) Examples of these systems range from supermicros (running SCO XENIX, for example) through DEC VAX machines to IBM 3090s. Figure 2-10 illustrates shared processing systems.

The major advantage of shared processing is that all users can share applications and data seamlessly. This is due to the fact that applications are held in areas of common memory and data reside on storage that is accessible to all qualified users (usually qualification is based on some kind of security criterion). Other advantages are related to the amount of data that the systems can process, their performance, and the overall availability of the data. Their major disadvantage, though, is cost. Mini and mainframe

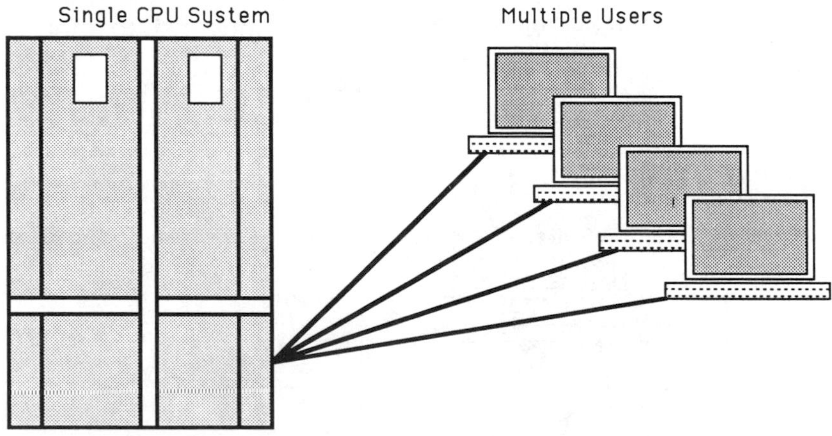

FIGURE 2-10 Shared processing systems

computers can be very expensive; in addition, the maintenance costs can be significant. Applications for these environments tend to be more expensive too, since they are more complex.

Distributed Processing

In **distributed processing**, processing functions are distributed over two or more independent computer systems. Thus the resources of more than one computer system are available to carry out the required tasks. Both client-based and client/server computing will be examined.

Client-based Computing In the early days, LANs were used (especially in PC environments) to share expensive peripheral devices such as laser printers and plotters. As the need for data sharing grew, LANs also were used to share data, but in a rudimentary way—mostly in the form of files with simple file locking capabilities. Central computers on the LAN hold all the resources to be shared by the users of the network. These computers are known as **file servers.**

File servers merely provide basic peripheral sharing; they service requests for data from the user computers, or **workstations.** These requests are for individual files only, since that is all the file server can handle. It is not aware of the contents of the files. This form of computing is called **client-based computing**. Here, all of the application processing occurs at the workstation; the file server computer simply handles requests for files.

Client-based computing—although it's not very different from single-processor stand-alone systems—enables data and peripheral resource sharing. Multiprocessor systems, despite multiple CPUs, are different from client-based computing since they are not truly distributed systems, because the CPUs are not independent. In client-based computing, users can request access to data on the file server, and the file is shipped by special network software to the workstation, where the user processes it however he or she wants.

Client-based systems do have limitations, however. One is that multiple users are still unable to update the same data simultaneously. Files can be shared to only one computer at a time.

While a file server is definitely more convenient than a sneaker net, it still has some of the same problems. Another problem is that the workstation is still required to do all the processing itself, which restricts the amount of data it can process. Remember, not only is the workstation responsible for supporting the application itself (which by itself is processor intensive), it must also be able to process the data that are coming across the LAN as files. The application processing these data cannot be expected to do everything in the most efficient manner possible—often performance suffers.

There is an another, less obvious problem with file servers in a LAN environment. Because file servers have no intelligence, they respond to requests for data by shipping entire files across the network. This increases traffic on the LAN unnecessarily; it wastes valuable network bandwidth. Consider the following example: A workstation is processing the user query "Retrieve all authors who live in Los Angeles." It ships the request to the file server, which responds by shipping the entire authors file to the workstation, which in turn processes the query against the file. So even if there are only five authors who live in Los Angeles of a total of five thousand authors in the authors file, the entire file is shipped. In a system with only a few nodes, it may not be a problem, but it definitely becomes a problem if fifty nodes are issuing simultaneous requests to the file server. The LAN, quite simply, bogs down and throughput and response time degrade rapidly.

There must be a better approach! Indeed there is. This alternative approach, known as **client/server computing,** combines the best of both PC workstation and mini and mainframe DBMS technology. It is the next logical step in the evolution of client-based computing just described. It remedies the major drawbacks of the file server approach. The next section discusses client/server computing in detail since that is the architecture on which SQL Server is based.

Client/Server Computing Client/server computing is a form of distributed processing, but takes the concept of client-based computing a bit further. Rather than having a server that is responsible only for file and peripheral sharing, the server now can act as a computer for running sophisticated network applications.

This is made possible by the client/server architecture, which distributes the processing functions between the workstation and server more efficiently. The server now not only returns files; it performs such data-handling functions as selection and index sorting.

The server is thus an intelligent server. It handles high-level requests for data and only returns the data required to answer the request across the LAN. Of course such a server has to have knowledge of more than raw data files; it has to understand and be capable of processing the high-level requests. Such a server is termed a **database server.** Figure 2-11 illustrates client/server computing.

This separation of the processing functions overcomes the major drawbacks of client-based computing. The problem of unnecessary network traffic is eliminated, since only the requested data are transferred across the LAN. This frees up network bandwidth that can be utilized by additional clients on the LAN. In

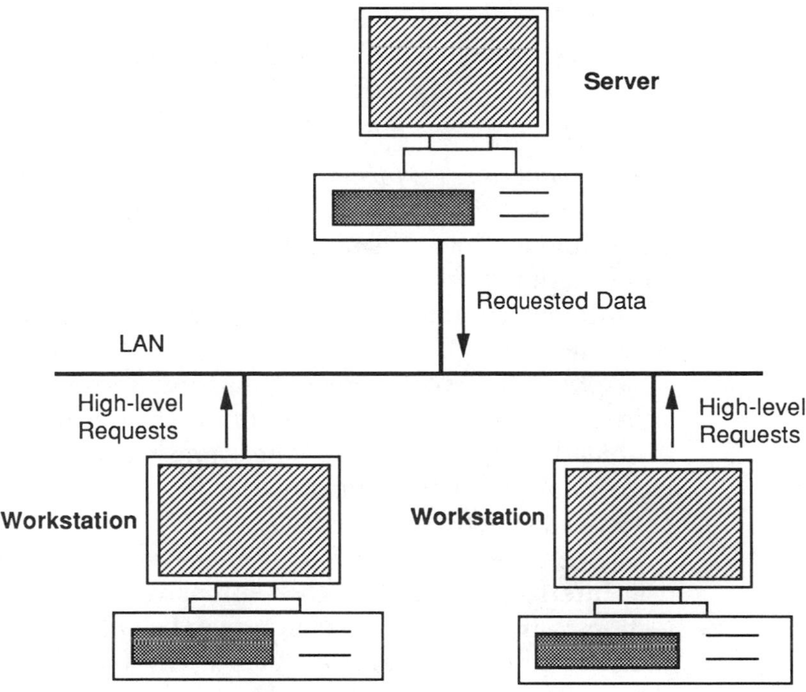

FIGURE 2-11 Client/server computing

addition, since the database server computer's primary purpose is to process requests for data, it can be optimized for this task, rather than serve as a general computer that handles applications as well. Since client computers need now handle only application-specific tasks, they too can be optimized for such tasks.

Benefits of Client/Server Computing The client/server architecture combines the benefits of centralized DBMS systems found in the shared processing environment of minis and mainframes with the user-friendliness and individual orientation found in PC environments. It is, as stated earlier, the next logical step in the evolution of client-based computing found in PC LAN environments. The client concentrates on such application-processing functions as user interface functions, reporting, and application logic. The server concentrates on such traditional DBMS functions as data definition and manipulation, security, backup and recovery, concurrency, and transaction management. The key benefits that result from a client/server architecture are superior performance, centralized administration, scalability, and an open platform. The following paragraphs briefly examine each in turn.

Superior Performance Client/server processing is based on the use of a database server, which significantly reduces LAN traffic and improves the performance of the overall system. Because database functions and application functions are clearly allocated to different computers, each can be optimized to perform their separate tasks.

For example, the client machine resources can be concentrated on providing the best possible user interface, without needing to consider database access. The server machine, conversely, is not responsible for supporting any user interface functions and can be optimized for DBMS activities.

As mentioned before, applications processing—especially user interface software—is CPU intensive. By relieving it from that responsibility, the server machine can be optimized for server functions. Here is one example: With many DBMSs it is possible to set configuration parameters in order to make use of all of the available memory on the machine. Because the server machine does not support any applications, all of the machine's memory can be used by the DBMS.

Database servers, unlike file servers, have knowledge of the tables, rows, and columns inside the database. Hence they can provide better concurrency controls to ensure that many users can access the same data at the same time. In file servers, the concurrency controls have to be at the level of files, since that is all the file server knows about. In database servers it is possible to have concurrency controls at a finer granularity—at the level of rows or pages, for example, rather than at the file or table level. This will significantly improve performance, especially in high update environments.

Centralized Data Administration The client/server model provides centralized data administration, since all the databases are managed and accessed by a central database server. This is a key component of the model, since all database processing is centralized in the server. The database server is responsible for such common DBMS functions as data concurrency, integrity, security, backup, and recovery in much the same way that they are handled by mini and mainframe DBMSs.

Scalability This benefit, though not so obvious, is nevertheless important. Since the processing of application and database functions is clearly separated in the client/server model, it is theoretically possible to replace the back-end database server with an identical server running on more powerful hardware and software, without affecting the front-end application. This concept is called **scalability**. Although a simple concept, it has big benefits. The first is that the front-end is virtually unchanged, and the user's investment in application software and training is protected. Another is that it offers you a low-cost growth path. If you start out on a 386 machine running OS/2, you can upgrade to a 486 machine or to a supermicro running UNIX, for example. Of course, the assumption is that the same protocol stacks are available for both the client and server environments.

Open Platform Most database servers have some form of published interface (the API discussed earlier) that can be used to develop applications for it. It is possible to take the stand-alone or file server versions of popular workstation programs and develop database server versions. This is really the client/server version of the product. All of the data reside in the database server, where they enjoy better data integrity, security, recovery, and so on, and all of the familiarity and power of the application are preserved.

SQL Server

This chapter and the preceding chapter have presented the basics of several different technologies that form the basis for SQL Server.

SQL Server is a high-performance, SQL-based, relational database server that is based on client/server architecture. Client applications formulate queries in SQL and ship them via the LAN to the SQL Server where they are processed. SQL Server processes the SQL request and returns to the application only the required data necessary to process the request.

In a PC LAN environment, there are several requirements for running SQL Server. The first is that SQL Server must run on an OS/2 computer. Additionally, SQL Server requires the named pipes interface in order to carry out communication on a network. It is NOS independent—that is, all communication with SQL goes through the named pipes interface. Thus, SQL Server will run on any LAN as long as the NOS supports named pipes. An alternative to OS/2-based LANs (such as 3Com 3+Open, Ungermann-Bass UB-NET ONE, or IBM's LAN Server) is Novell's NetWare.

Novell provides named pipes support in the form of an OS/2 requestor that basically allows a machine running OS/2 on a NetWare LAN to run SQL Server on the machine. The named pipes interface frees applications developers from having to write low-level NOS calls to enable IPC between client applications and SQL Server.

It should also be pointed out that SQL Server by no means runs only in PC LAN environments; in fact, it was first developed for UNIX and VMS minicomputer environments using TCP/IP and DECNET protocols. The basic client/server architecture of the SQL Server, however, is still the same on all the platforms. Another important point is that client/server architecture offers a scalable and open platform. With client support for different protocols stacks in LAN Manager and with LAN Manager's availability on key server platforms—LM/X under UNIX and LAN Manager on DEC hardware, you can have a truly heterogenous solution that allows different client workstations to talk to SQL Servers running under different back-end environments.

Summary

This chapter discussed LANs and their role in enabling distributed computing. Several forms of computing, specifically two forms of distributed computing, client-based and client/server, were described. SQL Server is a relational database server that is based on the client/server model and forms the back-end server component. Client communication with the server is through the high-level named pipes protocol. The next chapter begins to look in depth at the SQL Server product itself, beginning with its architecture.

CHAPTER 3

Architectural Overview

Introduction

As indicated in the first two chapters, SQL Server is a high performance, multiuser, relational database server based on SQL. It is built on client/server architecture, which implies a front-end, or client component, and a back-end, or server, component. SQL Server itself forms the back-end component in this architecture and is responsible for providing all the standard DBMS functions. The client component, for which there are many different possibilities, is responsible for providing all of the user-interface and application-processing functions. The language used to communicate between clients and SQL Server is called TRANSACT-SQL. TRANSACT-SQL is generally a superset of the two primary SQL standards mentioned in Chapter 1.

SQL Server was developed for the **on-line transaction processing** (OLTP) environment. This environment is characterized by a large number of concurrent users, large databases (several gigabytes), and applications with high transaction rates. OLTP systems are different from **decision support systems**, which are retrieval oriented, in that they are less demanding on the DBMS. SQL Server was designed for performance, with several features specifically intended for OLTP environments. These features will be discussed in this chapter.

It was pointed out earlier that the focus of this book is SQL Server in PC LAN environments. That means that the operating systems, network operating systems, and client applications discussed are from the PC environment. SQL Server has essentially the same architecture and features in different environments and is fairly well insulated from the underlying network layers. Thus, to a large extent, the statements made about SQL Server in this book hold true for other environments, too. In fact, although the version numbering schemes of SQL Server differ in PC and other environments, the intent is to keep the functionality in the different environments synchronized. Thus the next major release of SQL Server for OS/2 environments will encompass most of the functionality of the SYBASE Release 4.0 for UNIX.

In the PC LAN environment, SQL Server runs on an OS/2-based machine and requires named pipes support provided by the network operating system for remote client application communication. The client computer (or workstation), however, can run on either DOS or OS/2. All communication between the client application and SQL Server uses TRANSACT-SQL. Figure 3-1 illustrates the relationship between the client application and SQL Server.

Since SQL Server is strictly a software product that does not require any specialized hardware, it can be run in many different configurations. This flexibility allows you to choose the configuration best suited for your needs. Some of the possibilities are:

- running SQL Server and client applications on the same computer
- running SQL Server on a dedicated computer, or on the the file server, supporting one or more client applications running on one or more workstations
- running multiple SQL Servers on dedicated computers, communicating with multiple client applications

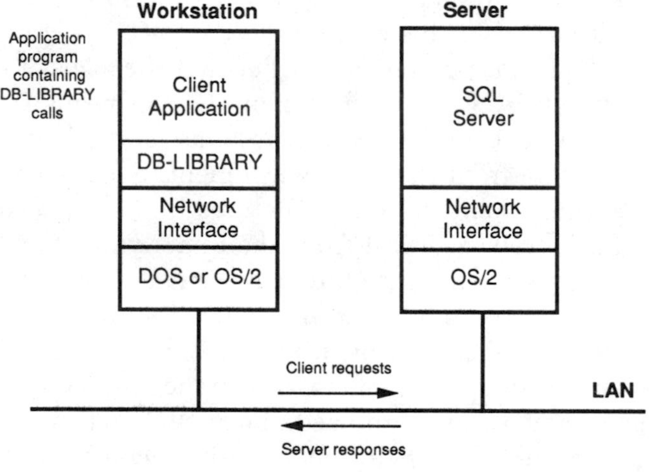

FIGURE 3-1 Client and SQL Server

This chapter presents a high-level architectural overview of the SQL Server environment, encompassing both the client and the Server, and outlines the salient features of SQL Server. Subsequent chapters explore these features in detail.

Server Architecture

Traditional DBMS architectures typically come in one of two forms—either a single-process architecture where users are handled by separate tasks or threads, or a multiprocess architecture where separate processes are spawned to manage additional users. The disadvantage of the first form is that all user requests are essentially single threaded through the DBMS, with the inherent potential for bottlenecks. (Note that this approach is fine for a single-user, workstation DBMS.) On the other hand, multiprocess architecture makes inefficient use of such system resources as memory, although it alleviates the single threading of the single process architecture in multiprocessor machines. With single processor computers, as additional users are added to the system, both response time and transaction throughput deteriorate rapidly.

SQL Server uses a **single-process, multithreaded** architecture—an architecture that uses multiple threads within a single process to service multiple users. This architecture has two key benefits. First, switching between the various user tasks (known as context switching) is much more efficient because it is handled within SQL Server internally. This allows multiple user requests to be processed concurrently, while context switching at the OS level (which occurs in multiprocess architectures) is minimized. The difference is shown in Figure 3-2.

Another benefit in this architecture is efficient use of memory. The memory overhead associated with multiple users is much smaller than that of multiprocess architectures. As a result, SQL Server achieves both a high transaction throughput that remains fairly constant as the number of users increases and a quick response time that increases linearly as users are added. See Figure 3-3. In contrast, the response time and transaction throughput of multiprocess architectures suffer significantly as the number of users increases.

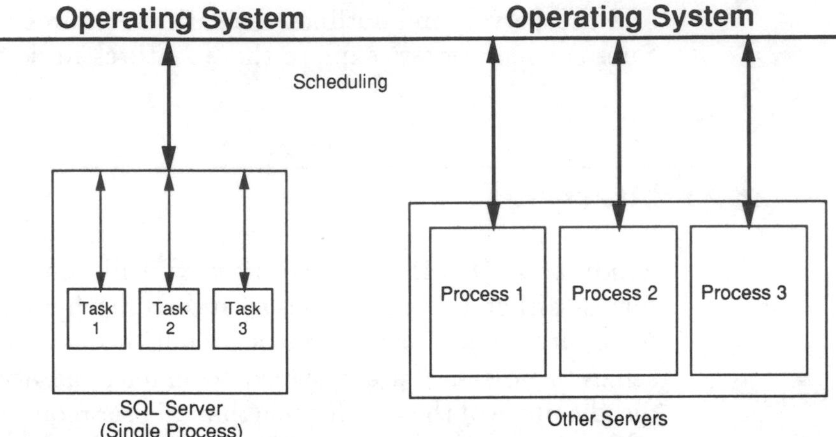

FIGURE 3-2 Multithreaded versus Multiprocess context switching

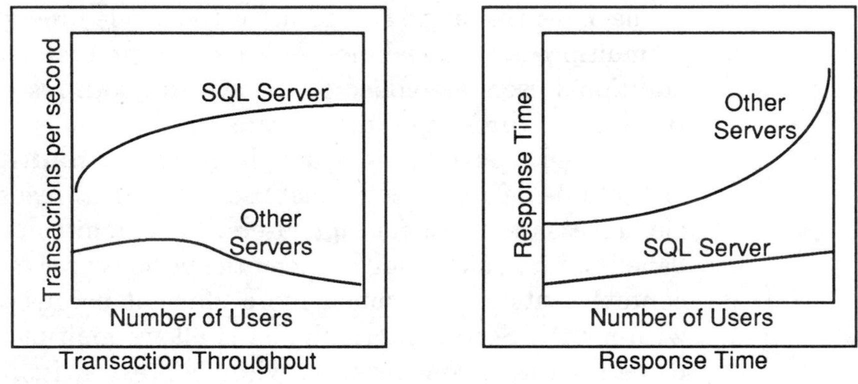

FIGURE 3-3 Transaction throughput and response time versus users

Server Components

The basic components of SQL Server are shown in Figure 3-4. As shown in the diagram, the Server comprises several key components. At the core of SQL Server is the **kernel**. The kernel is responsible for many of the functions normally performed by the operating system—scheduling, task switching, disk caching, locking, and so on. By implementing these functions efficiently in its

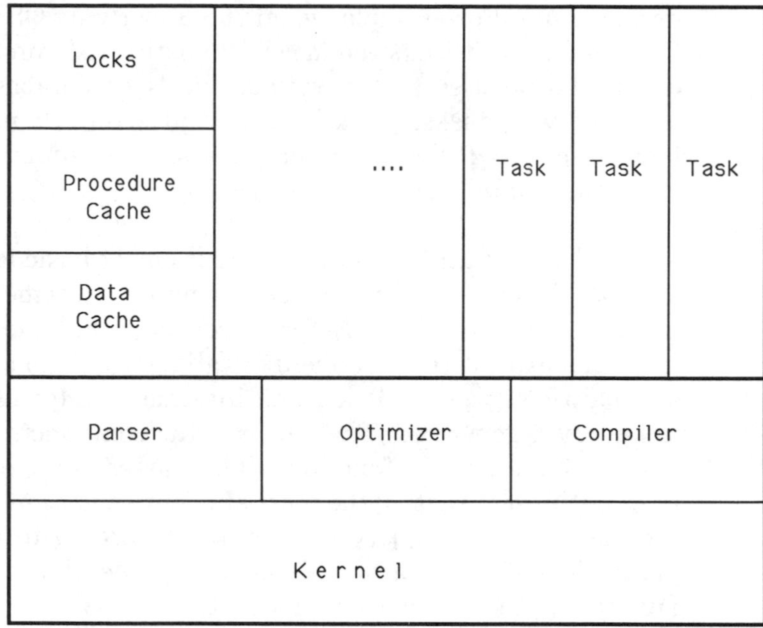

FIGURE 3-4 Basic SQL Server architecture

own kernel, SQL Server avoids any inefficiencies in the underlying OS. This makes it perform identically in different environments.

The other key components are the **parser**, the **optimizer** and the **compiler**. These components and their functions will be explained later in this chapter. In addition, there are several system tasks that the Server uses to manage its resources, for example, network-related tasks and disk management tasks. In addition, every client connection constitutes a task at the Server end. The functions of the core components of the Server are discussed in the next sections.

Optimized Kernel The kernel is the heart of the SQL Server. It is a highly optimized kernel that performs many of the functions that are normally the responsibility of the operating system. The kernel is responsible for task scheduling, context switching, buffer and cache management, and, ultimately, for executing the compiled queries themselves. By handling many of these OS functions itself, the Server is able to provide a very high level of performance. For example, when the underlying OS is responsible for scheduling, it lacks the means to distinguish among and assign different priorities to the various kinds of database tasks (user tasks, network tasks, recovery tasks, and so on). By managing these tasks itself, SQL Server is able to assign scheduling priorities to these tasks intelligently.

Parser and Compiler At its most basic level, the job of any DBMS can be viewed as executing the statements that make up its database language. Before executing a statement, the DBMS must ensure that the statement is valid, both from a syntactic and a semantic viewpoint. If it is, an intermediate (or parsed) form of the query is generated. The parser is the component of the DBMS responsible for these functions. The parsed form of the query is then optimized, that is, the most efficient execution plan is chosen for the query. The query is compiled according to this execution plan. This yields the actual machine code that is executed by DBMS to process the user's request.

In SQL Server, too, the parser performs these functions. Whenever a TRANSACT-SQL statement is received from a front-end client, the parser is invoked to check its correctness. It first ensures syntactic correctness—that valid keywords are used and the syntax of the statements is valid. Beyond that the parser ensures that all object references in the query are valid—that the tables, views, and columns all exist (or don't exist). If everything checks out, the parser generates the intermediate form of the query.

Cost-based Optimizer An essential component of every database management system is a **query optimizer**. (The term query encompasses both retrieval and modification statements in the DML.) This is especially true for DBMSs that provide a non-procedural database language such as SQL. Remember that in SQL, you specify what data you want to retrieve or modify; not the steps required to achieve it. Therefore, some component of the DBMS must be responsible for figuring out the most efficient way of processing a statement. This component is called the query optimizer.

A query optimizer's task is much like that of a motorist trying to get from one point in a city to another in the shortest possible time. The motorist must evaluate several alternative plans, taking into account several factors that will affect the time it takes to get from the point of origin to the destination. Some of these factors are the distances of alternative routes, the number of stop lights for each route, the average wait at each stop light, the current traffic pattern, and so on. Based on all of these factors, the motorist determines the optimum plan (or route) and then follows this plan.

SQL Server's query optimizer behaves much like the motorist. When a query is received by SQL Server, it is parsed and an internal form of the query is generated. Next, permissions are checked. If the user does not possess the required permissions, the query processing is aborted. Otherwise, the query passes through the optimization stage. SQL Server's query optimizer then generates a series of alternative strategies to process the query. It calculates an estimated cost (in terms of disk access) associated with processing the query according to each strategy. The cost is typically a weighted average of the amount of disk accesses due to various factors. Some of the factors that affect the cost are: whether or not an index can be used to speed up the retrieval, what percentage of the rows will be selected, the number of rows in the tables, and the distribution of the key values in the tables. The optimizer then picks the strategy with the lowest cost. This is the execution plan for the query. It is used by the compiler to generate the compiled form of the query.

SQL Server's query optimizer is unique in two ways. First, it is cost based, that is, it calculates an estimated cost for each alternative before picking one. Many optimizers are simplistic in evaluating their alternative strategies, which often leads to less than optimal execution plans. Second, the Server maintains statistical information about the distribution of the key values (by ranges) that provides the optimizer a much finer estimate of the number of rows that will be selected at various stages of the execution plan. As a result, the optimizer's estimates are much more accurate those of other systems. Figure 3-5 shows how the Server maintains distribution statistics.

Salient Features

The previous section discussed the core components of SQL Server. Here we focus on the salient features of the Server. There are many

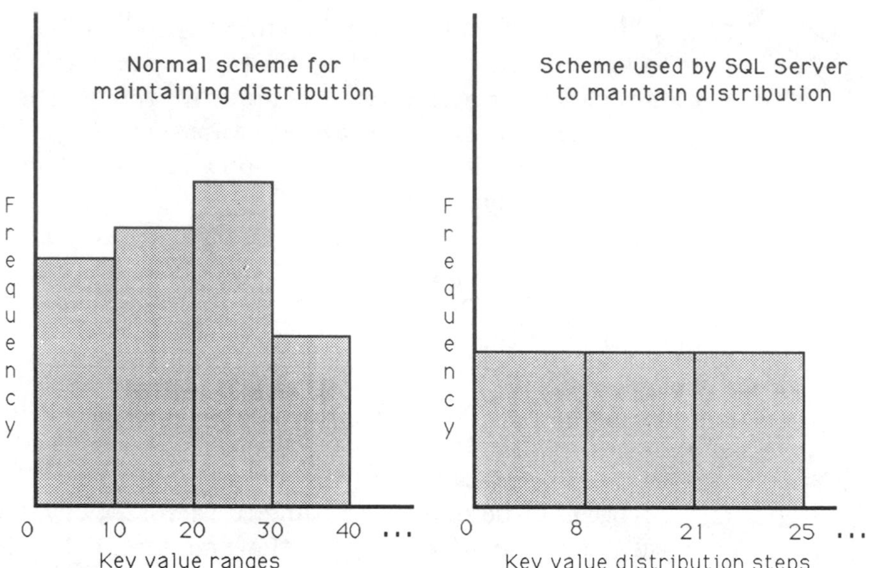

FIGURE 3-5 Distribution statistics maintained by the Server

features that you expect from any DBMS—a database language, transaction processing, recovery, security, and so on—and the SQL Server provides all of these features. Rather than discuss all of these features here, we will concentrate on features that set SQL Server apart from the rest of its competitors. They can be classified into performance, Server enforced integrity and security, high availability, and an open, scalable, distributed architecture. These are discussed in turn.

Performance Features SQL Server was designed specifically for mission-critical, online transaction processing applications. These applications require high transaction throughput, quick response times, and the ability to maintain the throughput without significant degradation, as the demands on the system grow. The designers of SQL Server, therefore incorporated several performance features to ensure that its performance objectives are met. They include a multi-threaded architecture, data and procedure caching, stored procedures, shared commits, and various tuning and configuration parameters.

The multi-threaded architecture has already been discussed earlier in the chapter. The key implications are that the Server makes much more efficient use of resources on the Server computer, and does not have the OS overhead associated with multiprocess architectures. For example, each additional megabyte of memory can accommodate 25 additional users. This frees up memory for data and procedure caching, thus improving performance. SQL Server also handles key OS functions such as locking and caching internally using threads, and hence does not have to rely on the underlying OS to perform these functions.

SQL Server has a configurable memory cache for improving disk access. A cache is simply a portion of allocated memory that is used to buffer disk pages. By trying to keep the required pages in the cache, and accessing them there, the amount of disk I/O is greatly reduced. Of course, updated cache pages must be periodically written to disk. We will define periodically more precisely in Chapter 11, when we discuss transactions and logging.

The cache in SQL Server is divided between data and procedures, and you can change the percentage allocated to each. The data cache is used for data, index, and log pages thus improving performance significantly.

One of the most significant enhancements provided by SQL Server is stored procedures. Stored procedures are a set of precompiled SQL statements stored in the Server's data dictionary. Stored procedures are executed by name, and can take parameters and call other **stored procedures**. When the procedure is invoked, it is executed without recompilation (unless objects that it references have changed). Thus, stored procedures offer significant benefits over regular SQL statements—improved performance and reduced network traffic. In addition, they are both shared and cached. That is, many users can execute the same procedure (provided they have the permission), and if an available copy of the procedure exists in cache, it will be used.

SQL Server also offers several configuration parameters and options that affect performance. They range from options that affect the overall Server performance, such as the recovery interval (for recovering a database) to setting individual query processing options that allow you to examine the number of disk and cache accesses made by a query. These options are discussed in Chapter 12.

Server Enforced Integrity and Security In OLTP environments, where there could potentially be a large number of concurrent users or applications, integrity and security are key concerns. Integrity ensures the accuracy, validity, and consistency of the data in the database. Security is concerned with defining authorized users and ensuring that all access to the data is authorized.

Security is an integral part of the functionality provided by most relational DBMSs. However, in the case of integrity, the reverse is true—support for integrity is either limited or absent at the DBMS level. In such environments, integrity is often enforced at the application level. In SQL Server, both integrity and security are enforced centrally using simple TRANSACT-SQL statements. This results in several benefits: the integrity and security checking of the Server cannot be circumvented, application development and maintainance costs are reduced, and potential inconsistencies in defining integrity are eliminated.

SQL Server uses several objects to enforce integrity and security. Some of them are defined using standard SQL statements, while others are defined with extensions to standard SQL provided by the Server. These objects include system data types, user-defined data types, null values, rules, defaults, triggers, views, procedures and statement and object permissions. These are discussed in detail in Chapters 7, 8 and 9.

High Availability In many environments, especially OLTP environments, it is expensive or even unacceptable to have the Server unavailable. Many DBMSs allow backups or design changes only when there are no users online, thus reducing availability greatly. SQL Server provides high availability by providing online maintenance and fast recovery. Online maintenance features allow you to perform dynamic backup and database design changes (that is, with users online). In addition, SQL Server also allows you to tune the maximum time it takes to recover a database from a system failure by setting a configuration parameter. All of these features significantly reduce down time, thus making SQL Server an ideal choice for mission-critical applications. In a future version,

SQL Server (under OS/2) will support disk mirroring of the database or transaction log to provide fault tolerance at the DBMS level. This functionality is already available on UNIX and VMS platforms.

Open, Scalable, Distributed DBMS Chapter 2 touched on some of the benefits of the client/server architecture—open architecture and scalable performance. Since SQL Server is based on this architecture, it too provides these benefits. By providing an open client interface for application development (discussed later in this chapter), it is possible for a wide variety of software products or custom applications to communicate with the Server. Some of the client applications that are in existence or being developed for the SQL Server are discussed in the following section. SYBASE also provides an Open Server interface for developing applications that are Server independent—that is applications written to this interface can access data from various back-end database servers.

The ability to run SQL Server on a different hardware platform without impacting client applications is termed **vertical scalability**. The ability to have multiple SQL Servers running on the same network is termed **horizontal scalability**. Both these abilities offer scalable performance. SQL Server is available from SYBASE for many different mini and mainframe software platforms (including UNIX and VMS) and hardware platforms (including Sun, VAX, and Pyramid computers). With client/server architecture there is clean separation of front-end user-interface and application processing functions from the back-end DBMS functions. Thus it is theoretically possible for a client application under OS/2 to access data on a SQL Server running under Ultrix (a UNIX flavor) in a VAX environment. Of course, the client and server must use common network protocols. Although not all of these protocols exist currently, it is SYBASE's intent is to provide complete vertical scalability with future versions.

Multiple SQL Servers are allowed on a network, thus allowing for distribution of data across the Servers. Two issues are important when dealing with distributed data—distributed retrievals and distributed updates. Most DBMSs provide little or no support for distributed data. SQL Server provides support for applications to perform both distributed retrieval and distributed updates through its client interface. However, this support does not exist at the level of SQL statements. SQL Server does however, allow you to access data in multiple databases simultaneously; a feature absent from many SQL implementations. In addition, it provides the two-phase commit protocol that is essential for guaranteeing the integrity and consistency of distributed updates.

Future versions of SQL Server will move toward providing more and more transparent support for distributed databases (databases on separate Servers). Some UNIX and VMS versions of SQL Server already allow Server-Server communication with **remote procedure calls** (RPCs)—by enabling a stored procedure on one Server to invoke a stored procedure on another Server. Unfortunately, this functionality is not yet available in the OS/2 version.

Client Components

Like SQL Server, the client application consists of several components. As discussed earlier, SQL Server provides an open platform on which a wide variety of client applications can be developed. The interface provided for writing these applications for SQL Server is known as DB-LIBRARY. DB-LIBRARY is a call-level interface (discussed in Chapter 1) that is available for DOS and OS/2 environments. It can be used for developing applications in many different languages—C, PASCAL, and COBOL to name a few. The next sections discuss two client applications, written using DB-LIBRARY, that are provided with SQL Server.

isql

The **isql** application is a simple command-line utility that interfaces to SQL Server. Both DOS and OS/2 versions are provided. The isql utility allows users to send TRANSACT-SQL statements to the Server and to view the results returned. It is a fairly rudimentary utility in that it has no built-in editing, formatting, or scrolling capabilities. If an error occurs in typing or executing a statement, it must be corrected by completely rekeying the statements. If column headings or data rows returned are larger than the screen width, they simply wrap onto the next line. Figure 3-6 illustrates the isql interface.

The isql utility can be invoked to establish a connection with the Server by simply typing isql at the operating system prompt, followed by any command-line options. There are several command-line options that can be specified–a list of the more common ones follows. These options allow you to specify, for example, the name of the Server you want to connect to, the Server login ID and password, or the input and output file names. In addition, external DOS or OS/2 editors such as EDLIN or MEP can be invoked from isql using the ed command once the appropriate environment variables have been set up. (The ed command is discussed shortly.)

Option	**Definition**
`/e`	echos input
`/c <batend>`	changes end of batch terminator to `<batend>`

```
1> use pubs
2> go
1> select pub_id, pub_name, city
2> from publishers
3> go

pub_id pub_name                   city
------ -------------------------- -------------
0736   New Age Books              Boston
0877   Binnet & Hardley           Washington
1389   Algodata Infosystems       Berkeley

(3 rows affected)
```

FIGURE 3-6 The isql interface

`/U <login_id>`	specifies the Server login ID
`/P <password>`	specifies the password for the login ID
`/S <server>`	specifies the server name
`/i <inp_file>`	specifies the input file name that contains the TRANSACT-SQL batch; the OS redirection symbol (<) can be used instead of /i
`/o <out_file>`	specifies the output file name for the results; the redirection symbol (>) can be used instead of /o

Once a user is connected to SQL Server, a line number and a line prompt (the > character) within isql is returned. TRANSACT-SQL statements can then be typed in, on one or more lines as desired (SQL statements are free form). A `go` on a line by itself signals an end of a command batch (one or more TRANSACT-SQL statements). Then isql sends the command batch to the Server. SQL Server processes the batch and returns the results for each statement in the batch to isql, which displays them. If errors are encountered in the batch, the appropriate error numbers and messages are returned. Stored procedures can also be executed through isql. isql itself does not preprocess the SQL statements in any way. It simply uses the DB-LIBRARY facilities for executing the batches, processing the results, and handling errors. A list of the isql commands follows.

Command	**description**
go	terminates command batch and sends it to SQL Server for processing
reset	clears the buffer of any statements
ed	invokes the editor (if defined)
!!<command>	executes an OS command
quit | exit	exits isql

The isql utility is a valuable tool for SQL Server primarily because it gives the user or developer a quick and ready interface to the Server. It provides, for example, an easy way to verify if a query will run or return the results expected. It can be used to verify the proper functioning of all the component parts of the Server environment. It is easy to isolate problems through the use of isql. For instance, you can quickly determine if a problem resides within a particular front-end application by checking whether or not the query can be run through a simpler utility—isql can serve the purpose.

System Administration Facility

The **Server Administration Facility** (SAF) is another front-end client application provided with SQL Server. It is a window-oriented, menu-driven, easy-to-use application intended primarily for administering the Server. It is written in C, using the DB-LIBRARY interface; it is available for both DOS and OS/2. The SAF provides menu selections for common administration tasks such as viewing currently logged-on users, adding a user, or backing up a database. Like isql, SAF allows users to execute TRANSACT-SQL statements (or stored procedures) through the interactive SQL Query window. However, it is much more window oriented than isql; it has an in-built editor and allows display of both the query and the results in different windows on the same screen. Figure 3-7 shows the SAF home screen.

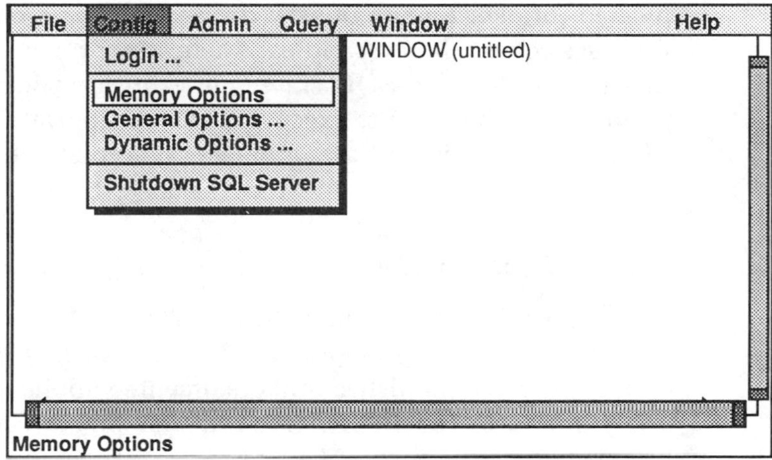

FIGURE 3-7 SAF home screen

The five major menus in the SAF are: File, Configuration, Administration, Query, and Window. The File menu allows the user to load a preexisting file containing TRANSACT-SQL statements into the Query window, or to save the current contents of the window to a specified file. It also allows printing the contents of the window to a specified printer. The Configuration menu allows the user to change global configuration parameters, to shut down the Server, or to log in to another Server. The Administration menu allows the user to perform several administrative tasks—to back up and restore databases, manage login IDs and users, view currently logged on users, and change database owners. The Query menu allows query execution and logging of queries and results in a file. Finally, the Window menu allows the user to control the size of the Query and Result windows on the screen. It should be pointed out that, to use any of these menus, the user must possess the appropriate permissions. In fact, the SAF conveniently grays out menu selections that are not accessible.

The SAF automates a number of frequently used administrative tasks that otherwise would require intimate knowledge of many TRANSACT-SQL statements. It provides both mouse support and shortcut keystrokes for the more commonly used menu options—these shortcuts are indicated next to the menu options. Operations such as backing up and restoring a database, changing configuration parameters, or system auditing can all be accomplished through the use of easy-to-use, point-and-click menus or a few keystrokes. However, an experienced user can choose to enter in the TRANSACT-SQL statements directly. For functions not provided by the menus, executing the appropriate TRANSACT-SQL statements is still the only way to accomplish them.

Other Client Applications

It was mentioned in the introduction that SQL Server provides an open platform for development of a wide variety of client applications. It has a published and documented applications programming interface, DB-LIBRARY, that developers can use to communicate with the Server. As a result, many vendors of popular PC programs—everything from spreadsheets to graphics programs to workstation DBMSs have pledged support for SQL Server. In addition, there are several custom vertical-market software systems (based on client/server architecture) that are being developed around SQL Server. This class of software is often described as **groupware**; it is software intended for a group of workstation users in a LAN environment.

A list of client software that is, or will be, available for SQL Server follows. The list is by no means comprehensive, but is an indication of the broad level of support that the Server enjoys. The front-ends that were being shipped at the time of publication are indicated by an asterisk; the others are all expected to be available within the next year or so (the exact availability can be confirmed by calling the vendor).

dBASE IV Server Edition (Ashton-Tate)
Paradox (Borland)*
DataEase SQL (DataEase)*
PC/Focus (Information Builders)*
Lotus 1-2-3 (Lotus Development)
Excel (Microsoft)
Advanced Revelation (Revelation Technologies)*
Object/1 (Micro Database Systems)*
Clipper (Nantucket)
FileShare (Saros Corporation)*
Forest and Trees (Channel Computing)*
SQR (SQL Solutions)*
ADS SQL Library (Automated Design)*
Capture and dBSQL-IV (Datawiz)*
SQLFILE (Vinzant, Inc.)*

The DB-LIBRARY Applications Programming Interface

DB-LIBRARY forms an important component of every client application, since it is the interface for developing applications for the Server. Basically, DB-LIBRARY is a set of functions written in C, that can be called from several different languages—C, PASCAL, and COBOL are examples. An easy way to think of it is that DB-LIBRARY is the component that manages the communication with the Server—it transmits client application requests in TRANSACT-SQL (the language that SQL Server understands) to the Server and manages the results returned.

DB-LIBRARY serves several important functions. First, it serves as a consistent programming interface for different languages. In other OS environments, where there is direct support for multiple languages, the DB-LIBRARY function calls are essentially the same from language to language. This makes it easy to port applications from one language to another. Second, DB-LIBRARY provides built-in network support; that is, it serves to shield users from the intricacies of underlying network protocols. For example, DB-LIBRARY provides high-level calls to connect to or disconnect from a Server, by making the appropriate calls to the network interface itself. In a sense, DB-LIBRARY allows an application to connect to or disconnect from a Server by name, rather than by network address. Third, it serves to insulate the client application from internal changes in the Server—as long as applications are written to the DB-LIBRARY interface, only the interface has to be changed.

DB-LIBRARY consists of a comprehensive set of function calls. The purpose of these functions is to allow the applications to manage the communication to and from the Server easily. These functions can be broadly classified into the following groups.

- initialization and housekeeping
- command setup and execution
- result processing
- error and message handling
- information retrieval
- miscellaneous
- advanced capabilities

Chapter 5 discusses the DB-LIBRARY functions in detail. For now, it should be pointed out that DB-LIBRARY is provided for several client environments—DOS, DOS with Windows, and OS/2—and is implemented differently in these environments. In DOS it is a **static library**. In DOS Windows and OS/2, it is a **dynamic-link library**. A static library is linked at compile time, whereas a dynamic-link library is linked to at run-time. The dynamic-link library is loaded on the first call to it.

TRANSACT-SQL

TRANSACT-SQL represents the flavor of SQL that is implemented by SQL Server. Like other database languages, it has two major components: data definition and data manipulation. Data definition provides for the creation, modification, and removal of database objects. Data manipulation provides for the retrieval and modification of the actual data that are stored in the database. In addition, TRANSACT-SQL has components that are concerned with defining data integrity constraints, defining privileges for executing statements and accessing data, and performing such administrative tasks as creating devices and backing up databases. Chapters 4 through 7 deal with the core components of the database language. Most of the statements and system procedures for data integrity, control, and administration are discussed in Chapters 8 through 12 of the book.

In general, TRANSACT-SQL is compatible with both the ANSI standard for SQL and IBM's SAA SQL standard (discussed in Chapter 1). It has many enhancements, however, that go beyond the two standards and beyond other commercial SQL implementations. These enhancements are discussed in the next section.

Extensions to Standard SQL

TRANSACT-SQL provides many useful extensions to standard SQL. Some are extensions to standard SQL statements such as SELECT or INSERT, which have been provided with enhanced functionality. Other extensions are entirely new statements that provide additional features or constructs. An outline of the major extensions follows. Examples of their usage are given in appropriate chapters throughout the book.

1. extensions to standard SQL
   - updates on views with minor restrictions
   - support for advanced data types, such as money, text, and image
   - definition of user-defined types based on system data types
   - creation of temporary tables
   - the ability to insert data in a table based on other data in the same or other tables
   - the ability to update or delete data in a table based on data in other tables
   - many additional built-in functions for manipulating data
2. a comprehensive **control-of-flow language** similar to that found in most programming languages, which provides the following statements
   - DECLARE
   - IF .. ELSE
   - WHILE
   - BEGIN .. END
   - BREAK
   - CONTINUE
   - RETURN
   - PRINT
   - GOTO
   - WAITFOR
   - RAISERROR
3. the COMPUTE clause in a SELECT statement, which when used with aggregate functions (SUM, MAX, MIN, AVG, COUNT), can generate control break reports
4. stored procedures, a named, precompiled set of TRANSACT-SQL statements that offers significant performance advantages

5. advanced data integrity mechanisms
   - defaults to provide values for columns automatically if none is provided
   - rules, which are mechanisms to enforce integrity constraints on data (can be used to enforce the concept of domains discussed in Chapter 1)
   - triggers, which are special kinds of stored procedures used to enforce referential integrity or integrity constraints that are based on business policy
6. the FOR BROWSE extension to the SELECT statement, which enables tables to be browsed from a DB-LIBRARY application
7. many global parameters, database options, and query processing options for monitoring and tuning performance

Summary

This chapter presented an architectural overview of both the client and server environments. It discussed the salient features of SQL Server and looked at two client applications—isql and SAF—that are provided as part of the SQL Server software. The role of DB-LIBRARY in providing the API for SQL Server was examined and the core language components in TRANSACT-SQL and the many extensions it provides over standard SQL were discussed. The next chapter discusses data definition—how to create, destroy, and modify the structure of objects in SQL Server.

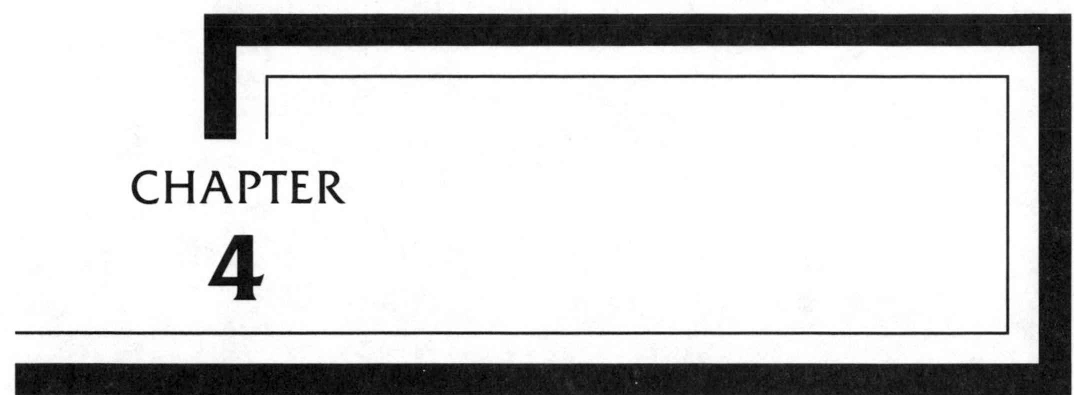

Data Definition

Introduction

This chapter focuses on the data definition component of TRANS-ACT-SQL. The DDL allows the user to create and drop database objects and modify their definition. What then is a database object? It is any object that is defined within the context of a database. SQL Server supports a rich set of database objects beyond those found in most relational DBMSs. They are:

databases	user-defined data types
tables	defaults
views	rules
indexes	stored procedures
	triggers

Managing the various database objects will be discussed later in the chapter. The next few sections describe how SQL Server's databases are organized and how objects are known within the context of these databases.

Databases in SQL Server

Databases are not, strictly speaking, database objects, but they can be considered as such for the purposes of the DDL. They are really objects within whose context other objects are defined. In addition, some objects depend on others for their definition—they may include references to other objects in their definition. Figure 4-1 shows the various database objects and their dependencies.

Every SQL Server installation can have many distinct databases. In fact, resources permitting, there can be 32,627 of them. There are basically two types of databases in SQL Server: **system databases**, which are created at server installation time, and **user databases**, which are created by users. The next two sections examine each in turn and explain how information about the databases and their objects are maintained on the server.

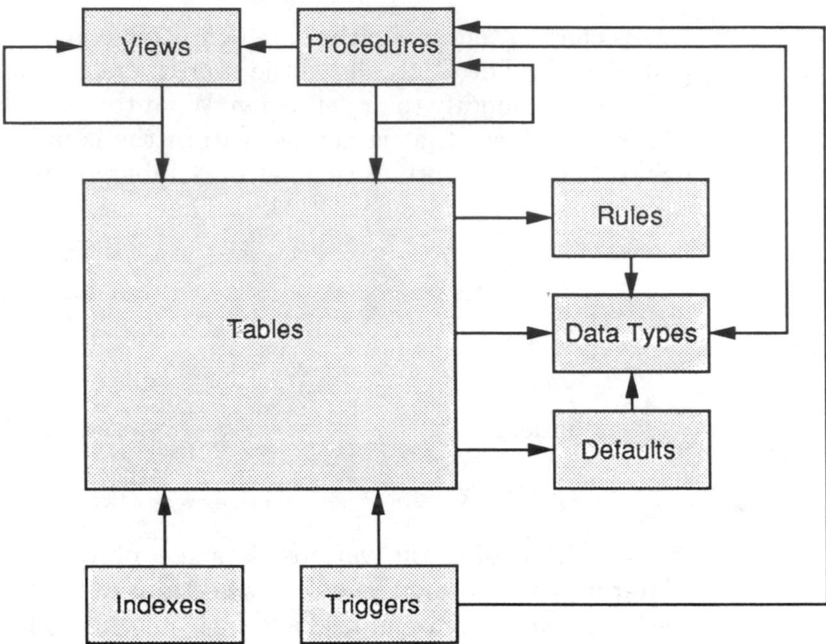

FIGURE 4-1 Database objects

System Databases

Three databases are created during SQL Server installation. These are special databases that are used by the server for different purposes and are called system databases. The three system databases are the master database (*master*), the model database (*model*) and the temporary database (*tempdb*). There is also an optional fourth database that can be installed, the sample *pubs* database; however, this is not a system database.

The master database is used to store information about the other server databases (both system and user) and to control the operation of the server as a whole–login ids and passwords, active processes, names and locations of databases, and so on. This information is recorded in a set of predefined tables known as the **system tables**, which form part of the server's data dictionary (discussed later in this chapter). The master database is owned by a special login ID called *sa* (for System Administrator or SA).

The model database serves as a template for creating other user databases. In fact, whenever a new database is created, a copy of *model* is made and the size of the copy is extended appropriately. The model database can be modified, both in size and content, to affect the structure of new user databases. For example, if you want each user database to start out with 4Mb of allocated space instead of the default 2Mb, you can modify *model* to be 4Mb in size.

The temporary database is used as storage for temporary objects created during server operation or for temporary objects explicitly created by the user. The temporary database is shared by all other databases on the server. Figure 4-2 shows the different kinds of databases.

User Databases

The primary task of the Server is to manage user databases, from the viewpoints of data definition and data manipulation. A user database is created by a user with the CREATE DATABASE statement. The creator of a database (or any database object) is its **owner** and is responsible for administering it. All user databases are created from the master database.

The act of creating a database allocates disk storage for the database and, hence, is an operation that is restricted. Initially,

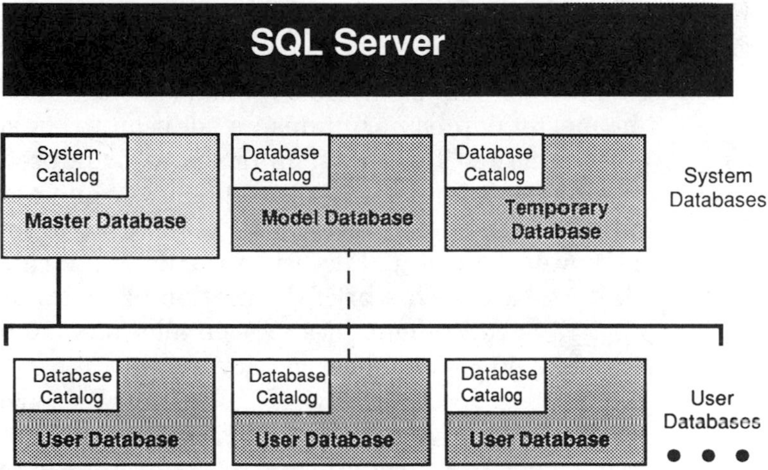

FIGURE 4-2 System and user databases

only the SA has permission to create databases. The SA can, of course, grant this privilege to other users or transfer ownership of a database to another login ID.

When created, a user database also contains a set of system tables—a subset of the set contained in *master*. These tables initially contain information describing the system tables themselves. The Server login ID that creates the database is assigned a special status in the database's system tables—that of a special database user, **dbo** (database owner or DBO). By virtue of being the DBO, the user is granted many special privileges and responsibilities for that database. Once a database is created, the various database objects listed at the beginning of the chapter can be created within it.

The act of dropping a database drops all of its objects and frees up the disk storage allocated for that database. Databases are dropped with the DROP DATABASE statement.

Data Dictionary

SQL Server, like any DBMS, has a data dictionary or catalog. In the case of the server, the data dictionary is actually distributed over the *master* database and the other databases. The catalog consists of nothing more than the system tables, which are predefined and part of the database at creation time. Every system and user database on the server has a set of thirteen system tables that are used to record database-specific information about its database objects (such as tables and views), users, permissions, and so on. This set of system tables constitutes the **database catalog**. The master database contains, in addition to the database catalog tables, nine additional system tables that are used to record such global server information as server login IDs and passwords, devices, and other server databases. This set of system tables constitutes the **system catalog**. The list of the database catalog and system catalog tables, with a brief description of their contents, follows.

The following tables exist in all system and user databases and make up the database catalog.

System table	Contents
sysalternates	contains server login id to database user mapping (aliasing) information

syscolumns	information about all the columns within tables or views or parameters in stored procedures
syscomments	definition of views, rules, defaults, triggers, and stored procedures
sysdepends	dependencies between stored procedures, views and triggers, and other stored procedures, views and tables
sysindexes	information on clustered and nonclustered indexes and tables with no indexes
syskeys	information on primary and foreign keys
syslogs	transaction log
sysobjects	information on tables, views, rules, defaults, triggers, procedures, logs, and temporary objects (in *tempdb* only)
syssegments	information on segments (named collection of disk pieces)
systypes	information on system and user-defined types
sysusers	information on database users

The following system tables exist only in the master database and make up the system catalog.

System table	**Contents**
sysconfigures	information on user-settable configuration parameters
syscurconfigs	current values of configuration parameters being used
sysdatabases	information on each database on the server
sysdevices	information on the database devices and dump devices for the server
syslocks	information on active locks
syslogins	information on server login accounts
sysmessages	information on server error messages and warnings

sysprocesses	information on active processes
sysusages	information on disk pieces allocated to databases

Changing Databases

Once a database is created, you can define database objects within the scope of that database. All database objects are created and known within the context of a database.

SQL Server uses the concept of a current database for each user connection. The term "user connection" can be considered a front-end client application connection with the server for now. It will be defined more precisely in Chapter 6 when discussing DB-LIBRARY. If you reference an object name in an SQL statement, by default it refers to an object in the current database. You can, however, reference objects in other databases by qualifying the object names. You can change your current database by issuing the USE statement. The USE statement changes the context from the currently active database to the database specified. The syntax of the USE statement is shown below.

Syntax

```
USE <database>
```

To connect to the server you must have a valid server login account, which comprises a login ID, password, and default database. The SA is responsible for administering the login accounts for the server. If no default database is specified when creating a server login account, the default database is set to *master*. When you first connect to the server, you are automatically put in your **default database**; it becomes your current database. For example, if your default database is *master* (not a good idea in general), and you want to make *pubs* the current database, you issue the following USE statement.

Example 4-1

```
USE pubs
```

```
OUTPUT
```

Qualification

It was mentioned earlier that objects are known within the context of a database on the server. In addition, each object is owned by the database user who creates the object. Two different users, Mary and Joe, for example, can both own tables named *publishers* in the *pubs* database. The process of making a reference to an object name unique by prefixing it with the database name or the owner name is called **qualification**.

There are two forms of qualification allowed for object names in SQL Server, depending on the usage of the object name within a particular TRANSACT-SQL statement. They are:

Syntax

```
[[<database>.]<owner>.]<object_name>

[<owner>.]<object_name>
```

Notice the period in the syntax between the three components. The qualifications `pubs.mary.publishers` or `mary.publishers` are both valid. In most cases, full qualification of object names is allowed; that is, both the owner name and the database name can be specified. However, in some cases (in DDL statements, objects can only be created in the current database, and hence only the second form of qualification is allowed.

Qualification enables you to reference objects in other databases. So you would be able, for example, to join two tables in different databases. Qualification also allows two database users to have the same object name (a phone directory table called *directory*, for example), instead of having to contrive a name to make it unique.

It is important to remember, however, that qualification is only required to uniquely identify an object and is therefore optional. If no ambiguity exists, you do not have to qualify the name. For example, if there is only one table called *publishers* in the *pubs* database, you can reference it as just *publishers*. The default value for thc `<database>` parameter is the current database and the default value for the `<owner>` parameter is the current user. Also, objects owned by the DBO (whose user name is *dbo*) need not be qualified.

Database Objects

This section looks more closely at the various database objects, discusses what they are used for, and examines how to create them, drop them, and alter their structure.

User Databases

It was mentioned earlier that the user can define multiple databases on a server. Chapter 10 examines at length how to create databases and allocate storage for them. However, for the sake of completeness, we will touch on it briefly here. Once a database is created, you can define objects within it using the DDL statements provided by TRANSACT-SQL.

Databases provide a means of grouping related objects (tables, views, and so on). For example, you can have a *payroll* database and an *inventory* database on the same server. Obviously, employee information that is part of *payroll* has nothing in common with parts information that is part of *inventory*. Putting unrelated information on separate databases, therefore, is good organization.

User databases are created with the CREATE DATABASE statement in the master database. Only users with appropriate permissions can create databases. Information about the databases is stored in the system catalog. The act of creating a database causes an empty database to be created. It is given a name and disk storage is allocated for the database and its objects. All disk storage in SQL Server is allocated from logical database devices (discussed in Chapter 10), which are made up of a set of units of physical disk space. This empty database is actually a copy of the *model* system database, with its preinitialized system tables.

Databases are removed with the DROP DATABASE statement from the *master* database. A user must be the DBO to drop a database. The SA can drop any database since the SA is treated as the DBO in every database. The act of dropping a database deallocates all of the storage for the database and its objects and removes all references to the database from the system catalog. The syntax for the CREATE DATABASE and DROP DATABASE statements follows.

Syntax

```
CREATE DATABASE <database> [ON {DEFAULT | <device>} = [<size>]
     [, <device> = [<size>]] ...]

DROP DATABASE <database>
```

You can allocate additional space for the database (for example, if the space allocated for it is used up) by using the ALTER DATABASE statement. However, there is no way to reduce the space allocated for a database other than dropping and recreating it. Of course, this would involve reloading the database, since dropping a database removes all its contents.

Syntax

```
ALTER DATABASE <database> ON {DEFAULT | <device>} = <size>
     [, {DEFAULT | <device>} = <size>] ...
```

Chapter 10 examines in more detail how to allocate space for databases and logs. For now, assume there exists a device called `userdev` on our server. The following example illustrates how to create a database `empdb` on it and how to extend it by 1Mb using the ALTER DATABASE statement.

Example 4-2

```
CREATE DATABASE empdb ON userdev = 2
ALTER DATABASE empdb ON userdev = 1
OUTPUT:
CREATE DATABASE: allocating 1024 pages on disk 'userdev'
Extending database by 512 pages on disk userdev
```

Data Types

The basic object in which to store data in a server database (as in any other relational database) is a table. Each table is composed of a fixed number of columns, and each column has an associated data type. The rows data in the table consist of column values that are derived from the data type of the column. Figure 4-3 shows a table with data organized in rows and columns.

The **data type** of a column specifies the kind of data the column can hold and the amount of storage required to hold the column value. For example, a column *store_id* of data type `char(4)` can hold character data (presumably the ID assigned to stores) up to four characters in length. Thus S321 or 7066 are valid column values, but 99615 is not.

The data type of a column is specified by the user as part of the table definition. Columns are not considered objects in their own right; they are part of the table definition. When you create a table, you specify its columns and their data types. This defines the structure of the table.

System Data Types SQL Server provides an extensive set of **system data types** for use in defining columns. System data types are the basic (or primitive) types provided by the server. These data types are predefined and exist at installation time. In addition, the server allows the definition of **user-defined data types** based on system data types. (This is discussed later in this

Stores Table

Stor_id Char(4) not null	Stor_name Varchar(40) null	Stor_address Varchar(40) null	City Varchar(20) null	State Char(2) null	Zip Char(5) null
7066	Barnum's	567 Pasadena Ave.	Tustin	CA	92789
7067	News and Brews	577 First St.	Los Gatos	CA	96745
7131	Doc-U-Mat: Quality Laundry and Books	24-A Avrogado Way	Remulade	WA	98014
8042	Bookbeat	679 Carson St.	Portland	OR	98076
6380	Eric the Read Books	788 Catamaugus Ave.	Seattle	WA	98056
7896	Fricative Bookship	89 Madison Ave.	Fremont	CA	90019

FIGURE 4-3 Tabular view of data

chapter.) The fourteen system data types and a description of the kind of data and the amount of storage needed for each type is presented in the following list.

Data type	**Description**	**Size of storage**
`char(n)`	fixed length character data (maximum length is 255 bytes)	*n* bytes
`varchar(n)`	variable length character data (maximum length is 255 bytes; however, the storage used is actual length)	0–*n* bytes
`int`	an integer value between $2^{31}-1$ and -2^{31} (2,147,483,647 and −2,147,483,648)	4 bytes
`smallint`	an integer value between 32,767 and −32,768	2 bytes
`tinyint`	a positive integer between 0 and 255	1 byte
`float`	a floating point number (range and precision is machine dependent)	8 bytes
`binary(n)`	binary data (maximum length 255 bytes)	*n* bytes
`varbinary(n)`	variable length binary data (maximum length 255 bytes; storage size is variable based on actual length of data)	0–*n* bytes
`bit`	binary digit (0 or 1)	8 per byte
`money`	money data (between 922,337,203,685,477.5807 and −922,337,203,685,477.5808 (precision is 4 digits)	8 bytes
`datetime`	date and time data	8 bytes
`text`	large text–printable character data (up to 2 gigabytes in length)	minimum 2K bytes (if allocated)

`image`	large image—binary data (up to 2 gigabytes in length)	minimum 2K bytes (if allocated)
`timestamp`	used to maintain timestamps for browse mode	

Nulls Chapter 1 introduced the concept of null values. A null value is basically an unknown or inapplicable value, which is distinct from any other value possible for the given data type. For example, in a personnel database there is a *phone_num* column in the employee table. For new employees the number may not be assigned for some time. During this time, it is appropriate to assign *phone_num* column for the employee the null value (unknown), rather than than some artificial value such as 000-0000, or 999-9999. In systems that do not support null values, the value is normally represented by a special value such as a zero or a blank character.

SQL Server, however, supports true null values and allows the user to specify on definition whether or not null values are allowed for a column or user-defined type. The following sections explain how this is done. The default status for nulls is that they are not allowed on column or user-defined type definitions. Null values are indicated, both on input and output (in such DML statments as INSERT or SELECT), by the keyword NULL.

User-defined Data Types In addition to the system data types, SQL Server supports user-defined data types. A user-defined data type is defined by a user based on a system data type. Once created, a user-defined type can be used any place a system data type is allowed.

User-defined types are useful in several ways. They enforce consistency across table definitions within a database, or even across databases. For example, you can use user-defined types to ensure a consistent definition of all phone number columns in a database. User-defined types also provide a higher level of abstraction than system types since you can restrict the range of values allowed by the underlying data type. For example, if you want to restrict salary columns to values between $10,000 and $300,000, you can define a user-defined type instead of using the system type money (which doesn't stop at $300,000!).

User-defined data types are added using the `sp_addtype` system procedure. When creating a user-defined data type, you can also provide an optional null specification. A null specification defines whether or not null values are to be allowed for columns of that user-defined data type.

Syntax

```
sp_addtype <type_name>, <base_type> [,<null_spec>]
```

For example, you can define a user-defined type *phone_type* for all phone number columns in the database. The definition allows for null values.

Example 4-3

```
sp_addtype phone_type, "char(14)", null

OUTPUT:
Type added.
```

Rules and Defaults

This section describes briefly two database objects, rules and defaults. (Chapter 8 discusses them in more detail). These objects can be bound either to user-defined data types or to columns in order to refine their definition. A **rule** is an object that serves to restrict further the pool of legal values that are allowed by the data type of a column. Rules are useful for enforcing business integrity constraints (salary must be less than $300,000, employee ID must fall in the range from 0 through 9999, and so on). Rules are useful in implementing the domain concept, as defined by the relational model.

A **default** allows the user to specify a value that the server automatically inserts for a column, when one is not provided explicitly. Defaults are useful for inserting common or unknown values (state defaults to CA, employee status defaults to exempt, and so on).

Tables

A table is the basic object in the server for storing data. A table consists of a fixed number of columns, each of a specified data type. The data type of a column can be either a system or user-defined data type.

Tables are created with the CREATE TABLE statement. The exact table design (as with other object) is the result of a process called logical database design. When you create a table, you specify the name of the table, its column names, their associated data types, and whether or not the columns can assume null values. The default is that null values are not allowed. The syntax follows.

Syntax

```
CREATE TABLE [<database>.[<owner>.]]<table>
     ( <column> <data_type> [NOT NULL | NULL]
     [, <column> <data_type> [NOT NULL | NULL] ...] )
```

For example, if you want to create an *employee* table that contains the employee's ID, first name, last name, date of birth, salary, and address, you can use the CREATE TABLE statement shown in Example 4-4.

Example 4-4

```
create table employee
     (emp_id          int         not null,
     emp_fname        char(15),
     emp_lname        char(15),
     emp_dob          date,
     emp_sal          money,
     emp_street       char(20)    null,
     emp_city         char(15)    null,
     emp_state        char(2)     null,
     emp_zip          char(5)     null)

OUTPUT:
```

Once the table is created you can load data into it. There are two ways to load data into a table—either through the INSERT statement in the DML (discussed in Chapter 6) or through the

Bulk Copy utility provided by SQL Server (discussed in Chapter 10).

When a table is no longer required, you can drop it with the DROP TABLE statement provided you have the required permission. Dropping a table causes all of the data in the table to be dropped and all related objects, such as indexes and triggers, defined on the table to be dropped.

Syntax

```
DROP TABLE [[<database>.]<owner>.]<table>
     [, [[<database>.]<owner>.]<table> ...]
```

For example, to drop the *employee* table created in Example 4-4, you issue the following statement:

Example 4-5

```
DROP TABLE employee
```

OUTPUT:

Once a table is created, it is possible to make certain limited modifications to its structure: You can rename a column or the table itself, or add additional columns to the table. You rename columns or the table with the `sp_rename` system procedure; you define additional columns with the ALTER TABLE statement. All added columns must allow null values, since this is the initial value of the column for all the existing rows in the table. It is not easy to drop columns or change the data type of a column because of the way space is allocated for the columns at the physical level. In fact, the only way to do so is to drop and recreate the table.

Syntax

```
sp_rename <old_name>, <new_name>

ALTER TABLE [[<database>.]<owner>.]<table>
     ADD <column> <data_type> NULL
      [, <column> <data_type> NULL]
```

The following example shows how to change the name of the *emp_sal* column in the *employee* table created earlier to *emp_salary*.

Example 4-6

```
sp_rename "employee.emp_sal", emp_salary

OUTPUT:
Column name has been changed.
```

In general, you should be cautious about changing object names. Other object definitions that reference it are not automatically fixed, so you need to remember to change them, too. For example, if a view definition references the *emp_sal* column in the preceding example, the view definition becomes invalid.

If you decide you need an additional column in the employee table for the employee's phone number, you can modify the table definition as follows. Note the use of the *phone_type* user-defined data type created earlier and the null specification. The NULL keyword could have been left out since *phone_type* allows null values.

Example 4-7

```
alter table employee
     add emp_phone  phone_type     null

OUTPUT:
```

Views

Views are virtual tables, in that data do not actually exist in the view. Instead, data are derived dynamically from the underlying tables, called base tables, when the view is referenced. A view can extract any subset of the rows and columns from one or more underlying tables.

Views are created with the CREATE VIEW statement and dropped with the DROP VIEW statement. A view definition is based on the SELECT statement, which is the data retrieval statement in TRANSACT-SQL. Views will be discussed further in Chapter 7.

Indexes

An **index** is an object that allows fast access to row data in a table based on column values. The basic concept of an index is found in many everyday situations—for example, a phone book to look up a phone number, or a filing cabinet to organize files for easy retrieval. An index consists of a key value and a pointer to the data. A key is a column (or list of columns) in a table. There are primary and foreign keys in a relational system (discussed in Chapter 1). Keys can be any set of columns to which fast access is desired.

There are many different kinds of indexes in database systems, and many different data structures used for indexes, each with advantages and disadvantages; however, most systems use some variation of the tree structure. SQL Server uses the B-tree structure (the B stands for Balanced).

The key values for an index are stored in index pages, and the actual rows of data are stored in data pages. An index entry in a B-tree structure typically consists of a key value and a pointer either to the next lower level index page or (at the lowest level of the index) to the actual data page itself. Indexes can also be **dense**, meaning that every key value is represented in the index, or **non-dense**, meaning that only certain selected key values on each data page (typically the highest key value or the lowest key value) appear in the index.

SQL Server allows you to define two kinds of indexes—**clustered** indexes and **nonclustered** indexes. A clustered index is one in which the order of the keys in the index (the logical or indexed order) is the same as the actual order, on disk, of the rows containing the keys (the physical order). In a nonclustered index, the physical order of the rows on disk do not match the logical order in the index.

The definition of a clustered index implies that there can be only one clustered index per table (since there can only be one order to the actual data in the table). In fact, the actual row data are part of the clustered index itself—the lowest level, or leaf level, of a clustered index consists of the actual data pages; the higher levels form the index pages. Since the rows are ordered according to key value, clustered indexes are nondense, and only the low key value on each page is recorded. Clustered indexes usually provide faster access to the data than nonclustered indexes and are also useful in answering queries involving ranges on the key column. Figure 4-4 illustrates clustered index structure.

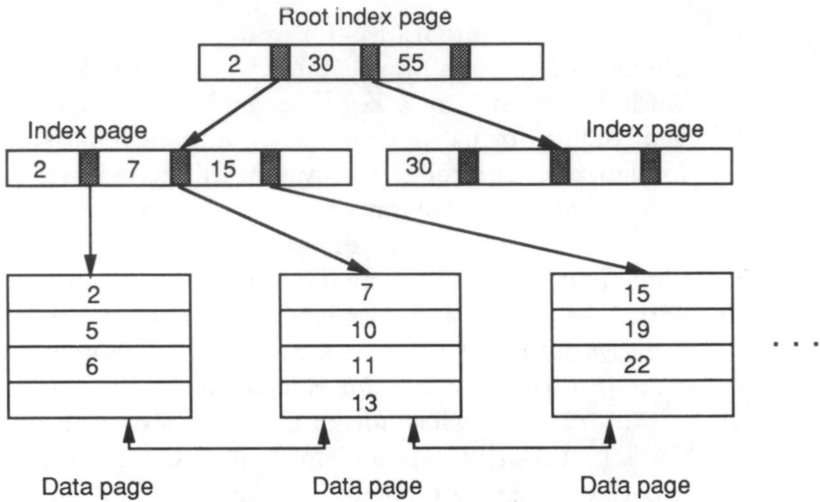

FIGURE 4-4 Clustered index structure

There can be several nonclustered indexes on a table (as many as 250). Nonclustered indexes are dense indexes, meaning that every key value is stored in the index (since the rows do not occur in any particular order). They are, therefore, larger and slower than clustered indexes. In general, you define a nonclustered index on a nonprimary key column through which fast access to the data is desired. Figure 4-5 illustrates nonclustered index structure.

Indexes are defined through the CREATE INDEX statement and dropped through the DROP INDEX statement. When creating an index, the user can also specify a FILLFACTOR (a percentage value) to specify how full each index and data page should be. Since SQL Server indexes are self-balancing, by lightly loading them at create time, users can avoid the overhead of page splitting at run time. Indexes can also be defined on multiple columns; these are called **composite indexes**. The syntax for defining and dropping indexes follows.

Syntax

```
CREATE [UNIQUE] [CLUSTERED | NONCLUSTERED] INDEX
     ON [[<database>.]<owner>.]<table>
     ( <column> [, <column> ] ... )
     [ WITH FILLFACTOR = <x> ]
```

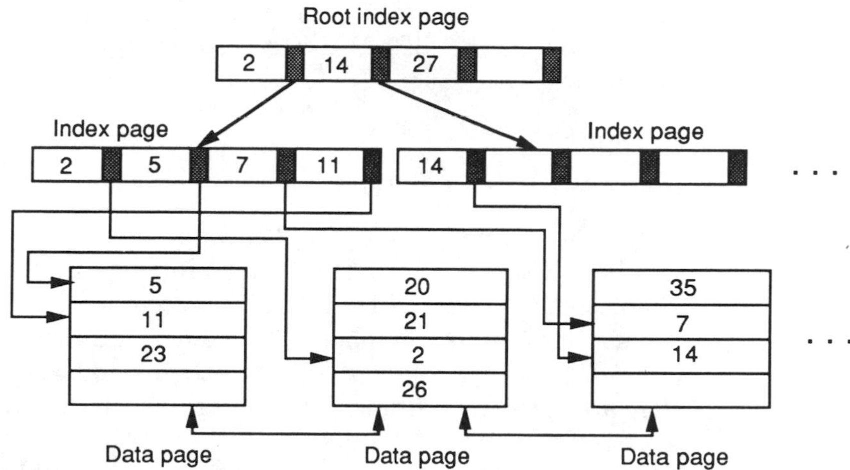

FIGURE 4-5 Nonclustered index structure

```
DROP INDEX <table>.<index> [ , <table>.<index>] ...
```

For example, you can define a clustered index on the *emp_id* column and nonclustered indexes based on the *emp_lname* and *emp_fname*, and *dept_id* columns of the *employee* table. This is shown in Example 4-8.

Example 4-8

```
create unique clustered index id_index
     ON employee (emp_id)
     with fillfactor = 50

create nonclustered index name_index
     ON employee (emp_lname, emp_fname)

create nonclustered index deptid_index
     ON employee (dept_id)
```

You can drop the *deptid_index* index just created as shown in Example 4-9. Index names do not follow the normal qualification rules for uniqueness; they have to be unique only by table. Thus two different tables in the same database can have an index called *deptid_index*. The index name must therefore be qualified by the table name on the DROP INDEX statement, as shown in the following example.

Example 4-9

```
drop index employee.deptid_index
```

A few final points should be made about indexes. The syntax for the CREATE INDEX statement in this example is somewhat simplified. The CREATE INDEX statement also allows several options for handling duplicate key values and rows; for details, see the *SQL Server Language Reference*. Also, indexes are not objects that are directly manipulated through the DML; rather they are used implicitly by SQL Server's query optimizer to improve performance. In fact, the output of any query should be exactly the same whether or not a particular index is used.

Stored Procedures

One of the most significant enhancements provided by SQL Server is the ability to create and use **stored procedures**. A stored procedure is a named, precompiled set of TRANSACT-SQL statements. The compiled form is stored in the server's data dictionary. From then on the procedure can be executed simply by name—the compiled form is retrieved from the dictionary and executed. Stored procedures provide many benefits and are discussed in detail in Chapter 7.

Stored procedures are created through the CREATE PROCEDURE statement and dropped through the DROP PROCEDURE statement. A procedure definition consists of a procedure name, a list of parameters, and the actual body of the procedure. Most of the TRANSACT-SQL statements (including the control-of-flow language statements) are allowed within the body of the procedure.

Triggers

A trigger is a special kind of stored procedure that is automatically executed whenever a prespecified event occurs. The event is basically any form of modification to a table—an insert, an update, or a delete.

It was mentioned earlier that rules can be used to enforce simple integrity constraints—for example, salary must be between $10,000 and $300,000, or author ID must be between 0 and 9999. These rules involve either a single column or multiple columns of the same user-defined data type. Triggers, on the other hand, allow you to enforce more complex integrity constraints, constraints that involve multiple columns or tables—for example, do not delete any authors who are currently authoring a book. This enforces the concept of referential integrity, or consistency among related tables.

Triggers are created using the CREATE TRIGGER statement and dropped using the DROP TRIGGER statement. Once created, the trigger is automatically enforced on all specified future forms of updates (INSERT, UPDATE, or DELETE) of the table. To modify the trigger definition, you must drop it and recreate it. Triggers are discussed in detail in Chapter 8.

Summary

This chapter discussed the data definition language of TRANSACT-SQL. It discussed how databases are organized in SQL Server and the concept of system and user databases. It showed what objects can be created in SQL Server and the purpose served by them. It showed how to create and drop most of these objects. Others were only discussed briefly because they are discussed in detail in later chapters. Specifically, views and procedures are discussed in Chapter 7; and defaults, rules, and triggers are discussed in detail in Chapter 8 under the topic of database integrity.

Data Retrieval

Introduction

The previous chapter discussed how to create, drop, and alter databases and database objects in SQL Server. This chapter focuses on how to manipulate the data within these objects. In general, data manipulation includes both retrieving data and modifying data (inserting, updating, or deleting) in the database. So data manipulation can be divided into two components, data retrieval and data modification. This chapter discusses the first component and leaves the second component to the next chapter.

Data retrieval is the process of retrieving data that exist within tables and views in Server databases. The SELECT statement in TRANSACT-SQL serves this pupose. As will be shown later, the SELECT statement, with its many clauses and options, is an extremely powerful statement. It was pointed out in Chapter 3 that TRANSACT-SQL offers several extensions to the standard SELECT statement. Most of these extensions are discussed in this chapter.

First, a reminder. SQL is primarily a database language; that is, it is a subset language concerned with defining and manipulating the objects and data within a database. In order to do anything significant with it (beyond querying the database), it must be supplemented with a full development language such as PASCAL, C, COBOL, or a fourth-generation language that provides all of the conditional execution statements, the looping constructs, display statements, and so on, that are necessary in order to develop a complete application.

The SELECT Statement

The data retrieval statement in TRANSACT-SQL is the SELECT statement. The complete form of the SELECT statement is fairly formidable, so the basic form is given here to start. The complete form will be given later. The basic form of the SELECT statement is simple; it consists of three clauses, the SELECT clause, the FROM clause, and the WHERE clause. The result of a SELECT statement is always a table; that is, the SELECT statement returns a variable number of rows of a fixed number of columns. The syntax of the basic SELECT statement follows.

Syntax

```
SELECT <target_list>
FROM <table_list>
WHERE <search_condition>
```

The semantics of the basic SELECT statement syntax are that the SELECT clause specifies the list of columns to be retrieved—this is the `<target_list>` parameter. The FROM clause specifies the tables from which the columns are chosen. This list constitutes the `<table_list>` parameter. It will be shown later that multiple tables can be specified in the FROM clause in certain kinds of SELECT statements. The WHERE clause specifies the condition that must be satisfied for a row to be included in the result table. (The result table isn't necessarily an actual table containing the results of the query. It may only be transitory or may not be created at all.) The condition in a WHERE clause can be very general and can include column names, expressions, arithmetic (+, −, /, *) and comparison (<, >, and so on) operators, conditions involving keywords (IN, LIKE, and so on); join conditions, and even other queries (known as subqueries). Any number of these individual conditions can be linked together using the logical operators AND, OR, and NOT. Thus, even in its simplest form the SELECT statement is very powerful.

Here is an example of how the SELECT statement can be used to do something useful. It uses the *pubs* database that you have seen already. Assume you want to find all publishers that are located in the state of California. You can enter the following SELECT statement (through either the SAF or the isql program) to retrieve the desired information. Figure 5-1 shows a basic SELECT statement.

Example 5-1

```
select pub_id, pub_name, city
from publishers
where state = "CA"
```

Columns in SELECT clause | Condition in WHERE clause

PUB_ID	PUB_NAME	CITY	STATE
1389	Algodata Infosystems	Berkeley	CA
0736	New Age Books	Boston	MA
0877	Binnet & Hardley	Washington	DC

Publishers Table

```
select pub_id, pub_name, city
from publishers
where state = "CA"
```

FIGURE 5-1 A basic SELECT statement

```
OUTPUT:

pub_id pub_name                                 city
------ ---------------------------------------- --------------------
1389   Algodata Infosystems                     Berkeley

(1 row affected)
```

In example 5-1, the SELECT clause contains the columns that are to be retrieved. The FROM clause contains the name of the table (in this case, a single table, *publishers*) that contains the desired columns. Finally, the WHERE clause specifies the condition–publishers in California–that must be true for rows to be included in the result. Each of these clauses is discussed a little further, before the more advanced capabilities of the SELECT statement are examined.

SELECT Clause

The SELECT clause is the only required clause in the SELECT statement, and it can be very general. It can include columns, column headings, constants, functions, and subqueries, and any combination of these, connected by operators. (A subquery is a restricted SELECT statement that is usually subordinate to another query.) Some examples to illustrate these capabilities are given in the following sections.

Retrieving Specific Columns In order to retrieve specific column information, the column names must be included in the SELECT clause. The columns appear in the result in the order specified in the SELECT clause; hence it is easy to reorder the data in any manner. The default column heading is the column name. For example, if you wish to retrieve specific information about certain titles—say the title, the type, and the price of all titles priced between $10 and $20 (noninclusive)—you enter the following query:

Example 5-2

```
select title, type, price
from titles
where price > $10 and price < $20

OUTPUT:
title                                              type                 price
-------------------------------------------------- -------------------- -----
The Busy Executive's Database Guide                business             19.99
Cooking with Computers: Surreptitious Balance Sheets business           11.95
Straight Talk about Computers                      business             19.99
Silicon Valley Gastronomic Treats                  mod_cook             19.99
Is Anger the Enemy?                                psychology           10.95
Prolonged Data Deprivation: Four Case Studies      psychology           19.95
Fifty Years in Buckingham Palace Kitchens          trad_cook            11.95
Sushi, Anyone?                                     trad_cook            14.99

(8 rows affected)
```

If you want to retrieve all of the columns in a table, there are two possible ways to do it. The first, of course, is to include all the column names in the table in the SELECT clause. A second, easier way is to use the shorthand notation SELECT *, which includes all columns. For example, to retrieve all the columns in the *publishers* table, execute the query shown in Example 5-3.

Example 5-3

```
select *
from publishers

OUTPUT:
pub_id pub_name                                 city                 state
------ ---------------------------------------- -------------------- -----
0736   New Age Books                            Boston               MA
0877   Binnet & Hardley                         Washington           DC
1389   Algodata Infosystems                     Berkeley             CA

(3 rows affected)
```

The columns in the result table appear in the order they were listed in the CREATE TABLE statement. If a different order is desired, the column names have to be explicitly listed in the SELECT clause. Notice also that the SELECT clause in Example 5-3 is missing the optional WHERE clause. If no WHERE clause is specified, all of the rows in the table (in the case of the *publishers* table, three rows) are returned. The semantics of a missing WHERE clause is equivalent to WHERE (TRUE), that is, every row in the table satisfies the condition and thus all rows in the table are returned.

Changing Column Headings At times you may want to provide a more meaningful column heading for the column data returned. By default, the column name is the column heading. This is the case in the examples just given. However, you can specify an optional column heading in the SELECT clause. There are two forms in which the column heading can be specified:

Syntax

```
<column_heading> = <column_name>

<column_name> <column_heading>
```

Example 5-4 retrieves the same information as Example 5-1—only the column headings are changed to ID, PUBLISHER, and CITY respectively.

Example 5-4

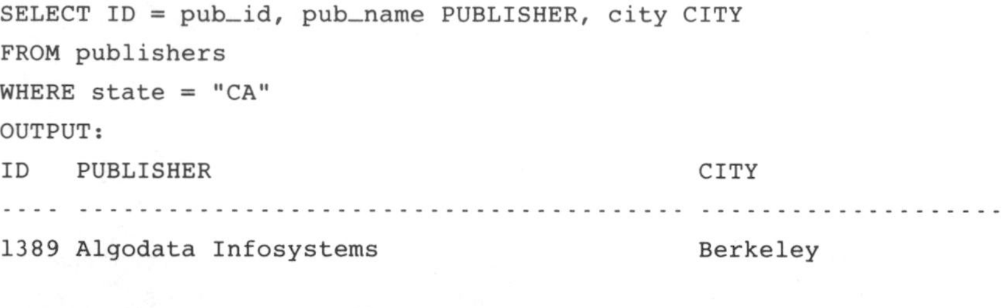

```
SELECT ID = pub_id, pub_name PUBLISHER, city CITY
FROM publishers
WHERE state = "CA"
OUTPUT:
ID   PUBLISHER                                CITY
---- ---------------------------------------- --------------------
1389 Algodata Infosystems                     Berkeley

(1 row affected)
```

Notice in the example that both forms of the syntax are used to change the column heading. The new column headings are entered in uppercase characters. Although the syntax implies that you can have column headings with embedded blanks, this results in a syntax error. Thus you cannot say `PUB ID = pub_id` in the SELECT clause in this example.

Expressions An expression returns a value. There are several kinds of expressions allowed in the various clauses of statements, including SELECT statements. Some examples are string, numeric, and Boolean expressions. They will turn up at various points in this chapter. For now, suffice it to say that expressions are very general and can include constants, column names, functions, and subqueries connected together with operators and keywords that have special meanings (such as IN and BETWEEN).

Numeric Computations The SELECT clause can include expressions that involve numeric computations. Numeric computations are also allowed in such other clauses as the WHERE clause and the GROUP BY clause. The computation can involve numeric constants, numeric data from the tables, or both. There are several numeric data types in SQL Server (as outlined in Chapter 4): `tinyint`, `smallint`, `int`, `float`, and `money`. In addition, there are the common arithmetic operators (+, −, /, *, %)

that operate on numeric data. The operators in sequence are addition, subtraction, division, multiplication, and modulo. The modulo operator returns the integer remainder on division (thus 10 % 4 = 2); it cannot be used with float or money data types.

When several operators exist in a numeric expression, a precedence determines in what order the operations are performed. The normal precedence is multiplication, division, and modulo first, followed by addition and subtraction. For operators at the same level, precedence follows from left to right. Of course, the normal precedence in a computation can be overridden by using parentheses. For example, if you want to find the number of titles that will have to be sold for authors to recoup their advances for titles published by Algodata Infosystems (`pub_id = 1389`), you can use the statements shown in Example 5-5.

Example 5-5

```
select TITLE = title, ADVANCE = advance, RECOUP = advance/price
from titles
where pub_id = "1389"

OUTPUT:
TITLE                                                ADVANCE  PRICE RECOUP
---------------------------------------------------- -------- ----- ------
The Busy Executive's Database Guide                  5,000.00 19.99 250.13
Cooking with Computers: Surreptitious Balance Sheets 5,000.00 11.95 418.41
Straight Talk about Computers                        5,000.00 19.99 250.13
But Is It User Friendly?                             7,000.00 22.95 305.01
Secrets of Silicon Valley                            8,000.00 20.00 400.00
Net Etiquette                                        NULL     NULL  NULL

(6 rows affected)
```

There are three important points to note. First, any computation involving the null value always yields a null. For example, NULL/5 is NULL or NULL * 2 is NULL. In Example 5-5, the recoup for the title Net Etiquette is NULL, because both advance and price are NULL. Second, since numeric expressions can be a part of many clauses in the SELECT statement, columns involved in computations can be drawn from several tables, not just from the target list. Third, when constants or columns of different data types are mixed in a numeric expression, the result data type is escalated to the higher type. For example, a numeric expression that combines `int` and `float` data types results in a `float` data type. The numeric data types from low to high are: `tinyint`, `smallint`, `int`, `money`, and `float`.

Eliminating Duplicate Rows By default, a SELECT statement displays all the rows that satisfy the condition in the WHERE clause, including duplicate rows (rows that have exactly the same values for all columns in the target list). Sometimes, however, you may be interested only in distinct rows in the result. TRANSACT-SQL provides the optional DISTINCT keyword after the SELECT keyword to indicate this. The exact syntax follows. The default is that all rows are returned, including duplicates. This can also be specified explicitly with the keyword ALL after the SELECT keyword.

Syntax

```
SELECT [ALL | DISTINCT] <target_list>
```

Note that null values are considered equal when the DISTINCT keyword is specified. Normally null values do not compare; that is, NULL is not equal to NULL. A comparison of two null values yields NULL. If DISTINCT is specified, however, only one row will appear in the result table even if multiple identical rows (with column values that are NULL) are returned. Example 5-6 shows the difference in output when you do and do not use the DISTINCT keyword on a query that selects all states that have stores.

Example 5-6

```
select state from stores
select distinct state from stores

OUTPUT:
state
-----
CA
CA
```

```
WA
OR
WA
CA

(6 rows affected)
state
-----
CA
OR
WA

(3 rows affected)
```

In the first case in Example 5-6, CA appears as many times as there are stores in California, WA as many times as there are stores in Washington, and so on. You are more likely to be interested in the set of distinct states that have stores (so that, for instance, you could target states that don't as potential new sites). The second query produces the information more concisely.

FROM Clause

The FROM clause specifies the tables or views that contain the columns in the target list of the SELECT clause. The order that you enter the tables or views has no significance and does not in any way govern the order in which the tables or views will be processed. The FROM clause follows the SELECT clause, except when there is the optional INTO clause, which is discussed later in the chapter. The syntax of the FROM clause follows.

Syntax

```
[FROM [[<database>.]<owner>.]{<table> | <view>} [HOLDLOCK]
   [, [[<database>.]<owner>.]{<table> | <view>} [HOLDLOCK]...]]
```

You can tell from the syntax that the FROM clause is optional. It is not required when there are no columns in the target list, that is, when the target list contains only constants, variables, or arithmetic expressions (see Example 5-7). In fact, if you do not know what else to do with TRANSACT-SQL, you can at least use it as a powerful (albeit expensive) means to balance your checkbook. The HOLDLOCK keyword is used in certain situations to instruct SQL Server to perform a special form of locking; it is discussed in Chapter 11. Example 5-7 shows how you can use an arithmetic expression in the SELECT statement to add 10 and 22. Example 5-8 shows how you can use the FROM clause to retrieve information on all the publishers in the *publishers* table.

Example 5-7

```
select "The sum of 10 and 22 is", 10+22 TOTAL

OUTPUT:                  TOTAL
----------------------- -----
The sum of 10 and 22 is 32

(1 row affected)
```

Example 5-8

```
select pub_id, pub_name, city, state
from publishers

OUTPUT:
pub_id pub_name                                 city                 state
------ ---------------------------------------- -------------------- -----
0736   New Age Books                            Boston               MA
0877   Binnet & Hardley                         Washington           DC
1389   Algodata Infosystems                     Berkeley             CA

(3 rows affected)
```

The FROM clause allows the fully qualified form of a table or view name. This means that tables in different databases can be referenced. In general, whenever multiple tables or views are referenced, the SELECT statement includes a restricting WHERE clause. Otherwise, the result is a product of the two tables, which can potentially be very large and which may not be very meaningful. (This product, called the Cartesian product, was discussed in Chapter 1. If two tables, R and S, contain r and s rows, the Cartesian product P contains r*s rows.) Multiple tables and view names are typically used when joining two tables based on a particular column in each table. For example, if you want to retrieve all the titles for a publisher you can draw the information from the *titles* and *publishers* tables, as in Example 5-9.

Example 5-9

```
select pub_name, title
from titles, publishers
where titles.pub_id = publishers.pub_id and
      publishers.pub_name = "Algodata Infosystems"

OUTPUT:
pub_name               title
---------------------- ------------------------------------------
Algodata Infosystems   The Busy Executive's Database Guide
Algodata Infosystems   Cooking with
                          Computers: Surreptitious Balance Sheets
Algodata Infosystems   Straight Talk about Computers
Algodata Infosystems   But Is It User Friendly?
Algodata Infosystems   Secrets of Silicon Valley
Algodata Infosystems   Net Etiquette

(6 rows affected)
```

In the example, the information requested resides in two separate tables and therefore must be materialized by joining the two tables based on the common column *pub_id*. Notice that the column name *pub_id* must be qualified in the two instances in the WHERE clause to make them unambiguous. On the other hand, since there is no ambiguity about *pub_name* and *title*, they need not be qualified even though they exist in two separate tables. The WHERE clause restricts the results to titles published only by Algodata Infosystems.

It should be noted that table and view names can be aliased (given another name). The alias follows the real name in the FROM clause and then is used in the WHERE clause. Since the alias can be an abbreviation, its use can save typing. Aliasing is required in certain kinds of join queries (self-joins) and subqueries, to distinguish different roles of table and view names. In example 5-10, the query produces exactly the same results as the query in Example 5-9, but is more concise.

Example 5-10

```
select pub_name, title
from titles t, publishers p
where t.pub_id = p.pub_id AND
      p.pub_name = "Algodata Infosystems"

OUTPUT:
pub_name               title
---------------------- -------------------------------------------
Algodata Infosystems   The Busy Executive's Database Guide
Algodata Infosystems   Cooking with
                          Computers: Surreptitious Balance Sheets
Algodata Infosystems   Straight Talk about Computers
Algodata Infosystems   But Is It User Friendly?
Algodata Infosystems   Secrets of Silicon Valley
Algodata Infosystems   Net Etiquette

(6 rows affected)
```

WHERE Clause

The WHERE clause within the SELECT statement specifies the search condition that has to be satisfied for rows to be included in the result table. The WHERE clause acts like a filter—without it, all rows are selected; with it, the condition in the WHERE clause is evaluated for each potential row in the result table. The condition must evaluate to TRUE for a row to be included in the result table. The syntax of the WHERE clause follows.

Syntax

```
WHERE <search_condition>
```

The <search_condition> parameter in the WHERE clause is very general and can include conditions involving comparison operators, ranges, lists, string matching, nulls, joins, and subqueries. In addition, the search condition can be a combination of any of these conditions connected together by the logical operators AND, OR, and NOT. In fact, about the only restriction on conditions in the WHERE clause is that aggregate functions are not allowed. Aggregate functions include SUM, AVG, MIN, MAX, and COUNT. They return a single (aggregate) value when they operate on a set of data. This chapter looks at the join and subquery conditions later. The following sections focus on the other kinds of conditions possible in the WHERE clause.

Comparison Conditions These conditions compare operands based on the standard comparison operators in the following list.

Comparison operator	Meaning
=	equal to
>	greater than
<	less than
>=	greater than or equal to
<=	less than or equal to
!=	not equal to
!>	not greater than
!<	not less than

The syntax of a WHERE clause involving a comparison condition follows. The operands in the comparison condition are not limited to columns or constants, but can be general expressions. Dates and character data can be compared, too. For dates, < means earlier in time and > means later in time. For character data, < means smaller in its ASCII representation (ASCII collating sequence), > means larger. The logical operator NOT can be used to negate the condition.

Syntax

```
WHERE <expression> <comparison_operator> <expression>
```

Examples 5-11 and 5-12 illustrate comparison operators. If you want to find all the authors who live in California, you execute the query in the first example. You can execute the second query to find all authors who do not live in California.

Example 5-11

```
select au_fname, au_lname, city
from authors
```

```
where state = "CA"

OUTPUT:
au_fname            au_lname                                 city
------------------- ---------------------------------------- --------------------
Johnson             White                                    Menlo Park
Marjorie            Green                                    Oakland
Cheryl              Carson                                   Berkeley
Michael             O'Leary                                  San Jose
Dick                Straight                                 Oakland
Abraham             Bennet                                   Berkeley
Ann                 Dull                                     Palo Alto
Burt                Gringlesby                               Covelo
Chastity            Locksley                                 San Francisco
Akiko               Yokomoto                                 Walnut Creek
Dirk                Stringer                                 Oakland
Stearns             MacFeather                               Oakland
Livia               Karsen                                   Oakland
Sheryl              Hunter                                   Palo Alto
Heather             McBadden                                 Vacaville

(15 rows affected)
```

Example 5-12

```
select au_fname, au_lname, city
from authors
where not (state = "CA")

OUTPUT:
au_fname            au_lname                                 city
------------------- ---------------------------------------- --------------------
Meander             Smith                                    Lawrence
Morningstar         Greene                                   Nashville
Reginald            Blotchet-Halls                           Corvallis
Innes               del Castillo                             Ann Arbor
Michel              DeFrance                                 Gary
Sylvia              Panteley                                 Rockville
Anne                Ringer                                   Salt Lake City
Albert              Ringer                                   Salt Lake City

(8 rows affected)
```

An equivalent way of writing the WHERE clause in Example 5-12 is: `where state != "CA"`.

Range Conditions Range conditions are constructed using the keyword BETWEEN and two values that signify the end points in the range. The values do not need to be constants; they can be expressions that evaluate to a single value. The condition evaluates to TRUE if the first operand value is within the specified end points, FALSE otherwise. The BETWEEN keyword specifies an inclusive range; that is, the two end points are included in the range. The syntax of a range condition follows.

Syntax

```
WHERE <expression1> [NOT] BETWEEN <expression2> AND <expression3>
```

Again, the logical NOT may be used to negate the condition; so the WHERE clause will evaluate to TRUE for values outside the range. The same query can be written using comparison operators; however, the BETWEEN form is more concise. You do need to use the comparison form to specify an exclusive range where the two end points are not included in the range. For example, if you want to find all titles in the price range $15 to $20, inclusive, you can write the query in Example 5-13.

Example 5-13

```
select title, price
from titles
where price between $15 and $20

OUTPUT:
title                                               price
--------------------------------------------------- ------------------
The Busy Executive's Database Guide                 19.99
Straight Talk about Computers                       19.99
Silicon Valley Gastronomic Treats                   19.99
Secrets of Silicon Valley                           20.00
Prolonged Data Deprivation: Four Case Studies       19.99

(5 rows affected)
```

The query can also be written using the comparison operators, as follows.

```
select title, price
from titles
where price >= $15 and price <= $20
```

List Conditions A list condition evaluates to TRUE if the operand matches any item in a list of values. List conditions are constructed using the IN keyword. The syntax of the list condition follows.

Syntax

```
WHERE <expression> [NOT] IN {<value_list> | <subquery>}
```

A list condition can always be written as a set of equality comparison conditions connected together with logical OR operators. The list of values can be a list of constants or a list of values returned by a subquery. For example, if you want to find all the authors who live in Palo Alto, Oakland, San Francisco, or Berkeley, you can write the query in Example 5-14.

Example 5-14

```
select au_fname, au_lname
from authors
where city in ("Palo Alto", "San Francisco", "Berkeley", "Oakland")

OUTPUT:
au_fname             au_lname
-------------------- ----------------------------------------
Marjorie             Green
Cheryl               Carson
Dick                 Straight
Abraham              Bennet
Ann                  Dull
Dirk                 Stringer
Stearns              MacFeather
Livia                Karsen
Sheryl               Hunter

(9 rows affected)
```

An equivalent form, using equality conditions with the OR operator is:

```
select au_fname, au_lname
from authors
where city = "Palo Alto" or
      city = "San Francisco" or
      city = "Berkeley" or
      city = "Oakland"
```

String-Matching Conditions The LIKE keyword along with special **wildcard characters** is used to construct string-matching conditions. These conditions allow you to search `char,varchar` and `datetime` data for a matching string pattern. The wildcard characters and their significance are:

Wildcard character	Meaning
%	matches any string of zero or more characters
_	matches any single character
[ ]	matches any single character specified within the square brackets
[^]	matches any character not specified within the brackets

Here are some examples to clarify the use of wildcard characters in constructing string-matching patterns.

Pattern	Meaning
`LIKE "20%"`	Any string beginning with 20, that is, 20 followed by one or more characters
`LIKE "20[%]"`	20%
`LIKE "B_n"`	B followed by any single character, followed by n, for example, Bin, Ben, Bun.
`LIKE "[KC]arson"`	Karson or Carson
`LIKE "[1-4]0"`	10, 20, 30, 40

You can specify the wildcard characters themselves by enclosing them within square brackets, as in the second example. The syntax of a string-matching condition follows.

Syntax

```
WHERE [NOT] <column_name> [NOT] LIKE <string_pattern>
```

In string-matching conditions the NOT operator can be specified either before the LIKE keyword or before the column name. Both forms have the same meaning. If you want to find all books that have Computer in their title, you can use the LIKE keyword and the % wildcard character to write the following query.

Example 5-15

```
select title, price
from titles
where title like "%Computer%"

OUTPUT:
title                                                               price
------------------------------------------------------------------- -----
Cooking with Computers: Surreptitious Balance Sheets                11.95
You Can Combat Computer Stress!                                      2.99
Straight Talk about Computers                                       19.99
The Psychology of Computer Cooking                                   NULL
Computer Phobic and Non-Phobic Individuals: Behavior Variations     21.59
```

Null Conditions Null conditions are used to determine whether a column value is NULL (unspecified or inapplicable) or not. This is distinct from comparing a `char` or `varchar` column for equality with the string value NULL. Null conditions are constructed using the NULL keyword. Obviously, checking a column for null values only makes sense if the column allows null values in the first place–specified when the table is created. The syntax of a null condition follows.

Syntax

```
WHERE [NOT] <column> IS [NOT] NULL
```

In general, computations where either operand is NULL yield NULL. Thus 2 + NULL = NULL, and 2 = NULL or even

NULL = NULL is NULL. However, in the case of a NULL condition, the IS operator does not signify an equality comparison, rather it checks for the existence of the NULL value. Hence all rows where the specified column value is NULL are returned. For example, if you want a listing of titles for which the royalty is undecided or unspecified–indicated by NULL values–you can write the query shown in Example 5-16.

Example 5-16

```
select title, royalty
from titles
where royalty is null

OUTPUT:
title                                    royalty
---------------------------------------- ----------
The Psychology of Computer Cooking       Null
Net Etiquette                            Null

(2 rows affected)
```

Logical Operators As indicated earlier, many conditions can be connected together by the binary logical operators AND or OR, or negated using the unary logical operator NOT. Logical operators are always evaluated after the arithmetic and bitwise operators. Within the logical operators, NOT is evaluated first, then AND, and finally OR. Of course, the precedence of evaluation can always be changed using parentheses. For example, if you want to find all the authors who live in Utah or authors who do not have contracts, you can write the query shown in Example 5-17.

Example 5-17

```
select au_fname, au_lname, state, contract
from authors
where state = "UT" or contract = 0

OUTPUT:
au_fname             au_lname                                  state contract
-------------------- ---------------------------------------- ----- --------
Meander              Smith                                     KS           0
```

```
Morningstar          Greene                          TN      0
Dirk                 Stringer                        CA      0
Heather              McBadden                        CA      0
Anne                 Ringer                          UT      1
Albert               Ringer                          UT      1

(6 rows affected)
```

It should be mentioned that, since SQL Server allows null conditions, the normal truth tables for evaluating expressions involving logical (Boolean) operators must be extended to include null values. The tri-state truth tables extended to include null values are shown below.

	NULL
NOT:	NULL

AND:	NULL	TRUE	FALSE
NULL	NULL	NULL	FALSE
TRUE	NULL	TRUE	FALSE
FALSE	FALSE	FALSE	FALSE

OR:	NULL	TRUE	FALSE
NULL	NULL	TRUE	NULL
TRUE	TRUE	TRUE	TRUE
FALSE	NULL	TRUE	FALSE

Thus NOT(NULL) is NULL, NULL AND TRUE is NULL, and NULL OR TRUE is TRUE. Although at first you may not grasp this intuitively, on closer inspection the truth tables do make sense. Because a null value actually represents an unknown value, a value that could be TRUE or FALSE, NULL AND TRUE is NULL. In other words, depending on the assumed value of NULL, the result can be different (FALSE AND TRUE = FALSE and TRUE AND TRUE = TRUE). Therefore the result is indeterminate or equal to NULL. Similarly NULL OR TRUE is TRUE, since the result is always TRUE no matter what the possible value the NULL might assume.

Additional Clauses

You have seen how the basic SELECT statement works. This section explores some of the additional clauses in the SELECT statement. These clauses serve such purposes as sorting data and grouping data. They are all optional, but together they provide much of the power of the SELECT statement. The next sections first describe the various functions that are built into TRANSACT-SQL. Some of them are typically used with the additional clauses. Then the additional clauses INTO, GROUP BY, HAVING, ORDERED BY, and COMPUTE will be described.

Built-in Functions

TRANSACT-SQL has a rich set of built-in functions that can be used within the various clauses in the statements. Aggregate functions have already been mentioned. There are several other kinds of functions that are useful for providing system information, manipulating data, or converting data form one data type to another. The built-in functions can be broadly classified into the following types: aggregate, system, string and text/image, mathematical, date, and type conversion. These functions are covered in detail in the *SQL Server Language* Reference manual. Here is a brief look at each category's function.

Aggregate Functions Aggregate functions provide a summary value based on a set of values. Aggregate functions include SUM, AVG, MIN, MAX, and COUNT. A list of the functions and their results follows.

Function	Result
`SUM([DISTINCT] <exp>)`	total of [distinct] column values
`AVG([DISTINCT] <exp>)`	average of [distinct] column values
`MIN(<exp>)`	the lowest value
`MAX(<exp>)`	the highest value
`COUNT([DISTINCT] <exp>)`	number of [distinct] non-null values
`COUNT(*)`	number of selected rows

Aggregate functions are most commonly used in GROUP BY and COMPUTE clauses to generate summary values. The expression in the function argument can be any combination of column names, constants, and functions, connected by arithmetic or bitwise operators. It can also be a subquery. The DISTINCT keyword can be used with SUM, AVG, and COUNT to eliminate duplicates before the function is applied. All functions ignore null values, except for the COUNT(*) function. The SUM and AVG functions can be used with numeric data types only (`tinyint`, `smallint`, `int`, `money`, and `float`); however, MIN and MAX can be used with other data types such as `datetime` and `char`.

An example will help to clarify some of the quirks and subtleties of aggregate function behavior, especially with respect to null values. Example 5-18 shows two queries that use the COUNT, SUM, and AVG aggregate functions with and without the DISTINCT option, along with the corresponding results.

Example 5-18

```
select CNT = COUNT(*), CNT_PRICE = count(price),
       SUM_PRICE = SUM(price), AVG_PRICE = avg(price)
from titles

select CNT = count(*),
       CNT_DPRICE = count(distinct price),
       SUM_DPRICE = sum(distinct price),
       AVG_DPRICE = avg(distinct price)
from titles

OUTPUT:
CNT         CNT_PRICE   SUM_PRICE                  AVG_PRICE
----------- ----------- -------------------------- --------------------------
         18          16                     236.26                      14.77

(1 row affected)

CNT         CNT_DPRICE  SUM_DPRICE                 AVG_DPRICE
----------- ----------- -------------------------- --------------------------
         18          11                     161.35                      14.67

(1 row affected)
```

In the first example, COUNT(*) returns the total number of rows (18) in the *titles* table. COUNT(price), on the other hand, ignores rows where the price is NULL, and thus returns 16. SUM(price) returns the sum of the price column for all non-null entries, and AVG(price) returns SUM(price)/COUNT(price), ignoring the null values.

The second example is like the first, except that adding DISTINCT to the function parameters results in duplicates being eliminated before the function is applied. Thus AVG(DISTINCT price) = SUM(DISTINCT price)/COUNT(DISTINCT price). In this case, too, null values are ignored.

System Functions System functions provide information about the Server's environment. This includes information that is global to databases (at a Server level) and information specific to the Server's databases. System functions are typically used in the SELECT clause, and many of them provide a convenient mechanism for retrieving information from system tables.

Syntax

```
<system_function> ( <parameter> [, <parameter>]... )
```

A listing showing some of the more commonly used system functions follows. If an optional parameter is not supplied, the default is to use the current database, the current Server login ID, or the current database user.

Function	Parameters	Result returned
DB_NAME	([<db_id#>])	database name
HOST_NAME	()	computer name
SUSER_NAME	([<suser_id#>])	Server login ID
USER_NAME	([<user_id#>])	user name
COL_NAME	(<obj_id#>,<col_id#>)	column name
COL_LENGTH	(<obj_name>,<col_name>)	column length
ISNULL	(<exp>, <val>)	substitutes the specified value for NULL entries
DB_ID	([<database_name>])	database ID number
SUSER_Id	([<suser_name>])	Server login ID number
USER_ID	([<user_name>])	database user ID number

The purpose of most of the functions is self-explanatory. The ISNULL function substitutes the value provided for NULL entries (see Example 5-21). The last three functions return internal numeric identifiers used in system tables for databases, Server login IDs, and database users. Here are three examples using the system functions. Example 5-19 displays the current database. Example 5-20 displays the current Server login ID. Example 5-20 finds the average price of all titles, substituting $15 for any NULL entries.

Example 5-19

```
select db_name()

OUTPUT:
-----------------------------------
pubs

(1 row affected)
```

Example 5-20

```
select suser_name()

OUTPUT:
-----------------------------------
anath

(1 row affected)
```

Example 5-21

```
select avg(isnull (price, $15))

OUTPUT:
-----------------------------------
14.79

(1 row affected)
```

String and Text/Image Functions String functions allow you to manipulate `character` or `binary` data, whereas text/image functions provide values for common operations on `text` or image data. Neither string-function names nor text/image function names are considered keywords in TRANSACT-SQL. That is, you can have an identifier name that is the same as the function name. String operations include concatenation, extraction of a substring, and conversion of a string to all uppercase or lowercase characters. A list of the more commonly used string functions follows.

Function	**Parameters**	**Result returned**
ASCII	(<char_expr>)	ASCII code value of leftmost character
CHAR	(<integer_expr>)	character equivalent of the ASCII code value; NULL otherwise
LOWER	(<char_expr>)	converts to all lowercase
UPPER	(<char_expr>)	converts to all uppercase
SUBSTRING	(<expr>,<start>,<length>)	extracts part of binary or character string
+		concatenates two or more character or binary strings or columns

Example 5-22 uses the + function to display California authors' last names followed by a comma, a space, and first name. Example 5-23 shows how to display a list of business book titles abbreviated to the first forty characters.

Example 5-22

```
select NAME = au_lname + ", " + au_fname
from authors
where state = "CA"

OUTPUT:
----------------------------------------
White, Johnson
Green, Marjorie
Carson, Cheryl
```

```
O'Leary, Michael
Straight, Dick
Bennet, Abraham
Dull, Ann
Gringlesby, Burt
Locksley, Chastity
Yokomoto, Akiko
Stringer, Dirk
MacFeather, Stearns
Karsen, Livia
Hunter, Sheryl
McBadden, Heather

(15 rows affected)
```

Example 5-23

```
select TITLE = (substring (title,1,40))
from titles
where type = "business"

OUTPUT:
TITLE
----------------------------------------
The Busy Executive's Database Guide
Cooking with Computers: Surreptitious Ba
You Can Combat Computer Stress!
Straight Talk about Computers

(4 rows affected)
```

The data types `text` and `image` support very large amounts of character or binary data. Text and image functions do not directly manipulate `text` or `image` data—the READTEXT and WRITETEXT statements do that. Rather, they return values that are useful in manipulating such data. The text and image functions are listed below.

Function	Parameters	Result returned
TEXTPTR	(<text_col>)	returns the valid text pointer value for specified text or image column

TEXTVALID	(<col_name>,<text_ptr>)	checks to see if text pointer is valid; returns 1 if so, 0 otherwise
PATINDEX	(<pattern>,<text_col>)	returns the starting position of first occurrence of the pattern; the pattern can include wildcard characters

The *pubs* database does not have any column of `text` or `image` data type. In order to illustrate how a text function works, assume that the *notes* column in the *titles* table is of `text` data type. Example 5-24 illustrates a use of the text/image function TEXTPTR. The example in plain English is: Read 20 bytes of the *notes* column starting at the 10th byte for the book "Cooking with Computers."

Example 5-24

```
declare @tptr varbinary(30)
select @tptr = textptr(notes)
from titles
where title like "Cooking with Computers%"
readtext titles.notes @tptr 9 20
```

The first statement declares a variable length binary local variable `tptr` that is used to hold the pointer retrieved in the next SELECT statement. This pointer points to the start of the text column *notes*. The READTEXT statement is then passed this pointer and retrieves 20 bytes starting at byte 10 (offset 9). Image data are manipulated the same way text data are.

Mathematical Functions TRANSACT-SQL provides most of the common functions needed for mathematical operations on numeric data. A comprehensive list is provided in the *SQL Server Language Reference* manual; a list of the more commonly used ones follows.

Function	Parameters	Result returned
ACOS ASIN ATAN	(<float_expr>)	angle in radians whose cosine, sine, or tangent is floating point value

COS SIN COT TAN	(<float_expr>)	the cosine, sine, cotangent, or tangent of the angle (in radians)
CEILING FLOOR	(<numeric_expr>)	smallest integer greater than or equal to, or the largest integer less than or equal to the specified value
LOG LOG10	(<float_expr>)	the natural logarithm or base 10 logarithm of value
ABS	(<numeric_expr>)	absolute value
ROUND	(<numeric_expr>, <integer_expr>)	rounds numeric expression to integer precision
SIGN	(<numeric_expr>)	returns whether value is positive (+1), negative (−1), or zero (0)
POWER	(<numeric_expr>,<y>)	the value of <numeric_expr> raised to power <y>
SQRT	(<float_expr>)	the square root of the specified value
RADIANS DEGREES	(<numeric_expr>)	conversion from degrees to radians and vice versa

Three examples using mathematical functions follow. Example 5-25 uses the ROUND function; Example 5-26 uses the FLOOR/CEILING function; Example 5-27 uses the TAN and RADIANS functions.

Example 5-25

```
select round(2345.6789, 2)
select round(2345.6789, -2)

OUTPUT:
--------------------
         2345.680000

(1 row affected)

--------------------
         2300.000000

(1 row affected)
```

Example 5-26

```
SELECT floor(234.56)
SELECT floor(-234.56)
select ceiling($234.56)
select ceiling(-234.56)

OUTPUT:
-------------------
         234.000000

(1 row affected)

-------------------
        -235.000000

(1 row affected)

-------------------
            235.000

(1 row affected)

-------------------
        -234.000000

(1 row affected)
```

Example 5-27

```
select tan(radians(45.0))

OUTPUT:
-------------------
           1.000000

(1 row affected)
```

Date Functions Date functions allow the user to manipulate `datetime` data. Date functions can be used in expressions in the SELECT clause or the WHERE clause. Datetime data are stored internally in a special format (to the accuracy of .003 milliseconds) and displayed in a default character format (Jan 12 1990 10:45AM). However, they can be entered in several different formats (see the next chapter) and displayed in a wide variety of alternative formats using the CONVERT function described later. The date functions are:

Function	**Parameters**	**Result returned**
`GETDATE`	`()`	current date and time in internal format
`DATENAME`	`(<date_part>,<date>)`	produces specified date part of specified date
`DATEPART`	`(<date_part>,<date>)`	produces specified date part of specified date as an integer
`DATEDIFF`	`(<date_part>,<date1>,<date2>)`	calculates number of date parts between two dates
`DATEADD`	`(<date_part>,<number>,<date>)`	Adds the number of date parts to the date

In date functions, the `<date_part>` parameter refers to the component of the datetime value in question, for example, hour, day, month. A list of the valid date parts, along with their valid abbreviations, and acceptable values follows.

Date part	**Abbreviation**	**Values**
year	yy	1753–9999
quarter	qq	1–4
month	mm	1–12
dayofyear	dy	1–366
day	dd	1–31
week	wk	1–53
weekday	dw	1–7 (Sunday–Saturday)
hour	hh	0–23
minute	mi	0–59
second	ss	0–59
millisecond	ms	0–999

Two examples will help clarify date function usage. For a comprehensive look at the structure of datetime data and the use of datetime functions, consult the *SQL Server Language Reference Manual.* Example 5-28 requests the current date. Example 5-29 extracts the current month and weekday from the current date.

Example 5-28

```
select NOW = getdate()

OUTPUT:
NOW
--------------------
 Apr 24 1990  5:04PM

(1 row affected)
```

Example 5-29

```
select datepart (month, getdate())
select datename (month, getdate())

select datepart (weekday, getdate())
select datename (weekday, getdate())

select datepart (dayofyear, getdate())
select datediff (day, "Dec 31, 1989", getdate())

OUTPUT:
----------
         4

(1 row affected)

----------
April

(1 row affected)

----------
         3

(1 row affected)
```

```
----------
Tuesday

(1 row affected)

----------
       114

(1 row affected)

----------
       114

(1 row affected)
```

The examples are fairly self-explanatory. The week begins with Sunday, so Tuesday corresponds to 3 for weekday. Notice that the last two date functions yield the same result.

Type Conversion Function The CONVERT function allows the user to convert expressions from one data type to another. Like date functions, CONVERT can be used in expressions in the SELECT clause and the WHERE clause. The syntax of the CONVERT function follows.

Syntax

```
CONVERT (<data_type>, <expr> [, <style>])
```

The `<data_type>` parameter specifies the data type to which the `<expr>` parameter is to be converted. Unfortunately, this doesn't apply to user-defined data types. The data type can be any valid system data type, such as `char(12)` or `int`. The optional `<style>` parameter is used to specify different display formats when converting `datetime` data to character format.

Not all possible conversions are legal. Some conversions are implicitly performed by SQL Server (for example, when comparing character data of different lengths in mixed-mode arithmetic). Figure 5-2 summarizes the all possible conversions that are allowed,

TO: FROM:	binary	varbinary	tinyint	smallint	int	float	char	varchar	money	bit	datetime	text	image
binary	-	I	I	I	I	N	I	I	N	N	N	N	E
varbinary	I	-	I	I	I	N	I	I	N	N	N	N	E
tinyint	E	I	-	I	I	I	E	E	I	I	N	N	N
smallint	E	I	I	-	I	I	E	E	I	I	N	N	N
int	E	E	I	I	-	I	E	E	I	I	N	N	N
float	N	N	I	I	I	-	E	I	I	I	N	N	N
char	E	E	E	E	E	E	-	I	E	E	I	E	N
varchar	E	E	E	E	E	E	I	-	E	E	I	E	N
money	I	I	I	I	I	I	I	I	-	I	N	N	N
bit	I	I	I	I	I	I	I	I	N	-	N	N	N
datetime	E	E	N	N	N	N	I	I	N	N	-	N	N
text	N	N	N	N	N	N	E	E	N	N	N	-	N
image	E	E	N	N	N	N	N	N	N	N	N	N	-

I Implicit conversion
E Explicit conversion. CONVERT function must be used.
N Conversion not allowed
- Conversion of a type to itself. Allowed but meaningless

FIGURE 5-2 Data type conversion chart

implicit, or can be explicitly achieved through the CONVERT function. Example 5-30 converts a `varchar` column to `char` data. Example 5-31 converts the current date to English format (dd/mm/yy).

Example 5-30

```
select SHORT_TITLE = convert (char(12), title)
from titles
where type = "Business"

OUTPUT:
SHORT_TITLE
------------
The Busy Exe
Cooking with
You Can Comb
Straight Tal

(4 rows affected)
```

Example 5-31

```
select ENGLISH_DATE = convert(char(10), getdate(), 3)

OUTPUT:
```

```
ENGLISH_DATE
------------
24/04/90

(1 row affected)
```

The INTO Clause

The SELECT statement provides a means to create new tables based on data that exist in current tables without having to define the table first through the CREATE TABLE statement. In other words, it allows you to create tables dynamically. Tables are created dynamically with the INTO clause. The INTO clause specifies the name of the new table to be created and contains the columns specified in the target list of the SELECT clause. The syntax of the INTO clause follows.

Syntax

```
[INTO [[<database>.]<owner>.]<table_name> ]
```

The INTO clause is optional; when used, it follows the SELECT clause. As indicated by the syntax, the INTO clause allows tables in other databases to be created. The table created can be a temporary or permanent table. A **temporary table** lasts only for the current session and is automatically dropped at the end of the session. Temporary table names begin with the # sign. A **permanent table**, on the other hand, exists until explicitly dropped. The INTO clause is often used to create temporary tables during query processing. To create a permanent table using the SELECT statement, a particular database option, the **select into/bulkcopy** option, must be set. The select into/bulkcopy option is discussed in Chapter 12. Example 5-32 shows how you can create a list of titles priced above $20.

Example 5-32

```
select *
into expensive_titles
from titles
where price > $20
```

```
OUTPUT:
(3 rows affected)
```

GROUP BY and HAVING Clauses

Aggregate functions were introduced earlier in this chapter. They are SUM, AVG, MIN, MAX, and COUNT. Aggregate functions produce a summary value from the set of data that is returned by a query. Aggregate functions can be used in the SELECT clause of a query; however, they are not allowed in the WHERE clause. A query with aggregate functions in the SELECT clause can, however, have a restricting WHERE clause. In this case the table is restricted before the aggregate functions are applied. For example, the following query returns the average price of all business books.

Example 5-33

```
select AVG_PRICE = avg(price)
from titles
where type = "business"

OUTPUT:
AVG_PRICE
--------------------
               13.73

(1 row affected)
```

Aggregate functions are mentioned again because they are normally used in conjunction with the GROUP BY and HAVING clauses. The GROUP BY clause is used to group data returned by a SELECT statement; the HAVING clause is used to restrict the groups returned. Here is an example to clarify the concept of grouping.

The *titles* table has information on several different kinds of books. You might want some information about these books as groups, for example, business books or psychology books. This is the purpose of the GROUP BY clause when it is used with aggregate functions. The HAVING clause then further restricts the groups based on some condition. If you want to view the average advance paid to the authors and the sum of the year-to-date sales, grouped by type of book, the query in Example 5-34 returns this information.

Example 5-34

```
select type, AVG1 = avg(advance), SUM1 = sum(ytd_sales)
from titles
group by type

OUTPUT:
type                                      AVG1        SUM1
------------- ------------------------ ----------
business                              6,281.25       30788
mod_cook                              7,500.00       24278
popular_comp                          7,500.00       12875
psychology                            4,255.00        9939
trad_cook                             6,333.33       19566
UNDECIDED                                 NULL        NULL

(6 rows affected)
```

Figure 5-3 illustrates how the GROUP BY and HAVING clauses work. First the data in the *titles* table are restricted by the WHERE clause, if there is one. In this case, there is no WHERE clause; so all the rows qualify for grouping. Next, the grouping occurs based on the type of title. The *titles* table shown is in fact grouped by type of title. If there is no aggregate function in the SELECT list, the query processing is complete at this point; that is, if GROUP BY is used without an aggregate function, it simply rearranges the rows into groups. Next, the aggregate functions are applied to the groups and a summary row is produced (one for each group). Finally, the summary rows are restricted by the condition in the HAVING clause. To state it simply, the result of a query that has GROUP BY and HAVING clauses is a summary row (with the aggregate values) for each group that satisfies the HAVING clause.

The syntax of the GROUP BY and HAVING clauses follows.

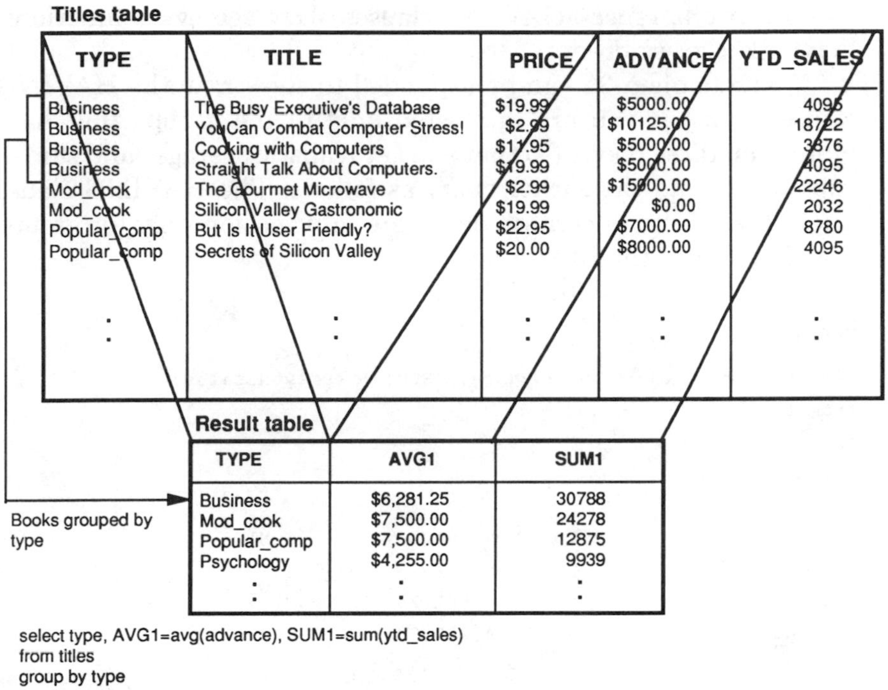

Titles table

TYPE	TITLE	PRICE	ADVANCE	YTD_SALES
Business	The Busy Executive's Database	$19.99	$5000.00	4095
Business	You Can Combat Computer Stress!	$2.99	$10125.00	18722
Business	Cooking with Computers	$11.95	$5000.00	3876
Business	Straight Talk About Computers.	$19.99	$5000.00	4095
Mod_cook	The Gourmet Microwave	$2.99	$15000.00	22246
Mod_cook	Silicon Valley Gastronomic	$19.99	$0.00	2032
Popular_comp	But Is It User Friendly?	$22.95	$7000.00	8780
Popular_comp	Secrets of Silicon Valley	$20.00	$8000.00	4095
:	:	:	:	:

Result table

TYPE	AVG1	SUM1
Business	$6,281.25	30788
Mod_cook	$7,500.00	24278
Popular_comp	$7,500.00	12875
Psychology	$4,255.00	9939
:	:	:

Books grouped by type

```
select type, AVG1=avg(advance), SUM1=sum(ytd_sales)
from titles
group by type
```

FIGURE 5-3 Grouping data

Syntax

```
[GROUP BY [ALL] <aggregate_free_expression>
     [, <aggregate_free_expression>...]
     [HAVING <search_condition>]]
```

As the syntax indicates, the entire GROUP BY clause is optional. The HAVING clause is really part of the GROUP BY clause; a HAVING clause with no GROUP BY clause is meaningless. The GROUP BY clause, if it exists, follows the WHERE clause in a SELECT statement. Also, multiple expressions are allowed in the GROUP BY clause as long as they do not include aggregates.

As indicated, the result table contains only summary rows that satisfy the HAVING clause. In this sense, the HAVING clause is similar to the WHERE clause. The HAVING clause restricts the groups (summary rows) specified by GROUP BY; the WHERE clause restricts the rows specified by SELECT. There is, however, one major difference—HAVING clauses allow aggregate functions; WHERE clauses do not.

Example 5-35 can be expanded to show how the HAVING clause works. If you are interested only in the groups that have more than three books (so that you get realistic averages and sums), you can expand the earlier query as follows. The HAVING clause filters the results to contain aggregate information only for groups that have more than three books.

Example 5-35

```
select type, AVG1 = avg(advance), SUM1 = sum(ytd_sales)
from titles
group by type
having count(*) > 3
OUTPUT:
type                                    AVG1          SUM1
------------ ------------------------ -----------
business                            6,281.25         30788
psychology                          4,255.00          9939

(2 rows affected)
```

You can also nest groups by including multiple columns in the GROUP BY clause. For example, by modifying the previous query you can form groups by type of book within publisher as shown in Example 5-36. Note that TRANSACT-SQL does not impose any restrictions on the target list of a query that has a GROUP BY clause. Hence, *pub_id* can be dropped from the target list, although the results would be somewhat confusing. On the other hand, it is perfectly allowable to include an additional column (say, *title_id*) in the target list. Many other implementations restrict the target list of GROUP BY queries to include only columns that are being grouped on and columns used with aggregate functions.

Example 5-36

```
select pub_id, type, AVG1 = avg(advance), SUM1 = sum(ytd_sales)
from titles
group by pub_id, type
```

```
OUTPUT:
pub_id type                                AVG1          SUM1
------ ---------- ---------------------- -----------
0736   business                       10,125.00         18722
0736   psychology                      3,568.75          9564
0877   mod_cook                        7,500.00         24278
0877   psychology                      7,000.00           375
0877   trad_cook                       6,333.33         19566
0877   UNDECIDED                           NULL          NULL
1389   business                        5,000.00         12066
1389   popular_comp                    7,500.00         12875

(8 rows affected)
```

ORDER BY Clause

The ORDER BY clause in a SELECT statement is used simply to sort or rearrange the order of the data in the result table. Remember, the relational model does not impose any ordering on the rows in a table. Different DBMSs are free to adopt the most efficient order for physically storing the data. In SQL Server, the physical order of rows in a table is determined by whether or not a clustered index is defined on it. If it does, the rows are stored in physically sorted order based on the clustered index key values. If the table doesn't have a clustered index, the rows are stored in the order they are added to the table; that is, the newest row is added to the end of the table. This structure is sometimes called a **heap**.

By default, there is no defined ordering for the rows returned by a SELECT statement. Typically the rows are returned in the order in which they are physically stored. No matter how the rows are actually stored or returned, the ORDER BY clause can be used to rearrange or sort the result rows based on column values. The syntax of the ORDER BY clause follows.

Syntax

```
ORDER BY [<table>.|<view>.]<column> | <select_list_no> |
          <expression> [ASC | DESC]
         [,[<table>.|<view>.]<column> | <select_list_no> |
          <expression> [ASC | DESC]]...
```

The ORDER BY clause, if it exists, follows the GROUP BY clause. As the syntax indicates, the result rows can be sorted based on columns or expressions and in ascending (ASC) or descending (DESC) sequence. NULLs always appear first in the sort order. The default order is ascending. The sort order can also be specified positionally (the `<select_list_no>` parameter in the syntax). For example, `ORDER BY 2` would mean sort on the second column in the target list. Example 5-37 shows how to retrieve the author information for all authors who have contracts in ascending zip code order. (Note that the *zip* column is not in the target list.) You can also sort the result data in nested fashion, for example, author last name within state, as shown in the Example 5-38.

Example 5-37

```
select au_fname, au_lname, phone, state
from authors
where contract = 1
order by zip

OUTPUT:
au_fname             au_lname                                 phone        state
-------------------- ---------------------------------------- ------------ -----
Sylvia               Panteley                                 301 946-8853 MD
Michel               DeFrance                                 219 547-9982 IN
Innes                del Castillo                             615 996-8275 MI
Anne                 Ringer                                   801 826-0752 UT
Albert               Ringer                                   801 826-0752 UT
Johnson              White                                    408 496-7223 CA
Chastity             Locksley                                 415 585-4620 CA
Ann                  Dull                                     415 836-7128 CA
Sheryl               Hunter                                   415 836-7128 CA
Akiko                Yokomoto                                 415 935-4228 CA
Livia                Karsen                                   415 534-9219 CA
Dick                 Straight                                 415 834-2919 CA
Stearns              MacFeather                               415 354-7128 CA
Marjorie             Green                                    415 986-7020 CA
Cheryl               Carson                                   415 548-7723 CA
Abraham              Bennet                                   415 658-9932 CA
Michael              O'Leary                                  408 286-2428 CA
Burt                 Gringlesby                               707 938-6445 CA
Reginald             Blotchet-Halls                           503 745-6402 OR

(19 rows affected)
```

Example 5-38

```
select au_fname, au_lname, phone, state
from authors
where contract = 1
order by 4 desc, 1 asc

OUTPUT:
au_fname             au_lname                                 phone        state
-------------------- ---------------------------------------- ------------ -----
Albert               Ringer                                   801 826-0752 UT
Anne                 Ringer                                   801 826-0752 UT
Reginald             Blotchet-Halls                           503 745-6402 OR
Innes                del Castillo                             615 996-8275 MI
Sylvia               Panteley                                 301 946-8853 MD
Michel               DeFrance                                 219 547-9982 IN
Abraham              Bennet                                   415 658-9932 CA
Akiko                Yokomoto                                 415 935-4228 CA
Ann                  Dull                                     415 836-7128 CA
Burt                 Gringlesby                               707 938-6445 CA
Chastity             Locksley                                 415 585-4620 CA
Cheryl               Carson                                   415 548-7723 CA
Dick                 Straight                                 415 834-2919 CA
Johnson              White                                    408 496-7223 CA
Livia                Karsen                                   415 534-9219 CA
Marjorie             Green                                    415 986-7020 CA
Michael              O'Leary                                  408 286-2428 CA
Sheryl               Hunter                                   415 836-7128 CA
Stearns              MacFeather                               415 354-7128 CA

(19 rows affected)
```

COMPUTE Clause

The COMPUTE clause is used with row aggregate functions to generate summary values whenever the values in specified columns change. These summary values are also known as control-break totals. They appear as additional rows in the result table, rather than additional columns as with the GROUP BY clause. Thus you can see both the detail and summary rows in the same set of results. The COMPUTE clause is a powerful TRANSACT-SQL extension;

most other SQL database systems require the use of a report writer to provide this capability.

Syntax

```
[COMPUTE <row_aggregate> (<column>)
     [, <row_aggregate> (<column>)] ...
     [BY <column> [, <column> ] ...]]
```

The COMPUTE clause is optional; when it exists it is the last clause in the SELECT statement. The row aggregate functions are the same ones used with the GROUP BY clause–SUM, AVG, MIN, MAX, and COUNT. You can produce control-break totals on grouped data (that is, the SELECT statement can have a GROUP BY clause) and you can specify more than one row aggregate for the same group.

Examples 5-39 and 5-40 show how the COMPUTE clause works and how it relates to the GROUP BY clause. Both queries are used to produce the sum and the average of the prices of titles by type. Notice that, although the same aggregate value is produced in both examples, in the COMPUTE example (Example 5-39) both detail and summary rows are produced, whereas in the GROUP BY example (Example 5-40) only a single row with summary columns is produced.

Example 5-39

```
select type, price
from titles
order by type
compute sum(price), avg(price) by type
compute sum(price), avg(price)

OUTPUT:
type                            price
------------ -----------------------
business                         2.99
business                        11.95
business                        19.99
business                        19.99
                                  sum
```

```
                            ------------------------
                                               54.92
                                                 avg
                            ------------------------
                                               13.73

type                                           price
------------ ------------------------
mod_cook                                        2.99
mod_cook                                       19.99
                                                 sum
                            ------------------------
                                               22.98
                                                 avg
                            ------------------------
                                               11.49

type                                           price
------------ ------------------------
popular_comp                                    NULL
popular_comp                                   20.00
popular_comp                                   22.95
                                                 sum
                            ------------------------
                                               42.95
                                                 avg
                            ------------------------
                                               21.48

type                                           price
------------ ------------------------
psychology                                      7.99
psychology                                     21.59
psychology                                      7.00
psychology                                     10.95
psychology                                     19.99
                                                 sum
                            ------------------------
                                               67.52
                                                 avg
                            ------------------------
                                               13.50
```

```
type                         price
------------ -----------------------
trad_cook                    20.95
trad_cook                    14.99
trad_cook                    11.95
                               sum
             -----------------------
                             47.89
                               avg
             -----------------------
                             15.96


type                         price
------------ -----------------------
UNDECIDED                     NULL
                               sum
             -----------------------
                              NULL
                               avg
             -----------------------
                              NULL
                               sum
             =======================
                            236.26
                               avg
             =======================
                             14.77

(25 rows affected)
```

Example 5-40

```
select type, count(*), sum(price), avg(price)
from titles
group by type

OUTPUT:
type
------------ ---------- ----------------------- -----------------------
business              4                   54.92                   13.73
mod_cook              2                   22.98                   11.49
```

```
popular_comp          3          42.95          21.48
psychology            5          67.52          13.50
trad_cook             3          47.89          15.96
UNDECIDED             1           NULL           NULL

(6 rows affected)
```

Certain restrictions apply to queries containing a COMPUTE clause. First, all the columns in the compute clause must appear in the target list. Second, you cannot have an INTO clause with the COMPUTE clause (since there are special summary rows in the result). Finally, if you have a BY in the COMPUTE clause, an ORDER BY is also required (see Example 5-39); the columns in the BY section must be the same or an orderly (left to right) subset of the columns in the ORDER BY clause. If no BY is used, grand totals are generated, and the ORDER BY clause is optional.

Advanced Queries

The previous section presented the various clauses in the SELECT statement and their purpose. This section discusses two of the more advanced types of SELECT statements–ones that involve joins and ones that involve subqueries.

Joins

A join is a relational operation that allows the user to retrieve data from two or more tables based on a comparison of column values in each of the tables. The result is a single table (a requirement of the relational model) that contains all the columns selected from the first and second table, and all the rows that satisfy the comparison condition. Figure 5-4 illustrates joins.

Joins are fundamental to relational databases. In a database of normalized tables (tables that do not exhibit redundancy), they represent the only way to retrieve data from more than one table. Relationships in a relational database are represented by key values (foreign keys and primary keys); joins provide the means for materializing these relationships. A simplified join syntax follows.

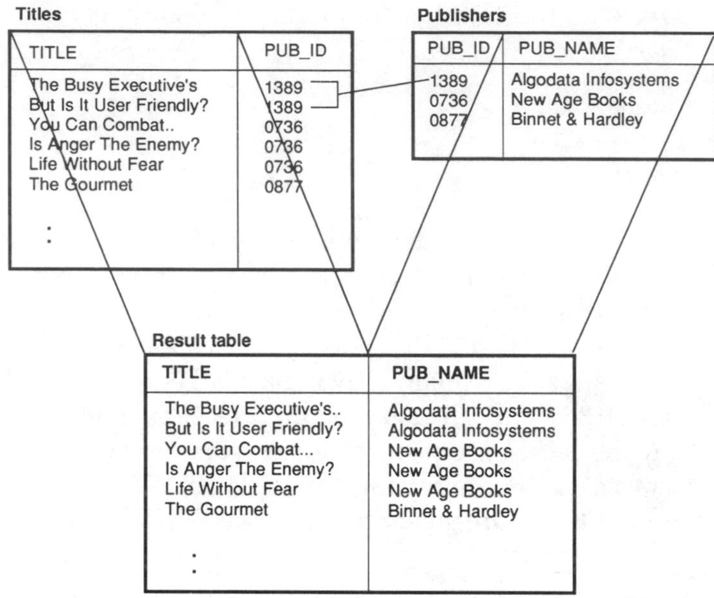


```
select title, pub_name
from titles, publishers
where titles.pub_id = publishers.pub_id
```

FIGURE 5-4 Joins

Syntax

```
WHERE [<database>.[<table>.|<view>.]]<column>
      <join operator>
      [<database>.[<table>.|<view>.]]<column>
```

The simplified syntax of a join condition forms the basis for joins. More than two tables can be joined in a single SELECT statement, and tables that exist in different databases can be joined. However, if the columns being joined have the same name, you need to qualify them to eliminate ambiguity. A SELECT statement that has multiple tables in the FROM clause, but no restricting WHERE clause, produces a product of the two tables. It can potentially contain a large number of rows even if moderate sized tables are joined.

There are several kinds of joins based on the join operator used in the join condition. The join operators supported are the standard comparison operators (see comparison conditions in the WHERE Clause section of this chapter). A list of the join operators follows.

Join operator	**Meaning**
=	equal to
>	greater than
<	less than
>=	greater than or equal to
<=	less than or equal to
!=	not equal to
!>	not greater than
!<	not less than
=*	outer join
*=	outer join

Joins based on equality (the most common) are called **equijoins**. A **natural join** is an equijoin with one of the redundant join columns removed. The last two operators in the list are **outer join** operators; which include all nonmatching rows from either one or the other table in the result (based on the outer join operator used). For example, if you want to find all authors and publishers in the same city, you can write the query shown in Example 5-41.

Example 5-41

```
select au_fname, au_lname, pub_name, authors.city
from authors, publishers
where authors.city = publishers.city

OUTPUT:
au_fname       au_lname       pub_name                  city
-------------- -------------- ------------------------- ----------
Cheryl         Carson         Algodata Infosystems      Berkeley
Abraham        Bennet         Algodata Infosystems      Berkeley

(2 rows affected)
```

To make absolutely sure that the authors and publishers are in fact from the same city, you can include the *state* column in the join condition.

Example 5-42

```
select au_fname, au_lname, pub_name, authors.city
from authors, publishers
where authors.city = publishers.city and
      authors.state = publishers.state

OUTPUT:
au_fname      au_lname      pub_name                 city
------------- ------------- ------------------------ ----------
Cheryl        Carson        Algodata Infosystems     Berkeley
Abraham       Bennet        Algodata Infosystems     Berkeley


(2 rows affected)
```

To find the publisher for all the business books you can write the following query.

Example 5-43

```
select title, type, pub_name
from titles, publishers
where titles.pub_id = publishers.pub_id and
      titles.type = "business"

OUTPUT:
title
type         pub_name
------------ ----------------------------------------
-----------------------------------------------------
------------ --------------------
The Busy Executive's Database Guide
business     Algodata Infosystems
Cooking with Computers: Surreptitious Balance Sheets
business     Algodata Infosystems
You Can Combat Computer Stress!
business     New Age Books
Straight Talk about Computers
```

```
business     Algodata Infosystems

(4 rows affected)
```

To find all books that are priced the same as any other book, you can execute the following query.

Example 5-44

```
select tl.title, t2.title, tl.price
from titles tl, titles t2
where tl.price = t2.price and
      tl.title_id < t2.title_id

OUTPUT:
title
title
price
------------------------------------------------
------------------------------------------------
------------------------
The Busy Executive's Database Guide
Straight Talk about Computers
                   19.99
The Busy Executive's Database Guide
Silicon Valley Gastronomic Treats
                   19.99
The Busy Executive's Database Guide
Prolonged Data Deprivation: Four Case Studies
                   19.99
Cooking with Computers: Surreptitious Balance Sheets
Fifty Years in Buckingham Palace Kitchens
                   11.95
You Can Combat Computer Stress!
The Gourmet Microwave
                    2.99
Straight Talk about Computers
Silicon Valley Gastronomic Treats
                   19.99
Straight Talk about Computers
Prolonged Data Deprivation: Four Case Studies
                   19.99
```

```
Silicon Valley Gastronomic Treats
Prolonged Data Deprivation: Four Case Studies
                   19.99

(8 rows affected)
```

To find all stores in the same city as that of a publisher and include stores that are not in the same city in the result, use the query in Example 5-45.

Example 5-45

```
select pub_name, stor_name, state = stores.state
from publishers, stores
where publishers.state =* stores.state

OUTPUT:
pub_name
        stor_name                                 state
----------------------------------------
       ---------------------------------------- -----
Algodata Infosystems
        Barnum's                                  CA
Algodata Infosystems
        News & Brews                              CA
NULL
        Doc-U-Mat: Quality Laundry and Books      NULL
NULL
        Bookbeat                                  NULL
NULL
        Eric the Read Books                       NULL
Algodata Infosystems
        Fricative Bookshop                        CA

(6 rows affected)
```

There are two important points about the examples worth mentioning. First, the order of the tables in the WHERE clause and the order in which the join columns are listed is not important. It is the job of the query optimizer to figure out the most efficient execution plan for the query. Second, if the column for city does not have the same name in both tables, the column name does not need to be qualified.

Example 5-42 shows multiple columns in the join. Example 5-43 shows a condition in the WHERE clause, in addition to the join condition. Example 5-44 shows a self-join (joining a table with itself). A self-join is like joining two instances of the same table, so instances have to be aliased. Example 5-45 shows an outer join that includes all nonmatching rows from the *stores* table. Note the NULL values for the publisher name for the nonmatching rows.

The concept of processing joins can be explained in terms of relational algebra operators—product, restrict, and project. This is useful in understanding what results a join query will generate. First, the Cartesian product of all the tables in the FROM clause is formed; all possible combination of rows from each of the tables are generated. The product of two tables contains as many rows as the multiplication of the rows in the first by the number of rows in the second. Second, the product is restricted based on the join condition, the column values are compared, and only those rows that satisfy the comparison are retained. The result is a large number of rows if no restricting join condition is specified in the WHERE clause. Finally, the result is projected on the columns in the target list to yield the final result.

In practice, the exact procedure or execution plan may differ from the preceding outline. It is dependent on both the query and the actual distribution of the data in the tables involved. In fact, much of the optimizer's job is to figure out the right sequence for processing the WHERE clause. Chapter 12 describes SQL Server's powerful performance tuning features that let you examine the optimizer's plan for a particular query. The `sp_helpjoins` stored procedure provides information on likely join columns in two tables. Two primary criteria are used to provide this information. The first is based on keys identified through the `sp_primarykey` and `sp_commonkey` stored procedures by the database designer. The second is based on whether or not the columns share the same name or data type. Example 5-46 shows how to find likely join columns in the *authors* and *publishers* tables.

Example 5-46

```
sp_helpjoins authors, publishers
```

```
OUTPUT:
first_pair
----------------------------- -----------------------------
city                          city
state                         state

(2 rows affected)
```

Subqueries

A subquery is a SELECT statement that is nested inside a SELECT, INSERT, UPDATE, or DELETE statement. A SELECT statement (the outer query) that contains one or more subqueries (the inner queries) is referred to as a **nested query**. The results of the outer query are evaluated based on the results of the inner subqueries. Figure 5-5 illustrates this concept.

Subqueries have a restricted SELECT statement syntax. They are normally enclosed in parentheses. They can return zero or more values or serve as existence tests based on the form of query within which the subquery is used. Subqueries are very powerful; they can themselves contain subqueries. They can also be used anywhere an expression is allowed, as long as they return a single value. However, many nested queries can be formulated as

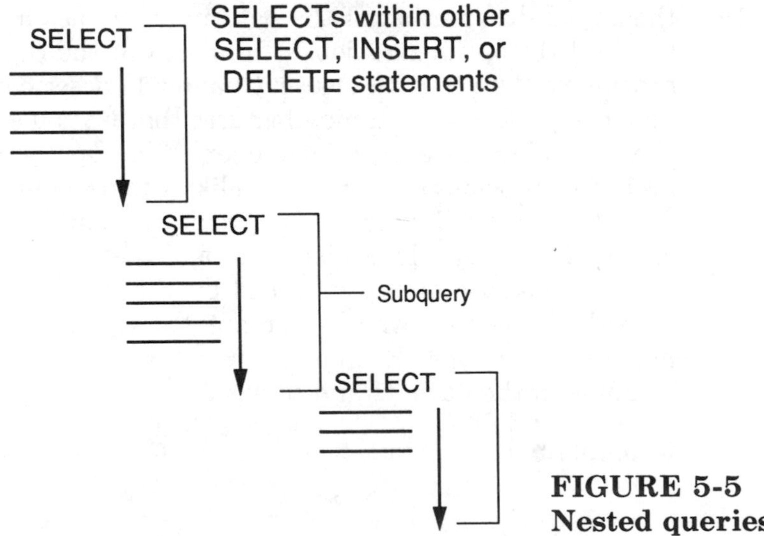

FIGURE 5-5
Nested queries

join queries and produce the same result. The syntax of a subquery follows.

Syntax

```
( SELECT [DISTINCT] <subquery_target_list>
  [FROM [[<database>.]<owner>.]{<table> | <view>} [HOLDLOCK]
     [, [[<database>.]<owner>.]{<table> | <view>} [HOLDLOCK]]...]
  [WHERE <search_condition>]
  [GROUP BY <aggregate_free_expr> [,<aggregate_free_expr>]...]
  [HAVING <search_condition>] )
```

There are three different forms of subqueries in the WHERE clause:

Syntax

```
WHERE <expression> [NOT] IN (<subquery>)
WHERE <expression> <comparison_operator>
 [ANY | ALL] (<subquery>)
WHERE [NOT] EXISTS (<subquery>)
```

The first form operates on lists; it can return a list of multiple values. The second form uses comparison operators and must return a single value unless it is modified with the keywords ANY or ALL. The third form serves as an existence test and is introduced by the keyword EXISTS. The three forms are described in the next three sections.

Subqueries with IN In this form, the inner query (the subquery) is evaluated first and returns a set of zero or more values to the outer query. The outer query then returns the rows that match the condition in the WHERE clause based on the values the subquery returned. Figure 5-6 illustrates how a nested query is used to return the publisher name for all publishers that publish business titles. The inner query returns the *pub_id* for all publishers that publish business titles. The outer query is then used to return the publisher name. If multiple values can be returned, the IN form must be used instead of the comparison operator =. For example, if you want all the titles written by Anne Ringer, use the nested query shown in Example 5-47.

Example 5-47

```
select title, price
from titles
where title_id in
     (select title_id
      from titleauthor
      where au_id in
           (select au_id
            from authors
            where au_lname = 'Ringer'
            and au_fname = 'Anne'))

OUTPUT:
title                                    price
---------------------------------------- ----------
The Gourmet Microwave                          2.99
Is Anger the Enemy?                           10.95

(2 rows affected)
```

Subqueries with Comparison Operators Subqueries can also be introduced with the standard operators used in comparison conditions. Example 5-48 shows how to find all titles that are published by Algodata Infosystems. The inner query returns the publisher id (1389) from the *publishers* table for Algodata Infosystems. The outer query then retrieves all titles with the publisher id 1389. The second query returns the same result using a join.

Example 5-48

```
select title, price
from titles
where pub_id =
     (select pub_id
     from publishers
     where pub_name = 'Algodata Infosystems')
select title, price
from titles, publishers
where titles.pub_id = publishers.pub_id
and pub_name = 'Algodata Infosystems'
```

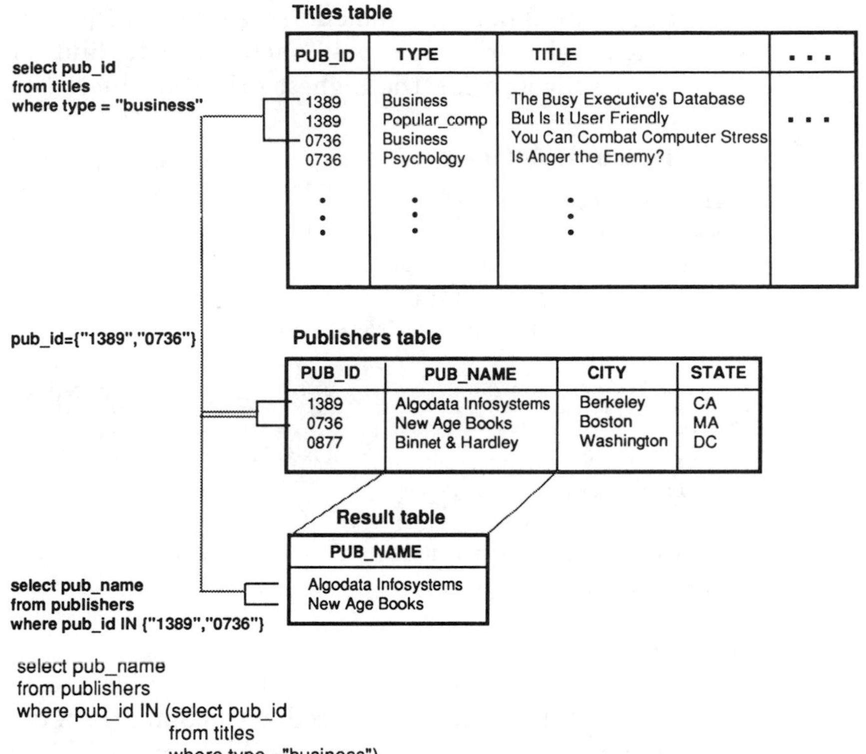

Titles table
PUB_ID
TYPE
TITLE
. . .
1389
1389
0736
0736
Business
Popular_comp
Business
Psychology
The Busy Executive's Database
But Is It User Friendly
You Can Combat Computer Stress
Is Anger the Enemy?
select pub_id
from titles
where type = "business"
pub_id={"1389","0736"}
Publishers table
PUB_ID
PUB_NAME
CITY
STATE
1389
0736
0877
Algodata Infosystems
New Age Books
Binnet & Hardley
Berkeley
Boston
Washington
CA
MA
DC
Result table
PUB_NAME
Algodata Infosystems
New Age Books
select pub_name
from publishers
where pub_id IN {"1389","0736"}
select pub_name
from publishers
where pub_id IN (select pub_id
from titles
where type ="business")

FIGURE 5-6 Subquery with IN

```
OUTPUT:
title                                                    price
-------------------------------------------------------- ----------
The Busy Executive's Database Guide                      19.99
Cooking with Computers: Surreptitious Balance Sheets     11.95
Straight Talk about Computers                            19.99
But Is It User Friendly                                  22.95
Secrets of Silicon Valley                                20.00
Net Etiquette                                             NULL

(6 rows affected)
```

Because subqueries introduced with a comparison condition can return only a single value to the outer query, they often include aggregate functions—remember, aggregate functions also return a single value. Example 5-49 shows how to find all titles that are priced higher than the highest priced business title.

Example 5-49

```
select title, price
from titles
where price > (select max(price)
               from titles
               where type = "business")

OUTPUT:
title                                                             price
----------------------------------------------------------------- ---------
But Is It User Friendly?                                              22.95
Secrets of Silicon Valley                                             20.00
Computer Phobic and Non-Phobic Individuals: Behavior Variations       21.59
Onions, Leeks, and Garlic: Cooking Secrets of the Mediterranean       20.95

(4 rows affected)
```

Subqueries introduced with comparison operators can also be modified with the keywords ANY or ALL, in which case they are referred to as modified comparison operators. Subqueries introduced with **modified comparison operators** can return multiple values and, hence, can also include the GROUP BY and HAVING clauses. For example, you can find the titles that are priced higher than all the business titles (using the > ALL form). This is the same as saying that the price is higher than the price of each and every business title.

Example 5-50

```
select title, price
from titles
where price > all (select price
                   from titles
                   where type = "business")

OUTPUT:
title                                                             price
```

```
------------------------------------------------------------ ----------
But Is It User Friendly?                                          22.95
Secrets of Silicon Valley                                         20.00
Computer Phobic and Non-Phobic Individuals: Behavior Variations   21.59
Onions, Leeks, and Garlic: Cooking Secrets of the Mediterranean   20.95

(4 rows affected)
```

On the other hand, you can find the titles whose prices are higher than any business title (using the > ANY form). This is the same as saying that the price is higher than the lowest priced business title.

Example 5-51

```
select distinct title, price
from titles
where price > any (select price
                   from titles
                   where type = "business")

OUTPUT:
title                                                            price
------------------------------------------------------------ ----------
Sushi, Anyone?                                                    14.99
Life Without Fear                                                  7.00
Is Anger the Enemy?                                               10.95
But Is It User Friendly?                                          22.95
Secrets of Silicon Valley                                         20.00
Straight Talk about Computers                                     19.99
Silicon Valley Gastronomic Treats                                 19.99
Emotional Security: A New Algorithm                                7.99
The Busy Executive's Database Guide                               19.99
Fifty Years in Buckingham Palace Kitchens                         11.95
Prolonged Data Deprivation: Four Case Studies                     19.99
Cooking with Computers: Surreptitious Balance Sheets              11.95
Computer Phobic and Non-Phobic Individuals: Behavior Variations   21.59
Onions, Leeks, and Garlic: Cooking Secrets of the Mediterranean   20.95

(14 rows affected)
```

If the subqueries in the preceding examples do not return any values, all rows in the outer query satisfy the condition. Also, the DISTINCT keyword is used in the outer query in Example 5-51 to suppress any duplicate rows that are generated.

Subqueries with EXISTS The third form of introducing subqueries uses the EXISTS keyword. Such subqueries do not return values; they serve as existence tests and return TRUE or FALSE. If the subquery returns TRUE, the row in the outer query is included in the result; if FALSE is returned, the row is not included. The subquery returns TRUE or FALSE based on whether or not any rows are returned by it.

Subqueries with EXISTS fall into the category of **correlated subqueries**. With most nested queries, the innermost query is evaluated first, the results are passed to the next outer query, and so on. In a correlated subquery, the evaluation of the inner query is dependent on the outer query and, in fact, refers to a table in the outer query. In such a case, the inner query is evaluated over and over with values from each row of the outer table. If the inner query returns any rows, that is, it returns TRUE, the outer row is included in the result table, otherwise it is not. Example 5-52 shows how to find all authors who live in a city with a publisher. Example 5-53 shows how to find all publishers that publish psychology titles.

Example 5-52

```
select au_fname, au_lname
from authors
where exists  (select *
               from publishers
               where publishers.city = authors.city)

OUTPUT:
au_fname                 au_lname
--------------------     ----------------------------------------
Cheryl                   Carson
Abraham                  Bennet

(2 rows affected)
```

Example 5-53

```
select pub_name
from publishers
```

```
where exists (select *
              from titles
              where titles.pub_id = publishers.pub_id and
                    titles.type = "Psychology")

OUTPUT:
pub_name
------------------------------
New Age Books
Binnet & Hardley

(2 rows affected)
```

Here are a few points to note. First, the EXISTS keyword is not preceded by any column name, expression, or constant. Second, since the subquery serves basically as an existence test, it uses the SELECT * syntax. Column names can be used in the target list, but there is no need to. Third, subqueries with EXISTS are always correlated subqueries. The keyword NOT can be used before the EXISTS keyword; in this case the WHERE clause is TRUE if no rows are returned by the subquery.

Subqueries in Data Modification Statements Subqueries can also be used in the WHERE clauses of the data modification statements INSERT, UPDATE, and DELETE the same way they are used in SELECT statements. Example 5-54 shows how to delete all sales for Cooking with Computers.

Example 5-54

```
delete from sales
where title_id =
     (select title_id
      from titles
      where title like 'Cooking with Computers%')

OUTPUT:
(1 row affected)
```

If publisher New Age Books decides it wants to give its customers a 20% discount on all psychology books, you can write the query shown in Example 5-55.

Example 5-55

```
update titles
set price = price * 0.8
where pub_id = (select pub_id
                from publishers
                where pub_name = 'New Age Books') and
                type = 'Psychology'
```

```
OUTPUT:
(4 rows affected)
```

Rules for Subqueries As mentioned earlier, a subquery has basically a restricted SELECT statement syntax. Most of these restrictions are understandable in light of the operators used in subqueries, and how they are processed. Some of these restrictions have been touched on in the preceding discussions. However, they are outlined here for completeness.

- The select list of a subquery can usually include only one column name or expression.
- The only exceptions are when the subquery is introduced with EXISTS or the IN keyword. Then you can use a SELECT * or several columns in the target list.
- Subqueries cannot use the INTO clause, the ORDER BY clause, or the COMPUTE clause.
- Subqueries introduced with unmodified comparison operators cannot have the GROUP BY or HAVING clause.
- The DISTINCT keyword cannot be used with subqueries that include a GROUP BY clause.

Except for these restrictions, subqueries are very general and can even be used in place of expressions in TRANSACT-SQL statements.

Summary

This chapter looked in some detail at the data retrieval component within the TRANSACT-SQL DML. The basic SELECT statement was discussed, and its three clauses–SELECT, FROM, and WHERE–were examined in detail. The chapter looked at how to group data and generate summary values using aggregate functions, and how to order data returned by the SELECT statement. Many of the more powerful options and forms of the SELECT statement, including the COMPUTE clause, joins, and subqueries were described. The next chapter focuses on data modification.

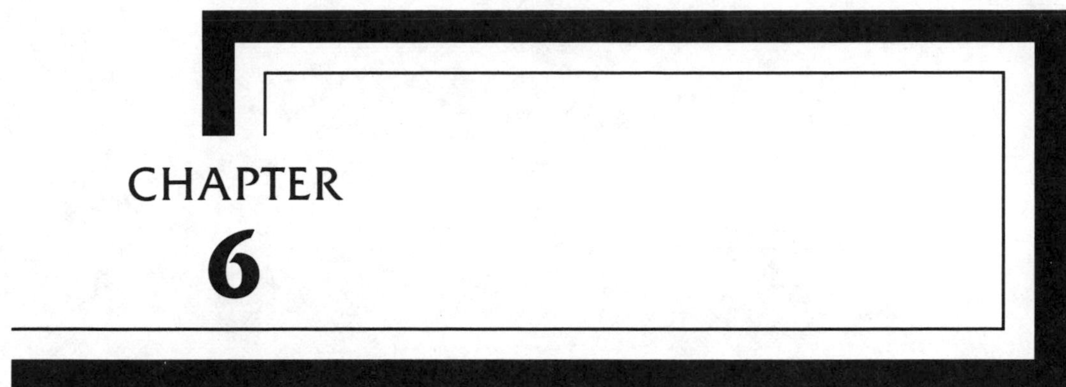

Data Modification

Introduction

Chapter 5 discussed data retrieval in TRANSACT-SQL. This chapter focuses on the other component of data manipulation–data modification. Data modification is the process of adding, modifying, and removing data within databases. The statements used in this process are termed data modification statements. This chapter also discusses the concept of transactions and the two kinds of transactions that are possible–implicit and explicit. Finally, it discusses the control-of-flow language (mentioned in Chapter 3) provided by TRANSACT-SQL.

The data modification statements in TRANSACT-SQL are INSERT, UPDATE, DELETE, and TRUNCATE. The INSERT statement adds a row to a table. The UPDATE statement allows a user to update columns selectively in rows in a table. The DELETE statement deletes a row from a table. The TRUNCATE statement is a fast way to delete all the rows in a table. TRANSACT-SQL provides many extensions to the standard SQL modification statements and even adds the TRUNCATE statement. The following sections discuss these extensions.

TRANSACT-SQL extends standard SQL with a set of statements that are collectively referred to as control-of-flow language. These statements provide the additional functionality necessary for writing simple programs in the areas of variable definition, looping, conditional execution, and display constructs. Control-of-flow statements are especially useful when you write stored procedures and triggers (discussed in Chapters 7 and 8). They include such statements as IF..ELSE, WHILE, PRINT, and DECLARE (variable definition). These statements are discussed under Control-of-Flow Language later in this chapter.

Data Modification Statements

Once you have created a table, you can insert, delete, or update rows in it using the data modification statements just mentioned. All of the data modification statements operate on only one table at a time. The INSERT statement allows you to add new rows to a table. The UPDATE statement allows you to modify data in columns within existing rows. The DELETE statement allows you to remove existing rows from a table.

All the data modification statements also operate on views—a view name can be substituted for a table name. However, when using data modification statements with views, you are limited by certain restrictions. These restrictions will be elaborated on in Chapter 7. The next section explains how data are entered in SQL Server. The following sections discuss the four data modification statements.

Entering Data

SQL Server supports several different system data types, and the user-defined data types based on them. The following rules apply when entering data in TRANSACT-SQL:

- All `char`, `varchar`, `text`, and `datetime` data must be enclosed in single or double quotes.
- `binary`, `varbinary` or `image` data must be preceded by 0x.
- `int`, `smallint`, and `tinyint` data are entered as is, but can also be entered in scientific notation.
- `float` data can be entered in the regular decimal notation (with a decimal point) or in the standard scientific or exponential notation.
- `money` data should be preceded by the dollar sign ($).

Here are some examples of how data of various types can be entered. Example 6-1 shows how `char` and `varchar` data are entered.

Example 6-1

```
"This is a short character string"
"It's time to quit"
'It''s time to quit'
```

Example 6-2 shows how `datetime` data are entered. `Datetime` data can be a date followed by a time, a time followed by a date, or the year at the end.

Example 6-2

```
"Apr[il] 20[,] [19]90"
'20] Apr[il][,] [19]90'
"4/20/1990"
"4-20-90"
"[19]90[0420]"

"14:45[:40:999]"
"4am"
"6 PM"
"[0]4[:40:30:675]AM"

"2:45PM Apr 20 1990"
"Apr 20 1990 2:45PM"
"Apr 20 2:45PM 1990"
```

Example 6-3 shows how to enter `binary`, `varbinary`, and `image` data; Example 6-4 shows how to enter `money` data; Example 6-5 shows how to enter `int`, `smallint`, and `tinyint` data; Example 6-6 shows how to enter `float` data.

Example 6-3

```
0xEF
0xABCDEF
```

Example 6-4

```
$20.50
$100.0045
```

Example 6-5

```
66
-64
12E3
```

Example 6-6

```
434.567
-.0004
12E3
12.2E-2
-4.02e4
+402e+2
```

Here are a few points to note. For `datetime` data the following defaults apply: time defaults to midnight, day to the first day of the month, month to January, and year to 1900. For `binary` and `varbinary` data a length of *n* in the data type specification means it can hold 2*n* characters. Thus a column of length 2 can hold 0x45AB. For `float` data the exact precision is dependent on the machine.

The INSERT Statement

As mentioned earlier, the INSERT statement allows you to add new rows to a table. There are two forms of the INSERT statement—one that allows you to enter explicit values for row data (the form that uses the VALUES keyword) and the other that add rows to a table based on other data in the same or other tables (the SELECT statement form).

Syntax

```
INSERT [INTO]
     [[<database>.]<owner>.]{<table> | <view>} [<column_list>]
     {VALUES (<constant_expression> [,<constant_expression>]...)
     | <select_statement>}
```

INSERT with VALUES The VALUES keyword allows you to specify explicit values for the columns of the table. Normally the column values must be specified in the order in which they were defined in the CREATE TABLE statement (Example 6-7). However, this order can be changed by first specifying the optional `<column_list>` parameter after the table or view name in the INSERT statement and then specifying the values in the order of the columns in the column list. Example 6-7 shows how to add the title The Guide to SQL Server to the *titles* table. Example 6-8 shows how to insert a title, The Fine Art of Programming. To the *titles* table leaving out the NULL values.

Example 6-7

```
insert into titles
values ("PC1470", "The Guide to SQL Server", "Computer",
        "0736", $24.95, NULL, NULL, NULL,
        "A comprehensive guide to the SQL Server", "06/15/90")

OUTPUT:

(1 row affected)
```

Example 6-8

```
insert into titles (title_id, title, type, pub_id, price,
                    notes, pubdate)
values ("PC1500", "The Fine Art of Programming", "Computer", "1389", $22.95,
        "Explores different programming philosophies", "02/01/89")

OUTPUT:

(1 row affected)
```

Normally in an INSERT statement all column values must be explicitly provided, or an error will occur. If, however, a column definition allows NULLs, or if a default is bound to the column, the column value need not be explicitly supplied. If a particular column value is not specified, one of three things happens. Depending on the null specification for the column, and on whether or not a default has been provided for the column, a NULL value is supplied, the default value is supplied, or an error occurs. The following table summarizes these actions. If the INSERT violates a rule or trigger, the row is not inserted into the table, and an error message is displayed.

	Not null	Null
Default	the default	the default
No default	error message	NULL

INSERT with SELECT This form of the INSERT statement allows you to insert data in a table based on other data in one or more tables. The data can even come from the same table being inserted into (a TRANSACT-SQL extension). The column list can be specified after the table name in the INSERT statement or in the target list of the SELECT statement (see Example 6-10). The rest of the SELECT statement defines where to take the data and what subset of data to extract.

You can have computed columns in an INSERT statement, for example, salary * 1.15. You can also specify column values selectively as long as no null definitions are violated and appropriate defaults are provided.

Here are some examples to illustrate the SELECT statement. Say you have a table called *newstores* that was created with information about new stores. The table has exactly the same definition as the *stores* table. You can add all of the rows in the *newstores* table to the *stores* table using either of the INSERT statements shown in Example 6-9.

Example 6-9

```
insert into stores
     select * from newstores
OR
insert into stores (stor_id, city, state, zip,)
     select * from newstores

OUTPUT:

(1 row affected)
```

Now, assume there was a table called *oldstores* containing stores that are not in business any longer. You want to reuse the store ids below 1000. You can use either of the statements in Example 6-10 to reinsert the store ids in the *stores* table.

Example 6-10

```
insert stores (stor_id, state)
     select stor_id, state from oldstores
     where stor_id < "1000"
```

```
OR
insert stores
     select stor_id, state from oldstores
     where stor_id < "1000"

OUTPUT:

(2 rows affected)
```

If you want to add another store location for Barnum's in Tustin, California, you can use the statement in Example 6-11 to insert the row and fill in the rest of the address later.

Example 6-11

```
insert into stores (stor_id, stor_name, city, state)
     select "7065", stor_name, city, state
     from stores
     where stor_name = "Barnum's"

OUTPUT:

(1 row affected)
```

The UPDATE statement

Once data is inserted into a table (with the INSERT statement), you can modify the table with the UPDATE statement. The UPDATE statement allows you to modify specific columns in a row by adding new data. The new data can consist of constant values or expressions, or they can be data extracted from other tables.

Syntax

```
UPDATE [[<database>.]<owner>.]{<table> | <view>}
SET   [[[<database>.]<owner>.]{<table>. | <view>.}]
        <column1_name> = {expression1 | NULL}
     [, <column2_name> = {expression2 | NULL} ]...
[ FROM [[<database>.]<owner>.]{<table> | <view>}
     [, [[<database>.]<owner>.]{<table> | <view>}]...]
[ WHERE <search_condition> ]
```

Without the FROM clause, the semantics of the UPDATE statement are simple—the SET clause determines the columns to be changed and their values, and the WHERE clause determines the rows to be changed. The optional FROM clause specifies where the data come from, when they are not drawn from the same table. For example, if you want to update Ann Dull's last name to Bright in the *authors* table you can write the UPDATE statement shown in Example 6-12.

Example 6-12

```
update authors
set au_lname = "Bright"
where au_lname = "Dull" and au_fname = "Ann"

OUTPUT:

(1 row affected)
```

Example 6-13 shows how you can lower the price by 10% and increase the royalty by 3% for all popular computing titles.

Example 6-13

```
update titles
set price = price * 0.90, royalty = royalty + 3
where type = "popular_comp"

OUTPUT:

(3 rows affected)
```

Example 6-14 shows how to change the publisher of the book Cooking with Computers to New Age Books.

Example 6-14

```
update titles
set pub_id = publishers.pub_id
from publishers
where titles.title like 'Cooking with Computers%' and
     publishers.pub_name = 'New Age Books'
```

```
OUTPUT:

(1 row affected)
```

The DELETE Statement

The DELETE statement allows you to remove rows from a table based on conditions involving data in either the same table or other tables.

Syntax

```
DELETE [FROM] [[<database>.]<owner>.]{<table> | <view>}
      [FROM [[<database>.]<owner>.]{<table> | <view>}
      [,    [[<database>.]<owner>.]{<table> | <view>}]... ]
      [ WHERE <search_condition> ]
```

The first optional FROM keyword is simply a "noise" keyword and is provided for compatibility with other SQL versions. The second FROM allows you to delete rows based on data in other tables. It is a TRANSACT-SQL enhancement. The WHERE clause specifies the condition that must be satisfied for deletion. If no WHERE clause is specified, *all* rows of the table are deleted. For example, if you want to delete all authors who live in Utah you can write the following query.

Example 6-15

```
delete from authors
where state = "UT"

OUTPUT:

(2 rows affected)
```

Example 6-16 shows how you can delete all sales for business titles.

Example 6-16

```
delete from sales
from sales, titles
```

```
where sales.title_id = titles.title_id and
     titles.type = "business"

OUTPUT:

(4 rows affected)
```

The TRUNCATE Statement

The TRUNCATE statement, unique to TRANSACT-SQL, is a fast, efficient way to delete all the rows in a table without dropping the table (or its associated objects). The TRUNCATE statement frees up the space used by the table and index data, but does not log the deletions, which enhances efficiency. Since the TRUNCATE operation is not recoverable (because deletions are not logged), permission defaults to the owner of the table and cannot be granted to another user. Transaction logging will be discussed in Chapter 11. For now it is sufficient to say that it is the mechanism by which recovery is provided. Permissions are discussed in Chapter 9. The TRUNCATE syntax follows.

Syntax

```
TRUNCATE TABLE [<database>.]<owner>.]<table>
```

Example 6-17 shows how you can remove all the rows from the *stores* table.

Example 6-17

```
truncate table stores

OUTPUT:
```

Transactions

So far, this chapter has discussed the data modification statements—INSERT, UPDATE, DELETE, and TRUNCATE. This section talks briefly about the related topic of transactions, although the implementation of transaction processing will be examined in depth in Chapter 11.

A **transaction** is a sequence of operations that is an integral unit of work to the DBMS; that is, it is either completed in its entirety or not at all. A transaction is an all or nothing proposition. There is no such thing as a partial transaction. Once it is applied (or committed), it cannot be undone (or rolled back).

Implicit Transactions

Transactions are a means whereby data consistency and data recovery are ensured in a multiuser environment. They can be **explicit**, using special user-defined statements that define transaction boundaries, or **implicit**, with automatically defined transaction boundaries. In TRANSACT-SQL, all data modification statements are treated as implicit transactions; that is, all data modification statements will either complete fully or not at all. In contrast, data retrieval statements are not considered transactions because they do not affect the state of the database. Example 6-18 shows a single INSERT statement, which is implicitly treated as a transaction by SQL Server.

Example 6-18

```
INSERT INTO stores
VALUES ("FFFF","Computerphile's Haven", "1234 Torrance Blvd.",
     "Torrance", "CA", "90501")

OUTPUT:

(1 row affected)
```

Treating data modification statements as implicit transactions has consequences that are not readily apparent, but that are crucial in any DBMS. It means that any update to the database (for any reason, including system failures) will not leave the database in an inconsistent or corrupted state. The modification also includes updates to any indexes on the table. If the system crashes part way through an INSERT statement, the database will not be left in state where only some of the column values exist, or where an index is not updated.

User-Defined Transactions

In addition to implicit transactions, SQL Server provides **user-defined transaction** capability through the use of such special statements as BEGIN TRANSACTION, COMMIT TRANSACTION, and ROLLBACK TRANSACTION. User-defined transactions allow users to group a set of TRANSACT-SQL statements into a transaction using the BEGIN TRANSACTION and COMMIT TRANSACTION statements. They also allow the user to define intermediate save-points within the transaction (useful for large transactions) using the SAVEPOINT statement. Finally, the user can undo a transaction completely or back to some previous save-point using the ROLLBACK TRANSACTION statement.

A transfer from a checking to a savings account illustrates the need for user-defined transactions. The transfer involves a debit of $300 from the checking account and a credit of $300 to the savings account. Both operations must happen, or neither. The user-defined transaction transfer uses a BEGIN TRANSACTION and a COMMIT TRANSACTION statement to group the two operations. Once the transaction is defined, it is up to the DBMS to guarantee that it is treated as a single integral unit of work.

The syntax of user-defined transaction statements follows.

Syntax

```
BEGIN TRANsaction
COMMIT TRANsaction
SAVE TRANsaction <save_point>
ROLLBACK TRANsaction   [ {<save_point> | <tran_name>} ]
```

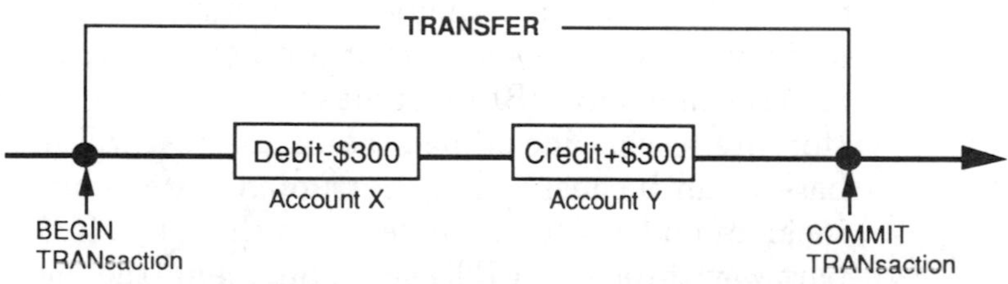

FIGURE 6-1 User-defined transaction transfer

Transactions cannot be nested. No permissions are required to define them, so any user can define transactions. Transactions can be undone completely or restored to some previously defined save point. The interaction of SAVE TRANSACTION and ROLLBACK TRANSACTION statements is illustrated in Figure 6-2.

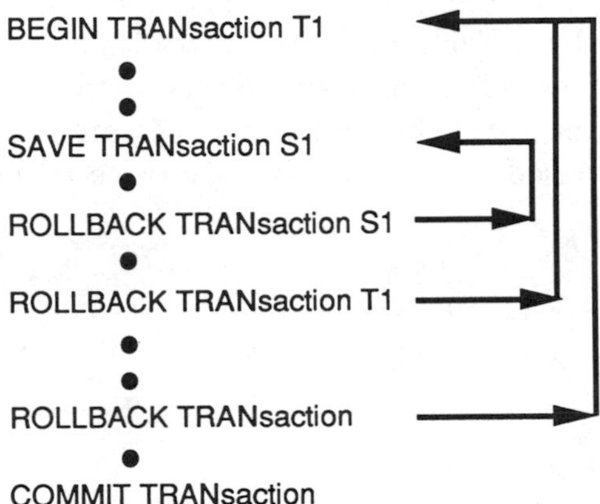
BEGIN TRANsaction T1
SAVE TRANsaction S1
ROLLBACK TRANsaction S1
ROLLBACK TRANsaction T1
ROLLBACK TRANsaction
COMMIT TRANsaction

FIGURE 6-2 Effect of SAVE and ROLLBACK statements

Certain statements are not allowed in user-defined transactions since the functions they perform are difficult to undo. Since, by definition, the transaction must be capable of being rolled back prior to a COMMIT TRANSACTION statement, such statements are precluded. They are:

- CREATE DATABASE, CREATE TABLE, or CREATE INDEX
- all DROP statements
- SELECT..INTO
- GRANT or REVOKE
- ALTER DATABASE, ALTER TABLE, TRUNCATE TABLE
- certain system administrator statements (DISK INIT, RECONFIGURE, LOAD DATABASE, LOAD TRANSACTION)

- user or system procedures that use the preceding statements

Most of these statements have been encountered by this point in the book. The GRANT and REVOKE statements won't be discussed until Chapter 9. They are used for assigning permissions. The SA statements, with various functions, are discussed in Chapters 10 and 11. Example 6-19 creates the user-defined transaction *raise_prices.* This user-defined transaction raises the prices of titles selectively, and the updated prices are either committed or rolled back, based on whether average price targets are met.

Example 6-19

```
begin transaction raise_prices
if (select avg(price) from titles) < $20
     begin
     update titles
     set price = price * 1.20
     where price < $15

     update titles
     set price = price * 1.10
     where price < $20
     end

if (select avg(price) from titles) < $20
     begin
     print "This repricing won't do"
     rollback transaction
     end
else
     begin
     print "Average price targets met"
     commit transaction raise_prices
     end

OUTPUT:

(0 rows affected)
(8 rows affected)
(13 rows affected)
```

```
(0 rows affected)
This repricing won't do
```

Control-of-Flow Language

Up to this point, the book has discussed individual SQL statements and procedures. It was pointed out in Chapter 3 that it is possible to process multiple SQL statements at one time by submitting the entire batch to the Server for execution. Batches can be submitted through both isql. or the SAF. Batches can also be submitted from custom application programs using the facilities that DB-LIBRARY provides.

TRANSACT-SQL provides a set of special statements, collectively referred to as a control-of-flow language, to alter the flow of execution of SQL statements in a batch, procedure, or trigger. These statements provide programming language such as constructs for declaring variables, conditional and unconditional execution, and displaying data. The following section examines batches more closely. The rest of the chapter looks at several control-of-flow statements.

Batches

A **batch** is a set of one or more SQL statements that is submitted to the Server for execution as a group. The Server executes each statement in the group in sequence and only returns the results to the client when all the statements have been executed. If an error occurs in processing any statement in the group, the entire batch is rejected. In isql, the end of a batch is indicated by a `go` on a line by itself. The `go` can be submitted interactively or through an OS file. This is really the same as what you type in after a single statement, but in a batch you can enter many statements before entering a `go`.

Here is an example of a batch.

Example 6-20

```
create table tmp (a int, b char(15))
create unique clustered index tmp_pk on tmp (a)
```

```
insert into tmp values (1, "This is row 1")
insert into tmp values (2, "This is row 2")
insert into tmp values (3, "This is row 3")
select * from tmp

OUTPUT:

(1 row affected)
(1 row affected)
(1 row affected)
a           b
----------- --------------
          1 This is row 1
          2 This is row 2
          3 This is row 3
(3 rows affected)
```

Batches provide several benefits. They can be used to automate long or repetitive tasks by storing the SQL statements in a file and submitting them for execution as required. They also make more efficient use of the network capacity, because the overhead of sending network messages is the same whether the message contains a single SQL statement or many. When many statements are batched together, a smaller portion of the message is overhead information—source and destination addresses, sequence numbers, and so on. Hence the network capacity is used more efficiently.

Certain restrictions apply to batches, but they are minor and don't prevent batches from being useful. You can create entire files of SQL batches that you can run through isql or the SAF to accomplish various tasks. In fact, this is how the Server creates *master*, *model*, and *pubs* at install time—the files for creating them (`instmstr.sql`, `instmodl.sql`, and `instpubs.sql`) are in the install subdirectory of the directory from which the Server is installed. The restrictions are:

- Certain statements—CREATE DEFAULT, CREATE RULE, CREATE VIEW, CREATE PROCEDURE, and CREATE TRIGGER—must be submitted in batches by themselves; that is, they must be single statement batches.

- The USE statement must be in a batch prior to the one in which objects in the database are referenced.
- An object cannot be dropped and then referenced or re-created in the same batch.
- Stored procedures that are not the first statement in a batch must be preceded by the keyword EXEC.
- Options changed with the SET statement do not take effect until the end of execution of the current batch. The SET statement is discussed in Chapter 12.

Example 6-21 shows a batch that violates the rules. It tries to make the *pubs* database the current database and then access the *stores* table.

Example 6-21

```
use pubs
select stor_id, stor_name, stor_address
from stores

OUTPUT:

Msg 208, Level 16, State 1:
Invalid object name 'stores'.
```

Control-of-Flow Statements

It was mentioned that control-of-flow statements provide many constructs that are similar to programming. More specifically they provide the ability to include comments, conditional and unconditional execution, looping, variable definition, display of data, and event-based execution. A list of the statements for these functions follows. They are described more fully in the following sections.

Statement	Purpose
`/* <comment> */`	comment delimiters; anything between these delimiters is ignored
`IF..ELSE`	allows conditional execution

`BEGIN`	begins statement block
`END`	ends statement block
`WHILE`	allows repeated execution (looping) while a condition is TRUE
`BREAK`	exits the next outermost WHILE loop
`CONTINUE`	restarts at the top of the WHILE loop
`DECLARE`	declares local variables
`GOTO <label>`	transfers execution to first statement after `<label>`
`RETURN`	exits unconditionally
`WAITFOR`	waits for a specified delay or event to resume execution
`PRINT`	displays user-specified messages
`RAISERROR`	sets the global variable `@@error` and displays a user-specified message

Comments Comments can be inserted anywhere in SQL text. A comment is delimited by the characters /* and */ (as in the C programming language). Comments have no maximum length. You can use them in your code to document the processing that occurs in a batch or procedure. Even a single SQL statement can have embedded comments. Example 6-22 shows the use of a comment.

Example 6-22

```
select title, price
from titles
/* find all the expensive titles (priced over $20) */
where price > $20

OUTPUT:

title                                                                price
------------------------------------------------------------------ ---------
But Is It User Friendly?                                                20.66
The Guide to SQL Server                                                 24.95
The Fine Art of Programming                                             22.95
Computer Phobic and Non-Phobic Individuals: Behavior Variations        21.59
Onions, Leeks, and Garlic: Cooking Secrets of the Mediterranean        20.95
(5 rows affected)
```

Conditional Execution The IF..ELSE construct is provided for conditional execution in TRANSACT-SQL. The syntax of the IF..ELSE statement follows.

Syntax

```
IF <boolean_expression>
     <statement_block1>
ELSE
     <statement_block2>
```

The semantics of the construct are the same as they are in any programming language. If the `<boolean_expression>` returns TRUE, `<statement_block1>` is executed; otherwise `<statement_block2>` is executed. The second statement block itself can be another IF statement; that is, IF statements can be nested. A statement block constitutes either a single SQL statement or one or more SQL statements enclosed by BEGIN and END. For example, if you want to determine if there are any authors who live in California, you can write the IF statement in Example 6-23.

Example 6-23

```
if exists (select * from authors where state = "CA")
     print "There are some authors who live in California"
else
     print "No authors live in California"

OUTPUT:

There are some authors who live in California
```

Statement Blocks As mentioned, a statement block is one or more statements enclosed by BEGIN and END statements. The block is then treated as a single statement in conditional execution statements, that is, it is executed entirely or skipped entirely depending on whether or not the condition is TRUE. Statement blocks can be nested.

Syntax

```
BEGIN
     [<statement>]...
END
```

A simple example of a statement block is given in Example 6-24. Statement blocks will turn up in the examples in the next chapter as well. In Example 6-23 it was determined that there are authors who live in California. If you want to print the information for these authors you can execute the modified IF statement in Example 6-24.

Example 6-24

```
if exists (select * from authors where state = "CA")
     begin
     print "There are authors who live in California"
     select au_id, city, zip
     from authors
     where state = "CA"
     end
else
     print "No authors live in California"

OUTPUT:

There are authors who live in California
au_id        city                 zip
----------- -------------------- -----
172-32-1176 Menlo Park           94025
213-46-8915 Oakland              94618
238-95-7766 Berkeley             94705
267-41-2394 San Jose             95128
274-80-9391 Oakland              94609
409-56-7008 Berkeley             94705
427-17-2319 Palo Alto            94301
472-27-2349 Covelo               95428
486-29-1786 San Francisco        94130
672-71-3249 Walnut Creek         94595
724-08-9931 Oakland              94609
724-80-9391 Oakland              94612
756-30-7391 Oakland              94609
846-92-7186 Palo Alto            94301
893-72-1158 Vacaville            95688
(15 rows affected)
```

Looping Repeated execution of a statement block, or looping, is achieved using the WHILE statement. The Boolean expression is evaluated at the top of the loop and, as long as it evaluates to TRUE, the statement block is executed. The syntax follows.

Syntax

```
WHILE <boolean_expression>
     <statement_block>
```

The BREAK and CONTINUE statements allow you to control the flow of execution within the loop. BREAK causes an exit from the loop; that is, execution continues with the next statement after the WHILE loop. CONTINUE causes the WHILE loop to restart, so any statements in the loop after CONTINUE are not executed.

Syntax

```
BREAK
CONTINUE
```

An example will clarify the usage of the WHILE..BREAK..CONTINUE construct. The example is somewhat artificial—it could be written more concisely—but is intentionally written this way for illustration. We will refine this example later. The DECLARE statement is used to declare a local variable and is discussed in the next section. If you want to raise the prices of all books until the average price is more than $20, or until the price has been raised three times you can write the batch in Example 6-25.

Example 6-25

```
declare @count int
select @count = 0
while (select avg(price) from titles) <= $20
begin
     select @count = @count + 1
     update titles
     set price = price * 1.20

          if (select avg(price) from titles) > $20
```

```
                    begin
                    print "Average price target met"
                    break
                    end
          else
                    begin
                    if (@count <= 3) continue
                    print "Maximum iterations exceeded"
                    end

          select @count
end

OUTPUT:

(1 row affected)
(0 rows affected)
(1 row affected)
(20 rows affected)
(0 rows affected)
(0 rows affected)
(1 row affected)
(20 rows affected)
(0 rows affected)
Average price target met
```

In the example, `@count` tracks the number of times the loop is executed. The price is raised by 20% through the UPDATE statement, then the average is checked to see if it is more than $20. If so, the loop is exited through the BREAK; if not, the loop count is checked to see if it has reached the maximum. If it hasn't, the loop is restarted at the top; if the maximum is exceeded, a message is displayed to that effect.

Local and Global Variables One of the nice features of the control-of-flow language is that it allows you to declare variables. There are two kinds of variables in TRANSACT-SQL: **local variables**, which are defined through the DECLARE statement and are assigned values through the SELECT statement, and **global variables**, which are predefined, system-supplied variables that contain various kinds of information.

Local variables are very useful when you are writing batches or stored procedures and triggers. They are so called because their scope is local to the batch or procedure where they are declared—they are only accessible within the batch or procedure. Local variables have names beginning with the @ character; the rest of the name follows the rules for identifiers. A local variable must be declared using the DECLARE statement, which provides its name and data type. Local variables are assigned values using the SELECT statement and displayed using the SELECT or PRINT statement. The syntax for declaration, assignment, and display are as follows.

Syntax

```
DECLARE <var_name> <data_type>
     [, <var_name> <data_type>]...

SELECT <var_name> = <expression>
     [, <var_name> = <expression>]...
     [<FROM_clause>]
     [<WHERE_clause>]
     [<GROUP_BY_clause>]
     [<HAVING_clause>]
     [<ORDER_BY_clause>]
     [<COMPUTE_clause>]

SELECT <var_name>
PRINT <var_name>
```

The next chapter contains many examples of local variable usage.

Global variables are predefined variables that contain system-related information. Global variables begin with two @ characters (for example, `@@rowcount`) to distinguish them from local variables. Some global variables are automatically maintained by the Server based on its operation (`@@procid, @@rowcount`, and so on); others can be set by the user to affect server operation (`@@textsize`) or indicate status of the last operation performed (`@@error`). Many of these variables are discussed in Chapter 12, especially the ones that provide a measure of Server activity. Some other global variables are listed here.

Global variable	Contents
`@@error`	the last error number generated by the system, typically used to check status of last statement executed on the server
`@@procid`	the procedure id of the currently executing stored procedure
`@@rowcount`	the number of rows affected by the last SQL statement
`@@version`	current version of SQL Server
`@@trancount`	the number of currently active transactions for the current user
`@@textsize`	the number of bytes returned for text data in a SELECT statement
`@@timeticks`	the number of microseconds per tick—each tick in OS/2 is 31.25 milliseconds (1/32 second)
`@@max_connections`	the maximum number of simultaneous connections allowed SQL Server in this configuration

Unconditional Branching The GOTO statement is used to achieve unconditional branching. When executed, it causes unconditional branching to a user-defined label. A label is an identifier that is followed by a colon. The label must be in the same batch or stored procedure in which the GOTO exists. The syntax of GOTO follows.

Syntax

```
<label>:
GOTO <label>
```

The following is a trivial example that uses the GOTO statement.

Example 6-26

```
DECLARE @count smallint
        @message char(40)
```

```
SELECT @count = 0

loop:
SELECT @count = @count + 1
SELECT @message = "This is a loop " + str(@count)
PRINT  @message

WHILE @count < 3
      GOTO loop

OUTPUT:

(1 row affected)
(1 row affected)
(1 row affected)
This is a loop          1
(1 row affected)
(1 row affected)
This is a loop          2
(1 row affected)
(1 row affected)
This is a loop          3
```

There can be no duplicate labels within a batch or procedure (for obvious reasons); they must be unique. They also cannot duplicate any TRANSACT-SQL keywords. In general, GOTO statements are used with IF or WHILE statements to avoid endless loops.

Unconditional Exit The RETURN statement is used to exit a query or stored procedure unconditionally. Statements following the RETURN are not executed. The RETURN statement is similar to the BREAK statement used within WHILE loops.

Syntax

```
RETURN
```

The following is an example of a stored procedure that uses the RETURN statement to exit if certain required parameters are not supplied.

Example 6-27

```
create procedure au_state @state char(2) = null as
if @state is null
     begin
     print "You must supply a state code"
     print "The syntax is 'au_state <state>'"
     return
     end
else
     begin
     select au_id, au_fname, au_lname
     from authors
     where state = @state
     order by au_id
     end
```

Event-driven Execution The WAITFOR statement allows event-driven execution of a statement block, procedure, or transaction. There are many kinds of events—TIME (when a specific time of day is reached), DELAY (after a specified time delay), or an ERROREXIT or PROCESSEXIT (system-generated events). If ERROREXIT is specified, SQL Server will wait until a process terminates abnormally. If PROCESSEXIT is specified, the server waits for any process to terminate for any reason. WAITFOR statements are often used by system processes for such functions as cleanup, maintenance, and statistics.

Syntax

```
WAITFOR {DELAY <time> | TIME <time> | ERROREXIT | PROCESSEXIT}
```

It is important for you to know that a WAITFOR statement implies a synchronous wait. That is, your task at the Server end is dormant; you cannot use your connection with the Server until the event occurs. The time portion for the DELAY and TIME options can be specified in any one of the valid datetime formats without a date part.

Example 6-28 uses WAITFOR in a small batch that monitors the number of active connections and transactions on the Server every 15 seconds.

Example 6-28

```
declare @count smallint, @msg varchar(80)
select @count = 0

loop:
     waitfor delay "00:00:15"
     select @count = @count + 1
     insert into act_monitor (time, connections, transactions)
     values (getdate(), @@connections, @@trancount)
     select @msg = "No of rows inserted = " + str(@count)
     print @msg
     if (@count < 5) goto loop
```

```
OUTPUT:

(1 row affected)
(1 row affected)
(1 row affected)
(1 row affected)
No of rows inserted =          1
(1 row affected)
(1 row affected)
(1 row affected)
No of rows inserted =          2
(1 row affected)
(1 row affected)
(1 row affected)
No of rows inserted =          3
(1 row affected)
(1 row affected)
(1 row affected)
No of rows inserted =          4
(1 row affected)
(1 row affected)
(1 row affected)
No of rows inserted =          5
```

Displaying Messages and Variables There are basically two statements in TRANSACT-SQL for displaying variables. They are the SELECT and PRINT statements. These statements, along with the RAISERROR statement, can also be used to display user-specified messages and variables in TRANSACT-SQL.

The SELECT statement can be used to assign a local variable its value and to display its value. The PRINT statement allows you to print a user-defined message, a local variable, or a global variable (of `char` or `varchar` type). The RAISERROR statement displays a user message or local variable and sets the global variable `@@error` to a user-supplied value to indicate a completion status. User error numbers must be greater than 20000, since values below that are reserved for system use.

Syntax

```
PRINT { <text_message> | <local_var> | <global_var> }
RAISERROR <number> { <text_message> | <local_var> }
```

You have already seen examples of the SELECT and PRINT statements. Example 6-29 shows an example of a message displayed through the SELECT statement. Example 6-30 shows how the RAISERROR statement may be used.

Example 6-29

```
DECLARE @message char(25)
SELECT  @message = "This is a short message"
SELECT  @message

OUTPUT:

(1 row affected)
-----------------------
This is a short message
(1 row affected)
```

Example 6-30

```
declare @store_count int
select @store_count = count(*) from stores
if @store_count > 1000
     raiserror 20010 "Please remove the inactive stores"

OUTPUT:

(1 row affected)
```

It should be made clear that the global variables are global to each user connection and not global to the server as a whole. Thus, if one user executes a SELECT statement that has an error, only his or her `@@error` variable is affected and set to the appropriate value. In Example 6-30 the `@@error` for the user who executes the batch is set to 20010, other `@@error` variables are unaffected.

The DB-LIBRARY Interface

Chapters 5 and 6 discussed the DDL and DML components of TRANSACT-SQL. The statements discussed can be executed from any ad-hoc interface such as isql or the SAF. Here we discuss how TRANSACT-SQL can be executed from within host language programs, using the DB-LIBRARY API provided by SQL Server. Chapter 3 introduced DB-LIBRARY and the various categories of functions it provides. This section expands on that discussion, and is intended to provide an example of developing an application using DB-LIBRARY. Thus, a simple C program that communicates with the Server is presented. Knowledge of C is assumed; if the reader is unfamiliar with C, this example can be skipped. For a more comprehensive discussion of DB-LIBRARY please refer to the *SQL Server Programmer's Reference.*

DB-LIBRARY is a set of functions and macros that handle various tasks—initialization, command setup and execution, results processing, error handling, information retrieval, and miscellaneous functions. In addition it provides many advanced capabilities—browse mode, text and image handling, bulk loading and unloading of data, and the two-phase commit. These capabilities are discussed later in this section. The other major component of DB-LIBRARY (other than the library that contains the functions itself) are the standard include (or header) files. The include files define the standard data types, data structures, return codes, and macros used to develop a DB-LIBRARY application.

DB-LIBRARY has several conventions in the naming of its macros, functions, data types and so on. Knowing the conventions aids in understanding DB-LIBRARY programs. All function names begin with the two lower case characters `db`. For example, the function to establish a connection with the server is `dbopen()`. Macro names begin with the same two letters, except that macro names are all upper case characters. Thus the macro to set a user name is `DBSETLUSER()`. DB-LIBRARY also provides standard type definitions (typedefs, in C parlance) for host language and server data types, and symbolic error codes. Host language data types begin with the upper case characters DB, and server data types begin with the upper case characters SQL. For example, a four-byte integer in SQL Server is the SQLINT4; an integer in C is DBINT. The purpose for having standard typedefs for data types for host languages (separate from native host language data types—short, long, etc.) is to provide platform independence. The DB-LIBRARY data types are mapped onto the appropriate native data types in the include files; the programs simply use the standard DB-LIBRARY data types. Error codes have no convention but are normally all upper case characters, for example, NO_MORE_ROWS or SUCCEED.

The following paragraphs provide an idea of the functions provided in each category. Initialization and housekeeping functions allow you to establish and close server connections, and use different databases on the server. They include functions like `dbopen()` and `dbclose()`. Command set-up and execution functions allow you to build, execute, and examine TRANSACT-SQL batches, and change command processing options. They include functions such as `dbcmd()`, `dbsqlexec()` and `dbsetopt()`. Results processing functions allow you to set-up to receive results, process the results, discard results, and a set maximum response time for receiving results from the server. They include functions such as `dbresults()`, `dbbind()`, `dbdata()`, and `dbsettime()`. Error handling functions allow you to dynamically install pre-defined error handlers for DB-LIBRARY and SQL Server errors. They include `dberrsghandle()` and `dbmsghandle()`. Information retrieval functions allow you to retrieve information about the result data being returned, or about the state of the command batch. They include functions such as `dbcolname()`, `dbcollen()` and macros such as `DBFIRSTROW()`, `DBCURROW()`, `DBCURCMD()`. Finally, the miscellaneous functions allow the control of process flow, data type conversion, and the reading and writing of disk pages directly. They include functions such as `dbsetbusy()`, `dbconvert()`, and `dbreadpage()`.

The following simple application program illustrates the typical use of the functions discussed. In general, DB-LIBRARY programs share a common framework, since steps that have to do with connecting to the Server, executing TRANSACT-SQL batches, processing results, disconnecting from the Server are similar. The actual processing of the data will of course, differ greatly depending on the application.

The steps are:

1. Logging in and establishing a connection with the Server
2. Building a TRANSACT-SQL command batch
3. Sending and executing the batch on the Server
4. Processing the next set of results
5. Processing the returned data
6. Closing the connection with the Server

One other step, not explicitly listed above, that spans all of the above steps, is error handling. Errors can be generated by SQL Server, the network OS, or by DB-LIBRARY itself. It is important to be able to handle errors and abnormal situations in your programs.

Using the framework outlined, we present a simple DB-LIBRARY application that retrieves the title, the price and the royalty percentage of the books in the *titles* table of the *pubs* database.

Example 6-31

```
/*
    Example 6-31 sends a query to the server for execution. It performs
    the following steps: connects to the server, executes the query, binds
    the results, prints the returned data and disconnects from the server.
*/
#define     DBMSOS2                    /* define OS2 mode */
#include    <stdio.h>
#include    <sqlfront.h>               /* standard include files */
#include    <sqldb.h>                  /* for DB-LIBRARY pograms */

#define     TITLE_LEN    32
```

```
extern      int     err_handler();      /* message and error handlers */
extern      int     msg_handler();      /* are external to this file  */


/*
    main program
*/

main (argc, argv)
        int argc;
        char *argv[];

{
    LOGINREC          *login;           /* LOGINREC pointer */
    DBPROCESS         *dbproc;          /* DBPROCESS pointer */


    DBCHAR            title[TITLE_LEN+1]; /* variables declarations */
    DBFLT8            price;            /* for returned data */
    DBINT             royalty;


    /* install error and message handlers */
    dberrhandle (err_handler);          /* for DB-LIBRARY errors */
    dbmsghandle (msg_handler);          /* for SQL Server errors */

    /* get LOGINREC structure; set component values */
    login = dblogin();
    DBSETLUSER (login, "sa");
    DBSETLPWD  (login, "sqldba");
    DBSETLAPP  (login, "example");

    /* establish connection with the server */
    if ((dbproc = dbopen (login, "sql_server")) == NULL)
    {
        printf ("server connection failed\n");
        exit (ERREXIT);
    }

    /* Change database context */
    dbuse (dbproc, "pubs");
```

```
    /* set up the query in the command buffer */
    dbcmd (dbproc, "select title, price, royalty ");
    dbcmd (dbproc, "from titles where price > $10 ");
    dbcmd (dbproc, "order by price ");

    /* send and execute the query */
    if (dbsqlexec (dbproc) == FAIL)
    {
        printf ("Query execution failed\n");
        dbexit(); exit (ERREXIT);
    }

    /* set up to receive data */
    if (dbresults (dbproc) == SUCCEED)
    {
        /*
           bind the column data to program variables.
           note that price (stored as money in the database)
           is automatically converted to floating point data
        */
        dbbind (dbproc, 1, STRINGBIND, (DBINT)TITLE_LEN+1, title);
        dbbind (dbproc, 2, FLT8BIND,   (DBINT)0,  &price);
        dbbind (dbproc, 3, INTBIND,    (DBINT)0,  &royalty);


        /* print the headings */
        printf ("TITLE                              PRICE     ROYALTY\n");
        printf ("--------------------------------   ------    -------\n");

        /* print the row data */
        while (dbnextrow (dbproc) != NO_MORE_ROWS)
        {
            printf ("%-32s    $%5.2f        %31d\n",
                    title, price, royalty);

        }
    }
}
```

The comments and the correlation to the steps outlined above should aid in the understanding of the program. The example is explained further here. The `#define DBMSOS2` indicates that the program is being compiled for OS/2. `<sqlfront.h>` and `<sqldb.h>` are references to the standard header files that have to be included in every DB-LIBRARY program. The variables are declared after the start of the program. There are two important data structures needed for establishing and communicating with the server: LOGINREC and DBPROCESS. The two variables `login` and `dbproc` are pointers to these structures. The structures are allocated by the `dblogin()` function which allocates and sets up the LOGINREC structure for connection to the server. The `dbprocess()` function establishes a connection to the server identified with the login ID and password (in this case `sql_server`, `sa` and `sqldba` respectively) in the LOGINREC. It returns a pointer to an allocated DBPROCESS structure on a successful connection; which is the first parameter in most DB-LIBRARY function calls.

The DBPROCESS structure is a key data structure in communicating with the Server. It contains the command batch, the data returned by the Server, descriptive information about this data and status and error information. Each connection to the server corresponds to a DBPROCESS structure in the client application. Several connections can be opened with one or more servers, and a connection is identified by the corresponding DBPROCESS pointer in subsequent DB-LIBRARY calls.

The `dbuse()` function changes the database context to the pubs database. The `dbcmd()` calls set up the command batch within the DBPROCESS structure. The `dbsqlexec()` call sends and executes the command batch. The `dbresults()` call sets up the results for the next command in the batch, and must be called once for each command in the batch. The `dbbind()` calls bind the columns in the target list of the query to program variables. It must be done once for each column that is retrieved; but also once for the entire set of data returned by the query. Once a column is bound to a program variable, the program variable automatically receives the value of that column on successive calls to the `dbnextrow()` function, which fetches successive rows. The standard `C printf()` functions are used to display fixed column headings, although this information could have been obtained using the information retrieval functions. This is exactly how isql displays its column headings. The function is called repeatedly to display rows until there are no more. The `dbexit()` function closes all connections with the server. The output produced as a result of executing the `example` program above is shown in Example 6-32.

Example 6-32

```
OS2[D:\SQL\DBLIB\SRC]example

OUTPUT:

TITLE                                PRICE      ROYALTY
------------------------------       ------     -------
Is Anger the Enemy?                  $10.95          12
Fifty Years in Buckingham Palace     $11.95          14
Cooking with Computers: Surrepti     $11.95          10
Sushi, Anyone?                       $14.99          10
Straight Talk About Computers        $19.99          10
Silicon Valley Gastronomic Treat     $19.99          12
The Busy Executive's Database Gu     $19.99          10
Prolonged Data Deprivation: Four     $19.99          10
Secrets of Silicon Valley            $20.00          10
Onions, Leeks, and Garlic: Cooki     $20.95          10
Computer Phobic and Non-Phobic I     $21.59          10
But Is It User Friendly?             $22.95          16
```

The `dbmsghandle()` and `dberrhandle()` functions allow you to dynamically install user-written message and error handler functions. Message handlers are invoked for SQL Server returned errors or messages. Error handlers are invoked for DB-LIBRARY and OS errors. The error handlers are omitted from the above program for simplicity. These functions are automatically invoked whenever a message or error is encountered. Depending on the value returned from the invoked handler, it is possible to either exit the program or continue with the execution.

Advanced DB-LIBRARY Features

DB-LIBRARY provides several advanced features, some of which are discussed here. The features are row buffering, reading and writing text and image data, bulk loading and unloading of data, and performing distributed updates (across Servers) that are treated as a transaction, using the *two-phase commit protocol.*

Row buffering allows the client application to buffer data rows returned. There may be situations when normal row-at-a-time processing is not adequate. Row buffering allows access to multiple rows simultaneously, and or access to rows in a different order than that returned by the Server. It is also more efficient to use row buffering if rows have to be accessed over multiple passes. The row buffering functions allow you to turn row buffering on or off dynamically. They allow you to adjust the buffer size dynamically; read rows at random, clear the buffer of rows, and determine what the first, last and current rows in the buffer are.

The READTEXT and WRITETEXT statement allow some manipulation of text and image columns at the TRANSACT-SQL level. DB-LIBRARY provides support for manipulating `text` and `image` columns within applications. These functions provide two additional advantages over TRANSACT-SQL. First, they allow processing of large size text or image data in smaller pieces. Second, they allow the application to manipulate the timestamp value associated with a `text` or `image` column. This prevents one user from inadvertently wiping out another user's update. Again, further information on these functions can be found in the *SQL Server Programmer's Reference.*

Browse mode is a capability provided by SQL Server, through which users can browse data retrieved from several tables and selectively update columns within it a row at a time. It is a mode that is commonly provided by several PC workstation DBMSs, such as dBASE IV. Because the row being browsed on the client is a copy of the row on the Server, there is a problem that arises with implementing browse mode in that multi-user concurrent environments. One user may overwrite the others updates. Locks cannot be used to ensure consistency since users may browse data for long periods of time, which is different from the case of a single UPDATE statement. The resolution used by the Server is timestamps. All browseable tables have a `timestamp` column associated with them. Each row in the table has a unique timestamp value associated with it. The timestamp is simply a system-generated monotonically increasing number, not a real timestamp. When the row is retrieved the timestamp is retrieved with it. When the row is updated and needs to be written to the database, the timestamp value in the row is compared to corresponding value in the database; if they compare and the update is allowed, the timestamp is updated. Otherwise it means that some other user already updated the table first; hence the update is disallowed.

Two conditions must be satisfied for a table to be browseable. First, the SELECT statement that retrieves the data must be appended with the special FOR BROWSE clause. This indicates to the Server that the data is going to be browsed. Second, the table from which the data is retrieved has to have a `timestamp` column and a unique index defined on it. The unique index is required for the Server to return a WHERE clause that uniquely identifies a row in the table. This WHERE clause is used to update the appropriate column value in that row. In addition, the columns being updated must not be derived columns; that is, there must be a direct correspondence between the result column and the database column.

Browse mode is conceptually simple. It involves retrieving result rows from one or more tables, updating the result rows where appropriate, and using the updated values in the result rows to update the database rows. In practice, this is implemented using special DB-LIBRARY browse mode functions. The steps involved in implementing a browse mode application are listed here; a discussion of the browse mode functions is outside the scope of this book. For additional details, refer to the *SQL Server Programmer's Reference*.

1. Establish the connections to SQL Server. Browse mode requires two connections (DBPROCESS structures) to be set up, one for retrieving data, and one for updating it.
2. Execute the appropriate SELECT..FOR BROWSE statement against the tables to retrieve the result data.
3. Retrieve the result data into program variables.
4. Modify any program variables as appropriate.
5. Execute an UPDATE statement with the column values corresponding to the updated program variables. The required WHERE clause for updating this row is obtained through a special browse mode function.

6. Repeat steps 3 through 5 for each row you want to update.

The other advanced capabilities of DB-LIBRARY mentioned are discussed later. The bulk copy functions allow you to develop a custom application for bulk loading of data into and out of the Server. They are discussed in Chapter 10. The two-phase commit functions allow an application to guarantee the integrity of distributed updates. The protocol is discussed in Chapter 11.

Summary

In this chapter the data modification statements—INSERT, UPDATE, DELETE, and TRUNCATE—were discussed. The basics of transactions, both those that are implicit and those that are explicit or user-defined, were covered, as well as the control-of-flow language within TRANSACT-SQL. Finally we provide an overview of the Host Language Interface of SQL Server, DB-LIBRARY.

CHAPTER 7

Views and Procedures

Introduction

The preceding chapters discussed how to define database objects and manipulate the data within them. The discussion of two objects—views and procedures—were deferred because they depend on concepts that had to be addressed first. Views depend on the SELECT statement for their definition; stored procedures use the control-of-flow language extensively in their definition. The SELECT statement and control-of-flow language were covered in Chapters 5 and 6. This chapter discusses how to create, drop, and use views, and examines the restrictions on their usage. It also explores the creation, removal, and usage of stored procedures. The benefits of views and stored procedures are evaluated and their use as security mechanisms is discussed.

Views

A view is a derived table that provides an alternate way of looking at data in one or more tables. Views are similar to tables from a data manipulation perspective, but they do not contain actual data. They serve many purposes, including simplifying or customizing an individual user's view of the data. They are provided by most RDBMSs.

Creating and Dropping Views

Views are created with the CREATE VIEW statement and dropped with the DROP VIEW statement. A view definition specifies what subset of the data in one or more tables is accessible through it. Since this is exactly what the SELECT statement returns, a view definition is based on the SELECT statement. Figure 7-1 illustrates a subset of data accessed by a view.

The CREATE VIEW and DROP VIEW syntax follows.

Syntax

```
CREATE VIEW [<owner>.]<view_name>
     [ ( <column> [, <column>] ... ) ]  AS
```

```
     <select_statement>

DROP VIEW [<owner>.]<view_name>
     [, [<owner>.]<view_name> ... ]
```

Views can be created only in the current database. (Notice the syntax has no database name in the qualification.) Their names must be unique in the set of all table and view names. Column names are optional in the view definition; if not specified, the column names in the view are the same as those in the underlying tables. In certain cases, however, the column names have to be specified:

- When columns are to be derived on the basis of expressions involving arithmetic operators, columns, or built-in functions.

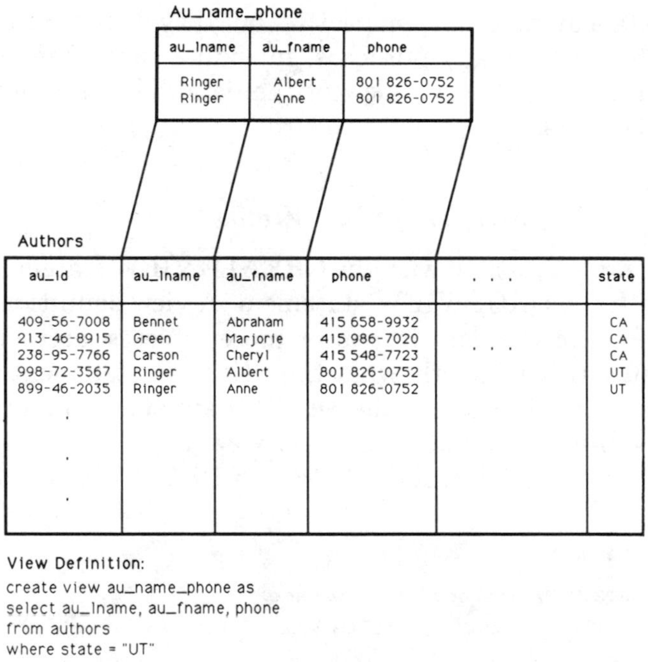

Au_name_phone

au_lname	au_fname	phone
Ringer	Albert	801 826-0752
Ringer	Anne	801 826-0752

Authors

au_id	au_lname	au_fname	phone	. . .	state
409-56-7008	Bennet	Abraham	415 658-9932		CA
213-46-8915	Green	Marjorie	415 986-7020	. . .	CA
238-95-7766	Carson	Cheryl	415 548-7723		CA
998-72-3567	Ringer	Albert	801 826-0752		UT
899-46-2035	Ringer	Anne	801 826-0752		UT
.					
.					
.					

View Definition:

```
create view au_name_phone as
select au_lname, au_fname, phone
from authors
where state = "UT"
```

FIGURE 7-1. Views: subset of rows and columns

- When duplicate column names would result, because columns with the same name in different tables are included in the view.
- When a different column name is desired, also achieved by providing a different column heading for the column in the SELECT statement (see Chapter 5).

If you want to look at selective author information for all authors who live in California, you can define the view as shown in Example 7-1.

Example 7-1

```
create view ca_authors as
     select au_id, au_fname, au_lname,
     au_city = city, au_state = state, au_contract = contract
     from authors
     where state = "CA"
```

In this example a subset of the columns from the *authors* table (the subset of interest to us) and of the rows (only California authors) is selected. Notice that two of the columns were renamed in the view: au_state and au_contract.

Views can contain derived columns—columns that are computed on the basis of arithmetic operators, built-in functions, and other columns. Views are not limited to a single table; multiple table views, typically involving a join, can be defined. Views can even be defined on other views. In fact, the full form of the SELECT statement is allowed in the view definition except for a few minor restrictions. It cannot have the DISTINCT keyword; it cannot reference temporary tables; and it cannot include the INTO, ORDER BY, or COMPUTE clauses. Some examples of view definitions follow.

Example 7-2 uses the *employee* table from Chapter 4 to illustrate a view with a derived column. In the next chapter, on the subject of triggers, it is suggested that you can dynamically update total salary (*emp_tsal* column) every time base salary (*emp_bsal*-column) or commissions (*emp_comm* column) changes, using a trigger. An alternate way to do the same thing is to define a view with a derived column. Which approach to use is determined by performance and usage considerations.

Example 7-2

```
create view emp_salary as
     select emp_id, emp_lname, emp_lname, emp_bsal, emp_comm,
            emp_tsal = (emp_bsal + emp_comm)
     from employee
```

```
OUTPUT:
```

Often, you need to access more than one table to obtain the desired information. Defining a multitable view might simplify the access. For example, a view that provides publisher and title information can be defined as follows:

Example 7-3

```
create view pub_titles as
     select pub_name, title, type, price
     from publishers p, titles t
     where p.pub_id = t.pub_id
```

```
OUTPUT:
```

A final example of view definition defines a view on an existing view. For a view with just authors who live in Oakland, you can define a view on *authors* directly (as in Example 7-1), or you can define a view on the *ca_authors* view as in Example 7-4. Notice that the view definition specifies a subset of both the rows and the columns in the *ca_authors* view.

Example 7-4

```
create view oakland_authors as
     select au_id, au_fname, au_lname, au_contract
     from ca_authors
     where au_city = "Oakland"
```

```
OUTPUT:
```

To define a view, the user must have the appropriate SELECT permissions (discussed in Chapter 9) on the columns being referenced in the definition. Once a view is defined, it can be used in data manipulation statements (both retrieval and modification), just like a table. In fact, permissions are defined on it just as they are on a table. In contrast to tables, you cannot define defaults, rules, triggers, or indexes on views. If you think about it, this makes sense because views themselves do not contain any data. This fact is not apparent to the user, who sees the data materialize when the view is referenced. In Example 7-5 all authors who live in California and have contracts can be selected by the following query written against the *ca_authors* view created earlier.

Example 7-5

```
SELECT au_fname, au_lname, au_contact
FROM ca_authors
WHERE au_contract = 1

OUTPUT:

au_fname             au_lname                                 au_contract
-------------------- ---------------------------------------- -----------
Johnson              White                                              1
Marjorie             Green                                              1
Cheryl               Carson                                             1
Michael              O'Leary                                            1
Dick                 Straight                                           1
Abraham              Bennet                                             1
Ann                  Dull                                               1
Burt                 Gringlesby                                         1
Chastity             Locksley                                           1
Akiko                Yokomoto                                           1
Stearns              MacFeather                                         1
Livia                Karsen                                             1
Sheryl               Hunter                                             1

(13 rows affected)
```

View Resolution

When you define a view, the Server ensures that the underlying tables and views are valid, the columns in the view are compatible with the underlying data types, and none of the restrictions on defining views is violated. The view definition is then stored, both in an internal form and in text form in the system tables. When a data retrieval or modification statement that includes a view reference is executed, the Server once again validates the object definitions (they may have changed) and also ensures that none of the restrictions on modifying data through views (discussed later) is violated. The Server then combines the original statement with the stored definition of the view and translates it to a statement on the underlying tables. This process is called **view resolution**.

SQL Server uses an intelligent view resolution algorithm. You can redefine intermediate views without invalidating views that are dependent on it, as long as the redefinition does not make it impossible to resolve the dependent view. Example 7-6 shows how the definition of the *ca_authors* view of the previous examples can be changed to include the phone number and to drop the state without affecting the *oakland_authors* view, since all of the columns in its SELECT statement target list are still valid.

Example 7-6

```
drop view ca_authors
<exec>

create view ca_authors as
        select au_id, au-fname, au_lname, au_phone = phone,
                au_city = city, au_contract = contract
        from authors
        where state = "CA"
<exec>
select * from oakland_authors
<exec>

OUTPUT:

au_id       au_fname            au_lname                             au_contract
----------- ------------------- ------------------------------------ -----------
213-46-8915 Marjorie            Green                                          1
274-80-9391 Dick                Straight                                       1
724-08-9931 Dirk                Stringer                                       0
724-80-9391 Stearns             MacFeather                                     1
```

```
756-30-7391 Livia              Karsen                    1

(5 rows affected)
```

You can rename a view using the `sp_rename` system procedure, in the same way that you rename any other database object. When you change the name of a view, the references to it in dependent view definitions are not automatically fixed. The next time you attempt to reference the dependent view, view resolution is attempted, and an error message is displayed. A similar result occurs if a table or view, on which another view definition is based, is dropped and the dependent view is referenced. If, however, a new table or view is created with the same name, the dependent view definition will use the new table or view, as long as view resolution is possible.

Data Modification through Views

It has been mentioned that the standard data modification statements–INSERT, UPDATE, and DELETE can be used on views. In fact, these modifications all resolve into updates on the underlying base tables. So there are certain restrictions on modifying data through views. Most of these restrictions are minor and seem reasonable, once they are explained. Many other systems are far more restrictive in the usage of views; in fact, some systems do not allow any updates through views, so that views are read only. A list of the restrictions follows.

1. UPDATE and INSERT statements on views are allowed only if they resolve to single base table, that is, all the columns must be from a single table.
2. Modifications (INSERT, UPDATE, DELETE) that reference derived columns (computed or derived using built-in functions) are not allowed.
3. Modifications to views that are based on aggregate functions and the GROUP BY clause are not allowed.
4. INSERT statements are not allowed on views unless they provide a value for every column defined as NOT NULL in the underlying table.

in the underlying table.

5. The WRITETEXT statement (special statement for text and image columns) is not allowed on views.

A discussion of the rationale for the restrictions will show that they are reasonable and even necessary. The first restriction stems from the fact that data modification statements are allowed only on a single table at a time. The second restriction is imposed because the Server cannot determine how to update the corresponding base table columns. For example, if the *emp_tsal* column is increased by 20% in the *emp_salary* view, SQL Server cannot deduce how to distribute this raise between the *emp_bsal* and *emp_comm* columns. The third restriction has a similar rationale—SQL Server is not able to figure out how to distribute the inserts or updates to the underlying rows and columns. For example, if an `AVG(salary)` column in a view defined on the *employee* table is increased, which employees in the *employee* table get the benefit of the raise in average salary? The fourth restriction is reasonable, since, if the INSERT does not provide the value and the column cannot be NULL, SQL Server cannot automatically supply a value for the column.

Information on Views

You can obtain information on views in several ways. The `sp_help` system procedure, which shows all objects defined in the current database, also displays views. Using the `sp_help` procedure with the view name shows such information as the view owner, when it was created, its columns, and any keys defined for it (you can define primary, foreign, and common keys on views).

Example 7-7

```
sp_help ca_authors

OUTPUT:

Name                           Owner                          Type
------------------------------ ------------------------------ ----------------
ca_authors                     dbo                            view
```

```
(0 rows affected)
Data_located_on_segment       When_created
----------------------------- --------------------


(0 rows affected)
Column_name     Type            Length Nulls Default_name    Rule_name
--------------- --------------- ------ ----- --------------- ---------------
au_id           id nocase           11     0 NULL            NULL
au_fname        varchar nocase      20     0 NULL            NULL
au_lname        varchar nocase      40     0 NULL            NULL
au_phone        char nocase         12     0 NULL            NULL
au_city         varchar nocase      20     1 NULL            NULL
au_contract     bit                  1     0 NULL            NULL
No defined keys for this object.

(0 rows affected)
```

Another system procedure, `sp_helptext`, allows you to retrieve the CREATE VIEW statement used to define the view. The text definitions of views, procedures, and triggers are stored in the *syscomments* system table; `sp_helptext` retrieves them.

Example 7-8

```
sp_helptext oakland_authors

OUTPUT:

         text

--------------------------------------------------------------------
--------------------------------------------------------------------
---------------------------------------
create view oakland_authors as
        select au_id, au_fname, au_lname, au_contract
        from ca_authors
        where au_city = "Oakland"

(1 row affected)
```

Finally, the `sp_depends` system procedure lists the objects in the current database that the view or table references. It also provides all the objects that reference the view or table. For example, the *ca_authors* view references the *authors* table; however *oakland_authors* depends on *ca_authors.*

Example 7-9

```
sp_depends ca_authors

OUTPUT:

Things the object references in the current database.
object                                type            updated selected
------------------------------------- --------------- ------- --------
dbo.authors                           user table      no      no

(0 rows affected)
```

Benefits of Views

The preceding discussion of views has not answered the question: What are the advantages of views? Views serve several purposes. They focus on data of interest; they customize an individual user's view of the data contained in the base tables. They simplify access to the data, especially when they are contained in more than one table. They can also serve as a security mechanism. Finally, perhaps least obviously, views provide logical data independence (although in a somewhat limited way); they shield users from changes in the logical structure of the underlying tables, if it becomes necessary.

What follows is an elaboration of the benefits of views mentioned in the preceding paragraph. For example, for a user concerned only with the name and phone number columns in the *employee* table, a view can be defined to focus on the specific columns *emp_fname, emp_lname,* and *emp_phone*; the user then need not deal with the remaining columns in the *employee* table. For the user interested in employee salary as well as name and phone number (assuming the user has proper authorization), another view can be defined to include this column. Thus each user's perception of the database can be customized.

Views can be used to simplify access to the database. For example, if you routinely retrieve information contained in two different tables (for example, publisher and author information), you can define a view that extracts the required columns by joining the two tables.

Views can be used to maintain derived information. If the *employee* table has two columns, one that contains salary and one that contains commissions, you can define a view with a computed column that is the employee's total salary, being the sum of the salary and commissions columns. Whenever the view is referenced, the sum of the two columns is computed from the data in the employee table. Hence, the data in a view are not static; they are recomputed every time the view is referenced.

Views can serve as powerful security mechanisms by granting users access to the view, but denying them access to the underlying base table. Chapter 9 discusss in detail how to accomplish this.

Finally, views provide logical data independence. For example, if you decide to maintain author data in two separate tables—one that contains the basic author information (*au_info*) and one that contains address information (*au_addr*), you can define a view, called *authors,* instead of the original authors table that provides both sets of information by joining the two tables on the basis of *au_id*. Applications that accessed the original authors table could now access the authors view and are unaffected, in fact unaware, that a change was made on the base tables. Unfortunately the logical data independence is only partial; it breaks down for some data modification statements.

Stored Procedures

Chapter 3 outlined the phases and components that a regular SQL statement (or batch of statements) goes through when it is processed by the Server—parsing, normalization, permissions checking, optimization, and, finally, compilation. The compiled form of the query is executed to return the results. This sequence of events is shown in Figure 7-2.

One of the most significant enhancements provided by SQL Server is the ability to create and use **stored procedures**. A stored

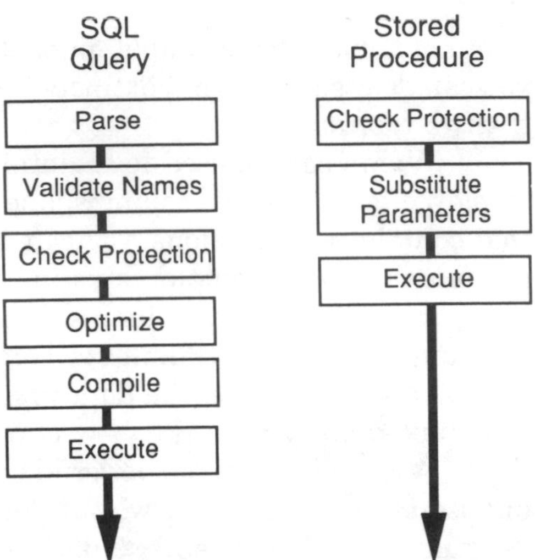

FIGURE 7-2. Ad-hoc query versus stored procedure execution

procedure is a named, precompiled set of TRANSACT-SQL statements (including control-of-flow statements), that is stored in the Server's data dictionary and executed simply by name. With stored procedures, the parsing, normalization, and optimization take place at definition time. The first time the procedure is run, an execution plan is generated. The compiled form, with this execution plan, is stored in the Server's data dictionary. From then on, the compiled form is retrieved from the dictionary and executed. This has significant performance benefits. In addition, procedures share a common cache which also improves performance. Multiple users do not share the same copy of the procedure code in cache, however if an unused copy exists in cache it is used; the procedure is recompiled only if the definition of the objects it references has changed. Stored procedures are very flexible because they can accept parameters and call other stored procedures, including themselves.

Creating and Dropping Stored Procedures

Stored procedures are created through the CREATE PROCEDURE statement and dropped through the DROP PROCEDURE statement. A procedure definition consists of a procedure name, a list of parameters, and the actual body of the procedure. Most of the TRANSACT-SQL statements, including the control-of-flow language statements, are allowed within the body of the procedure. Procedures can be created only by users with the appropriate permission (discussed in Chapter 9). The syntax follows.

Syntax

```
CREATE PROCEDURE [<owner>.]<procedure> [;<number>]
     [ [(] <parameter> <data_type> [= <default>]
     [, <parameter> <data_type> [= <default>]]... [)] ]
     [WITH RECOMPILE] AS
     <sql_statements>
```

As the syntax implies, procedures can be created only in the current database. The complete syntax has many options, some of which will be discussed later in the chapter. Procedures can take parameters, and default values can be specified for the parameters. In its simplest form, however, a stored procedure can have no parameters and consist of a single SQL statement. If you often want a list of the login IDs defined on the Server, you can define a procedure, `sp_users`, to retrieve this information (Example 7-10). In this case the procedure has no parameters and is, in fact, a single SQL statement. However, it still makes sense to define this statement as a stored procedure, because when it is executed repeatedly, it offers performance improvements.

Example 7-10

```
create proc sp_users as
select users=name from sysusers

OUTPUT:
```

If you often retrieve information about specific authors from the *pubs* database, you can define a procedure called `author_info`, which retrieves the desired information for an author. This procedure has a parameter, the author's last name, to narrow the scope of the returned information.

Example 7-11

```
create procedure author_info @last_name varchar(30) as
     select au_fname, au_lname, state, phone, contract
```

```
    from authors
    where au_lname = @last_name
```

OUTPUT:

The `@last_name` parameter is the only parameter (of type `varchar(30)`) in the procedure. Parameters can also be user-defined data types. The SELECT statement is the body of the procedure. At execution time the value of the parameter is substituted in the SELECT statement. Of course, this example is fairly trivial; procedures can be much more complex. For a more complex example, you can retrieve all titles in a particular category (say, business or psychology) within a particular price range, by defining the procedure that follows.

Example 7-12

```
create procedure titles_type_range
    @type varchar(15), @high money, @low money =  0 as
    select title, type, price
    from titles
    where type = @type
    and   price between @high and @low
```

OUTPUT:

In this case, the procedure has three parameters. The default value 0 is specified for the parameter `@low`. (Of course, you could specify a different value for `@low` at execution time.) If no default value is provided, the parameter value must be provided on execution. The null value can be specified as a parameter default; in fact, this is often used within the procedure to detect whether or not a parameter value is supplied, and to trigger an appropriate course of action. Parameter values can include wildcard characters. In Example 7-13 the definition of `author_info` is modified to specify a NULL default value for `@last_name` and to use the LIKE keyword in the WHERE clause, to allow wildcard characters.

Example 7-13

```
create procedure author_info @last_name varchar(30) = null as
    if @last_name is null
```

```
          print "you must supply a last name pattern"
     else
          select au_fname, au_lname, state, phone, contract
          from authors
          where au_lname like @last_name
```

OUTPUT:

Executing Stored Procedures

Procedures are executed using the EXECUTE statement. There are two ways to execute stored procedures, depending on how you specify the parameter values. Parameter values can be specified positionally, in which case the parameter names are optional, or they can be specified by parameter name, in which case they can occur in any order. The syntax of the EXECUTE statement follows. Parameter names follow the convention used in local variables, in that they that begin with the @ sign; the rest of the parameter name follows the rules for identifiers.

Syntax

```
[EXECute] [[<database>.]<owner>.]<procedure>[;<number>]
          [[ <parameter> = ]<value>
          [, <parameter> = ]<value>] ...]
          [WITH RECOMPILE]
```

Examples 7-14 and 7-15 show how to execute the `sp_users` stored procedure and the `authors_info` procedure created earlier.

Example 7-14

```
sp_users
```

```
OUTPUT:

users
------------------------------
public
guest
dbo

(3 rows affected)
```

Example 7-15

```
exec author_info "Green"

OUTPUT:

au_fname       au_lname                          state phone        contract
-------------- ------------------------------ ----- ------------ --------
Marjorie       Green                             CA    415 986-7020        1

(1 row affected)
```

In the syntax of the EXECUTE statement, the EXECUTE keyword is optional. In Example 7-14, the EXECUTE keyword is not used to execute `sp_users`. This is possible only if the procedure name is by itself or is the very first statement in a TRANSACT-SQL batch. In all other cases the EXECUTE keyword is required. To be safe, you can always specify the EXECUTE keyword (abbreviated EXEC). The modified `author_info` procedure of Example 7-13 can be executed to find all authors with last names beginning with G as follows.

Example 7-16

```
exec author_info "G%"

OUTPUT:

au_fname       au_lname                          state phone        contract
-------------- ------------------------------ ----- ------------ --------
Marjorie       Green                             CA    415 986-7020        1
Burt           Gringlesby                        CA    707 938-6445        1
Morningstar    Greene                            TN    615 297-2723        0

(3 rows affected)
```

Procedure Definition Options

Two aspects of procedure definition and execution can be examined now—procedure groups and the WITH RECOMPILE option. It is useful in defining stored procedures in SQL Server to group together a set of related procedures into a **procedure group**. SQL Server allows you to assign a name to the group. For example, a group of procedures that deals with employee pay increases can be called `raises`. The procedures within the group are then assigned unique numbers (1, 2, 3, and so on). The individual procedure name consists of the group name followed by a semicolon and the number; for example, `raises;1`, `raises;2`, and so on.

An advantage of procedure groups is that you can easily identify related procedures. In addition, the entire set of procedures can be dropped with a single DROP PROCEDURE statement (discussed shortly). Thus the statement `drop procedure raises` drops the entire set of procedures within the procedure group `raises`. In fact, dropping individual procedures within the group is not allowed.

The optional WITH RECOMPILE clause can be used in both the CREATE PROCEDURE and EXECUTE PROCEDURE statements. However, it has a different meaning depending on where it occurs. If you do not include the WITH RECOMPILE clause in a CREATE PROCEDURE statement, SQL Server stores the execution plan that it generates the first time the procedure is run with the parameters supplied for the first execution. The assumption is that these parameters are indicative of the typical use of the procedure.

However, if it is likely that each run will have parameters that result in significantly different execution plans, the user can specify WITH RECOMPILE in the CREATE PROCEDURE statement. You would do this if there are no typical parameters or if the tables referenced in the stored procedure are very dynamic, undergoing constant change. Specifying the WITH RECOMPILE clause prompts SQL Server not to save a plan for the stored procedure; it generates the execution plan and recompiles the procedure each time it is executed.

There are times when a particular execution of a stored procedure differs from the norm—in its parameters, for example—but the stored execution plan generated on the first run is adequate otherwise. In such a case, the user can specify WITH RECOMPILE in the EXECUTE statement. This causes SQL Server to generate an execution plan and recompile the stored procedure for the current run *only*; the generated execution plan is not saved for future runs.

Dropping Stored Procedures

Stored procedures can be dropped using the DROP PROCEDURE statement. If a procedure that invokes another procedure is run and the other procedure has been dropped, SQL Server displays an error message. If a new procedure with the same name is defined, SQL Server will automatically use the new occurrence. The syntax of DROP PROCEDURE follows.

Syntax

```
DROP PROCedure [<owner>.]<procedure>
     [, [<owner>.]<procedure>] ...
```

Multiple procedures can be dropped in a single DROP PROCEDURE statement. (If you just want to rename the procedure, you do not have to drop it and recreate it; you simply rename it using the `sp_rename` system procedure.) For example, if you do not need it any longer you can drop the `author_info` procedure as shown in Example 7-17. Of course, a user must have the appropriate permission to drop a procedure.

Example 7-17

```
drop procedure author_info
```

When an object referenced by a stored procedure is renamed, the reference is not automatically fixed up. The stored procedure may work fine until it is recompiled. It is advisable to drop a procedure and recreate it, if objects that it references are renamed.

Information on Procedures

The system procedures that provide information on views can also be used with stored procedures. The `sp_help` procedure provides information about the owner and parameters of a stored procedure.

Example 7-18

```
sp_help author_info

OUTPUT:

Name                          Owner                          Type
----------------------------- ------------------------------ ----------------
author_info                   dbo                            stored procedure

(0 rows affected)
Data_located_on_segment       When_created
----------------------------- --------------------

(0 rows affected)
Parameter_name  Type            Length Param_order
--------------- --------------- ------ -----------
@last_name      varchar             30           1

(0 rows affected)
```

The sp_helptext system procedure retrieves the text of the CREATE PROCEDURE statement used to create the stored procedure. The sp_depends system procedure provides information about all the objects referenced by the stored procedure and other objects, including stored procedures, that depend on the stored procedure.

Example 7-19

```
sp_helptext title_type_range
<exec>
sp_depend author_info
<exec>

OUTPUT:

         text

--------------------------------------------------------------------------------
--------------------------------------------------------------------------------
--------------------------------------
CREATE PROCEDURE titles_type_range
```

```
        @type varchar(15), @high money, @low money =  0 AS
        select title, type, price
        FROM titles
        WHERE type = @type
        AND   price BETWEEN @high and @low

(1 row affected)

Things the object references in the current database.
object                                    type            updated selected
----------------------------------------- --------------- ------- --------
dbo.authors                               user table      no      no

(0 rows affected)
```

Rules for Procedures

As with views, there are certain rules that must be followed when stored procedures are created. This section briefly discusses these rules. They are:

- The CREATE PROCEDURE statement must be in a batch by itself.
- The body of a CREATE PROCEDURE cannot include the statements CREATE VIEW, CREATE DEFAULT, CREATE RULE, CREATE TRIGGER, or CREATE PROCEDURE.
- Other database objects such as tables and indexes can be created and referenced in the same procedure. However, an object cannot be created, dropped, and then referenced in the same procedure.
- Procedures can call other procedures (up to 32 levels), and objects in the called procedure can reference objects in the calling procedure.
- Procedures can reference objects in other databases (including procedures).
- There can be a maximum of 40 parameters, local variables, and global variables in a procedure.

- Temporary tables can be referenced within a procedure. You can create a temporary table in a procedure; it is dropped when you exit the procedure.

Except for these restrictions, procedures can contain any TRANSACT-SQL statements, including the flow-of-control language statements discussed in Chapter 6. This makes them very powerful.

Two other points should be made about procedures. First, stored procedure can call itself; that is, recursive procedures are allowed. Of course, some logic must exist to terminate the recursion, or else an error will occur when the available resources (such as memory or disk space) are used up or the nesting depth is exceeded.

Second, when many users are likely to be executing a stored procedure, care should be taken to qualify object names in certain statements (referred to as utility statements) within the procedure body. The reason is that these object names are resolved when the procedure is run; hence the user name of the person running the procedure is used for qualification. For example, if user *john*, who owns table *employee*, creates the procedure that follows, he must qualify the table name as shown. If he doesn't, when *mary* runs the procedure, the table name becomes qualified with *mary*.

Example 7-20

```
create procedure upd_stat_employee as
     update statistics john.employee
```

The utility statements are CREATE TABLE, ALTER TABLE, DROP TABLE, TRUNCATE TABLE, CREATE INDEX, DROP INDEX, UPDATE STATISTICS, and DBCC. Object names on other TRANSACT-SQL statements (SELECT, INSERT, DELETE, and so on) are resolved when the procedure is compiled and hence do not need to be qualified.

Benefits of Procedures

Procedures serve many useful purposes. Probably the most important is that they offer significant performance gains. They reduce network traffic, since only the short statement to execute the procedure is sent across the network, not the entire procedure body of TRANSACT-SQL statements (which can potentially be very large). Also, they execute faster than regular SQL statements or batches because they are both precompiled and cached. Another less obvious benefit is that the compiled form of the procedure can be shared by many front-end applications and users. This is because it is stored on the Server and not on the client. Users must possess the appropriate permission to execute a stored procedure (discussed in Chapter 9).

Stored procedures can automate complex or long transactions. For example, you can define a procedure with three parameters to transfer money from one account to another—the source account, the destination account, and the amount of the transfer. However, procedures in themselves are not transactions, therefore, they are not guaranteed to execute completely, and they are not recoverable. Therefore, the specific update statements in the procedure must be defined within a user-defined transaction. Of course, each individual data modification within the procedure body is still treated as an implicit transaction.

Procedures can serve as security mechanisms by defining permissions to allow users access to the stored procedure and revoking permissions on the underlying tables. In this way only operations defined by the stored procedure are allowed. For example, users may be allowed to transfer money between accounts only through the transfer stored procedure and not allowed to update the underlying tables directly. This approach can also be used with the Server's system tables, where an incorrect or invalid update may potentially be catastrophic. In this way all updates to the system tables are made directly either through the DDL statements or through system procedures that guarantee that affected system tables are updated consistently.

System Procedures

Because of the many benefits provided by stored procedures, SQL Server provides an array of predefined procedures that perform many of the commonly needed user functions and administrative tasks. These procedures are called **system procedures** and are created when you install the server. System procedures are created in the *master* database and owned by the SA. As a convention they have names beginning with `sp_`.

System procedures allow users to retrieve information about database objects (tables, views, procedures, and so on) or perform such tasks as adding a user or group to the database. In most cases, these tasks require multiple retrievals and updates to one or more system tables—operations too risky to be done directly on the system tables. System procedures, therefore, provide two major benefits—they hide the structure of the system tables from the user, and they protect the integrity of the system tables by preventing meaningless or invalid updates, and incomplete transactions.

For example, adding a user to a database requires multiple updates to the *sysusers* table. If the updates are done directly (even by an experienced user), an update can accidentally be omitted, compromising the integrity of the system tables. There are too many opportunities for incorrect or invalid updates against the system tables to occur. By encapsulating this function in the `sp_adduser` system procedure and providing it with the appropriate parameters, the required updates are controlled and problems avoided.

Syntax

```
sp_adduser <login_id>, [, <user_name> [, <group>]]
```

In Example 7-21, the Server login ID `mary` is added as database user `mary` in the *pubs* database.

Example 7-21

```
sp_adduser mary, mary

OUTPUT:

New user added.
```

The many system procedures can be classified into two groups—those concerned with data definition and those concerned with system administration. A list of these system procedures follows. Most of them are discussed at some point in the book. A complete list of the system procedures, along with their syntax, is included in Appendix B.

The system procedures for data definition allow the following operations on databases and database objects.

- renaming database objects.
- binding and unbinding rules and defaults.
- adding and dropping user-defined types and retrieving their definition.
- retrieving information on databases and database objects.

The procedures in this category are:

```
sp_addtype        sp_foreignkey    sp_helpsql
sp_bindefault     sp_help          sp_helptext
sp_bindrule       sp_helpdb        sp_primarykey
sp_commonkey      sp_helpindex     sp_rename
sp_depends        sp_helpjoins     sp_unbindefault
sp_dropkey        sp_helpkey       sp_unbindrule
sp_droptype
```

The system procedures for administration are typically used by the SA, the DBO, or object owners to perform administrative tasks such as:

- adding and dropping login ids and changing passwords and default databases.
- user management: adding, dropping, and reporting on database users, groups, and aliases.
- performing storage management: adding devices and monitoring space usage.
- monitoring and tuning the server environment.

The procedures in this category are:

```
sp_addalias          sp_dropalias     sp_helpprotect
sp_addgroup          sp_dropdevice    sp_helpuser
sp_addlogin          sp_dropgroup     sp_lock
sp_adduser           sp_droplogin     sp_logdevice
sp_changedbowner     sp_dropuser      sp_password
sp_changegroup       sp_helpdevice    sp_monitor
sp_configure         sp_helpgroup     sp_who
sp_defaultdb
```

There are additional system procedures that are invoked by the system procedures above; however they cannot be invoked directly by users. For example, the two-phase commit procedures—`sp_abort_xact`, `sp_commit_xact`, `sp_remove_xact`, and `sp_stat_xact`—are used to coordinate a distributed transaction across multiple servers.

There is nothing magic about system procedures. They are created in the *master* database and owned by the SA. System procedures can be run from any database (including other system databases and user databases). The references to systems tables are automatically mapped to the current database. So if you execute `sp_addtype` to add a user-defined type in *empdb*, the type would be added to *empdb..systypes*.

Permissions on system procedures are set and controlled in the *master* database. Certain system procedures (mostly the administrative kind) can be executed only by the SA or the DBO. However, other system procedures can be executed by users at large. A user can be granted permission to execute a system procedure in all databases or in none. The procedure to disallow a user from executing a stored procedure is discussed in Chapter 9.

A final example illustrates how you can write a system procedure and add it to the Server's set. It also illustrates some of the control-of-flow features used in procedures. Basically, the intent is to develop a procedure that allows the user to add and drop a text comment for a database object, including columns in tables and views. The *syscomments* system table, which exists in every database, is used for storing the text. The *syscomments* table has an *id* column (the object id), a *colid* column (the column id, 0 otherwise), and a *text* column (for storing text up to 255 characters). There are two other columns—*number* (for multiple text lines) and texttype (for system versus user text—that are not used; they are set to 0 and 1, respectively. The definition of the procedure, called sp_addesc, follows.

Example 7-22

```
/* the procedure has two parameters, the object name, and the
description. If the object name is of the forms "a.b", it
   is assumed to be a column name
*/
create procedure sp_addesc @objname varchar(61)  = NULL,
                           @desc varchar(255)    = NULL
as
/* neither parameter can be null */
if (@objname = NULL or @desc = NULL)
   begin
   print "Object name and description are required."
   print "Syntax: sp_addesc <objname> <desc>"
   return
   end

set nocount on

declare @colspec tinyint
select  @colspec = 0

/* is the object a column ? */
if (@objname like "%.%")
   select @colspec = 1

declare @objid int, @colid int

declare @tabname varchar(30), @colname varchar(30)

select @colid = 0

/* if object is not a column */
if (@colspec = 0)
   begin

/* get object id */
   select @objid = id
```

```
   from sysobjects
   where name = @objname

   if (@objid = NULL)
      begin
      print "No such object exists in the current database"
      return
      end

/*record description in syscomments */
   insert into syscomments values
      (@objid, 0, @colid, 1, 0, @desc)
   end
else   /* column specification */
   begin
   select @tabname = substring (@objname, 1,
                                    charindex(".",@objname)-1)
   select @colname = substring (@objname,
                                    charindex(".", @objname)+1, 61)

/* determine object id and column id */
   select @objid = id
   from sysobjects
   where name = @tabname

   select @colid = colid
   from syscolumns
   where name = @colname and
         id = @objid

   if (@objid = NULL or @colid = NULL)
      begin
      print "Table or column does not exist in current database"
      return
      end

/*record description in syscomments */
   insert into syscomments values
      (@objid, 0, @colid, 1, 0, @desc)
   end
```

The procedure is fairly simple and progresses as follows: it first checks to see if either parameter is not provided; if so, it exits with an error message. Otherwise, it determines whether or not the object is a column specification. If not, it gets the object id from *sysobjects* and inserts the description in the *syscomments* table. If the object is a column, it gets the column id value from *syscolumns* as well, and uses that value for the *colid* column in *syscomments*. The complementary procedure `sp_dropdesc`, which drops a description, is also needed, but it is not included here.

Summary

This chapter looked at two database objects, views and stored procedures, in detail. It examined how to create and drop views and discussed their purpose and benefits. It explained how view resolution takes place in the Server. It set forth some restrictions in using views—both in defining them and in using them in data modification statements. It explained how to create and drop stored procedures, a valuable extension in TRANSACT-SQL. The usage and some restrictions in the definition of stored procedures were examined. Their many advantages, including improved performance and their ability to invoke other procedures and take parameters, were explored. The way in which both views and procedures can be used as security mechanisms was touched upon. The chapter finally discussed how system procedures are created and managed, and included a list of some system procedures.

CHAPTER
8

Integrity Features

Introduction

This chapter explores the integrity features of SQL Server. While most traditional RDBMSs provide little or no support for data integrity, SQL Server provides integrity features that are unique in two ways. First, SQL Server provides DBMS-enforced integrity. What this means and how it is useful are discussed. Second, it provides extensive support for integrity in the form of null values, user-defined types, defaults, rules, and triggers. NULL was discussed in Chapter 4; the remaining objects are discussed here.

Data Integrity

A database is only as useful as the quality—or integrity—of the data within it. Data integrity, simply defined, is the accuracy, correctness, and validity of the data in the database. Accuracy has to do with how closely the data model the truth. For example, if your inventory database tells you you have 40 parts, do you really have 40? If the actual quantity is 50 you would incorrectly reject an order for 45 parts. Correctness, which is related to accuracy, implies that the data truly represent the facts about the real world entities being modeled; for example, that Joe's social security number really is 123-45-6789. Validity has to do with the logical consistency of the database. For example, if Susan works for the accounting department, not only must the accounting department exist, but also Susan must be correctly related to accounting. The system (used in a general sense to encompass both the client and server) therefore must provide integrity features that protect the data from accidental corruption that would cause it not to model real world entities and relationships accurately.

Kinds of Integrity

There are primarily two kinds of integrity to be concerned with in databases, especially in relational systems. The first kind is intrinsic to the database; it is an integral component of the data. In relational databases, all relationships are represented by primary and foreign key values; there are no explicit system-maintained pointers in the rows. While this provides the advantages of a simple data model and a high degree of data independence, it also means that when key values change, they must be changed every place they occur in the database. For example, in a personnel database, if the department number (*dept#* column in the department table) for accounting changes from 020 to 040, every place it is referenced in the database (all foreign that reference *dept#*) must be changed to 040, for integrity to be maintained. Otherwise, you have key values that reference nonexistent or incorrect departments.

The second kind of integrity is extrinisic to the database; it enforces the rules of the application or business domain being modeled. Every business has rules, policies, and procedures that must be enforced. For example, there may be a rule that no employee should be paid more than $100,000, or that spouses cannot work in the same department. These are rules that typically vary from business to business, but that need to be enforced to ensure the validity of the data.

Application versus DBMS-Enforced Integrity

A major concern with integrity is how and where it should be effected. Integrity can be effected in application code, or it can be specified at the forms or even the database definition level. The location of the code or procedure or definition constraint that actually enforces the integrity must also be chosen. Intrinsic integrity is best enforced at the DBMS level, as long as there is some way to specify the relationships (foreign and primary keys). It is less apparent where to enforce extrinsic integrity—in the application or at the level of the DBMS. (There has been little support to enforce this kind of integrity at the DBMS level, especially for complex business rules.) In most DBMS environments, it is largely up to the client or front-end application to ensure that the data entering the database are valid. In fact, large parts of many application systems are devoted to complex code for enforcing such integrity.

Every system (both application and DBMS) should guarantee the integrity of the data it manipulates. Ensuring data integrity implies enforcing the semantics of the real world or the particular environment within the actual data. What this usually means is that any update to the data is constrained to fit certain rules. These rules are referred to as **integrity constraints**. For example, employee salaries may be constrained to $20,000 to $150,000. Another example may be simply ensuring that every employee's social security number is either not known (NULL), or that the number conforms to the pattern 999-99-9999.

The applications that create and maintain the data should also maintain the data's integrity. Integrity logic can be coded into the application to prevent invalid or incorrect data from ever getting to the database. In fact, it is commonly the case that the application programs of a system bear the burden of enforcing most of the integrity rules of the application environment. Thus if the salary constraint just mentioned needs to be enforced for a payroll system, all application programs in that system that create or modify rows in the *employee* table can incorporate code to enforce it. The approach of enforcing integrity through application code—although simple in concept—has several drawbacks:

- Applications must devote significant amounts of code to data integrity logic, especially for complex constraints.
- The integrity logic must be enforced consistently by all front-end applications—it only takes one nonconforming application to corrupt the integrity of the database.
- Updates to the database from ad-hoc interfaces (using the DML) must be carefully controlled and monitored to ensure that none of the integrity constraints is violated.
- If the integrity constraints change they affect multiple applications.

DBMS-enforced integrity, on the other hand, is the ability to enforce data integrity at the level of the DBMS (or Server). This capability is provided by allowing various kinds of integrity constraints to be specified through the data definition language. Once defined, these constraints are stored in the DBMS's data dictionary and enforced automatically by the DBMS on any updates to databases (in INSERT, UPDATE, and DELETE statements). Figure

8-1 contrasts integrity enforced at the application and DBMS levels.

There are many advantages to enforcing integrity at the DBMS level. Most of the problems that arise from application-enforced integrity are eliminated. Since business rules really model the application environment (or data) and have little to do with the application programs themselves, it seems logical to specify and enforce them at the database level, rather than at the application level. In the salary integrity constraint mentioned earlier, salary must range from \$20,000 to \$150,000. This fact relates to the salary data and not to any applications that use the data (such as a pay raise application).

The advantages that result from DBMS-enforced integrity are:

- Integrity constraints are specified in one place using simple DDL statements instead of redundantly in many applications using code.

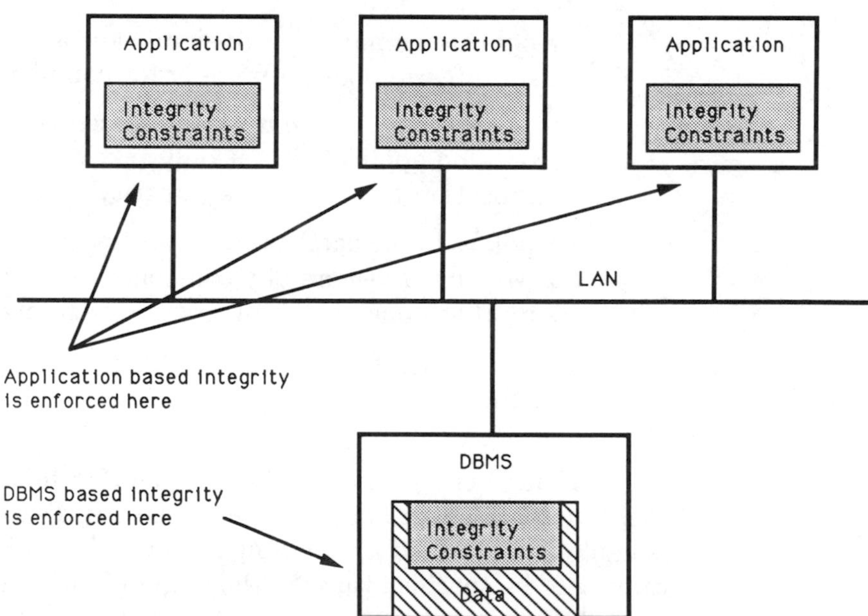

FIGURE 8-1 Application-enforced integrity versus DBMS-enforced integrity

- The constraints are enforced centrally by the DBMS and shared by all front-end applications. Thus they are enforced consistently for all applications (including ad-hoc interfaces).
- If the rules change, the integrity constraints have to be modified in only one place.

In practice, few DBMSs provide a comprehensive set of features to enforce data integrity. This probably causes so many systems to enforce integrity constraints in the applications. SQL Server, on the other hand, provides a powerful set of features that allow you to specify a wide range of integrity constraints—from simple range conditions on columns to complex business integrity rules that span multiple columns or tables. In fact, these features can be broadly categorized into those that are defined on single columns and those that span multiple columns (in, possibly, multiple tables). The rest of this chapter discusses these SQL Server features.

Single Column Integrity

SQL Server provides several features for enforcing data integrity at the column level. These features include allowing null values, user-defined data types, defaults, and rules. Chapter 4 already introduced these concepts. How the objects can be created and dropped, and how they are used for the purposes of data integrity are now examined.

Nulls

The concept of null values has been discussed. To elaborate, a null value is simply a nonentry, an unknown or inapplicable value. NULL is different from blanks (" ") or the zero value (0), and the DBMS must represent them as such. Null values are basic to the relational model and are part of the ANSI SQL standard. A column definition specifies whether or not a column value can be NULL. You can use this to enforce constraints either by prohibiting null values—for example, "part number cannot be null"—or by allowing null values—"phone number is null if not known."

User-defined Data Types

User-defined data types allow users to define their own types based on system types. This integrity feature provides a higher level of abstraction and consistency in the definition of an object. Let us use storage of telephone numbers to illustrate this idea. Telephone numbers occur several places in our database; there are phone numbers for stores, authors, and publishers. The columns containing them can be defined in several ways. They can be character columns of 10, 12, or 13 characters, the number depending on whether you include just digits, 1234567890; digits with dashes, 123-456-7890; or digits with parentheses and dashes, (123)456-7890. The point is that column definitions can vary, even within the same database. When they are defined differently, they have to be manipulated differently.

To enforce consistency in the column definitions a user-defined data type can be created. The user-defined type, `phone_type`, in this illustration, applies to all columns that hold phone numbers. User-defined types can allow a null specification; that is, the user can specify whether or not to allow null values when the user-defined type is created. (This definition can be overridden at column specification time within a CREATE TABLE statement.) This is also useful in ensuring the consistency of definition of the user-defined data type. In our telephone number illustration, if you do not expect to have phone numbers for all rows, you would want to allow null values. You can define `phone_type` as follows.

Example 8-1

```
sp_addtype phone_type, 'char(10)', null

OUTPUT:

Type added.
```

Once defined, the user-defined type `phone_type` can be used every place a phone number column occurs in the database (in our database, the *authors, publishers,* and *stores* tables). User-defined types can even be used to enforce consistency across multiple databases—for example, a part number definition in an inventory control database, a manufacturing database, and an accounts receivable/payable database. This can be done by including the user-defined type in the *model* database; then every new user database (which starts out as a copy of *model*) contains the user-defined type.

Defaults

In relational systems, every column must have a value. The value can be NULL, and it may or may not be explicitly provided. A default supplies a predefined value for a column, when one is not supplied explicitly. Once created, the default can be bound either directly to columns, or indirectly to all columns of a particular user-defined data type. Although defaults can be created at any time, they are only effective while they are bound to columns. If a default is no longer applicable, it can be unbound from any columns to which it was bound; if it is not bound to any column it can be dropped from the database.

Creating and Dropping Defaults Defaults are created through the CREATE DEFAULT statement. Default names follow the rules for identifiers; however, they can be created only in the current database. The syntax of the CREATE DEFAULT statement follows.

Syntax

```
CREATE DEFAULT [<owner>.]<default>
     AS <constant_expression>
```

A default value can be an expression, as long as it does not reference a database object or column. Functions can be used within the expression, as long as they do not have parameters that reference database objects. For example, if you want to define the default value for the *state* column in the *authors* table to be CA (since most authors appear to live there), you can create the following default.

Example 8-2

```
create default state_default as "CA"
```

```
OUTPUT:
```

When you specify the constant value, you must follow the normal rules for entering data in SQL Server. (See Chapter 6.) Characters and dates must be enclosed in quotes, money data must be preceded by the $ sign, and so on. You can also specify NULL as a default value.

A default is dropped using the DROP DEFAULT statement. Of course, for a default to be dropped, it cannot be bound to any column or user-defined type, and the user must have proper permission. However, you do not have to unbind and drop a default in order to bind a new default to a column; binding the new default overrides the old one. The syntax of the DROP DEFAULT statement follows.

Syntax

```
DROP DEFAULT [<owner>.]<default>
        [, [<owner >.]<default> ]...
```

Binding and Unbinding Defaults Once a default is created, you can bind it to one or several columns, or all columns of a user-defined type, using the `sp_bindefault` system procedure. The default has no effect if the user provides an explicit value for a column to which the default is bound. Also, it only affects column values in new rows added to the table after the default is bound, existing column values are not changed.

Syntax

```
sp_bindefault <default>, <object> [,FUTUREONLY]
```

The `<default>` parameter is the default name, and `<object>` specifies the name of the column or user-defined type to which the default is bound. The `<object>` parameter can either be of the form `<table>.<column>` or `<user_defined_type>`; if it is not of the first form, it is assumed to be a user-defined type. The optional FUTUREONLY keyword can be used when binding to a user-defined type to control whether or not existing columns of that type are affected by the default. If FUTUREONLY is specified, existing columns of that user-defined type are not affected; the only other columns that are not affected are those that have defaults bound to them directly.

For example, you can bind `state_default` created earlier to the *state* column in the *authors* table. Once the default is bound, if a value for the *state* column is not provided, the value CA is automatically entered by the Server.

Example 8-3

```
sp_bindefault state_default, "authors.state"

OUTPUT:

Default bound to column.
```

A default can be bound only to a column of compatible type. For example, `state_default` cannot be bound to a column of integer data type. If the column data type is user-defined, the default value must be compatible with the base type of the user-defined data type (`char, int`, and so on). Otherwise an error will occur—not when you bind the default, but when the Server tries to insert the value.

Defaults can also be bound to several columns or to a user-defined data type. This allows several columns to inherit the default value. For example, if you want all state columns (in *authors, stores, and publishers* tables) to default to CA, you can bind `state_default` to all of them. Alternatively, you can define `state_type`, a user-defined type, and bind the default `state_default` to it. From then on, all columns defined using that user-defined data type inherit that default.

Example 8-4

```
sp_bindefault state_default, state_type

OUTPUT:

Default bound to datatype.
```

Defaults cannot be bound to system types. If you could, the range of columns affected would be too large. (Imagine binding a default to `int`!) Defaults bound to specific columns of a user-defined data type, take precedence over a default bound to the user-defined data type.

Defaults are unbound from columns or user-defined data types using the sp_unbindefault system procedure. Unbinding a default does not cause the default to be dropped, even when the default is no longer bound to any columns or user-defined data types. If you want to drop the default, you must do it explicitly. Another way to unbind a default from a column or user-defined data type is simply to bind a new default to it; the old one is automatically unbound. The syntax of the sp_unbindefault system procedure follows.

Syntax

```
sp_unbindefault <object> [,FUTUREONLY]
```

The <object> parameter is interpreted as a column name or user-defined data type the same way it is in the sp_bindefault procedure. FUTUREONLY works in reverse when defaults are unbound from user-defined data types—if FUTUREONLY is specified, existing columns of that data type do not lose their binding. Also if the default on a particular column of that user-defined data type has been changed, and the default is being unbound from the user-defined data type, it does not affect the column.

An example will clarify the preceding statements. Assume that the *state* column in the *authors, stores,* and *publishers* tables are all of the user-defined data type, state_type, and the default state_default is bound to state_type. A new state default, called new_state_default, is bound to *publishers.state.* If you unbind the default state_default from state_type, as shown in Example 8-5, *publishers.state* still has new_state_default bound to it, although *authors.state* and *stores.state* no longer have any defaults. If FUTUREONLY is specified, all existing columns retain the defaults.

Example 8-5

```
sp_unbindefault state_type
```

```
OUTPUT:

Default unbound from datatype.
```

Interaction of Defaults and Nulls The action taken by SQL Server when a value is not provided for a column on insert depends on whether or not a default is bound to the column (either directly or indirectly), and on the null specification for the column. SQL Server does one of three things–provide a null value, insert the default value, or return an error. The following table summarizes the actions.

Column definition	NULL		NOT NULL	
	No default	Default	No default	Default
No entry	null	default	error	default
NULL entry	null	null	error	error
Value	value	value	value	value

A good way to think of this is, if an explicit value is provided in an INSERT (NULL or NOT NULL), that value is used if the column definition allows it, otherwise an error occurs. If no value is provided but a default is, the default value is used (regardless of the null specification). If no default is provided, the null value is inserted, if allowed (NULL column specification), otherwise an error occurs (NOT NULL column specification).

Rules

In any DBMS, the system data types provide a very basic form of integrity check. They prevent the user from entering character data for numeric or bit fields, for example. SQL Server provides a rich set of system types (see Chapter 4). In addition, it provides user-defined data types to allow for consistency and a higher level of abstraction in defining types. **Rules** are mechanisms to enforce simple integrity constraints that go beyond the data type (whether system or user-defined) of a column. A rule can be bound to one, several, or all columns or a particular user-defined type, much like a default. It serves to restrict further the range of legal values allowed by the column's data type.

Rules, in conjunction with system and user-defined types, allow **domain integrity** to be enforced in SQL Server. The concept of domains is basic to the relational model; every column has an underlying domain that represents the set of all possible values from which the column value is drawn. Domains are usually more restrictive than the base data type of the column. For example, the single character sex column in an employee table would have the domain `{ "M", "F" }`. You can define the column's data type as `char(1)` (the base type). However, to limit the values to that allowed by the domain `"M"` or `"F"`, you can use rules. It is unfortunate that the support for domain integrity is limited in today's RDBMSs.

Creating and Dropping Rules Rules are created with the CREATE RULE statement and dropped with the DROP RULE statement. Like defaults, they can be created only in the current database, and their names must conform to the rules for identifier names. The syntax of the CREATE RULE and DROP RULE statements follows.

Syntax

```
CREATE RULE [<owner>.]<rule> AS
     <boolean_expression>
DROP RULE [<owner>.]<rule>
     [, [<owner>.]<rule> ]...
```

A rule definition specifies the rule name and the integrity constraint that must be satisfied on every insert or update to a column to which it is bound. The constraint is basically a Boolean expression that evaluates to TRUE (the constraint is satisfied) or FALSE (it is not). If it is not satisfied, the insert or update is disallowed, and an error message is displayed. Rules can be created and bound at any time. They do not affect data that already exist in the table.

For example, you can define a rule, `price_rule`, that constrains all book prices to the range $0 to $500 (a reasonable range), as follows:

Example 8-6

```
create rule price_rule as
@price between $0 and $500
```

The `@price` is a symbolic name for the column value at definition time; the actual value is used in evaluating the expression on the actual INSERT or UPDATE. Any name that follows the rules for identifiers and is preceded by the @ character can be used for the symbolic name. The constraint that is part of the rule definition in the Server is very general—almost any expression that is valid in a TRANSACT-SQL WHERE clause is allowed. It can include conditions involving comparison operators, arithmetic operators, the IN keyword, the BETWEEN keyword, the LIKE keyword, and so on. The only exception is that it cannot include object names (tables and columns) or built-in functions that reference object names. Rules can be defined to constrain column values to a particular range or a list of values (as shown later) or to fit a particular pattern. For example, if you have a column holding social security numbers defined as `char(11)` in a table and you want the values to fit the pattern 999-99-9999, you can define `ssno_rule` as follows.

Example 8-7

```
create rule ssno_rule as
     @ssno like '[0-9][0-9][0-9]-[0-9][0-9]-[0-9][0-9][0-9][0-9]'
```

When a rule is no longer needed, it can be dropped from the database using the DROP RULE statement. It must be unbound from all columns or user-defined types before you can drop it; otherwise an error occurs. A rule does not need to be unbound or dropped in order to bind a new one in its place; the new rule can simply be bound in place of the old one. For example, if the rule created in Example 8-7 is not bound to any columns or user-defined types, you can drop it using the DROP RULE statement that follows. Only owners of rules can drop them; permission cannot be granted to anyone else.

Example 8-8

```
drop rule price_rule
```

Binding and Unbinding Rules Once a rule has been defined, it can be bound to one or several columns, or all columns of a user-defined type using the sp_bindrule system procedure. Rules cannot be bound to system data types, however, for the same reason that defaults cannot be bound to them—the target range of columns would be too broad. The syntax of the sp_bindrule system procedure follows.

Syntax

```
sp_bindrule <rule>, <object> [,FUTUREONLY]
```

The first parameter, <rule>, is the name of the rule object, which must exist in the database. The interpretation of <object> varies based on its form—if it is not of the form <table>.<column>, it is assumed to be a user-defined type. FUTUREONLY has exactly the same meaning as that in the sp_bindefault system procedure (discussed earlier), except that it applies to rules.

For example, if you want to ensure that all titles have a price range of $0 to $500, you bind price_rule created earlier to the *price* column in the *titles* table as follows.

Example 8-9

```
sp_bindrule price_rule, "titles.price"

OUTPUT:

Rule bound to table column.
```

Once a rule is bound to a column, SQL Server insures that any modification to that column meets the constraint specified in the rule definition. This means that on every INSERT or UPDATE of the *price* column in the *titles* table, SQL Server checks to make sure that the price is between $0 and $500. If not, the INSERT or UPDATE is disallowed, and the user is notified with an error message. The error message points out the exact column, table, and database where the conflict occurs, as illustrated by the unsuccessful update to the *titles* table that follows. An important point to note is that rules are not retroactive; that is, they do not apply to data that already exist in the *titles* table.

Example 8-10

```
INSERT INTO titles VALUES
     ("AA9999", "A test of wits", "psychology", "0736", $555.00,
          null, null, null, null, "05/15/90")

OUTPUT:

Msg 513, Level 16, State 1:
 A column insert or update conflicts with a rule imposed by a previous
CREATE RULE command. The command was aborted. The conflict occurred in
database 'pubs', table 'titles', column 'price'
Command has been aborted.
```

Rules, like defaults, can also be bound to user-defined data types, in which case columns of that user-defined data type inherit the rule. For example, if you want to constrain the values of all the state columns to only the western states (AZ, CA, NV, OR, WA), you can define a rule, `state_rule`, and bind it to the user-defined type `state_type` created during the discussion of defaults.

Example 8-11

```
CREATE RULE state_rule AS
     @state IN ("AZ", "CA", "NV", "OR", "WA")
<exec>
sp_bindrule state_rule, state_type
<exec>

OUTPUT:

Rule bound to datatype.
```

Before we leave the subject of integrity defined at the level of single columns, **entity integrity** should be mentioned. Entity integrity is intrinsic to the relational model and specifies that no part of a primary key may be NULL. This requirement stems from the fact that rows must be identifiable; if nulls were allowed, there would be no way to distinguish rows that had NULL primary key values. SQL Server does support the definition of a primary key using the `sp_primarykey` system procedure. However the procedure is currently just a documentation aid; it does not enforce the true meaning of a primary key—do not allow NULLs and enforce uniqueness among key values. However, the same result can be achieved by defining all primary key columns as NOT NULL and defining a unique index (usually the clustered index) on the primary key columns.

Multiple Column Integrity

So far, this chapter has discussed integrity that pertains to a single column or a set of columns treated as a single unit. Often, there is a need to specify more complex integrity constraints that span multiple columns, often in multiple tables. Some examples of these constraints are: Only allow orders for titles that exist; ensure that all employees work for existing departments; make sure that there are no more than five authors for a book. None of these constraints can be enforced by a simple rule. They require a more advanced data integrity mechanism. In DBMSs that do not provide a mechanism, such constraints are typically enforced in the application, using additional code. However, application-enforced integrity has all the drawbacks mentioned earlier.

SQL Server provides the capability of enforcing these complex constraints through the use of triggers. You can think of triggers as an advanced form of rules—rules that possibly span multiple tables. Triggers have broad applications; they can also be used to perform functions other than enforcing integrity. The next section explores some of these uses.

Triggers

A trigger, as mentioned in Chapter 4, is nothing more than a special kind of stored procedure automatically executed whenever a prespecified event occurs. The trigger can check to see if the integrity constraint (the trigger condition) is met and, based on that, perform certain actions (trigger actions). The trigger action can be, for example, to disallow an update, by rolling it back and printing an error message. The prespecified event can be any modification to a table, an INSERT, UPDATE, or DELETE. Since a trigger is basically a stored procedure, the full power of TRANSACT-SQL, including the enhancements discussed in Chapter 6, is available to the user for defining the trigger condition and actions.

Triggers are created using the CREATE TRIGGER statement. The statement specifies the table on which the trigger is defined and the events (INSERT, UPDATE, or DELETE) for which the trigger will fire. The actual body of the trigger follows the AS keyword and contains the statements that are executed when the trigger fires. Once defined, a trigger is automatically invoked by SQL Server whenever the prespecified event occurs. This is unlike rules or defaults, which must be bound before they are effective. The only way to prevent the trigger from firing is to drop the trigger. Triggers are dropped using the DROP TRIGGER statement.

Syntax

```
CREATE TRIGGER [<owner>.]<trigger>
     ON [<owner>.]<table>
     FOR {INSERT | UPDATE| DELETE}
     [, {INSERT | UPDATE | DELETE} ] ...
     AS
     <statement_block>

DROP TRIGGER [<owner>.]<trigger>
```

The `<statement_block>` is the body of a trigger; it can be as simple as merely printing an informational message to the user. However, since triggers are basically stored procedures that are defined by the user, they are very flexible and powerful mechanisms that can enforce much more complex integrity constraints (such as the ones presented earlier in this chapter) and perform other tasks as well. Here are some of the uses for triggers:

- They can enforce referential integrity, that is, the consistency of database values across multiple tables or databases. This can be achieved by disallowing updates that cause inconsistencies or by propagating changes to other tables in the database.

- They can keep summary data or derived data current. For example, if you have a derived column, *sales,* for a title in the *titles* table, which is the product of *price* and *ytd-sales,* you can use a trigger to recompute the sales column automatically every time a new row is inserted or every time the *price* or *ytd_sales* column is updated.
- They can control updates to a table based on values of the updated row prior to and after the update. For example, if you want to disallow updates that increase the price of a title by over 25%, you can use a trigger to enforce this constraint. Note that if you want simply to constrain the price of a title to a range, a rule would be adequate.

Referential integrity is crucial in relational databases. Since all relationships are represented as foreign to primary key value mapping in tables, it is very important that the key values are consistent—that there are no references to nonexistent values or that, if a key value changes, all references to it are changed consistently throughout the database.

There are several possible scenarios that could violate referential integrity. One is the modification or deletion of a primary key that could have matching foreign key values in other tables. Another is the addition or update of a foreign key, the value of which must match some primary key value. If it doesn't, it would point to a nonexistent entity. Thus in the *pubs* database, if the *pub_id* for a publisher changes, you want to ensure that *pub_id* is updated every place in the database that it is referenced. This is known as a *cascading update.* If you delete a title from the *titles* table, you want to delete all foreign key references to it. This is known as a *cascading delete.*

In addition to referential integrity rules, there may other business integrity rules that span multiple columns (or multiple rows). These rules are usually more complex than the simple column constraints for domain integrity discussed earlier and, hence, are often referred to as **complex business integrity** rules. An example of such a rule in the *pubs* database might be: There must always be a second source (store) in every major city for computer titles. Or the example mentioned earlier that there must be no more than five authors for any title.

Triggers provide a way to enforce these complex constraints at the DBMS level, although in some cases it may require a fair amount of TRANSACT-SQL programming. Triggers provide two special features that are not available with stored procedures. They have access to two special tables (*inserted* and *deleted*) and a special statement called the IF UPDATE statement. Both of these features are available only within the body of a trigger.

The *inserted* and *deleted* tables are special tables, referred to as trigger test tables. They contain the rows affected by the original event (the INSERT, UPDATE, or DELETE statement) that caused the trigger to fire. Since they are accessible inside the trigger, it is easy to determine values in the affected rows. The *inserted* table contains rows being inserted, and the *deleted* table contains the rows being deleted. (As has been shown, all data modification statements are treated as implicit transactions. Thus it is possible to roll back invalid transactions with a trigger.) Update statements are treated as a DELETE followed by an INSERT—the values of the row prior to the update are placed in the *deleted* table, and the values of the row after the update are placed in the *inserted* table. These tables will be used in the examples that follow. Figure 8-2 illustrates *inserted* and *deleted* tables.

The IF UPDATE statement allows you to see if a particular column within the row is being updated. It allows trigger actions to be associated with updates to specified columns. The column name is part of the syntax of the statement. The statement returns a TRUE if the column is being modified (in an INSERT or UPDATE statement), otherwise it returns a FALSE. The IF UPDATE statement is never TRUE for a DELETE statement.

Syntax

```
IF UPDATE (<column_name>)
```

With INSERT statements, the IF UPDATE statement returns TRUE whenever the column is assigned a value in the SELECT clause or VALUES clause of the INSERT statement. Explicit null values, or values provided by defaults thus cause the

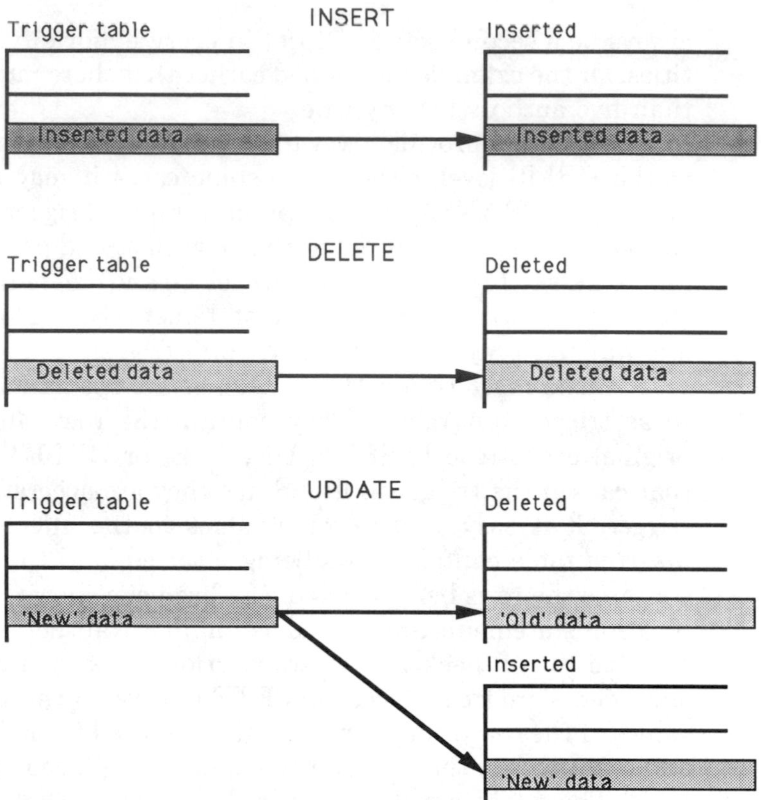

FIGURE 8-2 ***inserted* and *deleted* tables**

IF UPDATE statement to return TRUE. An implicit null value (one not provided by the query or default) returns a FALSE, however.

Examples of Triggers

This section provides examples of the ways in which triggers are used to enforce integrity in SQL Server, using the *pubs* database. The definition of the trigger in TRANSACT-SQL is shown.

Referential Integrity Example 8-12 shows how triggers can be used to enforce referential integrity. Whenever a user modifies a *stor_id* in the *stores* table, that change is propagated to all other tables—in this case specifically the *sales* table. What is more common, however, is that the update of the primary key would be disallowed, and the row in the *stores* table would need to be dropped and recreated with the new store id.

Example 8-12

```
create trigger stores_update
on stores
for update
as
if update (stor_id)
     if (select count(*) from deleted, stores where
          deleted.stor_id = stores.stor_id) > 0
     update sales
          set sales.stor_id = inserted.stor_id
     from sales, inserted, deleted
     where sales.stor_id = deleted.stor_id
```

Cascading Delete If you delete a particular title, you want to ensure that there are no longer any references to that title in the database (the classic dangling reference). Here is a trigger that deletes all references to that title in the *sales* table.

Example 8-13

```
create trigger delete_titles
on titles
for delete
as
     delete sales
     from sales, deleted
     where sales.title_id = deleted.title_id
```

For simplicity, references to the title are deleted only from the *sales* table. To complete the trigger, you would also delete references to the title from the *titleauthor* and *roysched* tables.

You might want to prevent the deletion of a title from the *titles* table if it has outstanding sales. This can be done as in the *pubs* database using the `deltitles` trigger. The `deltitles` trigger checks the *sales* table to see if the title being deleted has any outstanding sales. If so, it disallows the deletion and prints a message, otherwise the deletion is allowed. The `deltitles` trigger definition follows.

Example 8-14

```
create trigger deltitles
on titles
for delete
as

/* check to see if any outstanding sales */
if (select count(*) from sales, deleted
    where sales.title_id = deleted.title_id) > 0
     begin
     /* disallow delete */
     rollback transaction
     print "You can't delete a title with sales"
     end
```

What may not be obvious is that the trigger body, comprising the executable statements, is automatically part of the explicit or implicit transaction that caused the modification to the trigger table. Thus the ROLLBACK statement rolls back the entire transaction and the update to the table is disallowed.

Keeping Derived Data Current Triggers can also be used to maintain derived information. For example, assume you have an employee table that contains three columns—total salary, base salary, and commissions. In the following example, the statements required to create these are shown first. The total salary is the sum of the base salary and the commission. You can use a trigger that is invoked every time a row is inserted or updated to compute the total salary and thus keep it current.

Example 8-15

```
alter table employee
     add emp_bsal   money null,
         emp_comm   money null

sp_rename "employee.emp_salary", emp_tsal
OUTPUT:
```

```
Column name has been changed.

create trigger current_tot_sal
on employee
for insert, update as
if (update(emp_bsal) or update(emp_comm))
begin
    update employee
    set emp_tsal = inserted.emp_bsal + inserted.emp_comm
    where employee.emp_id = inserted.emp_id
end
```

Triggers can also be used to enforce constraints based on the state of a table before and after it is modified. For example, you can enforce a constraint that says, do not allow price increases of more that 25% on any title within a single update. Triggers have access to the values before and after the update and, using this information, can decide either to roll back the update transaction or to allow it to complete.

As a second example, assume you have an additional column *ytd_revenue,* that stores the year-to-date dollar sales in the *titles* table. The figure is computed by multiplying the price by the total number of year-to-date sales for that title. You can compute this in the application, the actual query, or the database itself. Assume that it is a frequent enough operation that the figure needs to be stored in the database. You can use the following trigger to keep this column current.

Example 8-16

```
create trigger sales_compute
on titles
for insert, update
as
if (update (price) or update (ytd_sales))
       update titles
       set titles.ytd_revenue = (in-
serted.price) * (inserted. ytd_sales)
       from titles, inserted
       where titles.title_id = inserted.title_id

OUTPUT:
```

Updating Data Based on Current and Future Values

Triggers can be used to control updates based on column values before and after an UPDATE. The following trigger disallows UPDATEs to the *titles* tables that raise prices by more than 25% of the existing value.

Example 8-17

```
create trigger reasonable_price_hike
on titles
for update
as
if update (price)
    if (select count(*) FROM inserted, deleted
        where inserted.title_id = deleted.title_id and
              inserted.price > (1.25 * deleted.price)) > 0
    begin
        print "Too much of a hike !"
        rollback transaction
    end

OUTPUT:
```

Information on Triggers

Information on triggers can be obtained in much the same way as it is for procedures—through the system procedures `sp_help`, `sp_helptext`, and `sp_depends`. The `sp_help` procedure displays the owner and the type of the object; the `sp_helptext` returns the actual text of the CREATE TRIGGER statement. The `sp_depends` procedure can find all objects (including triggers) that reference a table or view and all objects referenced by a trigger. The example that follows shows all objects referenced by the `deltitles` trigger.

Example 8-18

```
sp_helptext deltitles
go

OUTPUT:

         text
```

```
-------------------------------------------------------------------------------------
-------------------------------------------------------------------------------------
--------------------------------------
create trigger deltitles
on titles
for delete
as
/* check to see if any outstanding sales */
if (select count(*) from sales, deleted
    where sales.title_id = deleted.title_id) > 0
        begin
        /* disallow delete */
        rollback transaction
        print "You can't delete a title with sales"
        end

(2 rows affected)

sp_depends deltitles
go

OUTPUT:

Things the object references in the current database.
object                                  type            updated selected
--------------------------------------- --------------- ------- --------
dbo.sales                               user table      no      no

(0 rows affected)
```

Rules for Triggers

In general, triggers are very similar to stored procedures. However, there are a few minor rules and restrictions they must follow.

- Triggers are automatically invoked once they are defined; they are not executed as stored procedures.
- They cannot take parameters.

- They cannot be nested. If one trigger performs an update that would cause a second trigger to fire, the second trigger will not fire.
- There are only three triggers allowed per table, one each for INSERT, UPDATE, and DELETE.
- The special tables *inserted* and *deleted* and the special IF UPDATE statement are usable only within the trigger body.
- The TRUNCATE statement does not activate a trigger, even though it acts like a DELETE. This is because the TRUNCATE statement is not logged and hence cannot be undone.
- Only the owner of the table can create or drop a trigger on it; permission cannot be granted to other users.

Except for the above restrictions, anything that is allowed within a stored procedure is allowed within a trigger. The only severe restriction is that nested triggers are not allowed; if such a need arises, the body of the second trigger should be added to the body of the first trigger. This restriction will be removed in a future version of the SQL Server.

Summary

This chapter discussed the meaning of database integrity, how it can be enforced either through the client application or through the DBMS, and how the two approaches compare. It discussed the features of SQL Server—null values, defaults, rules, and triggers—that can be used to provide DBMS-enforced integrity. It discussed how null values, defaults, and rules can be used to enforce simple integrity constraints, and how triggers can enforce more complex integrity constraints. Examples of trigger definition were presented, and restrictions in their usage were listed.

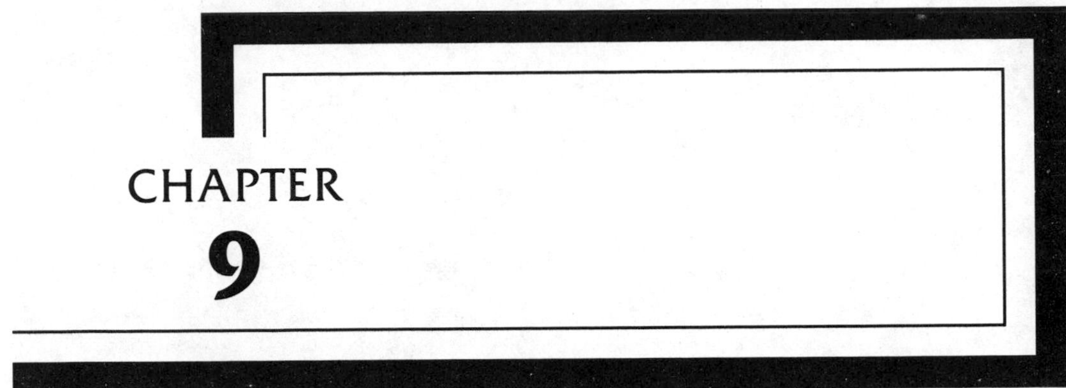

CHAPTER

9

Security

Introduction

Several preceding chapters have alluded to the appropriate permissions required to perform certain database operations. It was mentioned that only the SA can perform certain actions, that users with appropriate permissions can perform certain statements, that only the object owner can drop an object. All of these issues relate to security in SQL Server. Security is based on user authentication and user levels in SQL Server. This chapter discusses security in detail. It includes discussions of the different types of users and how to grant and revoke permissions to users. In addition, permissions on view and stored procedures is discussed.

User Structures

In any database environment, security is an important concern. Security is different from integrity (discussed in the previous chapter), which has to do with preventing inconsistent or invalid updates to the data in a database. Security deals with preventing unauthorized alternation of or access to the data within a database.

There are various forms of security in computing environments, and they can be provided at many levels. For example, actual physical access to the computer system on which a database exists may be restricted with a key card system. User names and passwords can be defined at the operating system level to restrict access to the computer system. The DBMS can provide security features independent from those of the OS for restricting access to all or parts of its databases.

In the SQL Server environment, too, there are various levels and forms of security. There is no logon security at the OS level (since OS/2 is a single user operating system), but access to the server machine can always be restricted by keeping it under lock and key. The lack of logon security can be circumvented by network OS security, by requiring the user to log on to the network before he or she can access the OS or database files. In some environments today (for example, the 3Com 3S/400 server), all local keyboard access can be prevented to the file server, and all administration must be performed remotely. This requires logging on to the network and going through network security. With current LAN Manager network servers (on which SQL Servers run), even users logging on locally will be required to sign on to the network and have proper network authorization, before they can access the file system. Since SQL Server is installed just as any other network service is, any network security measures available can be used to control access to the server. Finally, there is the security offered by SQL Server itself, in addition to the security at the OS and network levels. SQL Server's security is the primary topic of this chapter.

User Identification

SQL Server provides a comprehensive set of security features to control access to the Server's environment (including its databases and database objects). SQL Server controls access at two levels. At the Server level, it allows only valid users access to the Server; at the database level, it allows the assignment of specific privileges to users within the databases.

SQL Server's security mechanism is based on a two-tiered user-identification scheme. First, every user who wishes to access a Server must have a valid Server **login** ID and **password**. Second, every valid server login id must be defined as valid database **user name** for every database the user needs to access. Within a database, the user must have the required permission to perform operations or access objects.

Server Login IDs

A Server login account is required for every individual who wishes to access the Server. The login account consists of three components—a server login ID, an associated password, and a **default database**. The login ID is any identifier that uniquely identifies the individual to the Server. The password can be any string that conforms to identifier rules. The default database for a login id is the database you are placed in when you first connect to the Server.

Login ids are created by the SA using the `sp_addlogin` system procedure. They can also be created through the SAF by selecting the Login id menu under the Admin menu. The `sp_addlogin` procedure has three parameters corresponding to the three components of a login account; however, the password and default database are optional and are set to NULL and *master*, respectively, if they are not provided. The syntax follows.

Syntax

```
sp_addlogin <login_id> [, <password> [, default_db>]]
```

For example, if the SA wants to add a login ID *jackm* (for Jack Mack) with the password *smooth,* he can use the syntax in Example 9-1. Since he did not specify a default database, it will default to *master*.

Example 9-1

```
sp_addlogin jackm, smooth

OUTPUT:

New login created.
```

Once a login account has been created, the SA, or the user himself can change his password or default database at any time using the `sp_password` or `sp_defaultdb` system procedures. The same actions can also be performed through menu selections in the SAF. The syntax of the two procedures follows.

Syntax

```
sp_password <old_password>, <new_password> [, <login_id>]
sp_defaultdb <login_id>, <default_db>
```

Since only the SA can alter any user's password, the third parameter on the `sp_password` procedure is optional. The SA can also specify NULL for the `<old_password>` parameter, no matter what the actual password is. The SA can change Jack's password to *shutout* and his default database to *pubs*, as follows:

Example 9-2

```
sp_password null, shutout, jackm
<exec>
```

```
sp_defaultdb jackm, pubs
<exec>

OUTPUT:

Password changed.
Default database changed.
```

A special predefined Server login ID *sa* is created at installation and recognized by the Server as the system administrator or SA. The SA is the super-user or overall administrator of the Server and is responsible for installation, managing users, storage management, backup and recovery, performance tuning, and so on. There is no checking for permissions for anyone logged in as *sa*. When the Server is first installed, there is no password assigned for the login ID *sa*, so it should be changed to something else to prevent other users from logging on as the SA.

The login account information for a Server is stored in the *syslogins* system table, which is part of the system catalog. There is no system procedure (such as `sp_helplogins`) to return all the login account information for a Server, but it is easy enough to query the *syslogins* table as follows.

Example 9-3

```
use master
<exec>
select LOGINID = name, PASSWORD = password, DEFAULTDB = dbname
from syslogins
<exec>

OUTPUT:

LOGINID                        PASSWORD                       DEFAULTDB
------------------------------ ------------------------------ --------------------
sa                             sqldba                         master
probe                          NULL                           master
anath                          sqldba                         pubs
aloke                          NULL                           master
mary                           NULL                           master
jackm                          shutout                        pubs

(6 rows affected)
```

Database User Names

It was stated earlier that every login id at the Server level must be defined as a database user name in the database the user needs to access. This allows an individual access to the database through a USE statement, or as the default database when he or she first connects to the Server. The `sp_addlogin` or `sp_defaultdb` procedures do not check to see if the login ID is defined as a database user in the default database; if the user does not have access to the database, an error occurs, and the user is put in *master*. Allowing a user access to a particular database does not mean he or she can access the objects in that database. The ability to perform operations on a database object and to create and drop database objects is controlled by special privileges. A privilege is permission to perform an operation on some object. All privileges in SQL Server must be explicitly granted; by default a user has no privileges. Even the privilege to use a database must be granted by the database owner, who does so by adding the user to the database. Figure 9-1 shows the two-level Server user authentication scheme.

Users are added to a database through the `sp_adduser` system procedure. The `sp_adduser` procedure maps a specific login id to a user name in the database; the procedure must be executed from that database. Users are dropped using the `sp_dropuser` system procedure. Users can also be added through the SAF using the Manage usernames menu within the Admin menu.

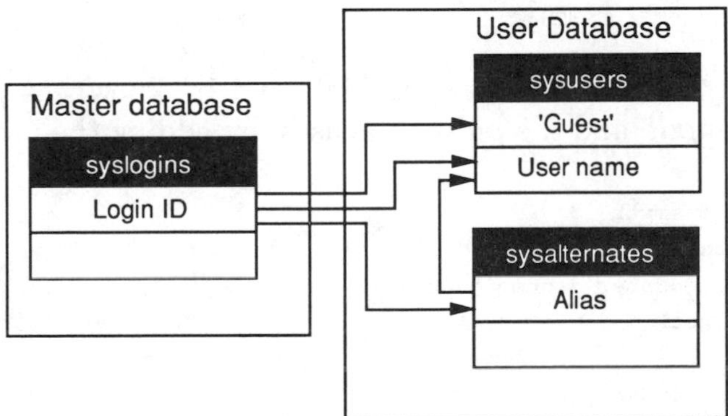

FIGURE 9-1 Server login IDs and database user names

Syntax

```
sp_adduser <login_id> [, <user_name> [, <group_name>]]
sp_dropuser <user_name>
```

If the <user_name> parameter is not supplied, it defaults to the login id. The <group_name> parameter specifies the group to which the user belongs. (Groups will be discussed in the next section.) If no group is specified, the user becomes part of the *public* group. Inside the database, the Server login ID is known by his or her database user name. For example, you can add the Server login ID *jackm* as the database user *ackm* in the *empdb* database and as *jackmack* in the *pubs* database.

Example 9-4

```
use empdb
<exec>
sp_adduser jackm
<exec>

use pubs
<exec>
sp_adduser jackm, jackmack
<exec>

OUTPUT:

New user added.
New user added.
```

Alternatively, *jackm* could be known as *jack* in both the *empdb* and the *pubs* databases, by adding the users as follows.

```
use empdb
<exec>
sp_adduser jackm, jack
<exec>

use pubs
<exec>
sp_adduser jackm, jack
```

```
<exec>

OUTPUT:

New user added.
New user added.
```

User names that are no longer needed can be deleted using the `sp_dropuser` system procedure. Users who own objects in the database cannot be dropped; the ownership must be changed or the objects dropped. For example, if the user name *Jack* is no longer needed in the *pubs* database, you can drop it as follows:

Example 9-5

```
use pubs
go
sp_dropuser jack
go

OUTPUT:

User has been dropped from current database.
```

There are two special user names that bear discussion. The first is *dbo*, which represents the database owner (DBO) of any database. The owner of the database has the user name *dbo* inside his or her database. Thus if Mary owns the *persondb* database, she is the DBO of the *persondb* database. The DBO generally is responsible for his or her database, allowing other users access to it, defining permissions to create objects in the it, setting up groups, and so on. The DBO inherits this set of default privileges for the database. The next section discusses these default privileges in further detail.

The other special user name is guest. Any valid Server login ID can access a database as a *guest*, even if he or she is not defined as a valid user in that database. Authorization to log in to a Server does not necessarily imply access to any database on that Server. The guest user mechanism is a convenient way to allow individuals with valid Server login accounts to access a database on the Server, without being defined as a user in that database. Often, it is impossible for the DBO to know at the outset all the login ids that may need access to the database. In fact, this is the mechanism whereby login ids are allowed access to the *master* and the *pubs* databases. The *guest* user name is added just as any other user name is (with the `sp_adduser` system procedure). Guest users are typically assigned limited permissions, since any login ID may access the database as the guest user.

Groups

The Server allows the definition of **groups** within a database. A group is a mechanism to assign the same privileges to several database users. The group is collectively granted privileges, in the same way they are granted to individual users. Every user in that group then inherits those privileges. The same result is obtained if you grant each individual user in the group the same privileges, but it is a time consuming and error-prone task, especially if the number of users is large.

A user can be assigned to a group when he or she is added to the database or at some later time. If no group is specified at user creation time, the user defaults to a special group called *public*. The public group is a predefined group in every database. Groups are added to a database using the `sp_addgroup` system procedure and dropped using the `sp_dropgroup` system procedure. However, the group must contain no users when it is dropped.

Syntax

```
sp_addgroup <group_name>
sp_dropgroup <group_name>
```

For example, if you want to allow certain individuals (John, Mary, and Sue) specific privileges to act as book reviewers, you can create a group called *reviewers* in the *pubs* database. You add *john, mary,* and *sue* as user names to the *pubs* database and assign them to the group *reviewers.* This eases the task of granting or revoking privileges to all reviewers.

Example 9-6

```
use pubs
<exec>
sp_addgroup reviewers
<exec>
sp_adduser john, john, reviewers
<exec>
sp_adduser mary, mary, reviewers
<exec>
sp_adduser sue, sue, reviewers
<exec>

OUTPUT:

New group added.
New user added.
New user added.
New user added.
```

The user's group assignment can always be changed later using the `sp_changegroup` system procedure. A user can belong to only one group, so changing a user to a new group removes him or her from the previous group.

Syntax

```
sp_changegroup <group>, <user_name>
```

The `sp_changegroup` procedure assumes that the group already exists. If you decide at some point that Sue should no longer have the privileges of a reviewer, you can drop her from the *reviewers* group by assigning her back to the *public* group. Later if you decide you don't need the *reviewers* group at all, you can drop the group itself, after dropping users *mary* and *john* from the group or changing them to another group.

Example 9-7

```
use pubs
<exec>
sp_changegroup 'public', sue
```

```
<exec>
sp_dropuser mary
<exec>
sp_dropuser john
<exec>
sp_dropgroup reviewers
<exec>

OUTPUT:

Group changed.
User has been dropped from current database.
User has been dropped from current database.
Group has been dropped.
```

Information on groups is recorded in the *sysusers* system table and can be obtained using the `sp_helpgroup` system procedure. If information on a specific group is requested, the users in the group are listed. If the `<group>` parameter is left out, all groups in the current database are listed.

Syntax

```
sp_helpgroup [<group>]
```

For example, if you run `sp_helpgroup` after you add the three reviewers to the *pubs* database, you will see the result shown in Example 9-8.

Example 9-8

```
sp_helpgroup reviewers

OUTPUT:

Group_name                Group_id Users_in_group            Userid
------------------------- -------- ------------------------- ------
reviewers                    16384 john                           3
reviewers                    16384 mary                           4
reviewers                    16384 sue                            5

(3 rows affected)
```

Aliases

An **alias** allows a login id to assume the identity of a user within the database. In this way, more than one login ID can be mapped to the same user name. The purpose of the alias is to allow an individual to assume the identity of some database user without the DBO having to add him or her as a user in the database. It is typically used in temporary situations. For example, if a temporary payroll administrator is filling in for the regular administrator, the person can be aliased to the user name of the regular administrator. Aliases can also be used to allow multiple login IDs to serve as the DBO of a database.

Aliases are created through the `sp_addalias` system procedure and dropped using the `sp_dropalias` system procedure. A login ID cannot be aliased to a user, if the user already exists in the database. An individual can be aliased to only one user at a time. If you want to be aliased to another user, you first must drop the existing alias.

Syntax

```
sp_addalias <login_id>, <user_name>
sp_dropalias <login_id>
```

For example, if Jack is filling in for Mary you can alias *jackm* to mary in *pubs* (provided he is not an existing user in that database).

Example 9-9

```
use pubs
<exec>
sp_addalias jackm, mary
<exec>

OUTPUT:

Alias user added.
```

Aliases are dropped using the `sp_dropalias` system procedure. For example, if you want to remove *jackm* as an alias to *mary* (since she is back from vacation), you can do the following.

Example 9-10

```
use pubs
<exec>
sp_dropalias jackm
<exec>

OUTPUT:

Alias user dropped.
```

You can find all users aliased to a user name in a database by using the `sp_helpuser` system procedure. The user name must be specified, or `sp_helpuser` returns all the user names in the current database. Alias information is recorded in the *sysalternates* system table.

Example 9-11

```
use pubs
<exec>
sp_helpuser dbo
<exec>

OUTPUT:

Users_name        ID_in_db Group_name        Login_name        Default_db
----------------- -------- ----------------- ----------------- ---------------
dbo                      1 public            sa                master

(0 rows affected)
```

User Levels

Several ways to identify users have been covered in the last few sections. Before discussing permissions, this section briefly discusses the levels, or classes of users that SQL Server recognizes. In SQL Server, the ability to grant certain permissions depends on a user's class. These different classes exist in a hierarchy, with the SA at the top and regular users at the bottom. The SA has, by default, privileges to do anything. On the other end, regular users have no privileges unless they are explicitly granted. As you go up the user class hierarchy, the set of privileges increases, as shown in Figure 9-2.

At the top of the hierarchy is the SA, who logs in with the special Server login ID *sa*. When the SA logs in, SQL Server does not check any permissions. The SA therefore has default permissions on everything. Initially when the Server is installed certain permissions default to the SA. Some of these privileges can be transferred to other database users, while others belong only to the SA and cannot be granted to other users.

The next level down in the hierarchy is the database owner. The DBO owns and is responsible for his or her database on the Server. This responsibility includes defining users, permissions, groups, and so on, for the database. In many database environments the SA and several DBOs together make up what is sometimes referred to as the database administrator (DBA). It is important to think of the SA and the DBO more as roles than persons since, in many cases, they all are assumed by one person. The SA may also be the DBO of all the databases on the Server. The SA is always the DBO of the *master* database. The concept of the DBO is important. Because SQL Server supports a large number of databases on one Server, the SA may want to assign different individuals (login IDs) to be DBOs of different databases on the server.

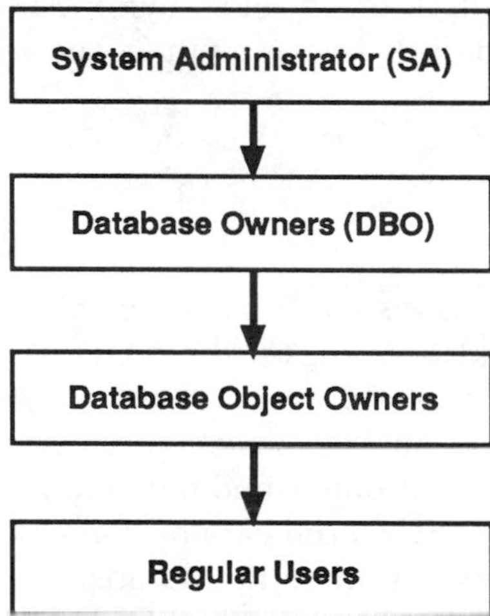

FIGURE 9-2 User levels

You can become a DBO in one of two ways. The first is for the SA to make you one. The SA creates a database and then transfers ownership to you (through a `sp_changedbowner` system procedure). The second is by actually creating a database, assuming you have the required permission to do so. This is in accordance with the principle that the creator of an object is its owner. The permissions that are required to do this are discussed in the next section. The DBO has global permissions on his or her database and on any owned objects in it. The SA is treated as the DBO, and has the same privileges as the DBO in each of the databases on the Server.

The next level down in the hierarchy consists of owners of database objects (tables, views, procedures, and so on). An object is owned by the database user who creates it. By default, the owner of an object has all permissions on that object. All other database users, including the DBO, must be explicitly granted permission to use that object. The DBO can get around this restriction by using the SETUSER statement (discussed later) to assume the identity of any user in the database.

At the lowest level in the hierarchy are the regular database users. These are users who do not own any databases or database objects and do not have any privileges other than those inherited by membership in a group or those explicitly granted to them by other users (the SA, DBO, or object owners). All database users belong to a group; by default they are put in the *public* group.

Permissions

SQL Server's permissions system is based on the concept of object ownership. Every object (including the database itself) in a database is owned by a user. The creator of an object is its owner and, by default, has all privileges on that object. Any other database user has no privileges to use that object and must be granted privileges explicitly in order to use it. In the case of databases, the creators can transfer their ownership after the databases are created. All permissions in SQL Server apply only to the database in which they are assigned. For example, if Mike has permission to create tables in the *pubs* database, he does not automatically have the right to create tables in the any other database.

There are two kinds of permissions that can be assigned to users in SQL Server. They are **statement permissions** and **object permissions**. A statement permission allows a database user to execute a particular TRANSACT-SQL language statement within that database, for example, permission to issue the CREATE TABLE statement in the *empdb* database. An object permission, on the other hand, allows a user to perform an operation specifically on that object, for example, permission to INSERT rows into the *authors* table in the *pubs* database. Both statement and object permissions are controlled through the GRANT and REVOKE statements. The GRANT statement is used to assign permissions and the REVOKE statement to take away permissions.

Statement Permissions

A statement permission defines which users can execute a particular Database language statement in the database. It is generally used to control which users can define database objects within the database, and applies mostly to such data definition statements as CREATE TABLE and CREATE RULE. Statement permissions can be granted for the following statements:

CREATE DATABASE
CREATE DEFAULT
CREATE PROCEDURE
CREATE RULE
CREATE TABLE
CREATE VIEW
DUMP DATABASE
DUMP TRANSACTION

Because creating a database allocates space for the database, it is a restricted statement–initially, only the SA has CREATE DATABASE permission. In certain Server environments the SA may want to delegate this responsibility to other users, in which case they can be granted CREATE DATABASE permission. The ALTER DATABASE statement permission, which can be used to increase the allocated space for a database, is transferred with CREATE DATABASE permission. Certain other statement permissions, such as CREATE INDEX and CREATE TRIGGER, belong only to the owner of the table on which it is defined and cannot be granted to other users.

Statement permissions are assigned with the GRANT and REVOKE syntax that follows. The keyword ALL in the syntax can be used only by the SA to indicate permission to execute all statements. This is because the ALL keyword includes the CREATE DATABASE permission, which can only be granted by the SA. If several statement permissions need to be granted or revoked, they can be listed in a single GRANT or REVOKE statement, separated by commas. The name list can include as many users and groups as needed. The keyword PUBLIC is not the same as the *public* group. It indicates all users in the current database regardless of their group, not all users who are members of the group *public*.

Syntax

```
GRANT {ALL | <statement_list>}
     TO {PUBLIC | <name_list>}

REVOKE {ALL | <statement_list>}
     FROM {PUBLIC | <name_list>}
```

For example, if the SA wants to give John permission to use all of the statements in the *pubs* database and Mary and Sue only the CREATE TABLE and CREATE VIEW permissions, the following GRANT statement accomplishes this.

Example 9-12

```
use pubs
<exec>
grant all to John
grant create table, create view to Mary, Sue
<exec>

OUTPUT:
```

Later, if the DBO decides that Mary is usurping the space allocated to the *pubs* database, he or she can revoke the CREATE TABLE permission from her as follows.

Example 9-13

```
revoke create table from mary
```

```
OUTPUT:
```

Object Permissions

Object permissions define the operations that users can perform on database objects. An object permission can be granted only by the object owner. These permissions define which DML statements can be executed against these objects. The exact statements that apply to the different objects are as follows.

Database object	**Statement**
Table	SELECT, INSERT, UPDATE, DELETE
View	SELECT, INSERT, UPDATE, DELETE
Column	SELECT, UPDATE
Procedure	EXECUTE

In contrast to statement permissions, object permissions are specific to the database object on which they are defined. Thus if Joe is given permission to SELECT from table *authors*, it does not imply that he has SELECT permission on other tables in the *pubs* database. On the other hand if Joe has CREATE TABLE permission in the *pubs* database, he can create a table with any name within the *pubs* database. Notice that SQL Server allows both SELECT and UPDATE permission to be defined to the granularity of columns. A column is, strictly speaking, not a database object since it does not exist by itself and is known only in the context of a table or view. However, SELECT and UPDATE permissions are definable at the level of a column. Of course, INSERT and DELETE permissions don't make sense on columns since they only add or delete rows. The EXECUTE permission gives the user permission to execute a stored procedure.

Object permissions, like statement permissions, are assigned with the GRANT and REVOKE statements. However, the syntax is slightly different for assigning object permissions.

Syntax

```
GRANT {ALL | <statement_list>}
     ON {<table> | <view> | <procedure>} [( <column_list> )]
     TO {PUBLIC | <name_list>}

REVOKE {ALL | <statement_list>}
     ON {<table> | <view> | <procedure>} [( <column_list> )]
     FROM {PUBLIC | <name_list>}
```

The `<statement_list>` parameter consists of the statements the users in the `<user_list>` parameter can perform on the objects (tables, views, columns, and procedures). The syntax allows certain combinations of statements on objects that are not legal. For example, it would not make sense to EXECUTE a table. Apart from that, the syntax of the GRANT and REVOKE statements for assigning object permissions is very similar to that for assigning statement permissions. As before, groups can be substituted for user names, and the keyword PUBLIC indicates all users in the current database, regardless of their group.

Granting a user a certain privilege does not give that user the right to confer that privilege to some other user. For example, if Joe is granted UPDATE permission on the *authors* table, he does not inherit the right to grant this permission to Mary. In some SQL implementations (for example, DB2), the WITH GRANT option is supported on the GRANT statement that provides this capability. In these systems, the REVOKE statement is recursive, so if Joe grants a privilege to other users and his privilege is revoked, the privilege is automatically revoked from the other users.

Here is an example of assigning object permissions. Assume that john and mary both belong to the reviewers group, and Sue belongs to the public group. You want the reviewers to have read access to all author information. Sue's job is to maintain the author information. The DBO decides that Sue should have SELECT (read) access to the *authors* table and INSERT and UPDATE permissions (on all columns), but no delete permission. Example 9-14 shows one way to assign the permissions.

Example 9-14

```
use pubs
<exec>

grant select on authors to reviewers
grant select, insert, update on authors to sue
<exec>
```

```
OUTPUT:
```

Note that the group name *reviewers* is used instead of the user names *john* and *mary,* since this is easier. Of course, this assumes that John and Mary are the only reviewers. If they are not, John and Mary must be named specifically to avoid assigning permission to the entire *reviewers* group. As noted earlier, you can grant and revoke multiple permissions in the same GRANT or REVOKE statement. The same is true for multiple users. Thus both Mary and John can be given both SELECT and UPDATE permission on *authors* in the same GRANT statement.

Example 9-15

```
GRANT SELECT, UPDATE ON authors TO mary, john
```

```
OUTPUT:
```

Permissions in SQL Server are cumulative; multiple GRANT and REVOKE statements simply add or delete privileges from the user's current set of privileges. A user can possess a set of default privileges by virtue his or her position in the user hierarchy. For example, the DBO always has CREATE TABLE permission in the database. A regular user, however, has no default privileges except those inherited from the group and so must be granted any additional privileges. There are several ways to assign a user the required privileges (some easier than others). For example, you can grant Sue the same set of privileges as in Example 9-14, using the statements as shown in Example 9-16 and 9-17.

Example 9-16

```
grant select on authors to sue
grant insert on authors to sue
```

```
grant update on authors to sue
```

```
OUTPUT:
```

Or you can give her ALL permissions (SELECT, INSERT, UPDATE, DELETE) on the *authors* table and then take away the DELETE permission, yielding exactly the same privilege set.

Example 9-17

```
grant all on authors to sue
revoke delete on authors from sue
```

```
OUTPUT:
```

In the same way, if *sue* is the only user you don't want to grant access to the *publishers* table, it is easy first to grant all users in the database SELECT access to the *publishers* table and then to revoke SELECT permission from *sue*.

Example 9-18

```
grant select on publishers to public
revoke select on publishers from sue
```

```
OUTPUT:
```

You can think of a user's privileges as a bag of goodies. Every GRANT statement adds goodies to the bag; every REVOKE statement takes away some.

Care should be taken when you assign permissions—the order in which the GRANT and REVOKE statements are executed affects the results. Two points should be remembered when you assign permissions. First, the permissions assigned to a group override the permissions assigned to individual members of the group. If you had assigned different permissions to the members of the *reviewers* group on the *titles* table, and you want to standardize their permissions, you can do so as shown in Example 9-19.

Example 9-19

```
revoke all on titles from reviewers
grant select on titles (title_id, title, type, pub_id, notes)
```

```
        to reviewers
```

```
OUTPUT:
```

The second point is that the keyword PUBLIC in GRANT and REVOKE statements includes all users, including the user assigning or revoking the permissions. If Sue executes the REVOKE statement that follows, she is left with no SELECT or UPDATE permission on *authors*.

Example 9-20

```
revoke select, update on titles from public
```

```
OUTPUT:
```

Information on Permissions

There are two kinds of information you are likely to need with respect to permissions. The first is the set of statement and object permissions that have been granted a particular user. The second is the set of users who have of permissions for a particular object. Both kinds of information can be obtained by the `sp_helprotect` system procedure. The syntax follows.

Syntax

```
sp_helprotect <object> [, <user>]
```

Example 9-21 shows the different forms of output that can be returned by `sp_helprotect`. The first part shows all the permissions defined on the *titles* table; the second shows all permissions possessed by Sue; the third shows the intersection of the two—permissions that Sue has on *titles*.

Example 9-21

```
sp_helprotect titles
<exec>
sp_helprotect sue
<exec>
sp_helprotect authors, sue
```

```
<exec>

OUTPUT:

type   action              user           column
------ ------------------- -------------- ---------
Grant  Delete              guest          All
Grant  Insert              guest          All
Revoke Delete              reviewers      All
Revoke Insert              reviewers      All
Revoke Select              public         All
Revoke Update              public         All

(6 rows affected)
type   action              object         column
------ ------------------- -------------- ---------
Grant  Create Table                       All
Grant  Create View                        All
Grant  Insert              authors        All
Grant  Select              authors        All
Grant  Update              authors        All
Revoke Delete              authors        All
Revoke Select              publishers     All

(7 rows affected)
type   action              user           column
------ ------------------- -------------- ---------
Grant  Insert              sue            All
Grant  Select              sue            All
Grant  Update              sue            All
Revoke Delete              sue            All

(4 rows affected)
```

Special User Privileges

Certain users—the SA, DBOs, and object owners—by virtue of their user class automatically inherit a set of default privileges. Some of these privileges can be given away to other users and some cannot. In general, the higher up you are in the user hierarchy, the more privileges you have.

The SA has permissions for everything. This includes several statements that are intended primarily for server administration, which only the SA can execute. Permission to execute them cannot be granted to other users. The complete set is:

CREATE DATABASE
ALTER DATABASE
DROP DATABASE
DISK INIT
DISK REINIT
DISK REFIT
KILL
RECONFIGURE

Permission to execute a CREATE DATABASE statement can be granted to other users. The ALTER DATABASE permission cannot be granted separately, but if a user is granted CREATE DATABASE permission, he or she automatically inherits the ALTER DATABASE permission. DROP DATABASE permission belongs to the DBO and cannot be transferred. Permission to execute the remaining statements (and several system procedures of a sensitive nature that are not listed here but are discussed later in this chapter and Chapter 10) belong only to the SA and cannot be transferred to other users.

The DBO, in general, inherits all statement permissions for the database, with or without CREATE DATABASE permission. Most of the statement permissions can be granted to other users; there are a few that cannot. The default set of DBO privileges is listed here. An X in the Grantable column indicates the privilege can be granted to other users.

Statement	**Grantable**
CREATE TABLE	X
CREATE VIEW	X
CREATE DEFAULT	X
CREATE RULE	X

CREATE PROCEDURE	X
DUMP DATABASE	X
DUMP TRANSACTION	X
GRANT and REVOKE (Object)	X
CHECKPOINT	
DBCC	
DROP DATABASE	
GRANT and REVOKE (Statement)	
LOAD DATABASE	
LOAD TRANSACTION	
SETUSER	

The SA assumes the identity of the DBO in every database and, hence, can assign any privileges that are grantable. The DBO has global permission in the database, except for objects created by other users. To access these objects, even the DBO must be granted the appropriate object permissions. Of course, the DBO can assume the role of any user in the database by using the SETUSER statement and, thus, perform any operation on that object. The SETUSER privilege is not transferable. If it were, the DBO could relinquish control of the database and lose it altogether.

Object owners have all privileges on their objects; the common object privileges (EXECUTE, SELECT, INSERT, UPDATE, DELETE) can be granted to other users. In fact, any other user, even the DBO, must be granted these privileges before he or she can use that object. Some privileges default to the object owner and cannot be transferred. For example, permission to drop an object belongs only to the object owner and is not transferable. The permission to TRUNCATE a table is another permission that cannot be transferred. Certain statement permissions to create related objects are inherited by the object owner. They cannot be transferred. For example, the owner of a table is the only user who can create an index or trigger on that table. The following is a list of privileges that default to the object owner. The Grantable column indicates which are transferable.

Statement	**Grantable**
ALTER TABLE	X
CREATE INDEX	

CREATE TRIGGER	
DROP (any object)	
GRANT (any object)	X
REVOKE (any object)	X
TRUNCATE TABLE	
UPDATE STATISTICS	
All object privileges	X

Permissions on System Tables and Procedures

When SQL Server is installed, the permissions on system tables are set up so that all users in user databases have permission to read the system tables. However, no update permissions (INSERT, UPDATE and DELETE) are granted to any user, including the DBO. This is to prevent direct updates to a system table, which could inadvertently compromise its integrity. As a result, all updates to the system tables are either performed through DDL statements directly or through system procedures that guarantee the integrity of their updates, as discussed in Chapter 7. The same is true for most of the system tables in *master*; all users can read them. Users do not have permission to read such sensitive information as passwords, contained in the *password* column of the *syslogins* system table.

Permissions on system procedures, as discussed in Chapter 7, are controlled in the master database, where the procedures are defined. Certain system procedures, such as those for adding and dropping logins or devices, can be executed only by the SA. Permission to execute them cannot be transferred. Other system procedures, such as those for adding or dropping users, can be executed only by the DBO. These procedures prevent any one other than the DBO of the current database from executing them. Users can be granted permission to execute these procedures in all databases, or in none. If a user name is not in *master*, the user is treated as the guest user, thereby automatically receiving EXECUTE permission on several system procedures such as all the sp_helpxxx procedures. To deny a user access to a stored procedure, the SA must first add the user to the master database and then revoke permission to execute that procedure from that user in *master*. For example, if you do not want Mary to look at database related information on the Server, you can execute the following statements.

Example 9-22

```
use master
<exec>
sp_adduser mary
<exec>
revoke execute on sp_helpdb from mary
<exec>

OUTPUT:

New user added.
```

Permissions with Dependent Objects

With dependent objects, such as views and procedures, it is not sufficient to check the permissions defined on the object only. Views can depend on other views or tables for their definition, and procedures can depend on other procedures, tables, or views for their definition. Checking permissions for dependent objects is not as simple as checking permissions on a table, because the object owners of a series of dependent objects may be different. For example, John can own procedure `titles_proc` which retrieves data from the view *title_view* owned by Mary, which depends on the titles table owned by Sue. If John grants Dave permission to execute his procedure, is Dave allowed indirectly to reference *title_view* and *titles* by executing the procedure?

The answer, of course, depends on whether Dave has been granted the appropriate permissions by Mary (who owns the view) and Sue (who owns the table). This series of object owners is often referred to as an ownership chain. If permissions on all dependent objects were to be checked, the process would be very time consuming, affecting performance adversely. SQL Server optimizes performance by not checking permissions in a dependent object chain if the corresponding owners are the same user. If there is a change of owners in the ownership chain or if there is a reference to an object in another database in the dependent object chain, the entire chain is checked for appropriate permissions.

In the scenario depicted in Figure 9-3, SQL Server checks to see if Dave has the appropriate SELECT permission on `titles_view` and on the *titles* table, since they both have different owners. If John owns both `titles_proc` and the *titles_view* table, and Dave executes the procedure `titles_proc`, SQL Server checks to see if Dave has the required permissions on only the `titles-_proc` procedure and the *titles* table.

Permissions management can get very complex, especially if the number of dependent objects gets large. As a general guideline, therefore, it is advisable to reduce administrative nightmares by

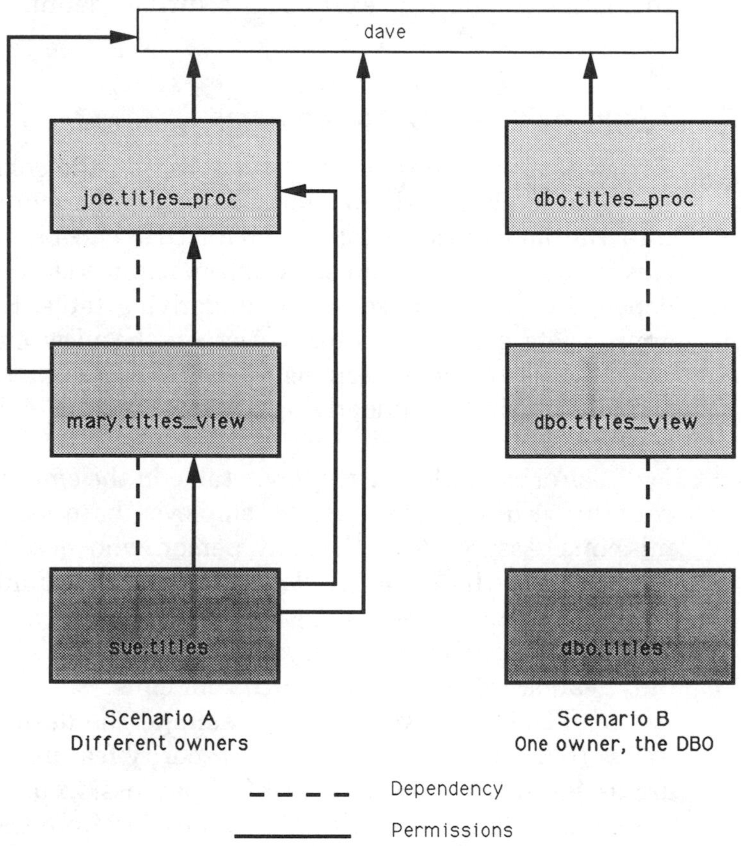

FIGURE 9-3 Ownership chains for the two scenarios

keeping ownership chains simple. In fact, it is highly recommended that—unless there is a good reason to do otherwise—all objects should be owned by the DBO, as shown in the second scenario in Figure 9-3.

Other Security Mechanisms

In addition to the security mechanisms discussed so far, views and stored procedures can also be used for security purposes in that they can limit access to data. In Chapter 7, it was suggested how this is done; here it is examined in further detail.

Views as Security Mechanisms

A view is a derived table that is a subset of the columns and rows in one or more underlying tables. A view is therefore like a window into the underlying data; only data that can be viewed through this window are accessible. Permissions on views are defined independently from those on the underlying table. By defining the appropriate permissions for a user on the view and revoking all permissions on the underlying tables, you can limit a user's access to the data in the underlying tables. Figure 9-4 illustrates this concept.

For example, the *employee* table in the *empdb* database may contain such sensitive data as employee base salaries and commissions. Assume that the only person who needs to retrieve or modify all of the employee data is the salary administrator, Sue. All other users of the database should not have access to the two sensitive columns, base salary and commission. They should have only read access to the rest of the columns.

There are several ways to achieve the desired results. One way is to use SQL Server's regular security features. First, all users are assigned the required SELECT permission on the entire employee table. Then the SELECT permission from the two sensitive columns is revoked. Finally Sue is granted the additional permissions.

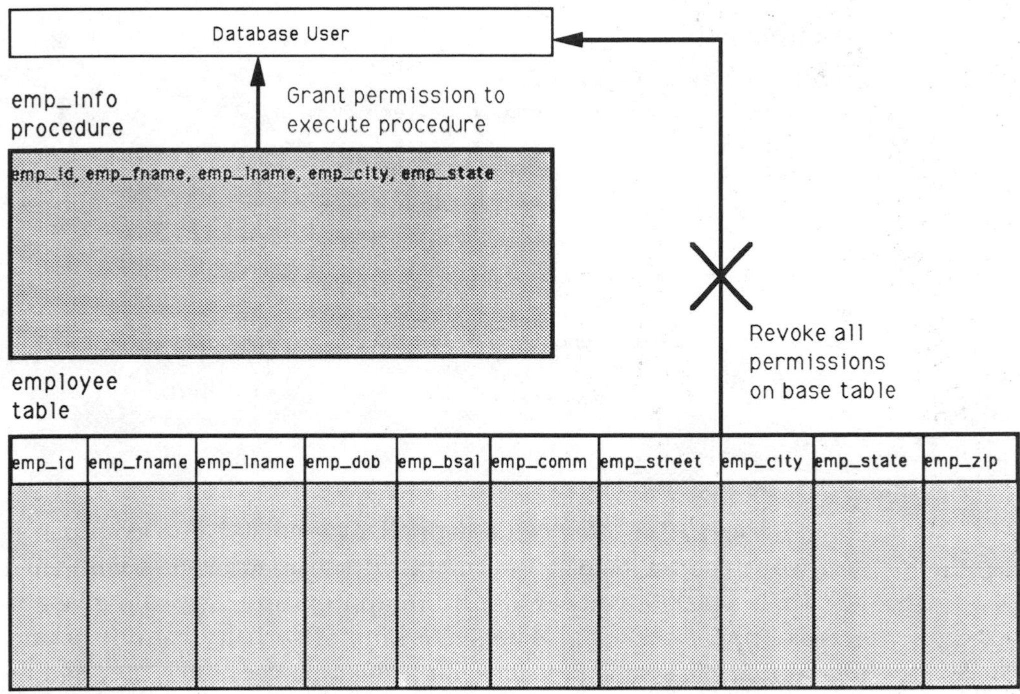

FIGURE 9-4 Views for security

Example 9-23

```
grant select on employee to public
revoke select on employee(emp_bsal, emp_comm) from public
grant select, insert, update, delete on employee to sue

OUTPUT:
```

Another way to achieve the same effect is to define a view on the *employee* table that excludes the sensitive columns. You then grant the appropriate permission on the view and deny access to the underlying table. In fact, users need not even know that *emp_view* is in fact a view (if it weren't so obviously named), or that the salary and commission columns even exist. Any user, other than Sue, who tries to access the employee table directly receives a permission-denied error.

Example 9-24

```
create view emp_view as
select emp_id, emp_lname, emp_fname, emp_dob,
       emp_street, emp_city, emp_state, emp_zip
from employee
<exec>

revoke all on employee from public
grant select on emp_view to public
grant select, insert, update, delete on employee to sue
<exec>

OUTPUT:
```

Views also offer value-dependent security. For example, if you want Joe to look at only data on those employees who earn less than $40,000, you can define an appropriate view and give Joe access only to the view. The same kind of security cannot be implemented using object permissions on employee, since they can be defined only at the table or column level.

Stored Procedures as Security Mechanisms

Security can also be provided through stored procedures in much the same way as through views. Since a stored procedure is user defined, the user can specify explicit legal operations within it. By granting users permission to execute the stored procedure and denying access to the underlying tables or views, the user's access to the tables can be controlled. Figure 9-5 illustrates how stored procedures work as security mechanisms.

For example, a stored procedure can be written to retrieve an employee's information, while leaving out such sensitive information as base salary and commissions. Users can then be allowed to access employee information only through the procedure, as shown in Example 9-25.

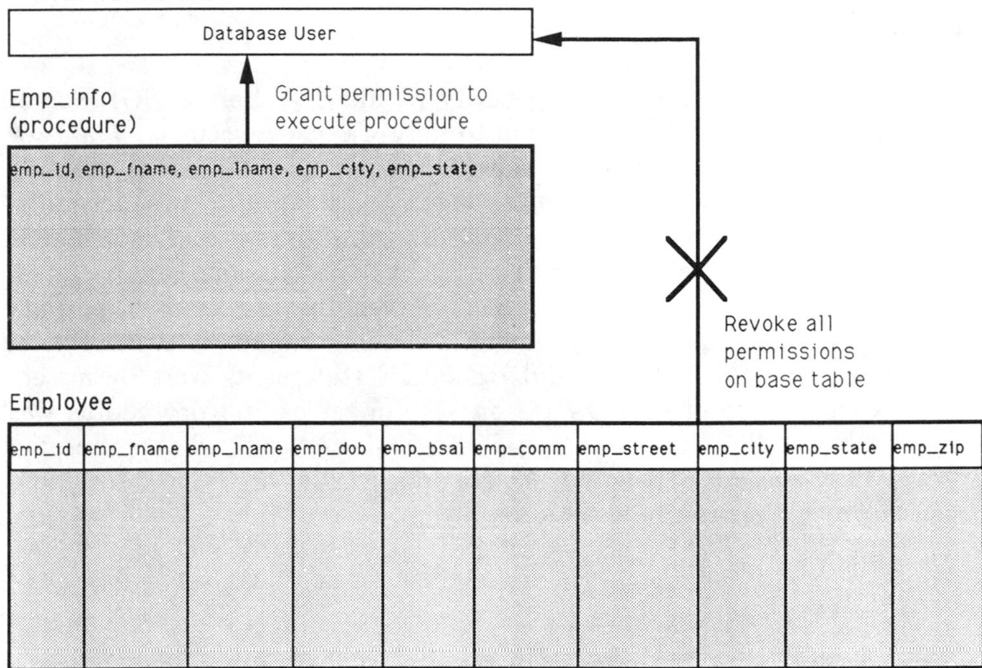

FIGURE 9-5 Stored procedures for security

Example 9-25

```
create procedure emp_info
    @empid_end int, @empid_start int = 0
as
select emp_id, emp_lname, emp_fname,emp_city, emp_state
from employee
where emp_id between @empid_start and @empid_end
<exec>

revoke all on employee from public
grant exec on emp_info to public
<exec>

OUTPUT:
```

Summary

This chapter focused on security within SQL Server. SQL Server provides security in addition to network or OS security. The two-level user authentication scheme used in SQL Server consists of Server login IDs and database user names. Groups, guest accounts, and aliases; their purposes and use were discussed. The different classes of users and the user hierarchy of permissions were outlined. The permission system in SQL Server, the two kinds of permissions—statement and object permissions—and how to control them through the GRANT and REVOKE statements were discussed. The set up of permissions on system tables and procedures was shown. The chapter discussed how SQL Server handles permission checking for dependent objects and, finally, how views and store procedures can be used for security.

CHAPTER
10

Server Installation and Storage Management

Introduction

The rest of the book deals with the operational aspects of SQL Server—installation and device management, transaction management, database backup and recovery, and tuning the Server. This chapter concentrates on the basic tasks of installing the Server and managing storage for its environment. Installing the Server by itself is a simple task, but it requires a fair amount of insight into several products for everything to function correctly and optimally. They include OS/2, the LAN operating system, SQL Server itself, and client application. Storage must be managed by allocating the devices and databases, loading and backing up the databases, and tuning and diagnosing space problems within the Server environment.

Not every user needs to be concerned with these issues. However, there should at least be one user, the SA, at every Server installation who is responsible for these issues. The SA can be thought of as a role that can be filled by one or more persons. The SA can be the same person as the network administrator, although this not common in installations with large LANs and numerous databases.

The SA is responsible for the overall Server environment—global Server issues such as installation, device management, user management, security issues, and database backup and recovery. In most DBMSs, especially those that support a single database per Server, the role of SA is more commonly referred to as the database administrator (DBA). In SQL Server, the traditional role of the DBA is broken into the roles of the SA and the individual database owners (DBOs), who may or may not be the same individual as the SA. The Server usually is installed by the SA.

Installation, Startup, and Shutdown

SQL Server is based on client/server architecture. The Server is the back-end component. The front-end component can be any application that provides SQL Server support, for example, a standard application such as a workstation DBMS, spreadsheet, word processor, or a custom application developed for the SQL Server environment (using the DB-LIBRARY API provided). The next section covers installation; the following section looks at various ways to start and shut down the Server.

Installation

An installation in the SQL Server environment is divided into two components: a back-end, or Server installation and a front-end, or client, installation. There can be more than one different front-end installation depending on which client applications are being installed. This section discusses the installation of the server and two client applications, isql and SAF, which are supplied with the SQL Server software.

Installing the SQL Server itself is a fairly straightforward process, provided all the other required software has been installed first, and it has the appropriate configuration. As many of you who have tried to install it may know, it can be more of a task than you would have thought.

SQL Server runs on top of both the operating system and the network operating system, as shown in Figure 10-1. Both OS/2 and the appropriate network software must be installed before SQL Server can be installed. The exact requirements for running SQL Server are provided in Appendix A.

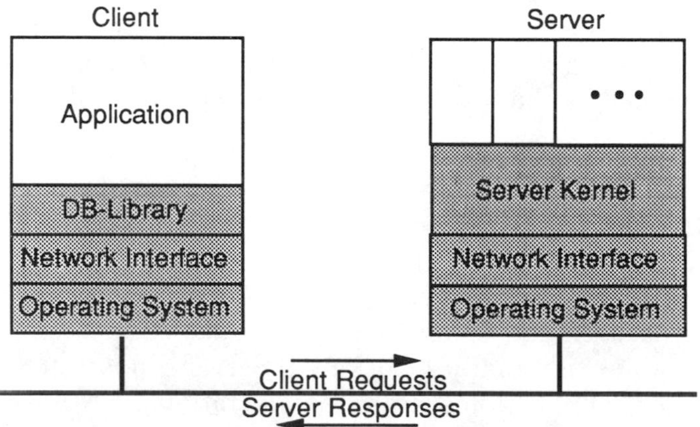

FIGURE 10-1. Server environment

In networks compatible with LAN Manager, this means installing the LAN Manager server software, including the named pipes support (discussed in Chapter 2). In networks using Novell this means installing the OS/2 requester that runs on top of the named pipes driver, which runs on top of Novell's native SPX/IPX protocol stack. A discussion of the installation of the OS or network products is outside the scope of this book; please refer to the product installation instructions from the vendor.

Once the appropriate base software is installed, installing SQL Server is a fairly simple process. To install the server, the user would follows these steps:

1. Insert the INSTALL diskette in drive A
2. Type `A:install`
3. Follow the instructions provided by the install program.

During the `install` program, the user is prompted to respond to such questions as amount of memory on the Server computer and amount of space for the `master` device. The appropriate values to be entered for most of these questions are discussed in detail in SQL Server *Getting Started*, the manual provided with SQL Server. What follows is a discussion of the possible configurations in which SQL Server can be run and some of the values for the requested parameters for these configurations.

There are basically three ways in which the SQL Server can be installed—on a separate, stand-alone computer (dedicated server), on a computer that also has the file server installed on it (nondedicated server), or on a computer that can be used as both a workstation and a server (concurrent server). The values for the different options depend on which of these configurations you choose.

Figure 10-2 summarizes the recommended values for various parameters based on the configuration and amount of memory available on the computer. Note that these are recommended values; the application or database environment may dictate other values. These values are a good starting point for tuning the configuration parameters for optimum performance.

Once the install program has successfully copied the SQL Server files into the appropriate directories on the disk, it builds

	Dedicated Computer					File/Print Server				User Workstation			
	6 Mb	8 Mb	10 Mb	12 Mb	16 Mb	8 Mb	10 Mb	12 Mb	16 Mb	8 Mb	10 Mb	12 Mb	16 Mb
SQL Server *memory* (Mb)	4	6.5	8	9.8	13.1	4	5	6	8	4	5	6	8
SQL Server *user connections*	Configure as needed					Configure as needed				Configure as needed			
SQL Server *procedure cache*	20%	20%	20%	20%	20%	20%	20%	20%	20%	20%	20%	20%	20%
Lan Manager disk cache (Kb)	0	0	0	0	0	512	1024	2048	4096	0	0	0	0
Lan Manager maxopen	*user connections* + 25					*user connections* + 64				*user connections* + 25			

6Mb is insufficient memory for File/Print Server and User Workstation Configurations

FIGURE 10-2 Recommended installation parameter values

the master device. The `master` device contains the system databases (*master, model*, and *tempdb*). It is needed to bootstrap the system, that is, to bring up the Server. The size of the `master` device is requested at install time (the default value is 10Mb). Once the master device is allocated, the *master, model*, and *tempdb* (and *pubs*, if requested) databases are created and loaded on this device. Actually the databases are created by running script files containing batches of SQL statements through the isql utility. The isql utility, can execute multiple command batches from an SQL script file. Once these databases are installed on the Server, the install program shuts down the Server to ensure that the Server can be both started and shut down successfully.

The client software, like the Server, runs on top of the LAN software, which runs on top of the operating system. In order for the client application to communicate with the Server, it must conform with the named pipes protocol. Currently, this support is available for both DOS and OS/2 workstations on networks running LAN Manager. For networks running Netware, only OS/2 support exists currently; DOS named pipes support is planned. In the future, Macintosh and Unix client workstation support is likely.

Depending on which client operating system is chosen, the appropriate LAN software must be loaded.

The first step in installing client software is installing the appropriate operating system. Once this step is completed, the appropriate client network software is loaded—either DOS or OS/2, depending on the environment. Then the actual client software is installed. Figure 10-3 shows the architecture of the client workstation.

SQL Server provides a single option during installation, which loads all the client workstation utilities and tools (including isql and the SAF). Loading these tools simply involves copying the executable to the appropriate directory, modifying the paths appropriately, and in the case of OS/2 installing any additional dynamic link libraries that are required.

Startup and Shutdown

Once the Server is successfully installed, it can be started and shut down in several ways, depending on the network environment. In

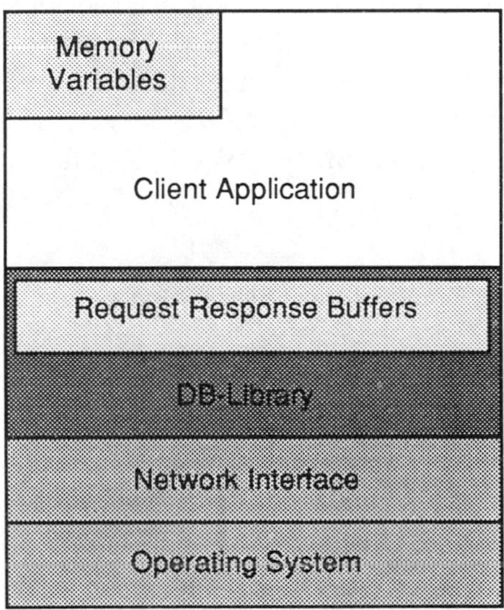

FIGURE 10-3 Client environment

LAN Manager environments, one way is through the SAF, a second uses the `net` command, and a third invokes the sqlserver executable (`sqlservr.exe`) directly. Let's look at them briefly. To start up SQL Server from the SAF, enter the server name, the login id, and the password on the Login to SQL Server dialog box. The SAF tries to connect to the appropriate server, senses it is not running, and asks if it should start it. If you select OK, it starts the requested server and then connects to it. The second way of starting the server is through the `net` command that is part of the network software. Since SQL Server is installed as a network service, it can be started and stopped like one. The command to start it follows, along with the output.

Example 10-1

```
OS2[D:\SQL]net start sqlserver
The SQLSERVER is starting............
The SQLSERVER was started successfully.
OS2[D:\SQL]
```

The `sqlserver` in the command is the name of the network service by which SQL Server is known. If there are multiple SQL Servers, they are installed as separate services, and named `sqlserver1`, `sqlserver2`, and so on. The third way to start up SQL Server is to invoke the executable directly. In Novell networks this is the only way to start up SQL Server, after the required network software is loaded on top of OS/2. The form is:

Syntax

```
sqlservr /d<master_dev_file_name> /e<errorlog_file_name>
```

The `/d` parameter specifies the master device file name; this is the name of the file that corresponds to the master device allocated at installation. The `/e` parameter specifies the name of the errorlog file; this is the file that SQL Server writes its startup and recovery messages to. `sqlservr` is the SQL Server executable name. Of course, it is assumed that directory where the executable resides is part of the path; this is set up during installation. An example of starting up the Server in this way is shown below.

Example 10-2

```
OS2[D:\BOOK\EXAM]sqlservr /dd:\sql\data\master.dat /ed:\sql\log\errorlog
Jun  8 1990 10:08AM kernel: :
        SQL Server 1.00
        Sat Apr 22 16:12:52 1989:3.4.
Jun  8 1990 10:08AM kernel: Confidential Property of Sybase, Inc.
Jun  8 1990 10:08AM kernel: Copyright (C) 1985-1989 Sybase, Inc.
Jun  8 1990 10:08AM kernel: Copyright (C) 1988,1989 Microsoft Corporation.
Jun  8 1990 10:08AM kernel: Copyright (C) 1988,1989 Ashton-Tate Corporation.
Jun  8 1990 10:08AM kernel: All rights reserved.
Jun  8 1990 10:08AM kernel: Use, duplication, or disclosure by the Government
Jun  8 1990 10:08AM kernel: is subject to restrictions as set forth in
Jun  8 1990 10:08AM kernel: subdivision (b) (3) (ii) of the Rights in Technical
Jun  8 1990 10:08AM kernel: Data and Computer Software clause at 52.227-7013.
Jun  8 1990 10:08AM kernel: Logging SQL Server messages in file
                            'd:\sql\log\errorlog'.
Jun  8 1990 10:08AM kernel: OS/2 SQL Server start address is 0x470000.
Jun  8 1990 10:08AM kernel: Using 1024 file descriptors.
Jun  8 1990 10:08AM kernel: Using 'd:\sql\data\master.dat' for configuration
                            information.
Jun  8 1990 10:08AM kernel: Master Database is Case Insensitive.
Jun  8 1990 10:08AM kernel: Using 'defaults' for network information.
Jun  8 1990 10:08AM kernel: Pipe name is '\PIPE\SQL\CONSOLE'.
Jun  8 1990 10:08AM kernel: Using asynchronous disk I/O for 'd:\sql\data\master.
                            dat'.
Jun  8 1990 10:08AM server: Number of buffers in buffer cache: 2050.
Jun  8 1990 10:08AM server: Number of proc buffers allocated: 512.
Jun  8 1990 10:08AM server: Number of blocks left for proc headers: 2456.
Jun  8 1990 10:08AM server: Opening Master Database ...
Jun  8 1990 10:08AM server: Recovering database 'master'
Jun  8 1990 10:08AM server: Activating disk 'empdev'
Jun  8 1990 10:08AM server: Activating disk 'emplog'
Jun  8 1990 10:08AM kernel: Using asynchronous disk I/O for 'd:\sql\data\empdev.
                            dat'.
Jun  8 1990 10:08AM kernel: Using asynchronous disk I/O for 'd:\sql\data\emplog.
                            dat'.
Jun  8 1990 10:08AM server: Activating disk 'userdev'
Jun  8 1990 10:08AM kernel: Using asynchronous disk I/O for 'd:\sql\data\userdev.
                            dat'.
Jun  8 1990 10:08AM server: Recovering database 'model'
Jun  8 1990 10:08AM server: Clearing temp db
Jun  8 1990 10:08AM kernel: Pipe name is '\PIPE\SQL\QUERY'.
```

```
Jun  8 1990 10:08AM server: Recovering database 'pubs'
Jun  8 1990 10:08AM server: Recovering database 'proxydb'
Jun  8 1990 10:08AM server: Recovering database 'costdb'
Jun  8 1990 10:08AM server: Recovering database 'empdb'
Jun  8 1990 10:08AM server: Recovery complete.
```

SQL Server can also be stopped in more than one way—through the SAF, using the TRANSACT-SQL shutdown statement, and through the `net` program. The Config menu in the SAF has a Shutdown SQL Server selection that can be used to shut down the server. This menu selection is available only to the SA. Choosing this selection causes a graceful shutdown; the currently executing statements finish execution, and then a CHECKPOINT is executed in every database before the server is shut down. The SAF connection is terminated, and the SA can either exit or log on to another server.

In LAN Manager networks, the `net` program can be used to stop SQL Server. This does not, however, perform a graceful shutdown; it brings down the Server immediately. It is equivalent to performing a SHUTDOWN with the WITH NOWAIT option (discussed shortly). Example 10-3 shows the results of executing this command.

Example 10-3

```
OS2[D:\SQL]net stop sqlserver

The SQLSERVER was successfully stopped.
OS2[D:\SQL]
```

Another way to stop the Server is to execute a TRANSACT-SQL statement called SHUTDOWN. Only the SA has permission to execute this statement. If the NOWAIT option is used, SQL Server shuts down immediately. Otherwise, the Server waits for all currently executing statements to complete, then it checkpoints every database, and only then does it shut down. The syntax of the SHUTDOWN statement follows.

Syntax

```
SHUTDOWN [WITH NOWAIT]
```

Storage Management

Having installed the SQL Server, the SA now has the important task of managing it. Two key aspects of managing the SQL Server environment are device, or space, management and user management. As discussed earlier, the SA may delegate some of these functions to other individuals, especially the individual DBOs. However, this and succeeding chapters will treat them as the SA's responsibilities.

Database Devices

In SQL Server, all disk space needed for databases and logs is allocated and managed in terms of logical database devices. A database device can be characterized as a set of contiguous area of a disk space (from logical disks) that is preallocated, or reserved, for SQL Server, and known to it by a logical name. In OS/2, a physical disk can be divided into logical disks, known by a logical disk identifier, such as `D:`. By preallocating and managing disk space, the Server does not have to request space from and return space to the OS dynamically, which improves Server performances.

Database devices are created using the DISK INIT statement. Only the SA has permission to create database devices; this permission cannot be granted to others. The SA must be in the *master* database when creating database devices. Information about a device is kept in the *sysdevices* system table that is part of the *master* database.

When a DISK INIT statement is issued, SQL Server performs a series of steps. The OS/2 file corresponding to the device is created, and the Server tries to allocate the space requested for the device to the OS/2 file. If there is insufficient space on the disk partition, the Server allocates the maximum amount of disk space possible on the partition. The Server then clears all the pages for database use, makes an entry in the *sysdevices* system table for the logical database device, and returns an indication to the SA of the amount of space allocated. The syntax of the DISK INIT statement follows.

Syntax

```
DISK INIT NAME = <"logical_name">,
          PHYSNAME = <"physical_name">,
          VDEVNO = <virtual_device_no>,
          SIZE = <number_of_blocks>,
          [, VSTART = <virtual_address> ,
             CNTRLTYPE = <controller_no>]
```

The <logical_name> parameter is the name by which the database device is known to SQL Server; it is the name used when you want to allocate space on this particular device (for example, in the CREATE DATABASE statement). The <physical_name> parameter is the full path name of the OS/2 file onto which the allocated space is mapped. Both the <logical_name> and <physical_name> parameters must be enclosed in quotes. VDEVNO is a unique number that identifies the database device on the Server. Currently, the Server allows the creation of nine database devices in addition to the master device (VDEVNO=0), which is created at startup. The sp_helpdevice system procedure displays information on database devices, including the device numbers in use. Size is the amount of space requested in 2K pages (2048 bytes). If you want to allocate a device of 10Mb, you request 5120 pages (5120 × 2K = 10Mb). VSTART specifies the virtual starting address, the page offset, whose default value is 0. CNTRLTYPE specifies the type of disk controller (default value 0). Neither of these values needs to be changed and, hence, can be left out. For example, if you want to create a device, acct_dev, approximately 16Mb in size, you can do as follows.

Example 10-4

```
disk init name="acct_dev", phsyname = "d:\sql\data\acct.dat",
        vdevno = 6, size = 4096
go

OUTPUT:
```

Default Devices A user often may be concerned only with the amount of space allocated for a database and not the exact allocation of this space on the device. For this purpose, SQL Server allows the SA to set up a pool of default database devices, which are used automatically if no explicit database device is specified in the CREATE DATABASE statement. These devices are known as default database devices. Database devices are added or removed from the default pool of devices using the `sp_diskdefault` system procedure. The syntax of the `sp_diskdefault` procedure follows.

Syntax

```
sp_diskdefault <database_device>, {DEFAULTON | DEFAULTOFF}
```

The `<database_device>` parameter is the device that is to be added or removed from the pool of default devices. DEFAULTON adds the device to the pool of default devices, DEFAULTOFF removes it from the pool of devices. Example 10-5 shows how the `acct_dev` device just created can be added to the pool of default devices.

Example 10-5

```
sp_diskdefault acct_dev, defaulton
go
```

```
OUTPUT:
```

The `master` device, created and assigned to the default pool when SQL Server is first installed, can be removed from the default pool as shown in Example 10-6. The SA may choose to do so to prevent user databases from using up the storage on the `master` device.

Example 10-6

```
sp_diskdefault master, defaultoff
go
```

```
OUTPUT:
```

Information on default database devices is kept in the *sysdevices* system table (in the *master* database). The `sp_helpdevices` system procedure indicates a status value of 3 for default devices.

Dump Devices

SQL Server databases and transaction logs can be backed up to special devices called **dump devices**. Databases and logs are backed up so that databases can be restored in case of unrecoverable, or catastrophic, media failure. The dump device can be stored on a floppy disk or on a fixed disk. These devices are similar to other devices in that they have a logical and physical name; however, they are used specifically for the purpose of storing backups. There are two dump devices that are predefined at installation—the `diskettedumpa` and the `diskettedumpb` devices. These devices map onto physical files a:\sqltable.dat and b:\sqltable.dat on diskette drives A: and B: respectively. Dump devices are added through the `sp_addumpdevice` system procedure. Its syntax follows.

Syntax

```
sp_addumpdevice {DISK | DISKETTE}, <logical_name>, <physical_name>,
          <cntrl_type> [, SKIP|NOSKIP [,<media_capacity>]]
```

DISK or DISKETTE specifies the kind of dump device. The `<logical_name>` parameter is the name by which the dump device is known to SQL Server; `<physical_name>` is the name of the underlying file to which it is mapped. The `<cntrl_type>` parameter specifies the controller number for type of device being added—it is 2 for disk dump devices, 3 or 4 for diskette dump devices. The NOSKIP or SKIP statement indicates whether or not ANSI tape labels are to be read. Media capacity, relevant only for diskette dump devices, specifies the storage capacity of the diskette (in Mb).

For example, you can create a dump device called `dumpd` on disk as follows:

Example 10-7

```
sp_addumpdevice "DISK", "dumpd", "d:\sql\data\dumpd.dat", 2

OUTPUT:

'Disk' device added.
```

To create a diskette dump device called `dumpb` for a 360KB floppy disk, you can add a dump device as follows:

Example 10-8

```
sp_addumpdevice DISKETTE, dumpb, "b:\dumpb.dat", 4, NOSKIP, .36

OUTPUT:

'Diskette' device added.
```

Dropping Devices

Over time, it may be necessary to drop existing devices and create new ones. One such situation occurs when a device is full. At this stage the SA may decide to create a new device for additional storage space or to drop and recreate a larger device. This is often the case in the current release of the Server, which allows only nine devices to be created. Both database and dump devices can be dropped using the `sp_dropdevice` procedure. Permission to drop a device defaults to the SA, but it cannot be transferred. Of course, all databases on the device must first be dropped. Once the device is dropped, SQL Server has no knowledge of it. However, you must still drop the physical OS/2 file to which the device is mapped (at the OS/2 command line), before storage for the device is freed. To do this it is necessary to stop SQL Server first. SQL Server opens the device files at startup, and hence OS/2 does not honor the delete request for the physical device file. The syntax of the `sp_dropdevice` system procedure follows.

Syntax

```
sp_dropdevice <logical_name>
```

The `<logical_name>` parameter corresponds to the logical device name. For example, to drop the `acct_dev` database device created earlier, you can enter the following command:

Example 10-9

```
sp_dropdevice acct_dev
```

```
OUTPUT:

Device dropped.
```

Information on Devices

You can obtain information on devices through the `sp_helpdevice` system procedure. The syntax is as follows.

Syntax

```
sp_helpdevice <logical_name>
```

For example, to obtain information on all devices on the Server, you can enter:

Example 10-10

```
sp_helpdevice
go

OUTPUT:

device_name                   physical_name
        description
        status cntrltype device_number low        high
----------------------------- -----------------------------------
       -------------------------------------------------------------
       ----- -------- ------------ ---------- ----------
diskdump                      nul
        disk, dump device
            16         2           0          0       20000
diskettedumpa                 a:sqltable.dat
        diskette, 1.2 MB, dump device
            16         3           0          0          19
diskettedumpb                 b:sqltable.dat
        diskette, 1.2 MB, dump device
            16         4           0          0          19
dumpb                         b:\dumpb.dat
        diskette, 0.3 MB, dump device
            16         4           0          0           5
dumpd                         d:\sql\data\dumpd.dat
```

```
        disk, dump device
            16          2              0            0            0
master                        d:\sql\data\master.dat
        special, physical disk, 10 MB
             2          0              0            0         5119
empdev                        d:\sql\data\empdev.dat
        special, physical disk, 34 MB
             2          0              4     67108864     67125247
emplog                        d:\sql\data\emplog.dat
        special, physical disk, 10 MB
             2          0              9    150994944    151000063
userdev                       d:\sql\data\userdev.dat
        special, physical disk, 4 MB
             2          0              5     83886080     83888127

(10 rows affected)
```

Most of the information displayed is stored in the *sysdevices* system table and is fairly self-explanatory. DEVICE NAME is the logical device name, and DEVICE NUMBER is the virtual device number discussed earlier. STATUS indicates the type of device—2 for database device, 3 for default device, and 16 for dump device, either disk or diskette. CNTRLTYPE is the controller number—0 for database device, 2 for disk dump device, and 3 or 4 for diskette dump device. LOW and HIGH indicate the starting and ending virtual page numbers for the device.

Database Space Allocation

As mentioned earlier, all storage space in SQL Server is allocated on devices. Chapter 4 already discussed how to create databases in some detail. This section focuses on considerations in allocating space for databases and transaction logs and the actual allocation process.

All databases are created in SQL Server from the *master* database. The default size for a database is 2Mb. If no explicit device is specified on the CREATE DATABASE statement, it is allocated sequentially from the default pool. This allocated space is shared by both the data and the transaction log unless steps are taken to ensure that the log is on a separate device.

Because the act of creating a database allocates space for it, the SA may want to restrict this operation. On the other hand (especially in large installations), the SA may want to grant a limited set of users the right to create databases. Another option is for the SA to create the databases and then transfer ownership to other users.

The creator of a database—whether the SA or a delegate—needs to have a rough idea of the amount of space he or she wants to allocate for the database and its transaction log, and how it should be allocated. These estimates do not have to be exact, since additional space can always be allocated for the database or the log. The size of the database includes all of the storage required by the objects within it—tables, indexes, procedures, and so on. The size can be estimated by looking at the maximum row sizes of the tables and indexes, estimating the number of rows in each, determining the number and size of the procedures, and so on. It is a good idea to allocate additional space up front to allow for growth.

Every database in SQL Server has an associated transaction log, and all transaction activity—updates, inserts, and deletes—are recorded in the transaction log. The size of the log, therefore, depends on the database environment and on both the amount of transaction activity (number of transactions per second on the average) and the rate at which transaction log dumps are made. Once a transaction log is dumped to a backup device, it is available for reuse. A good rule of thumb for the initial size of the log is 25% of the size of the database; you can always allocate additional log space if you need it.

The syntax of the CREATE DATABASE is repeated here for convenience, followed by the steps the Server takes to allocate a database.

Syntax

```
CREATE DATABASE <database> [ON {DEFAULT | <device>} = [<size>]
     [, <device> = [<size>]] ...]
```

When allocating space for a database, SQL Server goes through the following steps.

1. It creates a row in the *master..sysdatabases* table, provided the database name is unique. Remember that databases must be created in the *master* database, and that database names must be unique on a Server.
2. It checks to see that the devices specified in the CREATE DATABASE statement are valid database devices— that they exist and are database devices. If no device is specified it looks for a default database device.
3. Finally, it allocates the requested space from the specified devices. If the amount of space requested on any device is not available, it allocates whatever it can on that device (this is not considered an error). Every unit of disk space allocated on a device for a database (through either a CREATE DATABASE or ALTER DATABASE) is called a device fragment. Thus the space allocated for a database could be made up of multiple device fragments, on possibly different database devices. The *master..sysusages* table tracks all the device fragments for a database.
4. The rows for allocated device fragments are added to the *master..sysusages* table.

SQL Server reserves space for database objects from the allocated space. In particular, the space is used for data and index pages. Figure 10-4 illustrates the components of the allocated space.

For example, if you want to allocate 3Mb of space for the *personnel* database from the default pool, you can execute the following statement:

Example 10-11

```
create database personnel on default = 3

OUTPUT:

CREATE DATABASE: allocating 1536 pages on disk 'data_dev'
```

If you want to allocate the space explicitly on the device called `data_dev` you can execute the following statement:

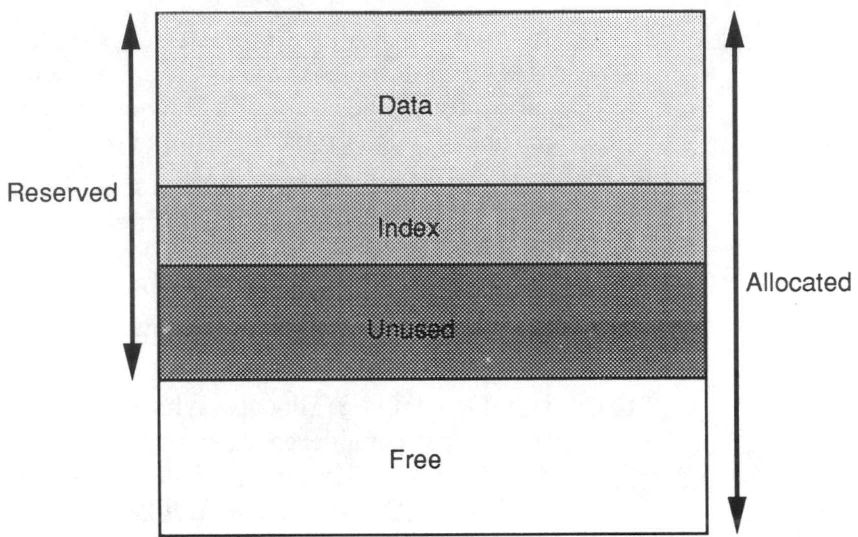

FIGURE 10-4 Database allocation information

Example 10-12

```
create database personnel on data_dev = 3
go

OUTPUT:

CREATE DATABASE: allocating 1536 pages on disk 'data_dev'
```

Storage space for databases is allocated in terms of allocation units—a contiguous area of a disk that is 256 pages (each 2K in size), that is, in 0.5 Mb units. The first page of each of these 256 page units is called the allocation page (for the allocation unit); it describes how the following 255 pages are used. For example, it specifies whether or not a page is allocated, whether it is an index page or data page, and so on. Figure 10-5 illustrates allocation pages and allocation units.

As mentioned earlier, the SA may want to create a database and transfer ownership of the database to some other user once it is created. The owner of a database has special privileges inside the database and has the special user name *dbo* inside the database.

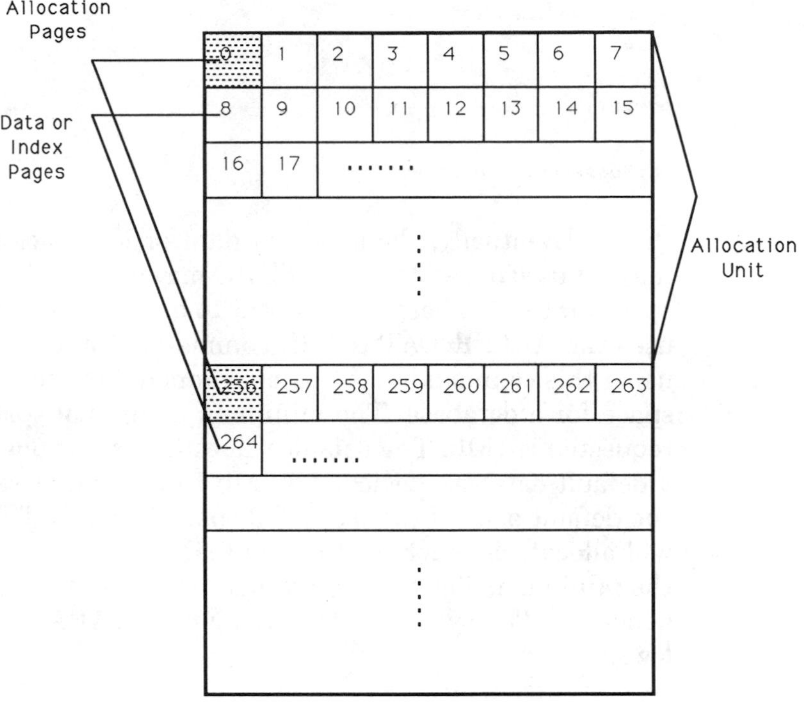

FIGURE 10-5 Allocation pages and allocation units

The SA transfers database ownership through the use of the `sp_changedbowner` system procedure.

Syntax

```
sp_changedbowner <login_id>
```

For example, if the SA wants to make John the owner of the *personnel* database, he or she executes the following sequence of statements:

Example 10-13

```
use personnel
<exec>
```

```
sp_changedbowner john
<exec>

OUTPUT:

Database owner changed.
```

Eventually, the allocated data or log space for a database may get used up, and the SA or DBO may need to allocate additional space for the database. An easy way to increase the size of a database uses the ALTER DATABASE command. You can only add space using this command–there is no command to reduce the allocated space for a database. The minimum additional space that can be requested is 1Mb. The default values for extensions are 1Mb from a default database device and 2Mb from a database device not in the default pool. If the requested space is not available, the Server will allocate as much as it can in 0.5Mb increments, with 1Mb as the minimum. The Server informs the user of the amount of space allocated. The syntax of the ALTER DATABASE command follows.

Syntax

```
ALTER DATABASE <database>
     [ON { DEFAULT | <device> } [= <size>]
     [, <device> [= <size> ]] ... ]
```

For example, if you run out of space in the *personnel* database, you can request 4Mb of additional space for it on the `data_dev` as follows:

Example 10-14

```
alter database personnel on data_dev = 4

OUTPUT:

Extending database by 2048 pages on disk data_dev
```

If the transaction log for a database is on a different device from the data, it may happen that the log runs out of space. The

ALTER DATABASE command, in conjunction with the `sp_logdevice` stored procedure, can be used to allocate additional space for the transaction log. A simple example is given here; however, the issue of transaction log allocation will be discussed in detail shortly.

Example 10-15

```
alter database personnel on log_dev = 2
<exec>
sp_logdevice personnel, log_dev
<exec>

OUTPUT:

Extending database by 1024 pages on disk log_dev
DBCC execution completed. If DBCC printed error messages, see your
System Administrator.
Syslogs moved.
```

The SA or DBO can drop a database using the DROP DATABASE statement. Dropping the database drops all of the objects within the database, frees up all the allocated space, and deletes all knowledge of the database. A database can be dropped only from the *master* database; there cannot be any current users in the database for it to be dropped. The syntax of the DROP DATABASE statement follows.

Syntax

```
DROP DATABASE <database> [, <database>]
```

For example, to drop the *personnel* database, you execute the following statements:

Example 10-16

```
use master
<exec>
drop database personnel
<exec>

OUTPUT:
```

Transaction Log Space

Chapter 6 discussed what transactions are. A transaction is a logical, indivisible unit of work comprising a sequence of database operations. A transaction is integral with respect to both concurrency—when multiple users concurrently access to the database—and recovery—in the event of system failure. The mechanism through which the DBMS guarantees recoverability and concurrency is called **transaction processing**.

Every database in SQL Server has an associated transaction log in which all changes to the database are recorded. This is the key to transaction processing. The transaction log is actually the *syslogs* system table in each database. The Server uses a write-ahead transaction log. This means that a record of the database change is written to the log before the actual database is modified. The change may be written to cache instead of disk for performance reasons, but the statement still holds. The interaction of transactions, logs, and caching is discussed in detail in Chapter 11.

In addition, all statements that affect the transaction state (BEGIN TRANSACTION, COMMIT TRANSACTION, ROLLBACK TRANSACTION, and so on) are recorded in the log as they occur. Thus, at any time the Server is aware of all active (uncommitted) and complete (committed) transactions. In case of a system failure, the Server goes through the transaction log, rolls back any uncommitted transactions, and rolls forward all committed transactions that are not guaranteed to be reflected on disk.

The default in SQL Server, is that the data and the log share the same allocated space. In other words, both the data and the log compete for the same disk space. In some environments this may not be an ideal situation. For example, in an high transaction volume environment, the log may get fairly large and consume all the database space, thereby preventing you from making any further modifications to the database.

SQL Server allows the backup of the data and the log within a database. It is put onto some other device, typically on another medium. This backup is critical to recovering from a catastrophic media failure. The commands provided for backing up and restoring databases are DUMP DATABASE, DUMP TRANSACTION, LOAD DATABASE, and LOAD TRANSACTION. The location of the transaction log is also important with respect to the DUMP and LOAD commands. If the database is not very large (less than 4Mb), the data and the log can be stored on the same device. In this case, the log cannot be backed up separately—you cannot use the DUMP TRANSACTION statement. The DUMP DATABASE statement is used to back up both the data and the log portions of the database. In the case of large databases, however, it is important to be able to allow incremental backups—backups of the modifications to the database from the last complete backup. In essence, this is a backup of the transaction log.

A simple example will illustrate this point. Assume that you have a *personnel* database for a large corporation. The data are approximately 500 Mb in size. The log is, on average, only about 5Mb in size, since the data are fairly static. Assuming a data transfer rate of 5Mb per second, the log takes about a minute to write, whereas the database backup takes approximately 100 minutes. If the data and log reside together, each database and log backup takes approximately 101 minutes. If they are backed up separately, a full database backup takes approximately 100 minutes, but the incremental backups take only a minute and can be performed much more frequently. For large databases, therefore, it is important that the log and the data reside on separate devices.

The following procedure places the data and the log on separate devices. First, you create the database with at least two different device fragments on two different database devices, that is, two different device names on the CREATE DATABASE statement. Then you use the `sp_logdevice` system procedure to assign one of the device fragments to the log.

The syntax of the `sp_logdevice` system procedure follows. Only the SA or the owner of a database has permission to execute the `sp_logdevice` system procedure for that database.

Syntax

```
sp_logdevice <database>, <database_device>
```

For example, if you want to allocate 6Mb of data space (on the `data_dev` device) and 2Mb of separate log space (on the `log_dev` device) for the *client* database, you can execute the following sequence of statements:

Example 10-17

```
create database client ON data_dev = 6, log_dev = 2
<exec>
sp_logdevice client, log_dev
<exec>

OUTPUT:

CREATE DATABASE: allocating 3072 pages on disk 'data_dev'
CREATE DATABASE: allocating 1024 pages on disk 'log_dev'
DBCC execution completed. If DBCC printed error messages, see your
System Administrator.
Syslogs moved.
```

If the transaction log runs out of space, you can expand the log space using the ALTER DATABASE statement and the `sp_logdevice` procedure mentioned earlier. Remember, this only makes sense if the log resides on a device separate from the data to begin with—otherwise it only competes with the database backup for the same space. For example, if you run out of log space for the *client* database, you can extend it as follows:

Example 10-18

```
alter database client on log_dev = 2
<exec>
sp_logdevice client, log_dev
<exec>

OUTPUT:

Extending database by 1024 pages on disk log_dev
DBCC execution completed. If DBCC printed error messages, see your
System Administrator.
Syslogs moved.
```

Information on Database Space Usage There are several system procedures that provide information on the space allocation and usage within a database. The `sp_helpdb` system procedure provides information on the device fragments allocated for the database. The syntax is as follows.

Syntax

```
sp_helpdb [<database>]
```

For example, if you run the sp_helpdb procedure for the *client* database, the following information is displayed:

Example 10-19

```
sp_helpdb client

OUTPUT:

name          db_size  owner                    dbid   created      status
------------------------ -------- ------------------------ ------ ----------- -----
--------------------------------------------------------------------------------------
client        10 MB    sa                          8 Jun  8 1990  no options set

(0 rows affected)
device_fragments              size          usage
------------------------------ ------------ --------------------
data_dev                             6.0 MB data only
log_dev                              2.0 MB log only
log_dev                              2.0 MB log only

(0 rows affected)
```

The sp_spaceused system procedure provides a summary of the space used by the current database or by a database object. The syntax of the sp_spaceused procedure follows.

Syntax

```
sp_spaceused [<object_name>]
```

To show how the space within the *client* database is used you can execute the following statements:

Example 10-20

```
use client
<exec>
sp_spaceused
```

```
<exec>

OUTPUT:

database_name                database_size
---------------------------- ------------------
client                       10 MB

(0 rows affected)
reserved        data            index_size      unused
--------------- --------------- --------------- ---------------
396 KB          34 KB           22 KB           340 KB

(0 rows affected)
```

The reserved, data, index_size and unused space sizes returned by the sp_spaceused procedure correspond to the components shown in Figure 10-4.

Transferring Data

The previous sections talked about how to allocate data and log space for databases. However, a database needs more than space to make it useful—it needs data. After all, the primary purpose of the Server is to provide efficient storage and access to data in its databases. This section focuses on how to transfer large amounts of data into and out of the Server databases.

As discussed in Chapter 6, the SQL Server DML provides the INSERT statement to add a row to a table. To insert a small number of rows, this is adequate. For a few hundred rows, you can define an isql batch with as many INSERT statements as you need, but this process quickly becomes cumbersome as the number of rows grows into the thousands or millions. In addition, it is often the case that the data currently reside in a OS file (created by some program or extracted from another database) and need to be imported into the current database. SQL Server provides two means for accomplishing this. You can use the bulk copy (BCP) utility program, which allows users to transfer large amounts of data in and out of the Server, or you can write a custom program using the bulk copy functions within DB-LIBRARY.

Bulk Copy Program

The bulk copy program is a generic, stand-alone, command line utility that allows the transfer of large amounts of data to and from the Server. The BCP utility's flexibility allows transfer of selected columns or data; it allows for customized definition of file formats (terminators, order of data, and so on); and it handles both ASCII (character) files and binary files on input and output.

There are several issues to consider when you use the BCP utility. Some have to do with the integrity and consistency of the data being loaded; others have to do with performance. The next two sections discuss these considerations.

Integrity and Consistency Issues The purpose of the bulk copy program is to import and export large amounts of data to and from the Server databases rapidly. In keeping with this design philosophy, on transfer of data into the Server, rules and triggers are not enforced when the data are loaded through the BCP utility. However, if defaults are defined they are used. Of course, constraints imposed by a column's data type are enforced.

Importing data into the Server is always dynamic—meaning that other users can be using the database. This poses no problem because the Server applies the normal locking protocols that it uses with any INSERT statement in a multiuser environment. This guarantees that there is no inconsistency, even when there are other users accessing and updating the same table while the data are being loaded.

Exporting data, however, must be static—no other users may be accessing the database. This ensures a consistent image of the database is exported. Otherwise a user can potentially modify one part of a table, while another part is being exported. You can ensure that no other user is in the database by using the `sp_dboption` system procedure to set the database option "dbo use only" to TRUE. Example 10-21 shows how to set the database option to allow the export of the *titles* table.

Example 10-21

```
use master
<exec>
sp_dboption pubs, 'dbo use only', true
<exec>

use pubs
<exec>
checkpoint
<exec>

OUTPUT:

Run the CHECKPOINT command in the database that was changed.
```

We have talked about multiuser integrity issues, but what if the system crashes during the loading of the data? Fortunately, the entire bulk copy is treated as a single transaction. Thus, all of the data are guaranteed to exist in their entirety or not at all. If the system crashes in the middle of the loading, none of the data will exist. Otherwise, all of it will exist.

Treating the entire bulk copy process as a transaction has some drawbacks, however. For example, if you are loading a million rows and the system crashes after 900,000 rows, the entire bulk copy would need to be restarted. For this reason, the bulk copy utility has a batch size option, which splits up the load into batches of the size specified. Each individual batch is then treated as a transaction, and a checkpoint occurs at the end of each transaction.

Performance Issues The bulk copy utility has two modes—fast and slow. The mode used for a bulk copy depends on certain conditions. The fast mode is used for bulk copies into tables that have no indexes; hence the row inserts are not written to the transaction log. The slow mode is used for tables that have at least one index, when the row inserts are written to the transaction log.

As a general rule, if large amounts of data need to be imported (typically more than 80% of table data), it is faster to drop all the indexes, load the table through bulk copy, and then rebuild the indexes. On the other hand, if a small amount of data (typically less than 20% of the table data) is being loaded, it is probably more efficient simply to load the data through bulk copy. For amounts of data in between, you can drop only the nonclustered indexes, load the data, and then rebuild the dropped indexes.

Permissions The bulk copy utility is like any other client program, in that you need a valid login id and password to connect to the Server. Once connected, however, you still need appropriate permissions to load data into or export data from a table in one of the Server databases.

For output to an OS file, the database user must have SELECT (read) permission on these objects: the table being exported and the *sysobjects, syscolumns*, and *sysindexes* tables in the *master* database. For input to a table, the user must have INSERT permission on the table being loaded.

Using Bulk Copy This section discusses how to use the bulk copy utility. In general, the steps involved in loading database tables are:

1. Set the SELECT INTO/BULKCOPY database option.
2. Drop database indexes (as determined by performance considerations).
3. Assuming you have the proper permissions, use the bulk copy utility to accomplish the transfer.
4. Repeat steps 2 and 3 for other tables in the database.
5. Back up the database using the DUMP DATABASE statement.
6. Reset the SELECT INTO/BULKCOPY database option.
7. Check the data in the tables to see that they do not violate any integrity constraints.

The syntax for invoking the bulk copy utility follows. A list of the parameters in the bulk copy utility and their explanation follows the syntax.

Syntax

```
BCP [[<database>.]<owner>.]<table> {IN | OUT} <data_file>
     [-m<max_err>] [-f<format_file>] [-e<err_file>] [-F<first_row>]
     [-L<last_row>] [-b<batch_size>] [-n] [-c] [-t<terminator>]
     [-r<row_term>] [-i<input_file>] [-o<output_file>]
     [-U<login_id>] [-P<password>] [-S<server>] [-v]
```

Parameter	Function
<table>	specifies the table into which data are being imported or from which data are being exported
IN | OUT	specifies the direction of the transfer
<data_file>	the full path name of the OS file from which data are being read or the file to which the data are being written

The invocation options allowed on the bulk copy utility are:

-m	maximum number of errors
-f	full pathname of a previously created format file
-e	full pathname of an error file
-F	number of the first row to copy
-L	number of last row to copy
-b	batch size for the transfer
-n	performs transfer using the database native types
-c	performs transfer with character type as default
-t	field terminator
-r	row terminator
-i	name of the file for redirected input to BCP
-o	name of redirected output file for BCP
-U	Server login ID
-P	password
-S	Server name
-v	reports version of BCP utility

Example 10-22 shows the use of the BCP utility. Assume you want to load the *sales* table in the sample *pubs* database. The data are in an OS/2 file called `sales.dat`, in which the column values are comma delimited. You can use bulk copy as follows.

Example 10-22

```
OS2[D:\SQL\BCP]bcp pubs.dbo.sales in sales.dat -Usa -Psqldba
 -Ssql_server -t\t -r\r\n

Enter the file storage type of field stor_id [char]:
Enter prefix-length of field stor_id [0]:
Enter length of field stor_id [4]:
Enter field terminator [\t]:

Enter the file storage type of field ord_num [char]:
Enter prefix-length of field ord_num [1]: 0
Enter length of field ord_num [20]:
Enter field terminator [\t]:

Enter the file storage type of field date [datetime]: char
Enter prefix-length of field date [0]:
Enter length of field date [26]:
Enter field terminator [\t]:

Enter the file storage type of field qty [smallint]: char
Enter prefix-length of field qty [0]:
Enter length of field qty [6]:
Enter field terminator [\t]:

Enter the file storage type of field payterms [char]:
Enter prefix-length of field payterms [1]: 0
Enter length of field payterms [12]:
Enter field terminator [\t]:

Enter the file storage type of field title_id [char]:
Enter prefix-length of field ord_num [1]: 0
Enter length of field ord_num [6]:
Enter field terminator [\r\n]:

Do you want to save this format information in a file? [Y/n] y
Host filename [bcp.fmt]: sales.fmt
```

```
Starting copy...

21 rows copied.
Clock Time (ms.): total = 1000   Avg = 47     (21.00 rows per sec.)

OS2[D:\SQL\BCP]
```

Custom Bulk Copy Program

For applications with nonstandard requirements such as critical speed requirements or interleaved loading of tables, the bulk copy interface may not be adequate. For these applications, DB-LIBRARY provides a special bulk copy interface, which is a set of functions to write a custom bulk copy program. Actually, the bulk copy utility utilizes this interface; however, because it is a generic program designed to handle a wide variety of needs, it doesn't perform adequately in all situations.

There are two modes of bulk copy that can be performed using the bulk copy functions. The first is for transfer to and from OS files; the second is for transfer to and from program variables. The first one is more common and is described here. The bulk copy functions used in this mode are:

`dblogin()`	establishes login structure
`bcp_init()`	specifies form of bulk copy transfer and name of the OS files
`bcp_columns()`	specifies custom format of the OS data file
`bcp_colfmt()`	specifies the specific column format
`bcp_exec()`	executes the bulk copy
`bcp_control()`	changes various control parameters for a bulk copy (maximum errors, batch size, and so on)
`bcp_moretext()`	writes part of large image/text value

Figure 10-6 provides an overview of the program structure and the bulk copy functions used in transferring to and from OS files. The overall flow is fairly simple; a list of the steps follows.

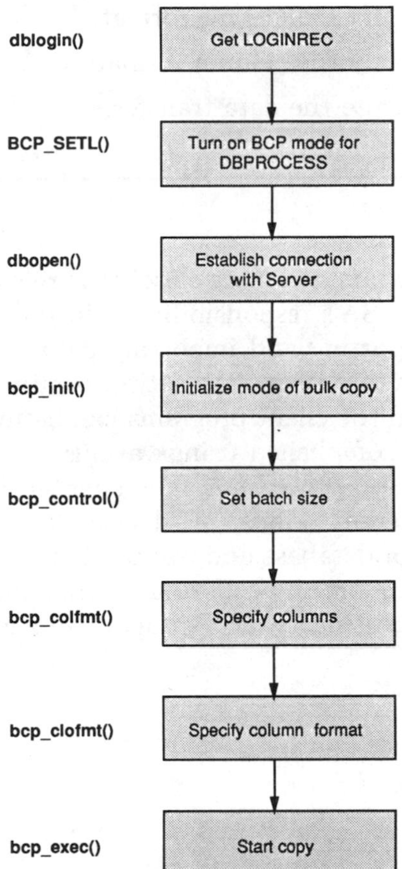

FIGURE 10-6 Bulk copy to/from OS files

1. Establish the login structure.
2. Set bulk copy mode in login structure before establishing connection to Server.
3. Establish connection to the server.
4. Initialize mode of bulk copy (OS file transfer).
5. Set batch size, maximum errors, and other parameters as required.

6. Specify the OS file format.
7. Specify the column formats.
8. Execute the data transfer.

Summary

This chapter examined more closely the role of the SA and focused on some of the SA's responsibilities—installation, storage management, and exporting and importing data into the Server. Installation requires the OS and the network software to be loaded before the Server and the client programs can be installed. Storage management is accomplished using various TRANSACT-SQL statements and stored procedures. The chapter discussed the management of different kinds of devices and their use and the management of database and transaction log space. Finally, it outlined how to import and export large amounts of data into and out of the database using the BCP program or a custom DB-LIBRARY program.

CHAPTER

11

Data Consistency and Recovery

Introduction

The notion of transactions was introduced in Chapter 6, when the TRANSACT-SQL DML was discussed. To repeat, transactions are logical units of work that are integral to both consistency and recovery. That means two things. First, two different concurrent transactions in a multiuser environment should not interfere with each other. Second, if a system failure occurs before a transaction is completed, the system should guarantee that the transaction will be reflected either in its entirety in the database or not at all. The mechanism through which the DBMS provides a transaction capability is known as transaction processing. This chapter explores transaction processing as it relates to consistency and recovery. It discusses the roles of locking and transaction logging and how page caching and checkpointing affect transaction processing.

Data Consistency

There are several problems that can arise when users access data concurrently in a multiuser environment. "Concurrently" is not the same as "simultaneously." It means in an interleaved manner, since in a single processor system, only one transaction can be executing at any instant in time. The classic concurrency problems are the **lost update**, the **uncommitted dependency**, and the **inconsistent analysis**. Figure 11-1 depicts these problems.

Concurrency Problems

The cases in Figure 11-1 illustrate the three kinds of concurrency problems that can occur. In case 1, users A and B both start transactions, retrieve the same piece of data ($X = 40$), and add 30 and 20 respectively to it. User A's update ($X = 70$) is written to the database at time $t4$, followed by user B's update ($X = 60$) at time $t5$. The result is that user A's update is lost at time $t5$. This is referred to as the lost update problem.

In case 2, user A starts a transaction and retrieves the datum ($X = 40$) as in case 1 and adds 30 to it (X is now 70). User B then

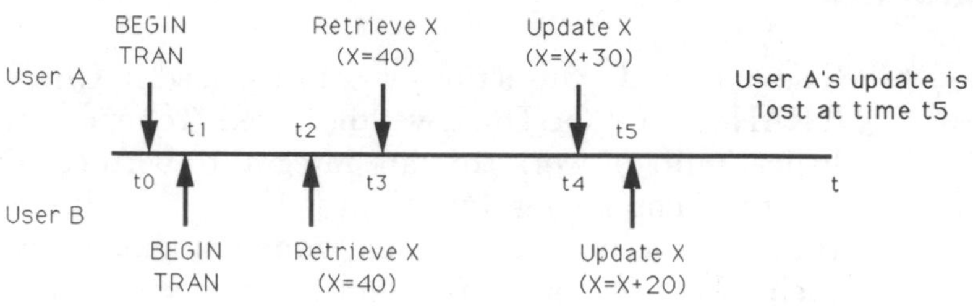

Lost Update

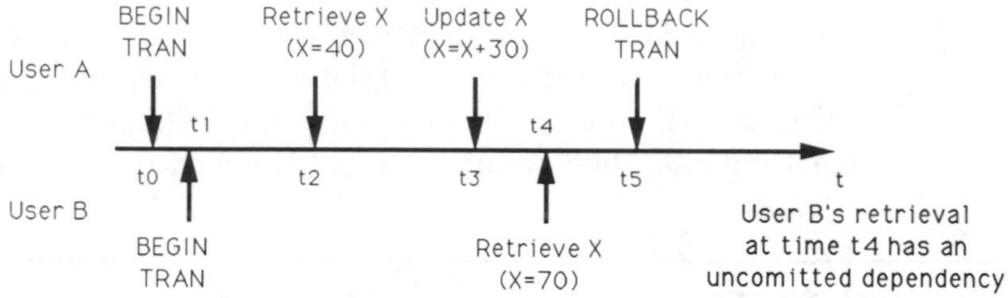

Uncommitted Dependency

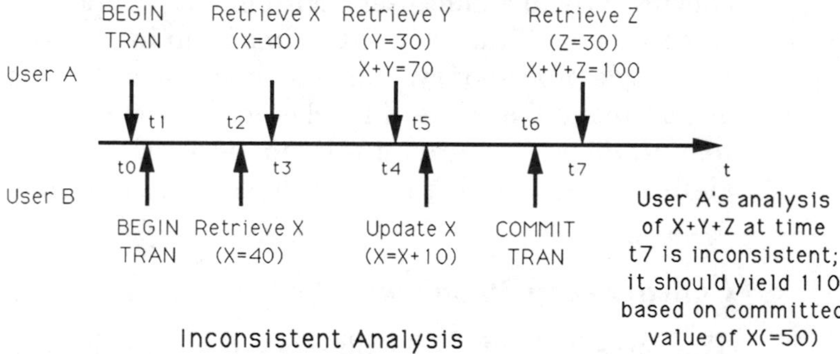

Inconsistent Analysis

FIGURE 11-1 Multiuser concurrency problems

decides at time *t*4 to fetch this value (subsequent to A's update) and perform some computation based on it. However, user A decides at time *t*5 to roll back the transaction (that is, to restore the value of *X* to 40). B's computation involves an uncommitted dependency since A can decide either to commit the update or to roll back the transaction.

In case 3, users A and B both fetch the same piece of data ($X = 40$). User A fetches *Y* and computes $X + Y$ at time *t*4, while user B updates X by adding 10 to it ($X = 50$) at time $t5$ and commits the transaction at time $t6$. At time $t7$, user A fetches Z ($= 30$) and computes $X + Y + Z$ yielding a total of 100, whereas based on the committed value of X, the total should be 110. This problem is known as inconsistent analysis.

It is obvious that the problem in a concurrent environment is basically one of interference. In order to achieve consistency, the concurrent transactions must be serialized; they must be executed serially *in some order.* The technique used to prevent concurrent users from interfering with one another is called **locking**. Locks are mechanisms to regulate access to shared objects in a concurrent environment. Typically, a user transaction requests, either implicitly or explicitly, a lock of a specific type from the system, in this case the Server, based on the operation being performed. If the lock is granted, the transaction proceeds. Otherwise it is queued until the resource is free. Locks of the same type are generally granted on a first-in-first-out (FIFO) basis, although in certain cases locks may be denied to prevent undesirable effects. These effects, known as **deadlock** and **livelock**, are discussed later in the chapter.

Shared and Exclusive Locks

There are two kinds of locks–shared and exclusive. A shared (read) lock means that the resource can be shared with other users. The lock is actually held by the user process on behalf of the user. This is the kind of lock utilized, for example, when a SELECT statement accesses a table. Since the rows are not being updated, other transactions can also read the table. An exclusive (write) lock is one that does not allow a resource to be shared with any other user. The exclusive lock is used, for example, when an UPDATE is being performed against a table.

Shared locks and exclusive locks are mutually exclusive. In other words, a shared lock can be granted to another transaction even if one transaction has a shared lock on the resource; however no exclusive locks can be granted until all shared locks are released. Conversely, exclusive locks can never be shared; that is, no more than one exclusive lock can be held on a resource. In addition, no shared locks can be granted until the exclusive lock is released.

An important criterion affecting locking is the granularity of locking—it can be performed at the level of a database, a table, a row, or even a column. In general, the coarser the granularity, the lower the degree of concurrency, and the finer the granularity, the more the overhead required to maintain the locking information. Most DBMSs avoid locking at the database or table level for concurrency reasons and avoid column locks for overhead reasons. Hence, they end up using some variation of row-level locking. In certain cases, a DBMS that normally uses row-level locking, may employ a table lock for efficiency reasons.

In SQL Server all locking is implicit, that is, the right type of locking is applied automatically to ensure data consistency in a multiuser environment. SQL Server locks are at the granularity of a page or a table. Locking at the level of a page rather than a row is sometimes referred to as **physical locking**. A page in SQL Server is a contiguous area of disk space 2K (2048) bytes in size; it may contain one or more rows. Page locking has slightly coarser granularity than row locking, since a page can contain one or more rows depending on the row size. (A row cannot span pages in SQL Server; the maximum row size is 1962 bytes.) However, with page locking the overhead is considerably less than with row locking. In certain extreme cases, when the number of page locks on a table gets large, SQL Server decides for efficiency reasons to escalate these several page locks to a single table lock, which prevents access to the entire table.

SQL Server allows you to look at the active locks through the `sp_lock` system procedure. The `sp_lock` system procedure queries the *syslocks* system table in the *master* database. The syntax of the `sp_lock` procedure follows.

Syntax

```
sp_lock [<spid1> [, <spid2>]]
```

Example 11-1 shows the output of the `sp_lock` system procedure. It indicates which server process holds the lock, whether it is shared (Sh) or exclusive (Ex), whether it is a page or table lock, the page number (if applicable), and the database on which the lock is held. The optional `<spid1>` and `<spid2>` parameters restrict the output to only those locks held by the process ids supplied. **Intent** or **extent locks** are two kinds of page locks in the server. Intent locks indicate the intention to update a page, even though the transaction may currently hold a shared lock on it. In this way no other transaction can acquire an exclusive lock on it. Extent locks are acquired during allocation and deallocation of extents (units of eight pages) during the creation or removal of database objects such as tables and indexes, and during the insertion of rows into a table. There is one other kind of lock—the **demand lock**—used to prevent additional shared locks from being granted when an exclusive lock is waiting to be granted. This is discussed further in the next section.

Example 11-1

```
sp_lock

OUTPUT:

spid   locktype             table_id    page        dbname
------ -------------------- ----------- ----------- ---------------
     1 Sh_table               672005425           0 pubs
     4 Sh_intent              464004684           0 master
     4 Ex_extent                      0          40 tempdb

(3 rows affected)
```

Locking prevents concurrent transactions from interfering with one another by executing them serially. This guarantees that one transaction does not overwrite another transaction's update; it does not recognize data that are in an inconsistent state (not committed or rolled back) in another transaction. In this way all of the concurrent access problems discussed at the beginning of the chapter are eliminated.

Repeatable Read Consistency

In normal situations when a transaction reads a page of a table or view (using SELECT), a shared lock is acquired on the page. Another transaction can also read the page by acquiring a second shared lock. However shared locks prevent any writer using INSERT, UPDATE, or DELETE statements from accessing the page until all the readers are done. Shared locks are only held while they are needed—while the data are being read. A writer in another transaction can obtain an exclusive lock and modify the page after the readers are done but before the first transaction is complete. Subsequent reads of the page can then potentially provide data that are different from those before the write. The problem, of course, does not arise with writes, since writes get exclusive page locks that are held until the end of a transaction.

In certain situations it is important to see the same data in a transaction every time they are read. This is known as **repeatable read consistency**; every time a column value is read within the transaction, its value is the same. SQL Server provides this through a more restrictive form of shared locking with the HOLDLOCK keyword on a view or table name in the FROM clause of a SELECT statement. Its syntax follows.

Syntax

```
SELECT ...
[FROM [[<database>.]<owner>.]{<table> | <view>} [HOLDLOCK]
    [, [[<database>.]<owner>.]{<table> | <view>} [HOLDLOCK] ]... ]
```

The HOLDLOCK keyword applies only to the table or view name after which it appears and causes shared locks (on the data page, table, or view) to be held until the end of the transaction, thus preventing the data from being modified. The HOLDLOCK keyword can also be used to provide **serial consistency** for operations that need to read several pages in sequence, for example, in an aggregate operation on all the rows of a table. Under normal circumstances, the shared locks on the pages are released after the pages are read. The HOLDLOCK keyword keeps the locks from being released. When a large number of shared locks have accumulated, the lock is escalated to a table-level lock.

Example 11-2

```
select type, avg(price)
from titles holdlock
where type in ("business", "psychology", "popular_comp")
group by type
```

```
OUTPUT:

type
----------- ----------------------
business                     13.73
popular_comp                 21.48
psychology                   13.50

(3 rows affected)
```

Deadlock and Livelock

Whenever concurrent processes request access to shared resources there is a potential for **deadlock.** A deadlock occurs when two processes attempt to access a resource that the other holds a lock on. Since each process has the other's resource, it is queued and theoretically will wait forever. In Figure 11-2, user A's process has page P locked and is trying to get a lock on page Q. User B's process, on the other hand, has page Q locked and is trying to get a lock on page P. Neither transaction can be completed and each user may wait indefinitely.

Fortunately, SQL Server provides automatic deadlock detection and resolution. SQL Server detects that the two processes are in a deadlock condition and resolves the situation by choosing one of the processes and aborting (rolling back) its transaction. That releases its lock, which allows the other process to get the resource it was requesting, thereby allowing its transaction to complete.

In order to resolve a deadlock condition, SQL Server must choose one of the two processes in the deadlock condition to be the victim process. The choice is based on which process has the lowest accumulated CPU time. The server then aborts its transaction and notifies the process of the action (with the infamous server message number 1205). The assumption is that this process has done the least work and hence is the best choice for abortion. In any multiuser environment, it is practically impossible to avoid deadlocks; however, it is important to minimize their possibility through proper database design and well-defined, consistent trans-

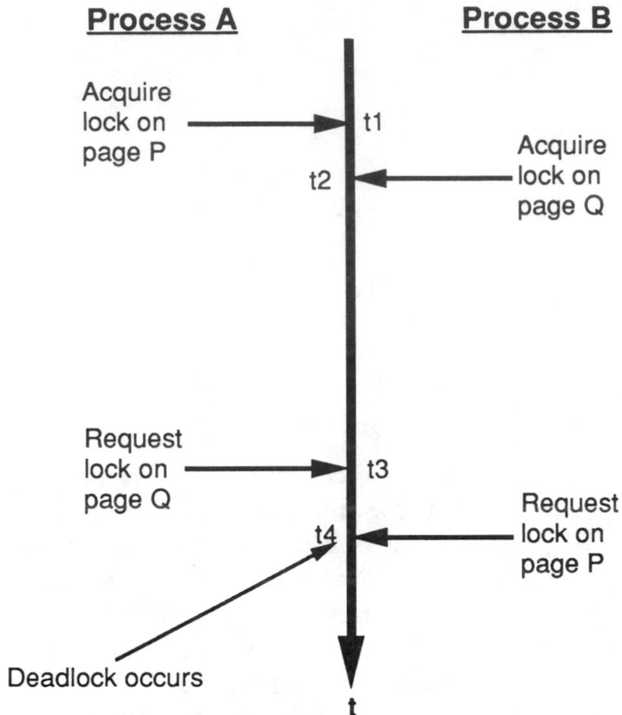

FIGURE 11-2 Deadlock

actions. Using stored procedures also helps, since they reduce the window for which locks are held.

Another situation that arises with shared and exclusive locks is known as livelock, or starvation. In this situation, a request for an exclusive lock keeps getting denied because a series of shared lock requests keeps getting granted, even though they are requested after the exclusive lock request. This is possible because several shared locks can be granted on the same page, while the exclusive lock has to wait until all shared locks are released. The user process requesting the exclusive lock is thus starved by the interfering shared locks.

SQL Server detects and resolves the livelock condition through the use of a demand lock. After four shared locks (a number that cannot be changed by the user) have been granted, the exclusive lock request is turned into a demand lock. This prevents any further shared locks from jumping ahead in the queue. When all the shared locks are released the exclusive lock is granted. The remaining shared locks are granted only after the exclusive lock is released.

Distributed Transactions

The concept of multiple SQL Servers installed on the same LAN has not been discussed, but in fact, there are many reasons why this might be desirable, or even necessary—performance, redundancy, or storage considerations. An example of a highly distributed database environment with LANs connected to other LANs through bridges, or to host machines through gateways, with SQL Servers in all these environments, each with multiple databases.

Multiple Servers and Databases In this distributed environment, you can have transactions spanning multiple databases on multiple servers. Imagine, for example, that the our *pubs* database is actually split across two Servers. One maintains the *titles, authors*, and *titleauthor* tables (*titledb*); the other contains the *publishers, stores,* and *sales* tables (*pubdb*). If you want to add a title published by a new publisher, you have to insert rows in both the *titledb* and the *pubdb* databases within the same transaction. Such a transaction is known as a distributed transaction. It is important that in distributed transactions both databases are updated or neither.

Two-Phase Commit Protocol The protocol used by many DBMSs to guarantee the integrity of a distributed transaction is known as **two-phase commit protocol.** Distributed updates are obviously more complex than distributed retrievals, since retrievals do not change the states of the databases involved. SQL Server provides both distributed retrieval and update capability at the application level, using the DB-LIBRARY interface. SQL Server provides special functions—the two-phase commit functions—to implement distributed updates.

The DB-LIBRARY functions will not be discussed in detail. This section provides a conceptual description of the protocol to give you an idea how the integrity of a distributed transaction is guaranteed. A distributed transaction is complex because independent resources are involved—multiple Servers, multiple separate logs, and multiple different databases. There are multiple, asynchronous updates occurring across multiple databases recorded in separate transaction logs. Any one of these components can fail—the servers, the updates, the log writes, and so on. This means that the entire transaction has to be rolled back. The first problem is how to know which individual Server updates are involved in the distributed transaction. Then some global status for the transaction must be maintained, and recovery must have some way to get at this status. (Remember, failure of any one of the updates implies failure of the distributed transaction). Finally, if the transaction does fail, recovery has to know exactly how to roll back the individual components of the distributed transaction. As you can see, providing a distributed transaction capability is no easy task.

A logical way to coordinate these separate updates is to appoint a leader and a place to hold the global status. In the two-phase commit protocol, the application and the Commit Server respectively perform these jobs. The Commit Server can be either one of the Servers in the transaction or an independent Server not affected by the transaction. The Commit Server is the place for holding global transaction status. The protocol itself is conceptually simple and consists of two phases—hence the term two-phase commit. In the first phase, the prepare phase, each of the participating Servers prepares to commit; in the second, commit phase, they actually commit, based on directions from the leader (the application). If any component fails during the prepare phase, each server rolls back its component of the transaction. If a failure occurs after the prepare phase, during the commit phase, the Commit server global status is used during recovery to roll back the individual server database updates.

There are several components that must work together in the two-phase commit protocol to guarantee the integrity of a distributed transaction—the application, the Commit Server, the participating Servers, and one other component called the probe process. The probe process (which is discussed later) is used during recovery to interrogate the Commit Server for global status (commit or rollback).

Figure 11-3 indicates graphically the stages in the two-phase commit protocol. A list of the steps follows.

1. Establish a connection with each server and designate one as the Commit Server (each connection requires a separate DBPROCESS structure).
2. Establish an ID and transaction name to identify the transaction to all the Servers, including the Commit Server. This also informs the Commit Server of the number of participating Servers.

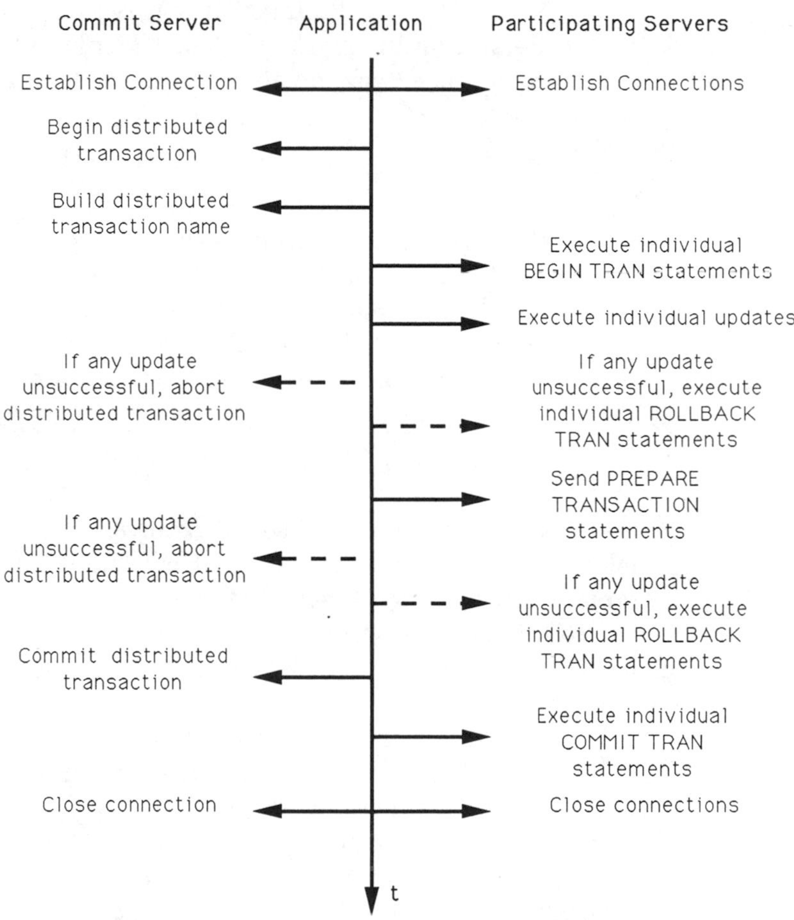

FIGURE 11-3 Two-phase commit protocol

3. Issue a BEGIN TRANSACTION to each participating server.
4. Execute the individual update statements on the respective participating Servers and check for successful execution.
5. Issue and execute a PREPARE TRANSACTION statement to the individual Servers. This is an indication to the Servers to get ready to commit.
6. Check the status returned by each Server. If the individual PREPARE TRANSACTION statements execute successfully, a commit status is recorded on the Commit Server, and it marks the start of phase two of the protocol. Otherwise, an abort status is recorded on the Commit Server.
7. Record the appropriate COMMIT or ROLLBACK status on the Commit Server.
8. After the global status is recorded, the appropriate COMMIT TRANSACTION to ROLLBACK TRANSACTION statements are executed on each participating Server, which is then removed from the list of active participating Servers in the transaction.
9. Close the connections with the Commit Server and each participating Server.

Although the protocol seems involved, it does in fact work, which is the important thing. If the PREPARE TRANSACTION statement stage is not reached, the application issues the individual ROLLBACK statements to the participating Servers. Even if the prepare stage is reached, there is still a possibility for one of the Servers to fail to respond successfully to the PREPARE TRANSACTION. Here too, the application issues appropriate ROLLBACK TRANSACTION statements to the Servers. The only other possibility is failure after the PREPARE, during phase two of the protocol. This can happen if any of the Servers fails to commit, or the Commit Server itself fails prior to the end of the transaction. In this case the global status recorded on the Commit Server is used during recovery to either commit or roll back the individual updates to the different databases. That is why the individual COMMIT TRANSACTION statements must be issued after the global status is recorded on the Commit Server.

It is during recovery of a distributed transaction that the probe process, mentioned earlier, plays a part. When the recovery detects a distributed transaction in phase two that needs to be recovered, it looks at the status on the Commit Server to decide whether to roll back or commit the transaction. This special process is initiated as part of recovery on the participating servers to interrogate the global status on the *master* database. The status itself is recorded in a special table called *spt_committab* on the *master* database. The process connects to the Commit server through a special login ID, known as *probe,* which has special permissions. Based on the status retrieved, the recovery process decides either to commit or to roll back the individual component of the distributed transaction on its Server.

Data Recovery

Data recovery entails recovering the database in the case of either a system failure, such as a system crash or malfunction, or a major media failure, where both the on-line database and transaction log are lost. The basic unit of recovery is a transaction, in that it is a logical unit of work integral to recovery and consistency. Transaction processing, therefore, includes recovery. Recovery guarantees that all incomplete transactions are undone completely from the database, whereas completed ones are guaranteed to exist in the database after recovery is complete (even the database did not reflect the updates just prior to the system failure). This kind of recovery, known as **automatic recovery**, or system recovery, is automatically provided by SQL Server. It is necessary for transaction processing.

Data recovery is also needed when the medium itself on which the database exists, that is, the disk, fails or is corrupted in a server environment. Such an event is catastrophic without some way to restore the server databases quickly and efficiently. Indeed, there is a way, but only at the expense of some additional operational procedures. They involve backing up the database and the transaction log on a periodic basis to some other medium (typically tape or other disk device). In case of a media failure, the database is restored from the most current database backup. Then the successive incremental transaction log backups are replayed to restore the database to a state as close as possible to its state at the time of the media failure. Complete recovery is not guaranteed, but at least it is better than having to recreate the entire database.

Transaction Logging

The primary component in the process of automatic recovery from a system or server failure is the **transaction log**. The transaction log is where all the changes to the database are recorded. The transaction log is actually another system table, the *syslogs* table.

In SQL Server, there is a separate transaction log for each database. All changes (INSERT, UPDATE, or DELETE) to a database are recorded in a log that is specific to it. Each modification to the database is a row in the table, written to the log in the temporal order in which it occurs. In addition, the execution of certain transaction-related statements such as BEGIN TRANSACTION, COMMIT TRANSACTION, ROLLBACK TRANSACTION and CHECKPOINT are recorded in the log.

SQL Server uses a **write ahead log** that is shared by all users of that database. Before any change is made to the database, the log is written. Physical, rather than logical, logging is used. This means that the offset and changed bytes within the changed page are logged, not the entire page. The changed data are used by recovery during system startup to restore the database automatically to a consistent state. Bringing the database to a consistent state means checking that all incomplete transactions are rolled back and all completed transactions are reflected in the database. It would seem that completed transactions should be reflected in the database as a matter of course. However, because of caching and I/O buffering, it is possible for a change to the database not to be reflected immediately. Therefore, recovery must be concerned with committed transactions, too. Why aren't the changes reflected immediately? A discussion of caching and I/O buffering follows.

Because SQL Server uses caching to improve overall performance, changes to the database are not always reflected in the database immediately. Caching uses memory to hold disk pages. It then reads and writes from memory, which is much faster than performing an I/O to the disk. Periodically, based on either an implicit time interval or an explicit system request, the pages are written to disk. In addition to page caching by the Server, the operating system buffers pages in memory before writing them out. In fact, the pages may not even be written when the transaction is committed.

This is why the write ahead log is necessary for recoverability. Without it, if a change is made to the database and the system crashes before the change is written to the log, there is no way to roll back that change. The log pages also must be **force written** at COMMIT TRANSACTION, since this is the only way to guarantee that the change is recorded in the transaction log. In force writing, the DBMS issues a call to the operating system to force the contents of the appropriate pages onto the hard disk. Then, even if there is a system failure before the actual change to the database is written out, the database can be recovered from the log.

Automatic recovery, then, is the process of ensuring that all uncommitted transactions are rolled back and that all committed transactions are reapplied if necessary. The next section examines the notion of page caching and checkpointing and how they interact with recovery and logging.

Caching and Checkpointing

Page caching was introduced in the previous section. This section expands on it further. A cache is nothing more than a portion of memory reserved for holding disk pages. Accessing (reading or writing) pages in memory is normally much faster than accessing them from disk. By keeping the frequently used pages in memory, caching improves the overall performance of the system. Caching can be at any level—Server, OS, or even hardware level. In deciding which pages to write out to make room for new pages, most systems, including SQL Server, use a least-recently-used (LRU) algorithm. In this scheme, the page least recently used (the farthest away in time) is written to disk if it has been modified, and its place in memory is used to bring in the new page. (The exact algorithm in the Server is a slight modification of the basic scheme presented here.) Figure 11-4 illustrates page caching.

In SQL Server, the page cache configuration is based on the amount of total system memory available. The configured cache is divided into two portions—one for data and index pages and one for precompiled stored procedures code pages. Configuring the cache size and the amount of cache allocated for procedures and data are explained in Chapter 12.

Checkpointing forces modified pages in the cache to be written to the disk. (It can be thought of as draining the cache.) Checkpointing causes the cache and the disk to become synchronized. The pages written can still be referenced in cache. Periodic

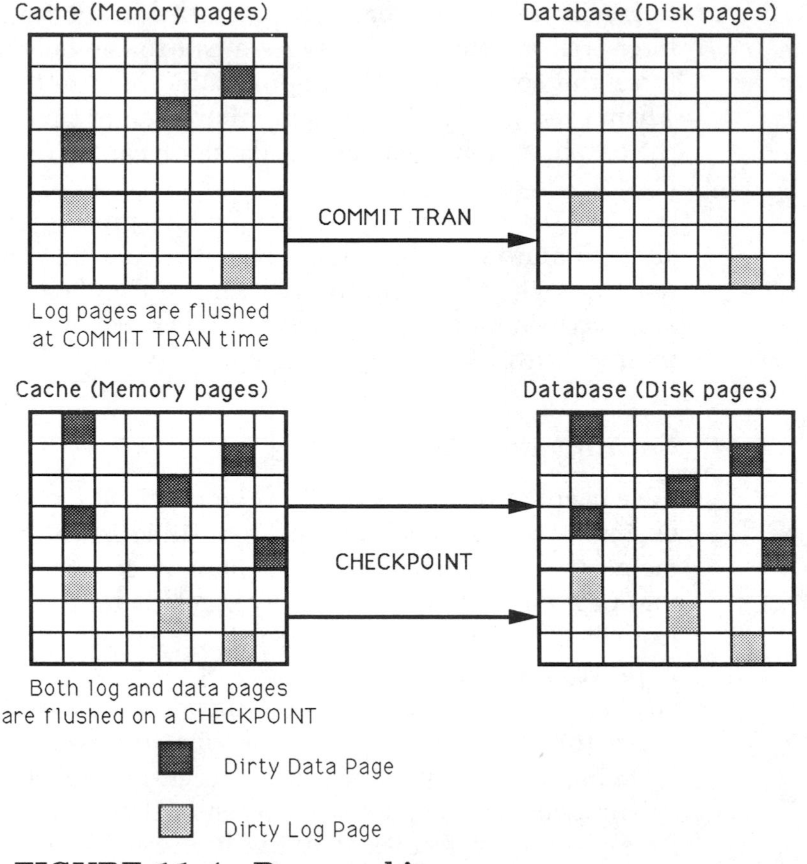

FIGURE 11-4 Page caching

checkpointing is performed by the Server automatically. The period is based on a maximum recovery interval set for the Server, which is a tunable configuration parameter that can be set by the SA. It specifies the worst-case recovery time per database during automatic system recovery. How checkpoints reduce the amount of work at recovery is explained in detail later. For now, it makes sense that since the cache and disk are synchronized at checkpoint time, recovery does not have to go beyond the checkpoint row in the log. With more frequent checkpointing, there is less recovery time. The Server actually calculates a checkpoint interval based on the recovery interval set—the smaller the recovery interval, the smaller (more frequent) the checkpoint interval.

The DBO or the SA can also issue an explicit CHECKPOINT command. An explicit checkpoint is no different from an implicit one that the Server performs periodically. However, if a large, nonlogged operation such as a bulk copy is performed on the database, explicit checkpointing may be advisable. In this case the changes to the database are not recorded in the transaction log, and a media failure would be catastrophic. In fact, the only way to restore the database would be to reload all the data, assuming that a backup was available prior to the load. Explicit checkpointing forces all the data pages in cache to be written to disk, thus ensuring that all changes are actually reflected on disk.

Checkpointing consists of several steps. First, all transactions that are updating the database are frozen. Next, the transaction log pages are written, the actual modified ("dirty") data pages are written, and a checkpoint record is written to the transaction log. Finally, all the frozen transactions in progress are unfrozen.

What are the implications of caching and checkpointing on transaction logging and recovery? When a COMMIT TRANSACTION is performed, the log pages must be written to disk, since the only way to guarantee recoverability is to have at least a record of the changes in the transaction log on disk. Updates, which are written to the data pages in cache, are only written out when room for a new page has to be made, or on a checkpoint. The discrepancy (in terms of the transactions) between the transaction log and the database since the last checkpoint is what needs to be recovered.

Figure 11-5 depicts graphically what happens at COMMIT TRANSACTION and CHECKPOINT time.

Automatic Recovery

As explained earlier, automatic recovery takes place every time the Server is restarted for each database that exists on the Server. The system databases are recovered first, beginning with *master*, then *model*. Then the *tempdb* database is cleared and intialized from *model*. User databases are recovered next. Recovery is intimately connected to the transaction log for each database (the *syslogs* table). It reads the transaction log for each database and determines whether to roll back or roll forward the transactions recorded. It

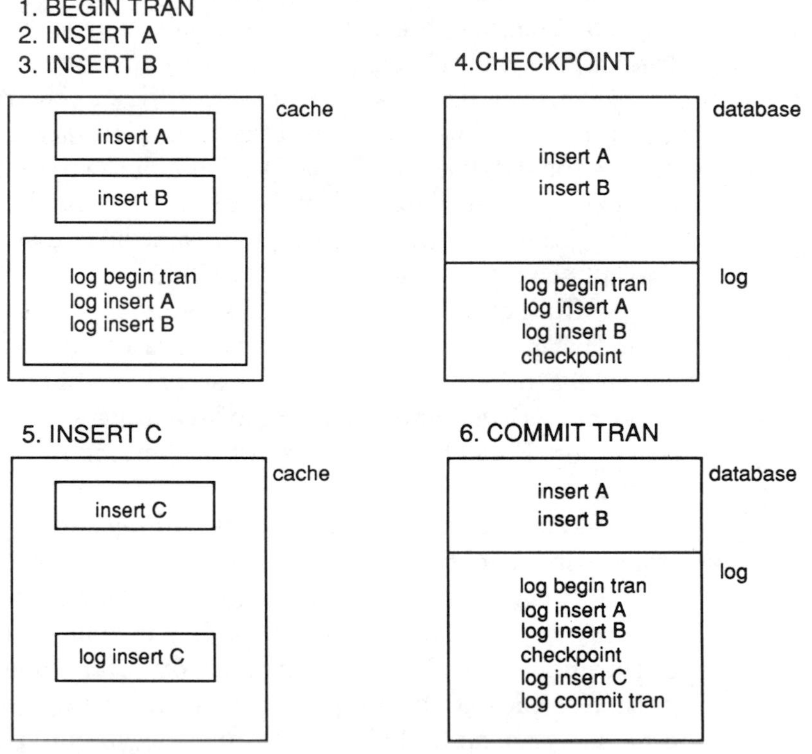

FIGURE 11-5 Commit transaction and checkpointing

rolls back all incomplete transactions and reapplies all committed transactions that are not present in the database. Finally, it makes a checkpoint entry in the transaction log.

Transaction Rollback and Rollforward You have some idea by now of what transaction rollback and rollforward are. Transaction rollback is a simple concept. If a transaction has not been committed at the time of the system failure it is rolled back—remember, transactions are an all or nothing proposition. It is perhaps not so easy to visualize why rollforward is required. The reason is that, even though a transaction may have been committed, it is not guaranteed to be written to disk.

The scenarios in Figure 11-6 will help explain which transactions in the log need to be rolled back or rolled forward and which can be skipped over. In scenario 1, both transaction A and transaction B are active at the time of the system failure; therefore both have to be rolled back. In scenario 2, transaction A is committed. However, no checkpoint occurred prior to the system failure. Therefore, transaction A has to be rolled forward. Transaction B is still active at the time of the failure and, hence, has to be rolled back during recovery. In scenario 3, transaction A is committed, there is a checkpoint subsequently, and then there is a failure. Transaction B is still active at the time of the failure. In this case, recovery can skip over transaction A (since it is already written to disk) and roll back transaction B.

There are two configuration parameters that affect automatic recovery. One is the recovery interval already discussed. The recovery interval is the worst case time (in minutes) per database for recovery. Recovery also writes a log of its processing to the errorlog file, and the recovery flag option controls the mode in which the Server writes to the errorlog file. The errorlog file is a file to which the Server writes its startup and error messages; it is discussed in further detail in Chapter 12. If the recovery flag is set to 1 (verbose mode), a detailed log of how recovery handles each transaction is written; if it is set to 0 (brief mode), only counts of transactions rolled back and forward are written.

Both options—recovery interval and recovery flag—can be changed either through SAF menus or by executing the

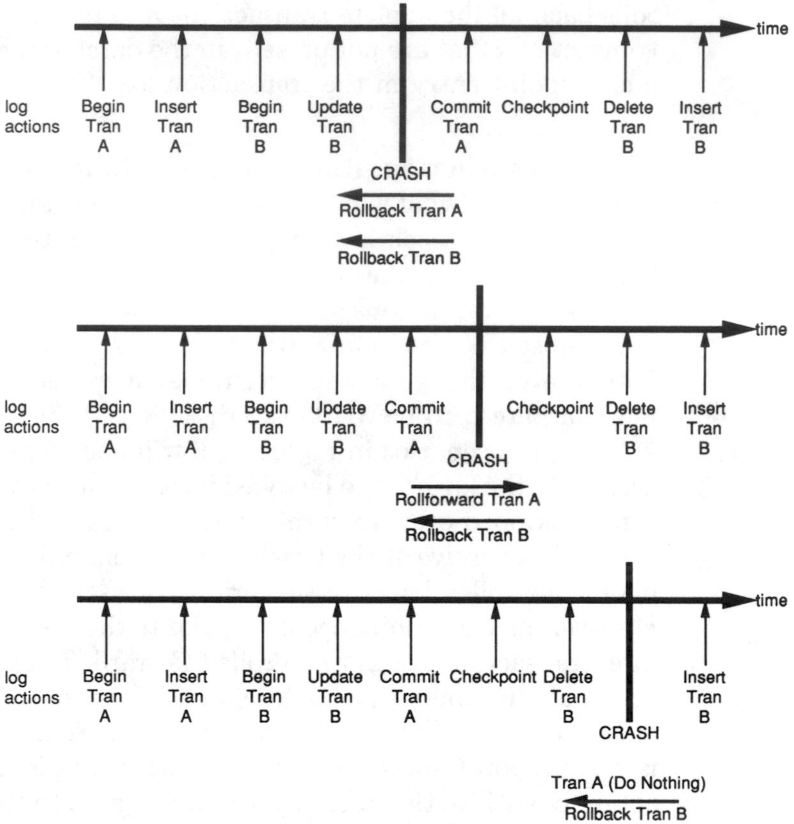

FIGURE 11-6 Rollback and rollforward

sp_configure system procedure. The syntax of the stored procedure is provided in the next chapter. Example 11-3 sets the recovery interval to 4 minutes and turns on the verbose recovery mode. Although the recovery interval is a dynamic configuration parameter whose setting takes effect immediately, the recovery flag parameter only takes effect on the next Server reboot.

Example 11-3

```
sp_configure "recovery interval", 4
<exec>
sp_configure "recovery flags", 1
<exec>
```

```
reconfigure
<exec>

sp_configure "recovery interval"
<exec>
sp_configure "recovery flags"
<exec>

OUTPUT:

Configuration option changed. Run the RECONFIGURE command to install.
Configuration option changed. Run the RECONFIGURE command to install.
name                 minimum     maximum     config_value run_value
-------------------- ----------- ----------- ------------ -----------
recovery interval              1       32767            4           4

(0 rows affected)
name                 minimum     maximum     config_value run_value
-------------------- ----------- ----------- ------------ -----------
recovery flags                 0           1            1           0

(0 rows affected)
```

Manual Recovery

So far, automatic recovery from system failures has been discussed. All such failures assume that the disk media (that hold the database and the log) remain intact. Of course, this is not always the case. If the disk is destroyed, how do you recover the databases that reside on the disk? Fortunately, most DBMSs provide a way of recovering from media failures. This recovery, termed manual recovery because it requires human intervention, is based on periodic backups, or **dumps** in SQL Server terminology, of the database and the transaction log to other dump devices on such media as tapes or disks. The term restore is often used to refer to manual recovery from media failures using backups. (Backups also serve other purposes, such as moving a database to other devices or even to other, similar Servers.)

There are several points to note about manual recovery. First, there is no way to restore a database if there are no previous backups. The process complementary to dumping the database and logs, known as **loading**, depends on reloading the backups in the right order. It is important to set up operational procedures that periodically back up the databases and logs. Second, restoration will not necessarily bring the database back to the instant in time that the media failure occurred. In fact, restoration can only be up to the most recent transaction log backup available; transactions after the last backup are lost.

Dynamic Backup The creation and deletion of dump devices were discussed in Chapter 10. This section discusses SQL Server's dynamic backup facility. This facility allows a backup of the database or log that is performed while users are using the database. This is a powerful feature of the Server, especially in on-line transaction processing environments, because it does not require users to be removed from the database. This results in a backup capability with a much higher availability than that of many DBMSs. In such systems it is necessary first to remove all the users in the database before dumping the database and then to bring the users back on-line again.

Dynamic database backups are performed through the DUMP DATABASE statement. They can also be performed through the SAF menus. The syntax follows.

Syntax

```
DUMP DATABASE <database> TO <dump_device>
```

The `<database>` parameter is the database being dumped, and the `<dump_device>` parameter is the device to which the dump is being performed. When SQL Server is installed, three predefined dump devices are created—two for dumping onto diskette drives A: and B: (they were discussed in Chapter 10) and one for dumping to disk. Of course, additional dump devices can be created. The unfortunate part is that, with the current version of SQL Server, there is no way to dump to a tape device. This is a serious limitation, especially for large databases in on-line transaction processing environments; however, this support is expected in the next release of the Server. In the meantime, the databases can be dumped to dump devices on disk, and the dump device files can be backed up using OS/2 facilities.

Dumping a database causes an automatic checkpoint to be performed. The exact state of the entire database at the time of the checkpoint is written out to disk. Transactions that are active (uncommitted) at the time of the checkpoint are written out; but they are rolled back during the load of the database. SQL Server uses a proprietary algorithm to ensure that a consistent image of the database is written out, even though user transactions may be executing at the time of the dump. In Example 11-4, the database *pubs* is dumped to the device `dumpdev`, which has been defined as a dump device.

Example 11-4

```
use master
<exec>
dump database pubs to dumpdev
<exec>

OUTPUT:
```

There are a few important points to remember about dumping. First, every time you dump to a device, the previous dump is overwritten. Second, dumps should be done frequently, especially since they can be performed dynamically. Third, a database should be dumped after certain events occur—such as when a nonlogged operation—a high speed bulk copy or a SELECT-INTO, for example—is performed, or when a large index is created. If the operation is nonlogged there is no way to recover if a media failure occurs subsequent to the operation. If a large index is lost, a LOAD TRANSACTION redoes all the transactions required to rebuild it, which can be time consuming. Executing dumps after such operations avoids these problems. Permission to dump a database belongs to the DBO, and is transferrable to encourage frequent dumps. A final point to remember is that both system and user databases should be backed up periodically.

Transaction logs, too, can—and should—be backed up. It can be argued that backups of transaction logs are not needed, since database backups are available. However, there are good reasons for using them: because database dumps can take a long time if the database involved is large, typically they are not performed very frequently. This leaves the database users open to a large window of vulnerability. If the disk is destroyed, the user must restore the database from the last database backup; everything since then is lost. This lost work can be significant if the last database backup was a long time ago.

Transaction log backups, on the other hand, are both incremental and dynamic—only the transaction activity in the log is written and users can be modifying the database at the time of the dump. This means transaction log dumps take much less time than database dumps. Basically, the time required to dump the transaction log is proportional to the size of the log, which in turn depends on the amount of transaction activity in that database environment. Dumping the transaction log also checkpoints the database and frees up space since it removes inactive transactions from the transaction log. Without this, the log would grow indefinitely and eventually run of space.

Syntax

```
DUMP TRANSACTION <database> TO <dump_device>
    [WITH TRUNCATE_ONLY]
    [WITH NO_LOG]
```

The DUMP TRANSACTION statement dumps the transaction log for the `<database>` specified to the `<dump_device>` specified. The WITH TRUNCATE ONLY option removes the inactive portion of the log without dumping it. It is used to free up space in the log. The WITH NO LOG option also removes the inactive portion of the log, however, it does not log the DUMP TRANSACTION activity. This option is used to free up space if the log is so full that there is no space even to log the DUMP TRANSACTION statement. There is also a database option, the TRUNCATE LOG ON CHECKPOINT option, that automatically truncates the log on every checkpoint. The option is set using the `sp_dboption` system procedure. This is useful for development environments, where backups of the log are not critical. There it is acceptable to have the log space freed up automatically. However, setting this option is not advisable in production environments, where backups of the logs are needed.

There is one other point that is worth mentioning. If the database and the log reside on the same device, the DUMP TRANSACTION statement is disabled, and the DUMP DATABASE statement dumps both the database and the log. This is the default case and is acceptable for small databases (<5Mb). For large databases, it is recommended that the database and the log reside on separate devices so that they can be dumped independently. The rationale for putting the database and the log on separate devices was outlined in Chapter 10 in the section on creating database devices.

Restoring Databases The process of rebuilding the database using the database and transaction log dumps is known as restoring or loading the database. Of course, this process is needed only if the database is destroyed because of media failure or if the database is being moved to some other device, either on the same or another Server.

The process of restoring a database is the reverse of dumping it. First the database must be created on the new medium or the existing medium, if it reusable. If the database already exists on the medium, it will have to be dropped using the DROP DATABASE or with the help of the database consistency checker (DBCC) utility (discussed in the next section) if DROP DATABASE is not successful. Then the database is loaded from the most recent database dump, and the transaction log dumps are loaded (reapplied) in the order they were performed.

The entire load of a database, using the LOAD DATABASE statement, is treated as a transaction by SQL Server. Loading a database overwrites the current contents of the database, so it should be used with some caution. Permission to load a database belongs to the DBO and cannot be transferred. During the database load, any uncommitted transactions are rolled back, and users are locked out from the database until the load is complete, so that it cannot be modified.

Syntax

```
LOAD DATABASE <database> FROM <dump_device>
```

<database> parameter is the database being loaded from the < dump_device> specified. This is normally the same device (disk or diskette) to which the dump was performed.

e the most recent database backup has been loaded, the transaction log backups can be applied to the database in the same order that were created. The transaction logs are loaded through the LOAD TRANSACTION statement. Since transaction log dumps are incremental, it is useless to perform a LOAD TRANSACTION, without first performing a LOAD DATABASE (or for that matter, a DUMP TRANSACTION without a DUMP DATABASE). Both the dumping and loading of databases and transaction logs can be accomplished through SAF menus.

Syntax

```
LOAD TRANSACTION <database> FROM <dump_device>
```

The <database> parameter is the database to which the log dump is being applied from the <dump_device> parameter. SQL Server checks the timestamps on the database and transaction log dumps to ensure that they are being loaded in order. Figure 11-7 shows two scenarios, one depicting automatic recovery, the other showing manual recovery.

In the first scenario, the database dump is performed at time *t*0, and transaction log dumps are performed at times *t*1 and *t*2, respectively. Then the system crashes at time *t*3. During restart, automatic recovery on the database is performed using the transaction log. At time *t*4, the database is recovered to point *t*3; that is, all committed transactions are reflected and all uncommitted ones are not.

In the second scenario, the same sequence of events occurs up to time *t*3 when a head crash occurs that renders the disk unusable. In this case, the database must be restored from the database and log dumps. Assuming that a new disk is installed along with the devices, and the database is created, the LOAD statements in Example 11-5 would be executed. Then at time *t*5 the database is restored to its state as of time *t*3.

Example 11-5

```
use master
<exec>
```

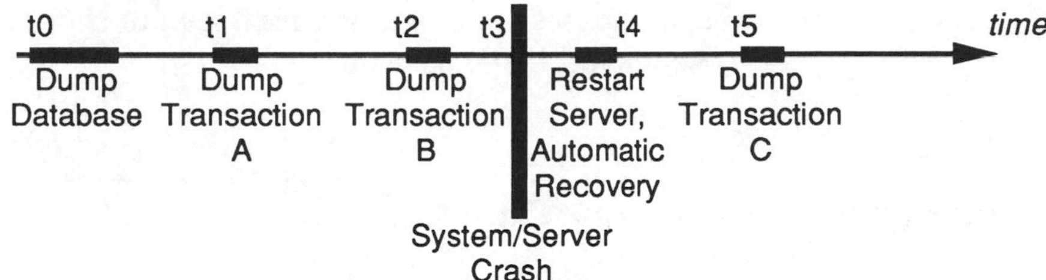

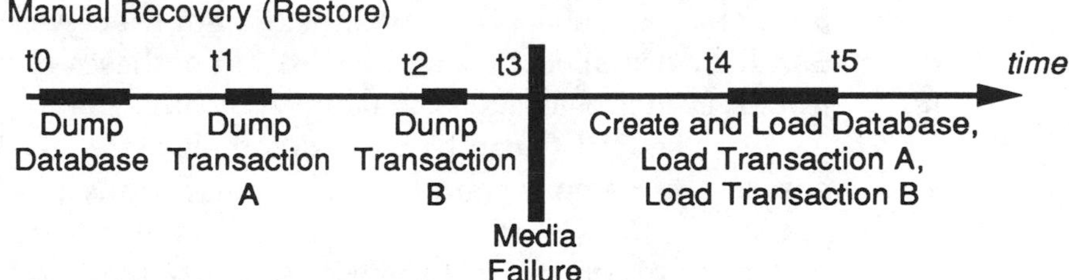

FIGURE 11-7 Automatic and manual recovery

```
load database testdb from dumpdev
<exec>
load transaction testdb from diskettedumpa                (Log Dump 1)
<exec>
load transaction testdb from diskettedumpa                (Log Dump 2)
<exec>

OUTPUT:
```

The *master* database should also be backed up, just like any other database, to ensure that it can be restored in case of a failure. However, the procedure to restore it is different from that of other databases, because it contains information about devices, other Server databases, login ids, and the like. The exact procedure varies based on when the last backup was done and is beyond the scope of this book. For readers interested in the exact procedure, please refer to the *SQL Server Administrator's Guide*. As a general rule, however, the procedure to recover the *master* database is greatly simplified if an up-to-date database backup is available. Whenever devices, databases, and login ids are added to the server, the *master* database should be backed up.

Database Consistency Checker

The database consistency checker (DBCC) is a diagnostic utility provided for the SA, the DBOs, and object owners to check various objects in the server environment for consistency in such areas as pointers, space allocation and indexes. For users who are intimately familiar with allocation and layout of databases and database objects it even provides a basic facility to patch the contents of pages.

The DBCC can be used as a diagnostic tool for many purposes. The SA may want to run it periodically to check the consistency of the server environment. It can also be run when a fatal system error occurs, or if the user suspects that a table or database might be corrupted. The DBCC can be run through either isql or through the SAF. There are several options to the DBCC (not all of which are included in the user documentation) that allow you to examine the consistency of database objects from different viewpoints.

Syntax

```
DBCC { CHECKTABLE (<table_name>)
    | CHECKDB [ (<database_name>) ]
    | CHECKALLOC [ (<database_name>) ]
    | CHECKCATALOG [ (<database_name>) ]
    | DBREPAIR (<database_name>, DROPDB) }
```

CHECKTABLE checks the specified table for correct data and index page linkage. CHECKDB performs a CHECKTABLE for all of the tables in the database specified. If no database is specified, the current database is assumed. CHECKALLOC checks to see that the allocation of pages to the database is consistent. CHECKCATALOG checks the consistency of the system tables for the specified database. DBREPAIR is used to drop damaged databases that cannot be dropped using a DROP DATABASE statement. Sample output reported by the CHECKTABLE, the CHECKALLOC, and the CHECKCATALOG options is shown in Example 11-6.

Example 11-6

```
use pubs
<exec>
dbcc checkdb
<exec>

OUTPUT:

Checking current database
Checking 1
The total number of data pages in this table is 2.
Checking 2
The total number of data pages in this table is 2.
Checking 3
The total number of data pages in this table is 4.
Checking 4
The total number of data pages in this table is 1.
Checking 5
The total number of data pages in this table is 12.
        .
        .
        .

Checking 512004855
The total number of data pages in this table is 1.
Checking 544004969
The total number of data pages in this table is 1.
Checking 576005083
The total number of data pages in this table is 2.
Checking 608005197
The total number of data pages in this table is 1.
Checking 640005311
The total number of data pages in this table is 1.
Checking 672005425
The total number of data pages in this table is 3.
```

```
Checking 704005539
The total number of data pages in this table is 1.
Checking 736005653
The total number of data pages in this table is 1.
DBCC execution completed. If DBCC printed error messages, see your
System Administrator.



dbcc checkalloc(pubs)

OUTPUT:

Checking pubs
Database 'pubs' is not in single user mode - may find spurious
allocation problems due to transactions in progress.
Alloc page 0 (# of extent=31 used pages=48 ref pages=48)
Alloc page 256 (# of extent=16 used pages=22 ref pages=22)
Alloc page 512 (# of extent=1 used pages=1 ref pages=1)
Alloc page 768 (# of extent=1 used pages=1 ref pages=1)
Total (# of extent=49 used pages=72 ref pages=72) in this database
DBCC execution completed. If DBCC printed error messages, see your
System Administrator.



dbcc checkcatalog(pubs)

OUTPUT:

Checking pubs
The following segments have been defined for database 4
(database name pubs).
virtual start addr      size      segments
--------------------    ------    --------------------------
3588                      1024
                                          0
                                          1
                                          2
DBCC execution completed. If DBCC printed error messages, see your
System Administrator.
```

Summary

This chapter discussed the problems of maintaining data consistency in multiuser transaction processing environments and how they are resolved using locking. It discussed the various types of locks employed by SQL Server—shared, exclusive, intent, and extent. SQL Server also provides automatic deadlock and livelock resolution and provides the HOLDLOCK keyword for repeatable read consistency. An overview of the two-phase commit protocol that can be used to implement distributed transactions in a DB-LIBRARY application was presented.

The chapter then focused on the two kinds of data recovery—automatic and manual. It discussed how the transaction log forms an important basis for providing recovery and how caching and checkpointing interact with data and log page writes. Automatic recovery is performed by Server on every restart. It rolls back all incomplete transactions at the time of the failure and rolls forward all transactions that are not reflected in the database. There is also manual recovery or restoration from a media failure; this is achieved through regular dumps of the databases and logs onto other media. Then, in case of a media failure, the database is restored from the most recent database dump and subsequent log dumps. Finally, the chapter discussed how the DBCC utility can be used to check the consistency of databases, tables, and systems and database catalogs, and to drop damaged databases.

CHAPTER 12

Tuning and Troubleshooting

Introduction

This chapter discusses the configuration parameters and options that can be used to tune the server for a particular application environment. Many of these options are available to regular users. Options that affect overall server performance can be used only by the SA. In addition, potential problems that can arise in the server environment are discussed; suggestions are made for their diagnosis and remedy.

Performance Tuning

Several configuration parameters and options can be set by users to affect the performance of the Server. They are used to maximize performance. Performance tuning can be accomplished at various levels—at the level of individual queries, at the database level, or even at the Server level.

Tuning Query Execution

There are various ways to affect the performance of SQL queries. The most basic is the structure of the query itself. This does not include the order in which the columns are listed in the SELECT clause or the order of the various conditions that appear in a WHERE clause—these are resolved by SQL Server's efficient cost-based optimizer. Instead, it is the way the query is formulated. The same results can often be obtained with differently formulated queries. You need to select the form that is most efficient for your application.

Using stored procedures optimizes the processing of frequently used transactions. As discussed in Chapter 3, a normal SQL query goes through several stages in its processing—parsing, protection checking, optimization, compilation, and execution. Since stored procedures are precompiled, the only steps that need to be processed are protection checking and execution. Of course, if parameters are passed to the stored procedure, parameter substitution has to take place prior to execution. Despite this, stored procedures generally execute faster than ad-hoc queries. This performance improvement is seen especially in queries whose execution time is short (usually less than a few seconds), since the time to parse and compile the query becomes a significant percentage of the total time to process the query. For queries that have a large execution phase, stored procedures may yield only minor gains.

To further optimize the processing of queries, SQL Server provides a variety of options that can be used to control and tune it. These options are available to all users—no permissions are required. They remain in effect only for the current session or until they are reset explicitly. A session is defined as a user connection to the Server. It is managed by a user task at the Server end. (A single client application may open multiple sessions with the server.) These options are controlled with the SET command. The syntax follows.

Syntax

```
SET {{ PARSEONLY | NOEXEC | SHOWPLAN | BACKGROUND |
       STATISTICS IO | STATISTICS TIME | NOCOUNT |
       ARITHABORT | ARITHIGNORE |
       OFFSETS {<keyword_list>} | PROCID}
      {ON | OFF} | ROWCOUNT <number> | TEXTSIZE <number>}
```

The SET command options can be classified into four categories:

- query-processing options
- options to display performance statistics
- exception-handling options
- options for application program use to interpret results

The next sections discuss these categories in turn.

Query-Processing Options

The options that control the way a query is processed are PARSEONLY, NOEXEC, SHOWPLAN, BACKGROUND, NOCOUNT, ROWCOUNT, and TEXTSIZE. The PARSEONLY option causes SQL Server to parse the query for syntactic and semantic correctness only, without optimizing, compiling, or executing it. This is useful for determining if a query has been formulated correctly, without actually having it compiled and executed.

The NOEXEC option performs all the steps through compilation, but does not execute the query. It is often used with the SHOWPLAN option to determine the execution plan generated for a query. This is especially useful for queries with large execution times. Once NOEXEC is set, no further statements are executed (including other SET statements), until the NOEXEC option is reset to OFF. Of course, it does not make sense to set both the PARSEONLY and the NOEXEC options to ON. Both PARSEONLY and NOEXEC are useful with large tables, where the query will take a long time to execute. These options are used to debug queries prior to their actual execution.

SHOWPLAN is probably the most useful query-processing option. It reveals the query execution plan generated by SQL Server's cost-based optimizer. The execution plan describes in fairly simple terms the exact plan the optimizer uses to process the query. It allows the user to see in what order the server processes join conditions and which of the defined indexes it uses. Thus the user could define additional indexes, or update the statistics maintained by server to optimize performance. A description of the criteria used by SQL Server's optimizer is beyond the scope of this book; it is sufficient to say that they are very sophisticated and include such criteria as the distribution of key values within an index. Once the plan is generated, the query is executed unless the NOEXEC option is set.

Example 12-1

```
use pubs
<exec>
set showplan on
<exec>

select au_lname, au_fname, city, state
from authors
where au_lname = "Ringer"
<exec>
```

```
OUTPUT:

STEP 1
The type of query is SELECT
FROM TABLE
authors
Nested iteration
Table Scan
au_lname                            au_fname             city                 state
----------------------------------- -------------------- -------------------- -----
Ringer                              Anne                 Salt Lake City       UT
Ringer                              Albert               Salt Lake City       UT
(2 rows affected)
```

The BACKGROUND option puts tasks generated by subsequent statements in the background and breaks the connection to the workstation. This option is useful, for example, if a long operational procedure is started by the SA every midnight. Instead of waiting for completion, the SA can initiate the procedure using the SET BACKGROUD ON and monitor the results at a more convenient time. Once the BACKGROUND is set to ON, the workstation session is terminated and the user must log on again to reestablish a session. This is true even for a SET statement executed from within a stored procedure; the session is not automatically reestablished when the stored procedure finishes executing.

If the NOCOUNT option is set to ON, the message displayed at the end of each statement execution indicating the number of rows affected by that statement—does not appear. This option is often used inside stored procedures or triggers that consist of several statements; it suppresses the row counts for the individual statements. The option, if set within a trigger or procedure, is only in effect within the body of that stored procedure or trigger. However, the global variable `@@rowcount` (which stores the number of rows affected by the last statement) is still updated, even if the NOCOUNT option is set to ON, so the information can be obtained if needed.

Finally, the SET ROWCOUNT option is used to specify the maximum number of rows the server should process. The Server stops processing additional rows when either the `number` specified is reached or there are no more rows to return. To reset the option to return all rows, the statement SET ROWCOUNT 0 is executed. The related option, SET TEXTSIZE is used to control the number of bytes returned by a query for a column of text or image data type. The `number` specified is stored in the global variable `@@textsize`, the default value being 255. You can display the current setting by executing the statement SELECT `@@textsize`. If `@@textsize` is set to 0, 32K bytes of data are returned (remember, text and image column data can be pretty large).

Statistics Options

Two options, STATISTICS TIME and STATISTICS IO, are used to monitor and display statistical information about the processing of TRANSACT-SQL statements. The default setting for both options is OFF. STATISTICS TIME displays times for parsing, compiling, and executing queries. The times, given in milliseconds, are useful in determining the individual components of processing. They can be used with the SHOWPLAN option to determine why a query takes an inordinately long time to execute.

The STATISTICS IO option displays several pieces of useful information: the number of table scans, the number of logical accesses (cache reads), the number of physical accesses (disk I/Os), and the total number of pages written, including log page writes. In general, all this information can be used to determine if the query is being executed efficiently. If not, the query can be formulated alternatively, or the cache size adjusted to improve performance. The number of table scans needed to process a query, for example, should be small. It indicates an efficient execution plan. The number of physical reads should be small compared to the number of logical reads, indicating efficient use of the cache. For update statements, the total number of pages written indicates the number of data and log pages written. Since the Server shares data and log page writes among users, this number may include writing other users' dirty data and log pages.

Example 12-2

```
use pubs
<exec>
set statistics time on
```

```
<exec>
set statistics io on
<exec>

select title, au_lname, au_fname
from titles, titleauthor, authors
where titles.title_id = titleauthor.title_id and
      titleauthor.au_id = authors.au_id and
      type = "business"
<exec>

OUTPUT:

Parse and Compile Time 0
SQL Server cpu time: 0 ms.
Parse and Compile Time 1
SQL Server cpu time: 31 ms.
title                                                 au_fname  au_lname
----------------------------------------------------- --------- ----------
The Busy Executive's Database Guide                   Marjorie  Green
The Busy Executive's Database Guide                   Abraham   Bennet
Cooking with Computers: Surreptitious Balance Sheets  Michael   O'Leary
Cooking with Computers: Surreptitious Balance Sheets  Stearns   MacFeather
You Can Combat Computer Stress!                       Marjorie  Green
Straight Talk about Computers                         Dick      Straight
Table: titles scan count 1, logical reads: 3, physical reads: 0
Table: titleauthor scan count 4, logical reads: 4, physical reads:0
Table: authors scan count 6, logical reads: 6, physical reads: 0
Total writes for this command: 0

Execution Time 2
SQL Server cpu time: 62 ms. SQL Server elapsed time: 90 ms.
(6 rows affected)
```

Exception Handling

The ARITHABORT and ARITHIGNORE options are used to control how the server handles exceptions during query execution. Setting the ARITHABORT option to ON causes the query to be aborted if a divide by zero or overflow condition occurs during execution. Setting the ARITHIGNORE option to ON returns a

NULL when either of the above exceptions occurs. No error message is returned. You cannot set both the options to ON. The default setting, both options set to OFF, causes SQL Server to return both an error message and a NULL.

Result Interpretation

The OFFSETS option and the PROCID option allow application programs to interpret results from the SQL Server. The OFFSETS option is used in DB-LIBRARY application programs to return the position, relative to the beginning of the query, of specified TRANSACT-SQL constructs in the command buffer. The command buffer is part of the DBPROCESS structure used to establish a connection to the Server (see Chapter 6). The keywords that can be specified are SELECT, FROM, ORDER, COMPUTE, TABLE, PROCEDURE, STATEMENT, PARAM, and EXEC. The OFFSETS option is useful, for example, if the program does not know the current contents of the command buffer, or if it wants to examine or replace part of the command buffer. For example, a program can check for the existence of a SELECT statement in the buffer by checking the offset of the SELECT keyword. In another example, the application may want to examine the ORDER BY clause in a SELECT statement by first determining its offset in the command buffer.

Setting the PROCID option returns the ID of the stored procedure to the DB-LIBRARY application before returning any rows generated as a result of the stored procedure. In this way the application can determine which stored procedure is being executed and the nature of the rows being returned to it by the procedure, before it actually receives the rows.

Database Tuning

There are several points the DBO or the database designer can keep in mind when optimizing performance at the database level. Some of them have been mentioned at different points throughout the book; most of them are discussed in this section.

A commonly overlooked area for optimizing database performance is database design. For example, the database designer can define appropriate indexes to improve the performance of frequently used queries or stored procedures. This is an area where it is useful to experiment with the SET options SHOWPLAN and STATISTICS IO. They can show how existing indexes are being used. It is generally advisable to define indexes on nonvolatile columns, or read-only columns, because there is minimal overhead in maintaining such indexes. On the other hand, you should avoid defining indexes on volatile columns (unless, of course, it is essential), since there is additional overhead in maintaining them.

Another area where performance can be improved is database object ownership. Although different objects within a database can be owned by different users, it is advisable to have a single user (typically the DBO) own all database objects. It has to do with the way permissions are checked for such dependent objects as views and procedures. The rules for checking permissions on dependent objects are discussed in Chapter 9. There are two reasons for advocating a single owner for all database objects. First, it simplifies the task of assigning permissions for accessing objects. Second, query execution against dependent objects is more efficient, since SQL Server checks permissions in a dependent object ownership chain only when the owners are different. If there is only one owner, it checks to see if the user has permission to access the dependent object only, which significantly reduces the time spent checking permissions during execution. Hence, from both a performance viewpoint and from the administrative viewpoint of assigning permissions, it is advantageous for the DBO to own all objects in a database.

Another important area of database optimization is the placement of the transaction log. By default, the database and the transaction log share the same space. Although this may be acceptable for small databases (less than a few megabytes), for larger databases it is advisable to put the transaction log on a device separate from that of the database. The log can then be backed up independently from the database, which allows incremental backups. The transaction log dumps can be performed more frequently, reducing the window of vulnerability in case of a media failure. Since the Server also allows dynamic dumps, it is easy to perform dumps frequently. In addition, when the transaction log is on a separate device on a physically separate hard disk with its own controller, there is no contention between the data and log page writes. This also produces performance improvements.

Database Options

There are several database options that the SA or the DBO can set for user databases to affect the state of the database. However, they cannot be changed for the *master* database. They are dbo use only, read only, select into/bulkcopy, single user, no chkpt on recovery, and trunc.log on chkpt. These options are set and their current values displayed using the `sp_dboption` system procedure; they must be changed from the *master* database. For the change to take effect, a CHECKPOINT must be executed in the database for which the options are changed. If `sp_dboption` is executed without any parameters, it displays a list of all the options that can be set. The syntax of the `sp_dboption` system procedure follows.

Syntax

```
sp_dboption [ <database>, <option_name>, { TRUE | FALSE } ]
```

The `<database>` parameter is the database for which the option is being changed, and `<option_name>` is the option being set. The *dbo use only* option restricts the use of the database to the DBO as long as the option is set. The *no chkpt on recovery* prevents the Server from writing a checkpoint record to the transaction log on recovery. The checkpoint record insures that recovery won't be rerun at system restart. The *no chkpt on recovery* option is useful when dual copies of the same database, a primary and a secondary, are maintained for redundancy reasons. Setting the option on the secondary database allows the log from the primary database to be applied to the secondary database; otherwise the checkpoint record that is added to the secondary database transaction log prevents this. The READ ONLY option allows users to retrieve data only; this prevents users from modifying database contents. This option is used only for static databases, for example, a historical database. Individual tables can also be made read only by revoking all INSERT, UPDATE, and DELETE privileges on the table from all users.

The *select into/bulkcopy* option is used to allow nonlogged operations on a database. These include the SELECT..INTO and the WRITETEXT statements and bulk copying of data. The SELECT..INTO statement creates a new table (either permanent or temporary) from other permanent tables. If it is a permanent table, the *select into/bulkcopy* option must be set. Temporary tables are created in the *tempdb* database, where the option is set by default. The *tempdb* database is never recovered; it is initialized at system startup. The WRITETEXT statement allows you to interactively update a text column within a table. WRITETEXT can be logged or nonlogged. Nonlogged WRITETEXT statements are desirable when large updates to text columns cause the log to grow rapidly. To permit the nonlogged operation the *select into/bulkcopy* option must be set for the database.

The bulk copy utility, as mentioned in Chapter 10, has two modes of operation, fast and slow. The fast mode is invoked automatically if the table being loaded has no indexes. In addition the *select into/bulkcopy* option must also be set for the database. Setting the option, of course, precludes the use of the DUMP TRANSACTION statement (since the operation is not logged). You must use the DUMP DATABASE statement to back up the entire database instead. This is recommended, especially after bulk loading large amounts of data. If there are indexes on the table being loaded, the slow mode is automatically invoked. In this case, the *select into/bulkcopy* option can be set to use logging or not.

The *single user* option, if set to TRUE, allows only one user at a time to access the database. This is different from *dbo use only,* which allows only the DBO to use the database. With *single user* any user can access the database, as long as there is no other user currently accessing it. This option can be used to perform sensitive operations on the database, when other users modifying the database at the same time would be disruptive.

The *trunc.log on chkpt.* option causes the inactive portion of the log (the committed transactions) to be cleared automatically on every checkpoint. Normally, the option is set to FALSE, and the only way to truncate the transaction log is to dump it. This option is useful in development environments, when transaction log dumps are not needed. In such environments, if the transaction log is never dumped, it continues to grow and would eventually runs out of space. Setting the option to TRUE prevents this. Of course, in this case the DUMP TRANSACTION statement does not work; so you must use the DUMP DATABASE statement instead.

These then are the database options that can be set with the `sp_dboption` system procedure. The default setting for all of these options is FALSE. To change the default value, change the value of the option in the *model* database; all databases created from then on will inherit the new value for the option. Example 12-3 shows how to set the *select into/bulkcopy* option for the *pubs* database to allow use of the bulk copy utility to load its tables.

Example 12-3

```
use master
<exec>
sp_dboption pubs, "select into", TRUE
<exec>

OUTPUT:

Run the CHECKPOINT command in the database that was changed.


use pubs
<exec>
checkpoint
<exec>

OUTPUT:
```

For the `<option_name>` parameter, any unique sequence of characters can be entered. Example 12-3 uses *select into* instead of the full name. To get a list of all options, you can execute `sp_dboption` with no parameters. You can also use the special option ALL SETTABLE OPTIONS to set all possible options. The current setting of these options for all the databases is recorded in the *sysdatabases* system table.

To look at the current settings of the options for any database, use the sp_helpdb system procedure. The output, as Example 12-4 indicates, shows which options are set.

Example 12-4

```
sp_helpdb

OUTPUT:

name               db_size  owner           dbid  created      status
------------------ -------- --------------- ----  -----------  ---------------------
costdb             2 MB     sa              6     Apr 22 1990  no options set
empdb              3 MB     sa              7     Apr 28 1990  no options set
master             3 MB     sa              1     Jan  1 1900  no options set
model              2 MB     sa              3     Jan  1 1900  no options set
proxydb            6 MB     sa              5     Jan  1 1900  no options set
pubs               2 MB     sa              4     May 30 1990  select into/bulkcopy
tempdb             2 MB     sa              2     Jan  1 1900  select into/bulkcopy
(0 rows affected)
```

Server Tuning

SQL Server provides a host of configuration parameters that affect various aspects of its performance. The default values for these configuration parameters provided by the setup program at installation, are based on the assumption that there is great deal of transaction activity and that there are few procedures in use. For environments where these assumptions don't apply, the SA can change all of these parameters in order to optimize the server's performance for any particular environment. The values selected depend on both the resources available to SQL Server and the usage characteristics of the environment.

Configuration Parameters

The configuration parameters can be classified broadly into dynamic and nondynamic parameters. Within nondynamic parameters there are both general and memory configuration parameters.

The dynamic parameters include *recovery interval* and *allow updates* (to system tables). The memory parameters include total *memory* available to the Server, maximum number of *user connections,* and percentage of total memory allocated to the *procedure cache.* The general parameters include *open databases, open objects,* maximum number of active *locks, fill factor* on indexes, *time slice* allocated for a task, default *database size, media retention, recovery flags,* and *serial number.*

The individual configuration parameters will be examined after a general discussion of how they work. Dynamic parameters take effect immediately after their values are set and a RECONFIGURE command is executed. Nondynamic parameters require the RECONFIGURE command to be executed, and only take effect on the next Server restart.

To understand how these parameters take effect, you need to know how they are maintained by the Server and how their current values are displayed and changed. The Server maintains two similar system tables in the *master* database—*sysconfigures,* used to store the currently configured value, and *syscurconfigs*, used to store the current run-time value. These tables are used to store configuration parameter values. The parameters themselves are displayed and changed through the `sp_configure` system procedure.

Syntax

```
sp_configure [<config_name> [, <config_value> ]]
```

The `<config_name>` parameter is the name of the parameter value being displayed or set, and the `<config_value>` parameter is the value to which it is being set. If neither parameter is specified, the current configured and run-time values of all parameters are displayed. If `<config_name>` is specified, the current values of that parameter are displayed. If both parameters are specified, the value is set to the value specified, provided it is in the range of legal values. Only the SA has permission to change global Server configuration parameters.

Example 12-5

```
sp_configure
```

```
OUTPUT:

name                minimum     maximum     config_value run_value
------------------ ----------- ----------- ------------ ---------
recovery interval            1       32767            4         5
allow updates                0           1            0         0
user connections             5        1024          100       100
memory                    1000       14000         5616      5616
open databases               5         100           20        20
locks                     5000       50000         5000      5000
open objects               100       10000          500       500
procedure cache              1          99           20        20
fill factor                  0         100            0         0
time slice                  50        1000          100       100
database size                2       10000            2         2
media retention              0         365            0         0
recovery flags               0           1            0         0
serial number                1      999999            0         0
(14 rows affected)
```

As you can see in Example 12-5, there are two values the Server maintains for each configuration parameter—the current configured value (in *sysconfigures*) and the current value it is using (in *syscurconfigs*). Once the parameters are changed, the RECONFIGURE statement must be executed for the new configured value to take effect. For the nondynamic parameters the Server must then be restarted for the new value to be used by the Server, since this is when the *syscurconfigs* table is built from the *sysconfigures* table. For dynamic parameters, however, the configured values are used immediately, they are set in *syscurconfigs* right after the RECONFIGURE command.

Memory Parameters The three parameters that together control how the memory allocated to the Server is used are *memory, user connections* and *procedure cache.* The memory parameter specifies the total memory available to the Server in pages (2K bytes). The default value is calculated and set by the setup program based on total memory available on the machine.

The memory available on the machine accommodates the operating system (OS/2), the network software, SQL Server, and any other applications running on it. With a dedicated SQL Server the overhead for the operating system and the network depends on the version of OS/2 and the network installed, as well as the network services installed on the Server machine. In general, the figure is approximately 4Mb, and the minimal SQL Server configuration is approximately 2Mb, which totals a minimal memory requirement of 6Mb. If additional software, such as Presentation Manager or some e-mail software, is installed, the figure must be proportionately higher to prevent excessive swapping.

The total memory allocated to SQL Server is used for many components. It loads the Server executable and allocates all its static memory needs—for the kernel, internal buffers, space for user tasks, and so on. The remaining memory is allocated to the cache, which is used for data and log pages and stored procedures. Figure 12-1 shows the different components that make up the total memory usage of the SQL Server. The total memory, of course, is the amount of memory allocated to the Server. Part of this memory is used by the Server itself, including the space it allocates statically at startup.

The user connection parameter determines the maximum number of simultaneous user connections to the server. Each user connection has an overhead of approximately 42Kb of memory on the server. This is for the server task that corresponds to the client connection. The number of user connections does not reflect the number of individual users logged on to the Server, but rather to

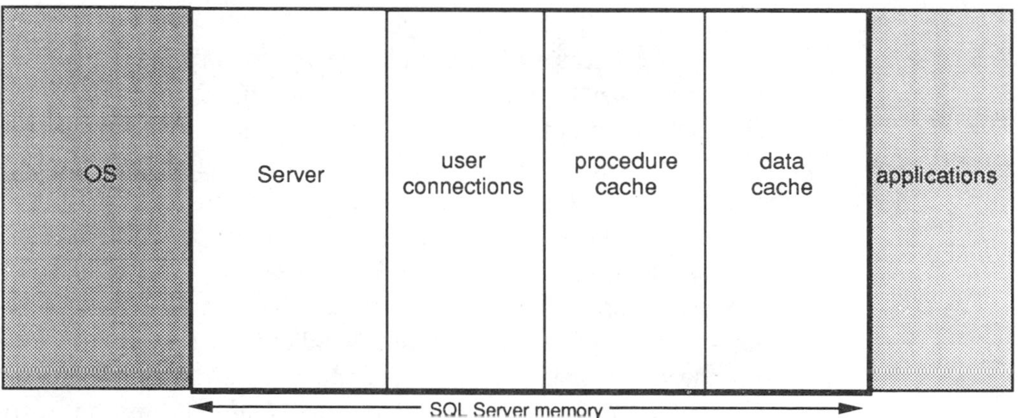

FIGURE 12-1 Memory usage of the SQL Server

each connection from a user application. Each connection requires a file descriptor; the maximum number of file descriptors allowed is 256. The current value of the maximum connections possible is stored in `@@max_connections`.

The way the application is programmed determines the exact number of connections established by each application. In a DB-LIBRARY application, each call to `dbopen()` yields a new DBPROCESS structure, which corresponds to a new user connection. Applications using browse mode, however, require a minimum of two connections, one for reading and one for updating. In addition, the Server uses a minimum of five connections—one each for the network listening socket, standard output, error logging, the *master* database device, and the console utility network listening socket. The Server also requires a connection for each device opened at startup.

The memory remaining after meeting the Server's needs and the user connection needs is allocated to the cache. The *procedure cache* parameter is the percentage of the total cache reserved for procedures; the remainder is used to cache data pages. The procedure cache is used both for executing stored procedures and for creating and compiling them. If SQL Server finds a procedure in cache, it does not need to read it from disk. The percentage can be varied to affect the size of the procedure cache in relation to the data cache. The data cache is used for data, index, and log pages.

General Parameters The memory parameters—*memory, user connections,* and *procedure cache*—have been discussed. The dynamic parameters—*recovery interval* and *allow updates*—will be discussed later. The remaining parameters fall into the general category. This section briefly describes each one. The *open databases* and *open objects* parameters depend on the environment. The default values for the maximum number are 20 and 500, respectively. Each open database occupies space in the disk cache; each open object requires approximately 40 bytes in memory. Other than that there is no significant overhead in raising these values if the environment so dictates. The maximum *locks* parameter is the maximum number of simultaneous locks that can be held by the

Server. The default value is 5000. If this is not sufficient, the number can be raised to a higher value. Raising this number has no significant impact on performance.

The *fill factor* parameter determines how full an index page is when one is being created. Every time a key value is inserted in an index page that is full, SQL Server splits the page and copies half of the new key values to the new page. This process consumes valuable resources. Therefore, in databases that are likely to grow rapidly, there is an advantage in creating lightly loaded index pages. The *fill factor* parameter specifies how lightly they should be loaded. Once set, the fill factor value is used whenever an index is created, until a different value is specifed in the CREATE INDEX statement (discussed in Chapter 4). The legal range of values is 0 to 100; the default is 0. When the value is 0, that SQL Server calculates an appropriate value for loading nonleaf pages in the index and completely fills leaf pages.

The *time slice* configuration parameter specifies in milliseconds the maximum CPU time a user task can run. Remember that SQL Server is single process and multithreaded, and it has its own scheduler to handle task or thread scheduling. The scheduler allows a task to run for a length of time up to a maximum amount specified by this parameter, before it switches to another task. (When the task does not need the entire time slice allotted to it, the switch occurs earlier.) The default value for this parameter is 100 milliseconds, and there is seldom reason to change it.

The *database size* parameter specifies the default size (in Mb) for every new user database. This value is used only if the size parameter is not specified in the CREATE DATABASE statement. The default value of database size is 2Mb. New databases are created by copying the *model* database, so the size of a new user database (if no size is specified) is either the same size as the *model* or the value specified by the *database size* parameter, whichever is higher. To specify a default size of 10Mb, you don't need to alter *model* to 10Mb. You simply specify a default size of 10Mb. If you leave the default set to 2Mb, you still get a database larger than 2Mb if *model* has increased in size beyond 2Mb (due to such additions as rules, defaults, procedures, and so on).

The *media retention* parameter specifies the number of days to retain each diskette that has been used for a database or log dump before allowing it to be reused. The parameter is simply a protection mechanism so that the diskettes are not accidentally overwritten before the specified number of days. If an attempt is made to overwrite the diskette before the specified number of days, a warning message is issued. The warning can, however, be overridden. The default value of 0 means the diskette can never be reused; a more typical value is 7 days. This parameter is more meaningful when tapes are used for backups. Tapes are typically recycled. In other words, they are used in a circular fashion for backing up databases and transaction logs; the oldest tape is used for the current backup. This parameter is also meaningful in the Server environment that backs up to cartridge tape.

The *recovery flags* parameter determines what information SQL Server writes to the errorlog file during startup. The default value is 0, which implies that the Server is in nonverbose, or brief, mode. This mode displays such minimal information as the time of startup, information on the devices it is using, and the databases it processes during recovery, along with the counts of transactions rolled forward and back. If the parameter is set to 1 (verbose mode), the Server additionally displays information for each individual transaction it recovers, including roll back or roll forward status.

The *serial number* parameter has been reserved for future editions of SQL Server. It is used to store the serial number for the SQL Server software being run. The *serial number* parameter is currently set to zero. The SA can change the value through the `sp_configure` system procedure. The parameter is not accessible through the SAF menus.

Dynamic Parameters Dynamic parameters are so named because they take effect immediately after the RECONFIGURE statement. The two dynamic configuration parameters are *recovery interval* and *allow updates.* The recovery interval parameter specifies the worst case time (in minutes) that will be required to recover a database during system startup. The default value for this parameter is 5 minutes per database. The range of permissible values is 1 through 32,767 minutes. The *allow updates* parameter determines whether or not the system tables can be updated directly through TRANSACT-SQL DML statements. By default, it is set to 0, indicating that it cannot.

SQL Server uses the recovery interval value to compute an automatic checkpoint interval for its own use. As discussed in Chapter 10, there is a close relationship between the recovery interval and the checkpoint interval. At the checkpoint, the cache and the database are synchronized. The amount of recovery work is roughly proportional to the transaction activity that takes place since the most recent checkpoint. In order for databases to recover quickly, checkpoints must occur often. If a system failure occurs just prior to a checkpoint, all the activity to the last checkpoint must be recovered. This represents the worst-case recovery time. SQL Server, using its proprietary algorithm, computes the checkpoint interval from the worst-case recovery time specified by the *recovery interval* parameter. A shorter recovery interval, therefore, yields a shorter checkpoint interval—checkpoints occur more frequently.

The *allow updates* parameter specifies whether or not the system tables can be updated directly. Normally, even the SA and DBO are not allowed to update the system tables directly using TRANSACT-SQL statements; they must do so using the system procedures. This acts as a safeguard against an accidentally incorrect or inconsistent update of the system tables. Since the system tables store vital system information, their corruption can harm the very operation of the Server. In some cases, however, it may be necessary for the SA or DBO to update the system tables directly. Such a case might be when the tables have been corrupted in the first place, due to some unpredictable circumstance. To perform such updates, the SA must first set the *allow updates* parameter.

The *allow updates* parameter is dynamic, meaning that it takes effect immediately after the RECONFIGURE statement is executed. Caution should be exercised when this parameter is used, since the system tables can be updated while it is set. Furthermore, any procedure (that updates the system tables) that is created while the parameter is set can update the system tables even after the parameter is reset. Hence, the *allow updates* parameter should be set only for the duration needed. As a general guideline, the Server should be brought up in single user mode whenever the parameter has to be set. This is achieved by directly starting the Server from the command line with the /m option (see Chapter 10). Once the required updates have been performed, the parameter can be reset and the Server restarted normally to allow the other users to log on to the Server.

Finally, it should be noted that all of these configuration parameters can be displayed and set easily by the SA through the Admin menu selection from the SAF. For other users these menu selections are not accessible (they are grayed out). When the SA wants to change any of the parameters, he or she selects the Config menu from the SAF main menu. On the Config menu the choices presented are Memory options, General options, and Dynamic option (corresponding to the three categories of parameters). If one of these options is chosen, the current run-time parameter values and the range of legal values for that category are displayed. To change a value, the new value is entered in the box where the old one is displayed and confirmed with an OK. For nondynamic options a message reminds the SA to restart the server.

Monitoring Server Activity

SQL Server maintains information about system activity in predefined global variables. Global variables are similar to local variables, except they can be accessed from any procedure and have variable names that begin with two at-signs (@@), for example, `@@cpu_busy`. There are several system procedures that SQL Server provides to monitor system activity. Two that have already been discussed are `sp_lock` (which displays active locks) and `sp_who` (which displays currently logged-on users). A third stored procedure used to monitor system activity is the `sp_monitor` stored procedure. It displays some of the global variables that store information about system activity.

The `sp_monitor` procedure has no parameters; it displays the variables in the format `<number>(<number>)-number%` or `number(number)`. The first number refers to a value relative to the last SQL Server restart. The number in parentheses refers to the change, or delta, in the value since the last time `sp_monitor` was run. The percentage number indicates the percentage of time since the last execution of `sp_monitor`.

Example 12-6

```
sp_monitor
```

```
OUTPUT:

last_run             current_run          seconds
-------------------- -------------------- -----------
 May 30 1990  2:55PM  May 30 1990 11:16PM       30073

(0 rows affected)
cpu_busy                  io_busy                   idle
------------------------- ------------------------- -------------------------
1695(1616)-5%            20(16)-0%                 0(0)-0%

(0 rows affected)
packets_received          packets_sent              packet_errors
------------------------- ------------------------- -------------------------
311(299)                  325(310)                  0(0)
(0 rows affected)

total_read          total_write         total_errors        connections
------------------- ------------------- ------------------- -------------------

341(186)            2030(1934)          0(0)                18(17)
(0 rows affected)
```

This is a list of the columns reported by sp_monitor.

Column	Meaning
last-run	clock time at which sp_monitor was executed
current_run	current clock time
seconds	seconds since last run
cpu_busy	number in milliseconds of CPU time used by SQL Server
io_busy	number in milliseconds of CPU time spent by SQL Server in doing I/O
idle	number in milliseconds of CPU time the Server has been idle
pack_received	number of packets received by SQL Server
pack_sent	number of packets written by SQL Server

`packet_errors`	number of errors detected by SQL Server in writing and reading packets
`total_read`	number of reads by SQL Server
`total_write`	number of writes by SQL Server
`total_errors`	number of errors detected by SQL Server
`connections`	number of logins or attempted logins into SQL Server

All of the values reported by `sp_monitor` are global variables of the same name (except for `last_run`, `current_run` and `seconds`). The values of these global variables can be reported using the SELECT statement. However, the values reported for global variables are in *ticks,* not milliseconds for the `@@cpu_busy`, `@@io_busy`, and the `@@idle` global variables. A clock tick in OS/2 is 31.25 milliseconds (1/32 second).

Example 12-7

```
SELECT @@pack_sent

OUTPUT:

 -----------
        328

(1 row affected)
```

Other global variables (`@@rowcount`, `@@error`, `@@textsize`, and so on) are not displayed by `sp_monitor`.

In tuning the Server, it is important to keep in mind that there should be sufficient memory on the machine not only to run the Server, but also to support the OS, network, and users for the server environment, and leave memory for the cache. Otherwise, the Server may swap in and out of memory, and performance suffers. If there isn't enough memory, you should seek other alternatives, one of which is to run a dedicated server, without other applications or additional network services. If all else fails, consider getting more serious hardware to meet your performance needs.

Troubleshooting

This section explores the potential problems the SA or DBO can encounter as caretakers of the Server or its databases. The tools and means available to diagnose and troubleshoot the system, and the possible actions to rectify them are examined. The various levels of error and warning messages returned from the Server and their associated levels of severity are presented.

Errors

SQL Server error messages are classified according to their severity into various levels. Whenever an error is returned by the Server, whether it is caused by user or system, several pieces of information are returned to the user application (which is basically a DB-LIBRARY application). The information includes the severity level, a message state, an error number, and the error text. Two kinds of errors can occur in a DB-LIBRARY application—those related to DB-LIBRARY usage (invalid function parameters, invalid usage of DB-LIBRARY functions, and so on), and those returned by the Server. The first is termed **errors** and the second **messages** in SQL Server terminology. This section talks about messages.

SQL Server error messages are stored in the *sysmessages* system table and have severity levels from 10 through 25 associated with them. Levels 10 through 16 are user errors, which are caused by some action of the user. They include syntax errors, invalid object names, inappropriate permissions, and so on. To correct these errors, the user must determine what caused the error and correct the situation.

Levels 17 through 24 indicate software or hardware errors. Levels 17 and 18 (explained in detail later in this section) are nonfatal errors. When these occur, the user can usually continue to work but may not be able to execute the statement that caused the error. Levels 19 through 24 are fatal system errors. When they occur, the process that caused the error is terminated and the connection to the user is broken. Depending on the severity of the problem, the user may or may not be able to reconnect. Fatal errors may cause damage to the database.

The following paragraphs briefly discuss each error severity level. Figure 12-2 shows the error message severity ranges and possible actions to rectify the errors. Level 10 indicates messages that are not really errors but status information. For example, the mes-

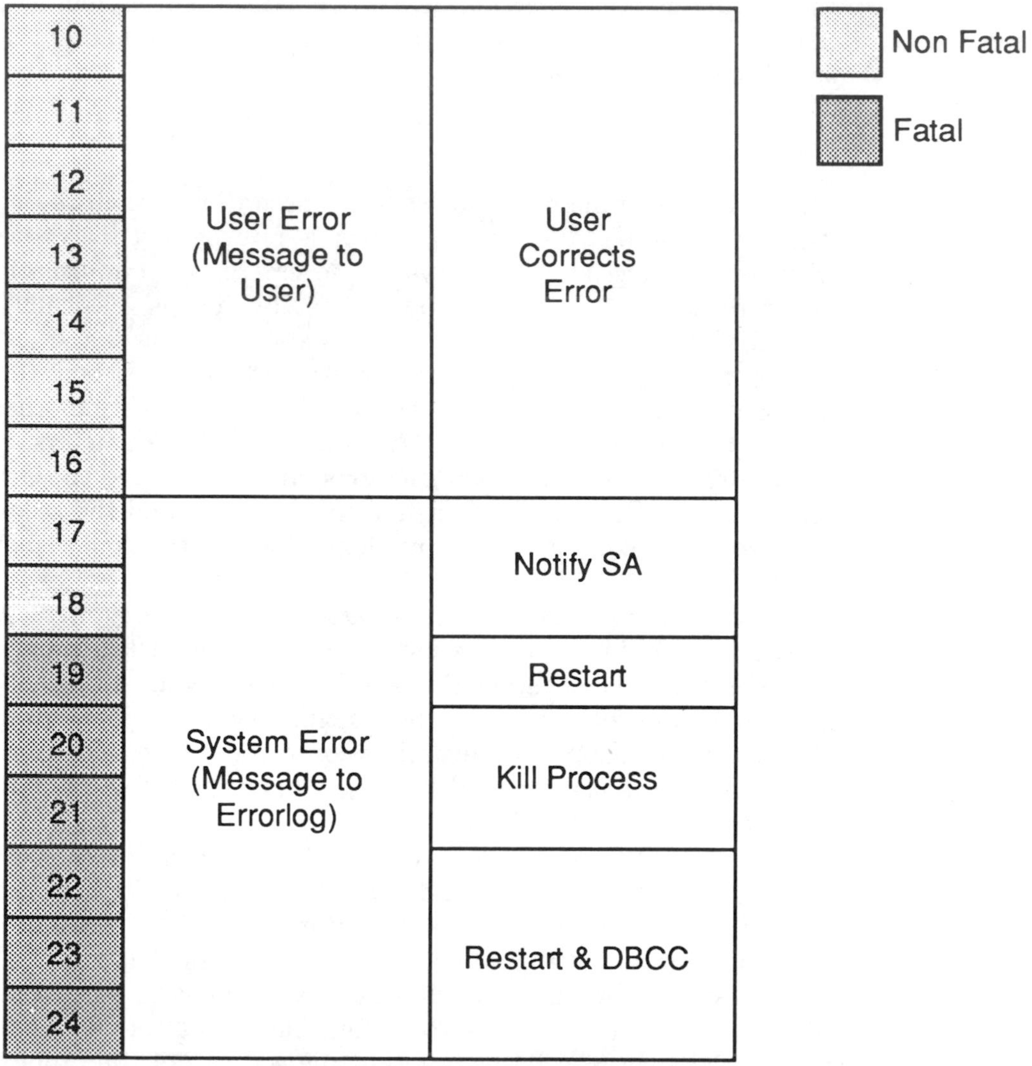

FIGURE 12-2 Error severity levels and possible actions

sage that indicates the number of pages allocated on a CREATE DATABASE statement falls within this category.

Severity level 11 indicates an invalid reference to an object, such as an invalid table name. An error may have resulted because the object does not exist, the name is misspelled, or the name is not qualified correctly. Level 12 indicates a data type error. A data type error can occur, for example, if a value of one data type is loaded into a column of an incompatible data type, or if values of incompatible types are combined in an expression. Level 13 is a transaction-related error. Such an error can be as simple as a missing BEGIN TRANSACTION statement or a more serious deadlock resolution. Level 14 is for invalid permissions. An example of an invalid permission error is an update to a table or an attempt to execute a procedure for which the user does not have permission. Level 15 is a syntax error in a TRANSACT-SQL statement. The error message indicates the line number and the word where the error is detected when the statement is parsed. Level 16 is for miscellaneous user errors that cannot be grouped into any of the preceding categories. For example, ambiguous column name references in a statement fall into this category.

Level 17 errors are resource errors. One example of a resource error is insufficient disk space on a device (either for data or the log). In another example, a resource error is returned when a system-configured value (for open databases, locks, objects, connections, and so on) has been reached. These problems can usually be corrected by the SA or DBO if resources are still available. Level 18 errors are internal nonfatal software errors. The statement that causes the error is allowed to execute to completion. Level 18 errors are not normal and should be reported to the developers of SQL Server.

Levels 19 through 23 are fatal system software errors. They can sometimes leave infected processes and break the connection to the user. Various actions can be taken to rectify the problem. The user, however, may not be able to continue the work from its status prior to the occurrence of the error. Level 19 is a fatal resource error in the Server, from which it cannot recover properly. The normal action is to restart the Server. Level 20 is a fatal software error in the current task, and level 21 is a fatal crror thc affects all the tasks for the database specified. These tasks are represented externally as processes; for example they are represented by SPID (Server process id) in the `sp_who` output. These SPIDs can be terminated by the KILL statement (discussed in the next section).

Levels 22 and 23 indicate that the integrity of the table or database is corrupted or suspect, because of some previous software or hardware problem. The first action is to run the DBCC, and examine its output to determine what objects are affected. In some cases, simply restarting the Server may rectify the problem (if the problem was limited to the cache, for example). In other cases, the object may need to be rebuilt, or the database restored from previous dumps.

Finally, level 24 is a fatal hardware or media failure. The hardware vendor may need to fix or replace the hardware or media. The DBCC should be run after the Server is restarted on all of the Server databases to ensure that they are still intact. Any damaged databases should be restored from previous dumps.

Error messages in SQL Server are returned to the user's terminal, written to the Server errorlog file, or both. Some action is required by the user, DBO, or SA to rectify the problem. Errors with severity levels 10 through 16 that are generated by the user can be corrected by the user. Levels 17 and 18 are reported to the user and should be passed to the SA or DBO. Levels 19 through 24 are written to the Server errorlog. The SA should make it a practice to review the errorlog file periodically for possible errors. The Server maintains the last seven errorlog files; however, a new errorlog file is created only when the Server is restarted. In environments where the Server is not restarted often, the errorlog file should be pruned regularly (maybe once a week), since it keeps growing.

Terminating Processes

In the context of the Server, a process is a task that is initiated and managed by the SQL Server kernel. Tasks are initiated by the Server for several reasons including managing its own resources (buffers, memory, and so on) and individual user connections. Each task has a unique Server process ID (SPID) that identifies it. Information about active processes are stored in the *sysprocesses* system table and can be displayed using the `sp_who` system procedure.

In certain situations it may be necessary to terminate a process. Examples of such situations are an infected process and an interfering user process. The SA can terminate such processes using the KILL statement.

Syntax

```
KILL <spid>
```

The `<spid>` parameter is the process ID for the Server process to be killed. The process ID can be identified with the `sp_who` system procedure. The `sp_lock` system procedure reports on current processes that hold locks. Only the SA has permission to execute the KILL statement; it cannot be transferred. Only user processes can be terminated; processes such as the network handler process or the checkpoint process cannot be terminated; requests to terminate these processes are ignored. The KILL statement is not reversible—the process cannot be reinitiated—therefore, it cannot be used inside a user-defined transaction.

Space and Access Considerations

This section discusses common space and access conditions that are encountered during the administration of the server and possible actions to handle them. Specifically, what do you do when you run out of database space and when a particular user cannot access the Server or a specific database?

Space Considerations

Chapter 10 discussed how space is allocated to databases. The Server does not enable you to monitor space usage at the device level easily. For example, there is no easy way to figure out how much space is unallocated on a device. This information is useful if you want to allocate a new database on the device. However, at the database level, you can always use the `sp_helpdb` and the `sp_spaceused` system procedures to monitor space usage. The first procedure displays how much total space is allocated to the database and what devices they are allocated on; the second shows how the space is used within the database. Example 12-8 shows the results of sp_spaceused for the *pubs* database.

Example 12-8

```
use pubs
<exec>
sp_spaceused
<exec>

OUTPUT:

database_name                  database_size
------------------------------ --------------------
pubs                           2 MB

(0 rows affected)
reserved        data            index_size      unused
--------------- --------------- --------------- ---------------
700 KB          84 KB           42 KB           574 KB

(0 rows affected)
```

By comparing the amount of space reserved versus the database size, you get an idea of the amount of space left over for expansion. The database size indicates the the space allocated for both the data and the log. When the space allocated for either the data or log is exhausted, a level 17 resource error is generated, indicating a database-full condition. Despite this, there may still be unused space for the database or log. The scenarios that follow describe the possible conditions and the steps to use to correct the situation.

There are basically four situations that can cause the database-full condition: when the data and log are on separate devices and the space allocated for (1) the data or (2) log is full, (3) when they share the same device and either the data or log space is full, and (4) when the *master* database is full. The following steps show what to do in each case.

In the first case (separate devices, data space full), the solution is simple. The space for data can be increased by allocating additional space on any available device (including default devices) using the ALTER DATABASE statement.

Step 1: `ALTER DATABASE <database> ON <device>= <size>`

In the second case (separate devices, log full), the procedure is a little more involved. The first step is to dump the log with the `no_log` option (since the log space itself is full). This also clears the log. The next step is a database dump. You then increase the space allocated for the database using the ALTER DATABASE statement, as in case 1, and allocate the additional space to the transaction log using the `sp_logdevice` stored procedure. The steps are:

Step 1: `DUMP TRANSACTION <database> TO <dump_device> WITH NO_LOG`

Step 2: `DUMP DATABASE TO <dump_device>`

Step 3: `ALTER <database> ON <log_device>=<size>`

Step 4: `sp_logdevice <database>, <log_device>`

In the third case (single device) either the data or log space is full. The first step is to dump the log with the `no_log` option. Then additional space is allocated using the ALTER DATABASE statement on the same or a different device. If a different device is used, one option is to move the transaction log for the database to the new device using the `sp_logdevice` procedure.

Step 1: `DUMP TRANSACTION <database> TO <device> WITH NO_LOG`

Step 2: `ALTER DATABASE <database> ON <device>= <size>`

Step 3 (optional): `sp_logdevice <database>, <device>`

The fourth case (*master* database full) is a special version of the first three cases, with the same permutations: separate devices, data space full; separate devices, log space full; single device full. In all cases, the first step is to dump the transaction log with the `no_log` option. The next step is to determine why the *master* database ran out of space (was it the data or log). This can be done using the `sp_spaceused` system procedure. Then you expand the space for the data, the log or both, as appropriate. The last step is required only if the transaction log for the *master* database is on a separate device.

Step 1: `DUMP TRANSACTION master TO <dump_device> WITH NO_LOG`

Step 2: Determine if data or log space is full, or both

Step 3: `ALTER DATABASE master ON <dump_device>= <size>`

Step 4 (log space full): `sp_logdevice master, <dump_device>`

Access Problems

This section looks at problems that concern users accessing the Server and its databases. Problems can exist at the Server level, at the level of the individual databases, or even at the level of access to objects within the database. Each is examined in turn.

There are a few probable causes why a user cannot connect to the Server. One, of course, is that the Server is not started. With such front-end tools as isql or bcp, the Server name, login name, and password are entered first, and only then is the connection made—or not made. The SAF, being more intelligent, senses the presence of SQL Servers on the network and provides a choice of Servers to connect to. It also starts the Server remotely, when it is not already started. Failure to connect is also caused by an incorrect login ID or password. After verifying both, the SA can check them by querying the *syslogins* table.

Once connected to the Server, the user is put in the context of his default database. If one is not defined, the user is put in the *master* database. Often the user may have a valid login ID and password allowing access to the Server, but be denied access to the default database due to oversight on the part of the SA or DBO. In this case, the Server returns an error message indicating that the user has been denied access to the default database. The user is put in the *master* database. The same situation results if the user tries to use the database with the USE <database> statement. In such situations, there are several possibilities for correcting the situation. The SA or DBO may, in fact, have intended to give the user access to the specified database. In this case, the SA or DBO adds the user to the database using the `sp_adduser` system procedure. If the SA or DBO wants the user to access the database only as the guest user, he or she must add the special user guest to the database and define appropriate permissions for it. The SA or DBO can also alias the user's login ID to some user name in the database using the `sp_addalias` stored procedure. Finally, the SA or DBO may, in fact, want to deny access to the database for the particular login ID, in which case the default database for the login ID should be changed appropriately.

Once in the context of a database, a user may still be denied access to a particular database object or part of an object, such as a column. In general, the error message returned indicates the nature of the problem. If the fully qualified form of the referenced object exists, the problem is usually some kind of permission violation, either directly on the referenced object or indirectly on some other object on which the referenced object depends. An example is a view or procedure reference that indirectly references an underlying table. The solution is for the DBO to check the user's permissions and redefine the appropriate permissions for the user or group.

Summary

This chapter provided an overview of the means available to tune the Server's environment at various levels. At the query level are the query processing, exception handling, and application processing options. At the database level are database options and considerations to improve performance. Finally at the Server level are configuration parameters and ways to monitor Server activity. The chapter also covered some basic techniques with which to troubleshoot the Server. It discussed error message severity levels and possible remedial actions. It discussed some space and access problems, their probable causes, and procedures to correct them. The possibilities and variations in the area of tuning and troubleshooting are so large, an entire book could be written on the subject.

System Requirements and SQL Server Limits

System Requirements

Server

Computer:
An IBM PC/AT or IBM PS/2 (or compatible) with an 80286 or 80386 microprocessor running OS/2

RAM:
6Mb memory (RAM)

Disk drives:
30Mb hard disk space, diskette drive(s) for installation and backup

Operating system:
MS OS/2 1.0, 1.1 or 1.2 (standard or adapted version)
IBM OS/2 1.1

MS OS/2 LAN Manager networks:
MS LAN Manager 2.0
3COM 3+Open 1.0
IBM OS/2 LAN Server 1.0
Ungermann-Bass Net/One 1.0
Later versions of the above networks may be usable.

SQL Server 1.0 or 1.1

Client

Computer:
DOS workstation – An IBM PC or compatible, with a hard disk
OS/2 workstation – An IBM PC/AT or IBM PS/2 (or compatible) with an 80286 or 80386 microprocessor running OS/2

RAM:
DOS workstation – 640Kb
OS/2 workstation – Minimum 2Mb; may be higher depending on OS/2 version

Disk drives:
10Mb hard disk space

Operating system:
DOS workstation – MS-DOS 3.2 or IBM PC-DOS 3.2 (or later)
OS/2 workstation – MS OS/2 1.0 or IBM OS/2 1.0 (or later)

Network software:
DOS workstation – MS LAN Manager DOS workstation
3Com 3+Open MS-DOS Manager
IBM PC LAN Program 1.3
Ungermann-Bass Net/One DOS Manager
OS/2 workstation – 3COM 3+Open 1.0
IBM LAN Server 1.0
Ungermann-Bass Net/One 1.0
MS LAN Manager 2.0

SQL Server Limits

Database:	
Maximum databases per SQL Server	32,767
Maximum database size	limited only by available disk space
Maximum databases spannned by one update	8
Maximum databases opened in one query	16
Maximum tables in a join	16

Tables:	
Tables per database	2 billion
Columns per table	250
Indexes per table	251 (1 clustered)
Rows per table	limited only by available disk space
Columns per composite index	16
Characters per database object name	30

APPENDIX

B

Syntax for TRANSACT-SQL and System Procedures

This appendix provides an alphabetical listing of the syntax for TRANSACT-SQL statements and system procedures. The following conventions are used.

- Uppercase letters are used for TRANSACT-SQL commands, functions, macros, and other portions of syntax that must be typed in exactly as shown.
- Mixed-case words indicate abbreviations for keywords. The uppercase letters show the required portion of the keyword; the lowercase letters show the optional portion (for example, TRANsaction).
- Lowercase is used for the names of database objects (columns, tables, databases, and so on), aliases, data types, filenames, group names, login IDs, database options, and passwords. If the Server is installed as a case-sensitive Server, the items will be case-sensitive.
- Brackets–[ ]–enclose optional items. Type only the information within the brackets, not the brackets themselves.
- Angle brackets–< >–enclose parameter names or argument names that you supply. Type in the information in place of the enclosed parameter or argument name. Note that you cannot use a blank space between words; use quotes to enclose them.
- The vertical rule– | –separates a list of required items. The vertical rule means you must choose one and only one item in the list.
- A comma separates items in a list. The comma means you can choose zero or more items in the list.
- The three-dot ellipsis . . . means that you can repeat the previous item as many times as necessary.
- <exec> executes one or more SQL statements. In SAF you execute statements by pressing Ctrl-E. In the isql program, you execute SQL statements with the go command. <execute> is assumed in most commands. It is shown only when multiple statements must be executed separately.

TRANSACT-SQL Syntax

```
/* text of comment */

ALTER DATABASE <database_name>
   [ON DEFAULT|<database_device> [= <size>] [,<database_device> [= <size>]...]]

ALTER TABLE [[<database>.]<owner>.]<table_name>
ADD <column_name> <data_type> NULL [,<column_name> <data_type> NULL...]

BEGIN
   <statement block>
END

BEGIN TRANsaction [<transaction_name>]

BREAK
   <statement>|<statement_block>

CHECKPOINT

COMMIT TRANsaction [<transaction_name>]

COMPUTE <row_aggregate> (<column_name>) [,<row_aggregate> (<column_name>)...]
   [BY <column_name> [,<column_name>...]]

CONTINUE

CREATE DATABASE <database_name>
   [ON DEFAULT|<database_device> [= <size>] [,<database_device> [= <size>]...]]

CREATE DEFAULT [<owner>.]<default_name>
   AS <constant_expression>

CREATE [UNIQUE] [CLUSTERED|NONCLUSTERED] INDEX <index_name>
   ON [[<database>.]<owner>.]<table_name>. (<column_name> [,<column_name>...])
   [WITH {FILLFACTOR = <x>, IGNORE_DUP_KEY,
      [IGNORE_DUP_ROW|ALLOW_DUP_ROW]}]

CREATE PROCedure [<owner>.]<procedure_name>[<;number>]
      [[(]<@parameter_name> <data_type> [=<default>]
```

```
      [,<@parameter_name> <data_type> [=<default>]...][)]]
   [WITH RECOMPILE]
   AS <SQL_statements>

CREATE RULE [<owner>.]<rule_name>
   AS <boolean_expression>

CREATE TABLE [[<database>.]<owner>.]<table_name>
      (<column_name> <data_type> [NOT NULL|NULL]
      [,<column_name> <data_type> [NOT NULL|NULL]...])

CREATE TRIGGER [<owner>.]<trigger_name>
   ON [<owner>.]<table_name>
   FOR {INSERT|UPDATE|DELETE} [, {INSERT|UPDATE|DELETE}]...
   AS <SQL_statements>|IF UPDATE (<column_name>)
      [AND|OR UPDATE (<column_name>)...]

CREATE VIEW [<owner>.]<view_name> [(<column_name> [,<column_name>...])]
   AS <SELECT_statement>

DBCC
   {CHECKTABLE (<table_name>)|
   CHECKDB [(<database_name>)]|
   CHECKALLOC [(<database_name>)]|
   CHECKCATALOG [(<database_name>)]|
   DBREPAIR (<database_name>, DROPDB)}

DECLARE <@variable_name> <data_type> [,<@variable_name> <data_type>]...

DELETE [FROM] [[<database>.]<owner>.]<table_name>|<view_name>
   [WHERE <search_conditions>]

DELETE [[<database>.]<owner>.]{<table_name>|<view_name>}
   [FROM [[<database>.]<owner>.]<table_name>|<view_name>
      [, [[<database>.]<owner>.]{<table_name>|<view_name>}]...]
   [WHERE <search_conditions>]

DISK INIT
   NAME = <"logical_name"> ,
   PHYSNAME = <"physical_name"> ,
   VDEVNO = <virtual_device_number> ,
   SIZE = <number_of_blocks>
```

```
   [, VSTART = <virtual_address> ,
   CNTRLTYPE = <controller_number>]

DISK REFIT

DISK REINIT
   NAME = <"logical_name"> ,
   PHYSNAME = <"physical_name"> ,
   VDEVNO = <virtual_device_number> ,
   SIZE = <number_of_blocks>
   [, VSTART = <virtual_address> ,
   CNTRLTYPE = <controller_number>]

DROP DATABASE <database_name> [,<database_name>]...

DROP DEFAULT [<owner>.]<default_name> [, [<owner>.]<default_name>]...

DROP INDEX <table_name>.<index_name> [,<table_name>.<index_name>]...

DROP PROCedure <procedure_name> [,<procedure_name>...]

DROP RULE [<owner>.]<rule_name> [, [<owner>.]<rule_name>]...

DROP TABLE [[<database>.]<owner>.]<table_name>
      [, [[<database>.]<owner>.]<table_name> ...]

DROP TRIGGER [<owner>.]<trigger_name> [, [<owner>.]<trigger_name>]...

DROP VIEW [<owner>.]<view_name> [, [<owner>.]<view_name>]...

DUMP DATABASE <database_name>
   TO <dump_device>

DUMP TRANsaction <database_name>
   [TO <dump_device>]
   [WITH TRUNCATE_ONLY]
   [WITH NO_LOG]

[EXECute] [[<database>.]<owner>.]<procedure_name>[<;number>]
   [[<parameter_name> = ] <value> [, [ <parameter_name> = ] <value>]]...
   [WITH RECOMPILE]
```

```
<label:>...GOTO <label>

GRANT {ALL|<permission_list>}
   ON {<table_name> [(<column_list>)]|<view_name> [(<column_list>)]|
      <stored_procedure_name>}
   TO {PUBLIC|<name_list>}

GRANT {ALL|<command_list>}
   TO {PUBLIC|<name_list>}

GROUP BY [ALL] <aggregate-free_expression> [,<aggregate-free_expression>]...
   [HAVING <search_conditions>]

IF <boolean_expression> <statement>
   [ELSE <statement>]

INSERT [INTO] [[<database>.]<owner>.]{<table_name>|<view_name>} [(<column_list>)]
   {VALUES (<constant_expression> [,<constant_expression>]...)|<SELECT_statement>}

KILL <spid>

LOAD DATABASE <database_name>
   FROM <dump_device>

LOAD TRANsaction <database_name>
   FROM <dump_device>

ORDER BY [{<table_name>.|<view_name>.}]{<column_name>|
      <select_list_number>|<expression>} [ASC|DESC]
      [, {[<table_name>.|<view_name>.}]{<column_name>|
<select_list number>|<expression>} [ASC|DESC]]...

PRINT {<"any_ASCII_text">|<local_variable>|<global_variable>}

RAISERROR <number> {<"text_of_message">|<local_variable>}

READTEXT [[<database>.]<owner>.]<table_name>.<column_name>
      <text_pointer> <offset> <size>
  [HOLDLOCK]
```

```
RECONFIGURE [WITH OVERRIDE]

RETURN

REVOKE {ALL|<permission_list>}
   ON {<table_name> [(<column_list>)]|<view_name> [(<column list>)]|
      <stored_procedure_name>}
   FROM {PUBLIC|<name_list>}

REVOKE {ALL|<command_list>}
   FROM {PUBLIC|<name_list>}

ROLLBACK TRANsaction [{<transaction_name>|<savepoint_name>}]

SAVE TRANsaction <savepoint_name>

SELECT [ALL|DISTINCT] <select list>
   [INTO [[<database>.]<owner>.]<table_name>]
   [FROM [[<database>.]<owner>.]{<table_name>|<view_name>} [HOLDLOCK]
      [, [[<database>.]<owner>.]{<table_name>|<view_name>} [HOLDLOCK]]...]
   [WHERE <search_conditions>]
   [GROUP BY [ALL] <aggregate-free_expression> [,<aggregate-free_expression>]...
   [HAVING <search_conditions>]
   [ORDER BY {[[[<database>.]<owner>.]{<table_name>.|<view_name>.}]<column_name>|
      <select_list_number>|<expression>} [ASC|DESC]
      [, {[[[<database>.]<owner>.]{<table_name>.]<view_name>.}]<column_name>|
      <select_list_number>|<expression>} [ASC|DESC]]...]
   [COMPUTE <row_aggregate>(<column_name>) [,<row_aggregate>(<column_name>)]...]
   [BY <column_name> [,<column_name>]...]
   [FOR BROWSE]

SET
   {{ARITHABORT|ARITHIGNORE|
   BACKGROUND|NOCOUNT|NOEXEC|
   OFFSETS <keyword_list>|PARSEONLY|PROCID|
   SHOWPLAN|STATISTICS IO|STATISTICS TIME}
      {ON|OFF|}
   ROWCOUNT <number>|TEXTSIZE <n>}

SETUSER [<"user_name">]

SHUTDOWN [WITH NOWAIT]
```

```
TRUNCATE TABLE [[<database>.]<owner>.]<table_name>

UPDATE [[<database>.]<owner>.]{<table_name>|<view_name>}
   SET [[[<database>.]{<owner>.]<table_name>.|<view_name>.}]
      <column_name1> = {<expression1>|NULL}
      [,<column_name2> = {<expression2>|NULL}]...
   [WHERE <search_condition>]

UPDATE [[<database>.]<owner>.]{<table_name>|<view_name>}
   SET [[[<database>.]<owner>.]{<table_name>.|<view_name>.}]
      <column_name1> = {<expression1>|NULL}
      [,<column_name2> = {<expression2>|NULL}]...(<select_statement>)
   [FROM [[<database>.]<owner>.]{<table_name>|<view_name>}
      [, [[<database>.]<owner>.]{<table_name>|<view_name>}]...]
   [WHERE <search_condition>]

UPDATE STATISTICS [[<database>.]<owner>.]<table_name> [<index_name>]

USE <database_name>

WAITFOR DELAY {<"time">|TIME <"time">|ERROREXIT|PROCESSEXIT}

WHERE <expression><comparison_operator> <expression>
WHERE [NOT] <column_name> [NOT] LIKE <"match_string">
WHERE [NOT] <column_name> IS [NOT] NULL
WHERE <expression> [NOT] BETWEEN <expression> AND <expression>
WHERE <expression> [NOT] IN (<value_list>|<subquery>)
WHERE [NOT] EXISTS (<subquery>)
WHERE <expression> <comparison_operator> ANY|ALL (<subquery>)
WHERE [NOT] <column_name> <join_operator> <column_name>
WHERE <boolean_expression>
WHERE <expression> AND|OR <expression>

WHILE <boolean_expression>
   {<statement>|<statement_block>}

WRITETEXT [[<database>.]<owner>.]<table_name>.<column_name>
      <text_pointer>
   [WITH LOG] <data>
```

System Procedures

```
sp_addalias <login_ID>, <user_name>

sp_addgroup <grpname>
```

```
sp_addlogin <login_ID> [,<passwd> [,<defdb>]]

sp_addtype <type_name>, <phystype>[,<null_type>]

sp_addumpdevice {"DISK"|"DISKETTE"}, <logical_name>, <physical_name>,
   <cntrltype> [, {NOSKIP|SKIP} [,<media_capacity>]]

sp_adduser <login_ID> [,<user_name> [,<grpname>]]

sp_bindefault <defname>, <objname> [, FUTUREONLY]

sp_bindrule <rule_name>, <objname> [, FUTUREONLY]

sp_changedbowner <login_ID>

sp_changegroup <grpname>, <user_name>

sp_commonkey <tabaname>, <tabbname>, <colla>, <collb>
   [,<col2a>, <col2b>,..., <col8a>, <col8b>]

sp_configure [<configname> [,<configvalue>]]

sp_dboption [<dbname>, <optname>, {TRUE|FALSE}]

sp_defaultdb <login_ID>, <defdb>

sp_depends <objname>

sp_diskdefault <database_device>, {DEFAULTON|DEFAULTOFF}

sp_dropalias <login_ID>

sp_dropdevice <logical_name>

sp_dropgroup <grpname>

sp_dropkey <keytype>, <tabname> [,<deptabname>]

sp_droplogin <login_ID>

sp_droptype <type_name>
```

```
sp_dropuser <user_name>

sp_foreignkey <tabname>, <pktabname>, <col1>
   [,<col2>, <col3>,..., <col8>]

sp_help [<objname>]

sp_helpdb [<dbname>]

sp_helpdevice [<logical_name>]

sp_helpgroup [<grpname>]

sp_helpindex <tabname>

sp_helpjoins <objname>, <objname>

sp_helpkey [<objname>]

sp_helprotect <objname> [,<user_name>]

sp_helpsql [<"topic">]

sp_helptext <objname>

sp_helpuser [<user_name>]

sp_lock [<spid1> [,<spid2>]]

sp_logdevice <dbname>, <database_device>

sp_monitor

sp_password <old>, <new> [,<login_ID>]

sp_primarykey <tabname>, <col1> [,<col2>, <col3>,..., <col8>]

sp_rename <objname>, <newname>

sp_renamedb <dbname>, <newname>

sp_spaceused [<objname>]
```

```
sp_unbindefault <objname> [, FUTUREONLY]

sp_unbindrule <objname> [, FUTUREONLY]

sp_who [{<login_ID>|<spid>}]
```

The Pubs Database

Pubs Database–Creation Script

The following isql script creates and populates the sample *pubs* database.

```
/*
** installpubs 46.1 1/9/89
**
** @(#)instpubs.sql     74.1     4/5/89
** Copyright Sybase, Inc., 1986, 1987, 1988, 1989
*/
set nocount on

if exists (select * from master.dbo.sysdatabases
          where name = "pubs")
begin
     drop database pubs
end
go
print 'Creating the "pubs" database'
create database pubs
go
use pubs
go
if exists (select * from master.dbo.sysdatabases
          where name = "pubs")
begin
     execute sp_addtype id, "varchar(11)", "not null"
     execute sp_addtype tid, "varchar(6)", "not null"
end
go
if exists (select * from master.dbo.sysdatabases
          where name = "pubs")
begin
     create table authors
     (au_id id,
     au_lname varchar(40) not null,
     au_fname varchar(20) not null,
     phone char(12),
     address varchar(40) null,
     city varchar(20) null,
```

```
     state char(2) null,
     zip char(5) null,
     contract bit)
end
go
grant select on authors to public
go
if exists (select * from master.dbo.sysdatabases
          where name = "pubs")
begin
     create table publishers
     (pub_id char(4) not null,
     pub_name varchar(40) null,
     city varchar(20) null,
     state char(2) null)
end
go
grant select on publishers to public
go
if exists (select * from master.dbo.sysdatabases
          where name = "pubs")
begin
     create table roysched
     (title_id tid,
     lorange int null,
     hirange int null,
     royalty int null)
end
go
grant select on roysched to public
go
if exists (select * from master.dbo.sysdatabases
          where name = "pubs")
begin
     create table sales
     (stor_id char(4),
     ord_num varchar(20),
     date datetime,
     qty smallint,
     payterms varchar(12),
     title_id tid)
end
```

```
go
grant select on sales to public
go
if exists (select * from master.dbo.sysdatabases
          where name = "pubs")
begin
     create table titleauthor
     (au_id id,
     title_id tid,
     au_ord tinyint null,
     royaltyper int null)
end
go
grant select on titleauthor to public
go
if exists (select * from master.dbo.sysdatabases
          where name = "pubs")
begin
     create table titles
     (title_id tid,
     title varchar(80) not null,
     type char(12),
     pub_id char(4) null,
     price money null,
     advance money null,
     royalty int null,
     ytd_sales int null,
     notes varchar(200) null,
     pubdate datetime)
end
go
grant select on titles to public
go
if exists (select * from master.dbo.sysdatabases
          where name = "pubs")
begin
     create table stores
     (stor_id char(4),
     stor_name varchar(40) null,
     stor_address varchar(40) null,
     city varchar(20) null,
     state char(2) null,
```

```
     zip char(5) null)
end
go
grant select on stores to public
go
if exists (select * from master.dbo.sysdatabases
          where name = "pubs")
begin
     create table discounts
     (discounttype   varchar(40) not null,
     stor_id         char(4) null,
     lowqty          smallint null,
     highqty         smallint null,
     discount        float)
end
go
grant select on discounts to public
go
create unique clustered index pubind
on publishers (pub_id)
go
create unique clustered index auidind
on authors (au_id)
go
create nonclustered index aunmind
on authors (au_lname, au_fname)
go
create unique clustered index titleidind
on titles (title_id)
go
create nonclustered index titleind
on titles (title)
go
create unique clustered index taind
on titleauthor (au_id, title_id)
go
create nonclustered index auidind
on titleauthor (au_id)
go
create nonclustered index titleidind
on titleauthor (title_id)
go
```

```
create nonclustered index titleidind
on sales (title_id)
go
create nonclustered index titleidind
on roysched (title_id)
go
create default typedflt
as "UNDECIDED"
go
sp_bindefault typedflt, "titles.type"
go
create default datedflt
as getdate()
go
sp_bindefault datedflt, "titles.pubdate"
go
create default phonedflt
as "UNKNOWN"
go
sp_bindefault phonedflt, "authors.phone"
go
insert authors
values('409-56-7008', 'Bennet', 'Abraham',
'415 658-9932', '6223 Bateman St.', 'Berkeley', 'CA', '94705', 1)
go
insert authors
values ('213-46-8915', 'Green', 'Marjorie',
'415 986-7020', '309 63rd St. #411', 'Oakland', 'CA', '94618', 1)
go
insert authors
values('238-95-7766', 'Carson', 'Cheryl',
'415 548-7723', '589 Darwin Ln.', 'Berkeley', 'CA', '94705', 1)
go
insert authors
values('998-72-3567', 'Ringer', 'Albert',
'801 826-0752', '67 Seventh Av.', 'Salt Lake City', 'UT', '84152', 1)
go
insert authors
values('899-46-2035', 'Ringer', 'Anne',
'801 826-0752', '67 Seventh Av.', 'Salt Lake City', 'UT', '84152', 1)
go
insert authors
```

```
values('722-51-5454', 'DeFrance', 'Michel',
'219 547-9982', '3 Balding Pl.', 'Gary', 'IN', '46403', 1)
go
insert authors
values('807-91-6654', 'Panteley', 'Sylvia',
'301 946-8853', '1956 Arlington Pl.', 'Rockville', 'MD', '20853', 1)
go
insert authors
values('893-72-1158', 'McBadden', 'Heather',
'707 448-4982', '301 Putnam', 'Vacaville', 'CA', '95688', 0)
go
insert authors
values('724-08-9931', 'Stringer', 'Dirk',
'415 843-2991', '5420 Telegraph Av.', 'Oakland', 'CA', '94609', 0)
go
insert authors
values('274-80-9391', 'Straight', 'Dick',
'415 834-2919', '5420 College Av.', 'Oakland', 'CA', '94609', 1)
go
insert authors
values('756-30-7391', 'Karsen', 'Livia',
'415 534-9219', '5720 McAuley St.', 'Oakland', 'CA', '94609', 1)
go
insert authors
values('724-80-9391', 'MacFeather', 'Stearns',
'415 354-7128', '44 Upland Hts.', 'Oakland', 'CA', '94612', 1)
go
insert authors
values('427-17-2319', 'Dull', 'Ann',
'415 836-7128', '3410 Blonde St.', 'Palo Alto', 'CA', '94301', 1)
go
insert authors
values('672-71-3249', 'Yokomoto', 'Akiko',
'415 935-4228', '3 Silver Ct.', 'Walnut Creek', 'CA', '94595', 1)
go
insert authors
values('267-41-2394', "O'Leary", 'Michael',
'408 286-2428', '22 Cleveland Av. #14', 'San Jose', 'CA', '95128', 1)
go
insert authors
values('472-27-2349', 'Gringlesby', 'Burt',
'707 938-6445', 'PO Box 792', 'Covelo', 'CA', '95428', 3)
```

```
go
insert authors
values('527-72-3246', 'Greene', 'Morningstar',
'615 297-2723', '22 Graybar House Rd.', 'Nashville', 'TN', '37215', 0)
go
insert authors
values('172-32-1176', 'White', 'Johnson',
'408 496-7223', '10932 Bigge Rd.', 'Menlo Park', 'CA', '94025', 1)
go
insert authors
values('712-45-1867', 'del Castillo', 'Innes',
'615 996-8275', '2286 Cram Pl. #86', 'Ann Arbor', 'MI', '48105', 1)
go
insert authors
values('846-92-7186', 'Hunter', 'Sheryl',
'415 836-7128', '3410 Blonde St.', 'Palo Alto', 'CA', '94301', 1)
go
insert authors
values('486-29-1786', 'Locksley', 'Chastity',
'415 585-4620', '18 Broadway Av.', 'San Francisco', 'CA', '94130', 1)
go
insert authors
values('648-92-1872', 'Blotchet-Halls', 'Reginald',
'503 745-6402', '55 Hillsdale Bl.', 'Corvallis', 'OR', '97330', 1)
go
insert authors
values('341-22-1782', 'Smith', 'Meander',
'913 843-0462', '10 Mississippi Dr.', 'Lawrence', 'KS', '66044', 0)
go
insert publishers
values('0736', 'New Age Books', 'Boston', 'MA')
go
insert publishers
values('0877', 'Binnet & Hardley', 'Washington', 'DC')
go
insert publishers
values('1389', 'Algodata Infosystems', 'Berkeley', 'CA')
go
insert roysched
values('BU1032', 0, 5000, 10)
go
insert roysched
```

```
values('BU1032', 5001, 50000, 12)
go
insert roysched
values('PC1035', 0, 2000, 10)
go
insert roysched
values('PC1035', 2001, 3000, 12)
go
insert roysched
values('PC1035', 3001, 4000, 14)
go
insert roysched
values('PC1035', 4001, 10000, 16)
go
insert roysched
values('PC1035', 10001, 50000, 18)
go
insert roysched
values('BU2075', 0, 1000, 10)
go
insert roysched
values('BU2075', 1001, 3000, 12)
go
insert roysched
values('BU2075', 3001, 5000, 14)
go
insert roysched
values('BU2075', 5001, 7000, 16)
go
insert roysched
values('BU2075', 7001, 10000, 18)
go
insert roysched
values('BU2075', 10001, 12000, 20)
go
insert roysched
values('BU2075', 12001, 14000, 22)
go
insert roysched
values('BU2075', 14001, 50000, 24)
go
insert roysched
```

```
values('PS2091', 0, 1000, 10)
go
insert roysched
values('PS2091', 1001, 5000, 12)
go
insert roysched
values('PS2091', 5001, 10000, 14)
go
insert roysched
values('PS2091', 10001, 50000, 16)
go
insert roysched
values('PS2106', 0, 2000, 10)
go
insert roysched
values('PS2106', 2001, 5000, 12)
go
insert roysched
values('PS2106', 5001, 10000, 14)
go
insert roysched
values('PS2106', 10001, 50000, 16)
go
insert roysched
values('MC3021', 0, 1000, 10)
go
insert roysched
values('MC3021', 1001, 2000, 12)
go
insert roysched
values('MC3021', 2001, 4000, 14)
go
insert roysched
values('MC3021', 4001, 6000, 16)
go
insert roysched
values('MC3021', 6001, 8000, 18)
go
insert roysched
values('MC3021', 8001, 10000, 20)
go
insert roysched
```

```
values('MC3021', 10001, 12000, 22)
go
insert roysched
values('MC3021', 12001, 50000, 24)
go
insert roysched
values('TC3218', 0, 2000, 10)
go
insert roysched
values('TC3218', 2001, 4000, 12)
go
insert roysched
values('TC3218', 4001, 6000, 14)
go
insert roysched
values('TC3218', 6001, 8000, 16)
go
insert roysched
values('TC3218', 8001, 10000, 18)
go
insert roysched
values('TC3218', 10001, 12000, 20)
go
insert roysched
values('TC3218', 12001, 14000, 22)
go
insert roysched
values('TC3218', 14001, 50000, 24)
go
insert roysched
values('PC8888', 0, 5000, 10)
go
insert roysched
values('PC8888', 5001, 10000, 12)
go
insert roysched
values('PC8888', 10001, 15000, 14)
go
insert roysched
values('PC8888', 15001, 50000, 16)
go
insert roysched
```

```
values('PS7777', 0, 5000, 10)
go
insert roysched
values('PS7777', 5001, 50000, 12)
go
insert roysched
values('PS3333', 0, 5000, 10)
go
insert roysched
values('PS3333', 5001, 10000, 12)
go
insert roysched
values('PS3333', 10001, 15000, 14)
go
insert roysched
values('PS3333', 15001, 50000, 16)
go
insert roysched
values('BU1111', 0, 4000, 10)
go
insert roysched
values('BU1111', 4001, 8000, 12)
go
insert roysched
values('BU1111', 8001, 10000, 14)
go
insert roysched
values('BU1111', 12001, 16000, 16)
go
insert roysched
values('BU1111', 16001, 20000, 18)
go
insert roysched
values('BU1111', 20001, 24000, 20)
go
insert roysched
values('BU1111', 24001, 28000, 22)
go
insert roysched
values('BU1111', 28001, 50000, 24)
go
insert roysched
```

```
values('MC2222', 0, 2000, 10)
go
insert roysched
values('MC2222', 2001, 4000, 12)
go
insert roysched
values('MC2222', 4001, 8000, 14)
go
insert roysched
values('MC2222', 8001, 12000, 16)
go
insert roysched
values('MC2222', 8001, 12000, 16)
go
insert roysched
values('MC2222', 12001, 20000, 18)
go
insert roysched
values('MC2222', 20001, 50000, 20)
go
insert roysched
values('TC7777', 0, 5000, 10)
go
insert roysched
values('TC7777', 5001, 15000, 12)
go
insert roysched
values('TC7777', 15001, 50000, 14)
go
insert roysched
values('TC4203', 0, 2000, 10)
go
insert roysched
values('TC4203', 2001, 8000, 12)
go
insert roysched
values('TC4203', 8001, 16000, 14)
go
insert roysched
values('TC4203', 16001, 24000, 16)
go
insert roysched
```

```
values('TC4203', 24001, 32000, 18)
go
insert roysched
values('TC4203', 32001, 40000, 20)
go
insert roysched
values('TC4203', 40001, 50000, 22)
go
insert roysched
values('BU7832', 0, 5000, 10)
go
insert roysched
values('BU7832', 5001, 10000, 12)
go
insert roysched
values('BU7832', 10001, 15000, 14)
go
insert roysched
values('BU7832', 15001, 20000, 16)
go
insert roysched
values('BU7832', 20001, 25000, 18)
go
insert roysched
values('BU7832', 25001, 30000, 20)
go
insert roysched
values('BU7832', 30001, 35000, 22)
go
insert roysched
values('BU7832', 35001, 50000, 24)
go
insert roysched
values('PS1372', 0, 10000, 10)
go
insert roysched
values('PS1372', 10001, 20000, 12)
go
insert roysched
values('PS1372', 20001, 30000, 14)
go
insert roysched
```

```
values('PS1372', 30001, 40000, 16)
go
insert roysched
values('PS1372', 40001, 50000, 18)
go
dump transaction pubs to diskdump with truncate_only
go
insert sales
values('7066', 'QA7442.3', '09/13/85', 75, 'On invoice','PS2091')
go
insert sales
values('7067', 'D4482', '09/14/85', 10, 'Net 60','PS2091')
go
insert sales
values('7131', 'N914008', '09/14/85', 20, 'Net 30','PS2091')
go
insert sales
values('7131', 'N914014', '09/14/85', 25, 'Net 30','MC3021')
go
insert sales
values('8042', '423LL922', '09/14/85', 15, 'On invoice','MC3021')
go
insert sales
values('8042', '423LL930', '09/14/85', 10, 'On invoice','BU1032')
go
insert sales
values('6380', '722a', '09/13/85', 3, 'Net 60','PS2091')
go
insert sales
values('6380', '6871', '09/14/85', 5, 'Net 60','BU1032')
go
insert sales
values('8042','P723', '03/11/88', 25, 'Net 30', 'BU1111')
go
insert sales
values('7896','X999', '02/21/88', 35, 'On invoice', 'BU2075')
go
insert sales
values('7896','QQ2299', '10/28/87', 15, 'Net 60', 'BU7832')
go
insert sales
values('7896','TQ456', '12/12/87', 10, 'Net 60', 'MC2222')
```

```
go
insert sales
values('8042','QA879.1', '5/22/87', 30, 'Net 30', 'PC1035')
go
insert sales
values('7066','A2976', '5/24/87', 50, 'Net 30', 'PC8888')
go
insert sales
values('7131','P3087a', '5/29/87', 20, 'Net 60', 'PS1372')
go
insert sales
values('7131','P3087a', '5/29/87', 25, 'Net 60', 'PS2106')
go
insert sales
values('7131','P3087a', '5/29/87', 15, 'Net 60', 'PS3333')
go
insert sales
values('7131','P3087a', '5/29/87', 25, 'Net 60', 'PS7777')
go
insert sales
values('7067','P2121', '6/15/87', 40, 'Net 30', 'TC3218')
go
insert sales
values('7067','P2121', '6/15/87', 20, 'Net 30', 'TC4203')
go
insert sales
values('7067','P2121', '6/15/87', 20, 'Net 30', 'TC7777')
go
insert titleauthor
values('409-56-7008', 'BU1032', 1, 60)
go
insert titleauthor
values('486-29-1786', 'PS7777', 1, 100)
go
insert titleauthor
values('486-29-1786', 'PC9999', 1, 100)
go
insert titleauthor
values('712-45-1867', 'MC2222', 1, 100)
go
insert titleauthor
values('172-32-1176', 'PS3333', 1, 100)
```

```
go
insert titleauthor
values('213-46-8915', 'BU1032', 2, 40)
go
insert titleauthor
values('238-95-7766', 'PC1035', 1, 100)
go
insert titleauthor
values('213-46-8915', 'BU2075', 1, 100)
go
insert titleauthor
values('998-72-3567', 'PS2091', 1, 50)
go
insert titleauthor
values('899-46-2035', 'PS2091', 2, 50)
go
insert titleauthor
values('998-72-3567', 'PS2106', 1, 100)
go
insert titleauthor
values('722-51-5454', 'MC3021', 1, 75)
go
insert titleauthor
values('899-46-2035', 'MC3021', 2, 25)
go
insert titleauthor
values('807-91-6654', 'TC3218', 1, 100)
go
insert titleauthor
values('274-80-9391', 'BU7832', 1, 100)
go
insert titleauthor
values('427-17-2319', 'PC8888', 1, 50)
go
insert titleauthor
values('846-92-7186', 'PC8888', 2, 50)
go
insert titleauthor
values('756-30-7391', 'PS1372', 1, 75)
go
insert titleauthor
values('724-80-9391', 'PS1372', 2, 25)
```

```
go
insert titleauthor
values('724-80-9391', 'BU1111', 1, 60)
go
insert titleauthor
values('267-41-2394', 'BU1111', 2, 40)
go
insert titleauthor
values('672-71-3249', 'TC7777', 1, 40)
go
insert titleauthor
values('267-41-2394', 'TC7777', 2, 30)
go
insert titleauthor
values('472-27-2349', 'TC7777', 3, 30)
go
insert titleauthor
values('648-92-1872', 'TC4203', 1, 100)
go
insert titles
values ('PC8888', 'Secrets of Silicon Valley',
'popular_comp', '1389', $20.00, $8000.00, 10, 4095,
"Muckraking reporting by two courageous women on the world's largest computer
hardware and software manufacturers.",
'06/12/85')
go
insert titles
values ('BU1032', "The Busy Executive's Database Guide",
'business', '1389', $19.99, $5000.00, 10, 4095,
"An overview of available database systems with emphasis on common business
applications.  Illustrated.",
'06/12/85')
go
insert titles
values ('PS7777', 'Emotional Security: A New Algorithm',
'psychology', '0736', $7.99, $4000.00, 10, 3336,
"Protecting yourself and your loved ones from undue emotional stress in the modern
world.  Use of computer and nutritional aids emphasized.",
'06/12/85')
go
insert titles
values ('PS3333', 'Prolonged Data Deprivation: Four Case Studies',
```

```
'psychology', '0736', $19.99, $2000.00, 10, 4072,
'What happens when the data runs dry?  Searching evaluations of information-shortage
effects on heavy users.',
'06/12/85')
go
insert titles
values ('BU1111', 'Cooking with Computers: Surreptitious Balance Sheets',
'business', '1389', $11.95, $5000.00, 10, 3876,
'Helpful hints on how to use your electronic resources to the best advantage.',
'06/09/85')
go
insert titles
values ('MC2222', 'Silicon Valley Gastronomic Treats',
'mod_cook', '0877', $19.99, $0.00, 12, 2032,
'Favorite recipes for quick, easy, and elegant meals, tried and tested by people
who never have time to eat, let alone cook.',
'06/09/85')
go
insert titles
values ('TC7777', 'Sushi, Anyone?',
'trad_cook', '0877', $14.99, $8000.00, 10, 4095,
'Detailed instructions on improving your position in life by learning how to make
authentic Japanese sushi in your spare time.  5-10% increase in number of friends
per recipe reported from beta test.',
'06/12/85')
go
insert titles
values ('TC4203', 'Fifty Years in Buckingham Palace Kitchens',
'trad_cook', '0877', $11.95, $4000.00, 14, 15096,
"More anecdotes from the Queen's favorite cook describing life among English
royalty.  Recipes, techniques, tender vignettes.",
'06/12/85')
go
insert titles
values ('PC1035', 'But Is It User Friendly?',
'popular_comp', '1389', $22.95, $7000.00, 16, 8780,
"A survey of software for the naive user, focusing on the 'friendliness' of each.",
'06/30/85')
go
insert titles
values('BU2075', 'You Can Combat Computer Stress!',
'business', '0736', $2.99, $10125.00, 24, 18722,
```

```
'The latest medical and psychological techniques for living with the electronic
office.  Easy-to-understand explanations.',
'06/30/85')
go
insert titles
values('PS2091', 'Is Anger the Enemy?',
'psychology', '0736', $10.95, $2275.00, 12, 2045,
'Carefully researched study of the effects of strong emotions on the body.
Metabolic charts included.',
'06/15/85')
go
insert titles
values('PS2106', 'Life Without Fear',
'psychology', '0736', $7.00, $6000.00, 10, 111,
'New exercise, meditation, and nutritional techniques that can reduce the shock of
daily interactions. Popular audience.  Sample menus included, exercise video
available separately.',
'10/05/85')
go
insert titles
values('MC3021', 'The Gourmet Microwave',
'mod_cook', '0877', $2.99, $15000.00, 24, 22246,
'Traditional French gourmet recipes adapted for modern microwave cooking.',
'06/18/85')
go
insert titles
values('TC3218',
'Onions, Leeks, and Garlic: Cooking Secrets of the Mediterranean',
'trad_cook', '0877', $20.95, $7000.00, 10, 375,
'Profusely illustrated in color, this makes a wonderful gift book for a
cuisine-oriented friend.',
'10/21/85')
go
insert titles (title_id, title, pub_id)
values('MC3026', 'The Psychology of Computer Cooking', '0877')
go
insert titles
values ('BU7832', 'Straight Talk About Computers',
'business', '1389', $19.99, $5000.00, 10, 4095,
'Annotated analysis of what computers can do for you: a no-hype guide for
the critical user.',
'06/22/85')
```

```
go
insert titles
values('PS1372',
'Computer Phobic and Non-Phobic Individuals: Behavior Variations',
'psychology', '0877', $21.59, $7000.00, 10, 375,
'A must for the specialist, this book examines the difference between those who
hate and fear computers and those who think they are swell.',
'10/21/85')
go
insert titles (title_id, title, type, pub_id, notes)
values('PC9999', 'Net Etiquette', 'popular_comp', '1389',
'A must-read for computer conferencing debutantes!')
go
insert stores
values('7066',"Barnum's",'567 Pasadena Ave.','Tustin','CA','92789')
go
insert stores
values('7067','News & Brews','577 First St.','Los Gatos','CA','96745')
go
insert stores
values('7131','Doc-U-Mat: Quality Laundry and Books','24-
A Avrogado Way','Remulade','WA','98014')
go
insert stores
values('8042','Bookbeat','679 Carson St.','Portland','OR','89076')
go
insert stores
values('6380',"Eric the Read Books",'788 Catamaugus Ave.','Seattle','WA','98056')
go
insert stores
values('7896','Fricative Bookshop','89 Madison St.','Fremont','CA','90019')
go
insert discounts
values('Initial Customer', NULL, NULL, NULL, 10.5)
go
insert discounts
values('Volume Discount', NULL, 100, 1000, 6.7)
go
insert discounts
values('Customer Discount', '8042', NULL, NULL, 5.0)
go
create rule pub_idrule
```

```
as @pub_id in ("1389", "0736", "0877", "1622", "1756")
or @pub_id like "99[0-9][0-9]"
go
sp_bindrule pub_idrule, "publishers.pub_id"
go
create rule ziprule
as @zip like "[0-9][0-9][0-9][0-9][0-9]"
go
sp_bindrule ziprule, "authors.zip"
go
create trigger deltitle
on titles
for delete
as
if (select count(*) from deleted, sales
where sales.title_id = deleted.title_id) >0
begin
     rollback transaction
     print "You can't delete a title with sales."
end
go
create view titleview
as
select title, au_ord, au_lname,
price, ytd_sales, pub_id
from authors, titles, titleauthor
where authors.au_id = titleauthor.au_id
and titles.title_id = titleauthor.title_id
go
create procedure byroyalty @percentage int
as
select au_id from titleauthor
where titleauthor.royaltyper = @percentage
go
grant execute on byroyalty to public
go
create procedure reptq1 as
select pub_id, title_id, price, pubdate
from titles
where price is not null
order by pub_id
compute avg(price) by pub_id
```

```
compute avg(price)
go
grant execute on reptq1 to public
go
create procedure reptq2 as
select type, pub_id, titles.title_id, au_ord,
 Name = substring (au_lname, 1,15),
 ytd_sales
from titles, authors, titleauthor
where titles.title_id = titleauthor.title_id
and authors.au_id = titleauthor.au_id
and pub_id is not null
order by pub_id, type
compute avg(ytd_sales) by pub_id, type
compute avg(ytd_sales) by pub_id
go
grant execute on reptq2 to public
go
create procedure reptq3 @lolimit money, @hilimit money,
@type char(12)
as
select pub_id, type, title_id, price
from titles
where price >@lolimit and price <@hilimit
 and type = @type or type like "%cook%"
order by pub_id, type
compute count(title_id) by pub_id, type
go
grant execute on reptq3 to public
go
grant create procedure to public
go
if exists (select * from master.dbo.sysdatabases
          where name = "pubs")
begin
     execute sp_adduser guest
end
go
if exists (select * from master.dbo.sysdatabases
          where name = "pubs")
begin
     grant all on publishers to guest
```

```
    grant all on titles to guest
    grant all on authors to guest
    grant all on titleauthor to guest
    grant all on sales to guest
    grant all on roysched to guest
    grant all on stores to guest
    grant all on discounts to guest
    grant exec on byroyalty to guest
    grant create table to guest
    grant create view to guest
    grant create rule to guest
    grant create default to guest
    grant create procedure to guest
end
go
use master
go
grant exec on sp_bindefault to guest
grant exec on sp_unbindefault to guest
grant exec on sp_bindrule to guest
grant exec on sp_unbindrule to guest
grant exec on sp_addtype to guest
grant exec on sp_droptype to guest
grant exec on sp_spaceused to guest
grant exec on sp_help to guest
grant exec on sp_helpgroup to guest
grant exec on sp_helpindex to guest
grant exec on sp_helprotect to guest
go
dump transaction pubs to diskdump with truncate_only
go
```

The following additions can be made to the instpubs.sql script that comes with SQL Server to add tables with `text` and `image` data types, and document the primary and foreign keys. These changes are from a future version of the pubs database creation script from SYBASE that is still not available in the OS/2 product.

These statements can be added to the pubs creation script after the definition and granting of SELECT permission on the discounts table. The tables can be populated with `text` and `image` data from OS files.

```
if exists (select * from master.dbo.sysdatabases
          where name = "pubs")
begin
     create table au_pix
     (au_id          char(11) not null,
     pic             image null,
     format_type     char(11) null,
     bytesize        int null,
     pixwidth_hor    char(14) null,
     pixwidth_vert   char(14) null)
end
go
grant select on au_pix to public
go
if exists (select * from master.dbo.sysdatabases
          where name = "pubs")
begin
     create table blurbs
    (au_id          id not null,
     copy            text null)
end
go
grant select on blurbs to public
go
execute sp_primarykey titles, title_id
execute sp_primarykey titleauthor, au_id, title_id
execute sp_primarykey authors, au_id
execute sp_primarykey publishers, pub_id
execute sp_primarykey roysched, title_id
execute sp_primarykey sales, stor_id, title_id, ord_num
execute sp_primarykey stores, stor_id
execute sp_primarykey discounts, discounttype, stor_id
execute sp_primarykey au_pix, au_id
execute sp_primarykey blurbs, title_id
go
execute sp_foreignkey titleauthor, titles, title_id
execute sp_foreignkey titleauthor, authors, au_id
execute sp_foreignkey roysched, titles, title_id
execute sp_foreignkey sales, titles, title_id
execute sp_foreignkey sales, stores, stor_id
execute sp_foreignkey titles, publishers, pub_id
execute sp_foreignkey discounts, stores, stor_id
```

```
execute sp_foreignkey au_pix, authors, au_id
execute sp_foreignkey blurbs, titles, title_id
go
```

The Sample Database *pubs*

The following pages indicate the table structures and the contents of the tables in the *pubs* database. The names of the eight tables are *publishers, authors, titles, titleauthor, sales, stores, discounts* and *roysched.*

The header for each column lists its datatype (including the user-defined data types *id* and *tid*), and its null/not null status. Defaults, rules, triggers, and indexes are noted where they apply.

publishers			
pub_id char(4) not null pub_idrule[1] clust. uniq	pub_name varchar(40) null	city varchar(20) null	state char(2) null
1389	Algodata Infosystems	Berkeley	CA
0736	New Age Books	Boston	MA
0877	Binnet & Hardley	Washington	DC

1. The *pub_idrule* states that the data must be 1389, 0736, 0877, 1622, or 1756, or must match the pattern 99[0-9][0-9].

authors								
au_id id not null clust, uniq	au_lname varchar(40) not null nonclust, composite	au_fname varchar(20) not null	phone char(12) not null UNKNOWN[1]	address varchar(40) null	city varchar(20) null	state char(2) null	zip char(5) null ziprule[2]	contract bit not null
409-56-7008	Bennet	Abraham	415 658-9932	6223 Bateman St.	Berkeley	CA	94705	1
213-46-8915	Green	Marjorie	415 986-7020	309 63rd St. #411	Oakland	CA	94618	1
238-95-7766	Carson	Cheryl	415 548-7723	589 Darwin Ln.	Berkeley	CA	94705	1
998-72-3567	Ringer	Albert	801 826-0752	67 Seventh Av.	Salt Lake City	UT	84152	1
899-46-2035	Ringer	Anne	801 826-0752	67 Seventh Av.	Salt Lake City	UT	84152	1
722-51-5454	DeFrance	Michel	219 547-9982	3 Balding Pl.	Gary	IN	46403	1
807-91-6654	Panteley	Sylvia	301 946-8853	1956 Arlington Dr.	Rockville	MD	20853	1
893-72-1158	McBadden	Heather	707 448-4982	301 Putnam	Vacaville	CA	95688	0
724-08-9931	Stringer	Dirk	415 843-2991	5420 Telegraph Av.	Oakland	CA	94609	0
274-80-9391	Straight	Dick	415 834-2919	5420 College Av.	Oakland	CA	94609	1
756-30-7391	Karsen	Livia	415 534-9219	5720 McAuley St.	Oakland	CA	94609	1
724-80-9391	MacFeather	Stearns	415 354-7128	44 Upland Hts.	Oakland	CA	94612	1
427-17-2319	Dull	Ann	415 836-7128	3410 Blonde St.	Palo Alto	CA	94301	1
672-71-3249	Yokomoto	Akiko	415 935-4228	3 Silver Ct.	Walnut Creek	CA	94595	1
267-41-2394	O'Leary	Michael	408 286-2428	22 Cleveland Av. #14	San Jose	CA	95128	1
472-27-2349	Gringlesby	Burt	707 938-6445	PO Box 792	Covelo	CA	95428	1
527-72-3246	Greene	Morningstar	615 297-2723	22 Graybar House Rd.	Nashville	TN	37215	0
172-32-1176	White	Johnson	408 496-7223	10932 Bigge Rd.	Menlo Park	CA	94025	1
712-45-1867	del Castillo	Innes	615 996-8275	2286 Cram Pl. #86	Ann Arbor	MI	48105	1
846-92-7186	Hunter	Sheryl	415 836-7128	3410 Blonde St.	Palo Alto	CA	94301	1
486-29-1786	Locksley	Chastity	415 585-4620	18 Broadway Av.	San Francisco	CA	94130	1
648-92-1872	Blotchet-Halls	Reginald	503 745-6402	55 Hillsdale Bl.	Corvallis	OR	97330	1
341-22-1782	Smith	Meander	913 843-0462	10 Mississippi Dr.	Lawrence	KS	66044	0

1. The default *UNKNOWN* is inserted if no data are entered.
2. The *ziprule* states that the zip code must match the pattern [0-9][0-9][0-9][0-9][0-9].

titles									
title_id tid not null deltitle[3] clust, uniq	title varchar(80) not null nonclust	type char(12) not null UNDECIDED[1]	pub_id char(4) null	price money null	advance money null	royalty int null	ytd_sales int null	notes varchar(200) null	pubdate datetime not null getdate()[2]
BU1032	The Busy Executive's Database Guide	business	1389	$19.99	$5000.00	10	4095	An overview of available database systems with emphasis on common business applications. Illustrated.	06/12/85
PC1035	But Is It User Friendly?	popular_comp	1389	$22.95	$7000.00	16	8780	A survey of software products for the naive user, focusing on the "friendliness" of each.	06/30/85
BU2075	You Can Combat Computer Stress!	business	0736	$2.99	$10125.00	24	18722	The latest medical and psychological techniques for living with the electronic office. Easy-to-understand explanations.	06/30/85
PS2091	Is Anger the Enemy?	psychology	0736	$10.95	$2275.00	12	2045	Carefully researched study of the effects of strong emotions on the body. Metabolic charts included.	06/15/85
PS2106	Life Without Fear	psychology	0736	$7.00	$6000.00	10	111	New exercise, meditation, and nutritional techniques that can reduce the shock of daily interactions. Popular audience. Sample menus included, exercise video available separately.	10/05/85
MC3021	The Gourmet Microwave	mod_cook	0877	$2.99	$15000.00	24	22246	Traditional French gourmet recipes adapted for modern microwave cooking.	06/18/85

(continued)

1. The default *UNDECIDED* is inserted if no data are entered in the column.
2. The *getdate()* function inserts the current date as the default if no data are entered in the column.
3. The *deltitle* trigger prohibits deleting a title if the *title_id* is listed in the *sales* table.

titles, continued									
title_id tid not null deltitle[3] clust, uniq	title varchar(80) not null nonclust	type char(12) not null UNDECIDED[1]	pub_id char(4) null	price money null	advance money null	royalty int null	ytd_sales int null	notes varchar(200) null	pubdate datetime not null getdate()[2]
TC3218	Onions, Leeks, and Garlic: Cooking Secrets of the Mediterranean	trad_cook	0877	$20.95	$7000.00	10	375	Profusely illustrated in color, this makes a wonderful gift book for a cuisine-oriented friend.	10/21/85
MC3026	The Psychology of Computer Cooking	UNDECIDED	0877	NULL	NULL	NULL	NULL	NULL	07/31/86
PC8888	Secrets of Silicon Valley	popular_comp	1389	$20.00	$8000.00	10	4095	Muckraking reporting by two courageous women on the world's largest computer hardware and software manufacturers.	06/12/85
PS7777	Emotional Security: A New Algorithm	psychology	0736	$7.99	$4000.00	10	3336	Protecting yourself and your loved ones from undue emotional stress in the modern world. Use of computer and nutritional aids emphasized.	06/12/85
PS3333	Prolonged Data Deprivation: Four Case Studies	psychology	0736	$19.99	$2000.00	10	4072	What happens when the data runs dry? Searching evaluations of information-shortage effects on heavy users.	06/12/85
BU1111	Cooking with Computers: Surreptitious Balance Sheets	business	1389	$11.95	$5000.00	10	3876	Helpful hints on how to use your electronic resources to the best advantage.	06/09/85
MC2222	Silicon Valley Gastronomic Treats	mod_cook	0877	$19.99	$0.00	12	2032	Favorite recipes for quick, easy, and elegant meals, tried and tested by people who never have time to eat, let alone cook.	06/09/85

(continued)

1. The default *UNDECIDED* is inserted if no data are entered in the column.
2. The *getdate()* function inserts the current date as the default if no data are entered in the column.
3. The *deltitle* trigger prohibits deleting a title if the *title_id* is listed in the *sales* table.

titles, continued									
title_id tid not null deltitle[3] clust, uniq	title varchar(80) not null nonclust	type char(12) not null UNDECIDED[1]	pub_id char(4) null	price money null	advance money null	royalty int null	ytd_sales int null	notes varchar(200) null	pubdate datetime not null getdate()[2]
TC7777	Sushi, Anyone?	trad_cook	0877	$14.99	$8000.00	10	4095	Detailed instructions on improving your position in life by learning how to make authentic Japanese sushi in your spare time. 5-10% increase in number of friends per recipe reported from beta test.	06/12/85
TC4203	Fifty Years in Buckingham Palace Kitchens	trad_cook	0877	$11.95	$4000.00	14	15096	More anecdotes from the Queen's favorite cook describing life among English royalty. Recipes, techniques, tender vignettes.	06/12/85
BU7832	Straight Talk About Computers	business	1389	$19.99	$5000.00	10	4095	Annotated analysis of what computers can do for you: a no-hype guide for the critical user.	06/22/85
PS1372	Computer Phobic and Non-Phobic Individuals Behavior Variations	psychology	0877	$21.59	$7000.00	10	375	A must for the specialist, this book examines the difference between those who hate and fear computers and those who think they are swell.	10/21/85
PC9999	Net Etiquette	popular_comp	1389	NULL	NULL	NULL	NULL	A must-read for computer conferencing debutantes!	12/31/86

1. The default *UNDECIDED* is inserted if no data are entered in the column.
2. The *getdate()* function inserts the current date as the default if no data are entered in the column.
3. The *deltitle* trigger prohibits deleting a title if the *title_id* is listed in the *sales* table.

titleauthor			
au_id id not null nonclust	title_id tid not null nonclust	au_ord smallint null	royaltyper int null
uniq, nonclust, composite			
409-56-7008	BU1032	1	60
213-46-8915	BU1032	2	40
238-95-7766	PC1035	1	100
213-46-8915	BU2075	1	100
998-72-3567	PS2091	1	50
899-46-2035	PS2091	2	50
998-72-3567	PS2106	1	100
722-51-5454	MC3021	1	75
899-46-2035	MC3021	2	25
807-91-6654	TC3218	1	100
486-29-1786	PS7777	1	100
486-29-1786	PC9999	1	100
712-45-1867	MC2222	1	100
172-32-1176	PS3333	1	100
274-80-9391	BU7832	1	100
427-17-2319	PC8888	1	50
846-92-7186	PC8888	2	50
756-30-7391	PS1372	1	75
724-80-9391	PS1372	2	25
724-80-9391	BU1111	1	60
267-41-2394	BU1111	2	40
672-71-3249	TC7777	1	40
267-41-2394	TC7777	2	30
472-27-2349	TC7777	3	30
648-92-1872	TC4203	1	100

sales					
stor_id char(4) not null	ord_num varchar(20) not null	date datetime not null	qty smallint not null	payterms varchar(12) not null	title_id tid not null nonclust
7066	QA7442.3	09/13/85	75	On invoice	PS2091
7067	D4482	09/14/85	10	Net 60	PS2091
7131	N914008	09/14/85	20	Net 30	PS2091
7131	N914014	09/14/85	25	Net 30	MC3021
8042	423LL922	09/14/85	15	On invoice	MC3021
8042	423LL930	09/14/85	10	On invoice	BU1032
6380	722a	09/13/85	3	Net 60	PS2091
6380	6871	09/14/85	5	Net 60	BU1032
8042	P723	03/11/88	25	Net 30	BU1111
7896	X999	02/21/88	35	On invoice	BU2075
7896	QQ2299	10/28/87	15	Net 60	BU7832
7896	TQ456	12/12/87	10	Net 60	MC2222
8042	QA879.1	05/22/87	30	Net 30	PC1035
7066	A2976	05/24/87	50	Net 30	PC8888
7131	P3087a	05/29/87	20	Net 60	PS1372
7131	P3087a	05/29/87	25	Net 60	PS2106
7131	P3087a	05/29/87	15	Net 60	PS3333
7131	P3087a	05/29/87	25	Net 60	PS7777
7067	P2121	05/15/87	40	Net 30	TC3218
7067	P2121	05/15/87	20	Net 30	TC4203
7067	P2121	05/15/87	20	Net 30	TC7777

stores					
stor_id char(4) not null	stor_name varchar(40) null	stor_address varchar(40) null	city varchar(20) null	state char(2) null	zip char(5) null
7066	Barnum's	567 Pasadena Ave.	Tustin	CA	92789
7067	News & Brews	577 First St.	Los Gatos	CA	96745
7131	Doc-U-Mat: Quality Laundry and Books	24-A Avrogado Way	Remulade	WA	98014
8042	Bookbeat	679 Carson St.	Portland	OR	89076
6380	Eric the Read Books	788 Catamaugus Ave.	Seattle	WA	98056
7896	Fricative Bookshop	89 Madison St.	Fremont	CA	90019

discounts				
discounttype varchar(40) not null	stor_id char(4) null	lowqty smallint null	highqty smallint null	discount float not null
Initial Customer				10.5
Volume Discount		100	1000	6.7
Customer Discount	8042			5

roysched			
title_id tid not null nonclust	lorange int null	hirange int null	royalty int null
BU1032	0	5000	10
BU1032	5001	50000	12
PC1035	0	2000	10
PC1035	2001	3000	12
PC1035	3001	4000	14
PC1035	4001	10000	16
PC1035	10001	50000	18
BU2075	0	1000	10
BU2075	1001	3000	12
BU2075	3001	5000	14
BU2075	5001	7000	16
BU2075	7001	10000	18
BU2075	10001	12000	20
BU2075	12001	14000	22
BU2075	14001	50000	24
PS2091	0	1000	10
PS2091	1001	5000	12
PS2091	5001	10000	14
PS2091	10001	50000	16
PS2106	0	2000	10
PS2106	2001	5000	12
PS2106	5001	10000	14
PS2106	10001	50000	16
MC3021	0	1000	10
MC3021	1001	2000	12
MC3021	2001	4000	14
MC3021	4001	6000	16
MC3021	6001	8000	18
MC3021	8001	10000	20
MC3021	10001	12000	22
MC3021	12001	50000	24
TC3218	0	2000	10
TC3218	2001	4000	12
TC3218	4001	6000	14
TC3218	6001	8000	16
TC3218	8001	10000	18
TC3218	10001	12000	20
TC3218	12001	14000	22
TC3218	14001	50000	24
TC3218	0	2000	10
TC3218	2001	4000	12
TC3218	4001	6000	14
TC3218	6001	8000	16
TC3218	8001	10000	18
TC3218	10001	12000	20
TC3218	12001	14000	22
TC3218	14001	50000	24

(continued)

roysched, continued			
title_id tid not null nonclust	lorange int null	hirange int null	royalty int null
PC8888	0	5000	10
PC8888	5001	10000	12
PC8888	10001	15000	14
PC8888	15001	50000	16
PS7777	0	5000	10
PS7777	5001	50000	12
PS3333	0	5000	10
PS3333	5001	10000	12
PS3333	10001	15000	14
PS3333	15001	50000	16
BU1111	0	4000	10
BU1111	4001	8000	12
BU1111	8001	10000	14
BU1111	12001	16000	16
BU1111	16001	20000	18
BU1111	20001	24000	20
BU1111	24001	28000	22
BU1111	28001	50000	24
MC2222	0	2000	10
MC2222	2001	4000	12
MC2222	4001	8000	14
MC2222	8001	12000	16
MC2222	8001	12000	16
MC2222	12001	20000	18
MC2222	20001	50000	20
TC7777	0	5000	10
TC7777	5001	15000	02
TC7777	15001	50000	14
TC4203	0	2000	10
TC4203	2001	8000	12
TC4203	8001	16000	14
TC4203	16001	24000	16
TC4203	24001	32000	18
TC4203	32001	40000	20
TC4203	40001	50000	22
BU7832	0	5000	10
BU7832	5001	10000	12
BU7832	10001	15000	14
BU7832	15001	20000	16
BU7832	20001	25000	18
BU7832	25001	30000	20
BU7832	30001	35000	22
BU7832	35001	50000	24
PS1372	0	10000	10
PS1372	10001	20000	12
PS1372	20001	30000	14
PS1372	30001	40000	16
PS1372	40001	50000	18

APPENDIX

D

The System Tables

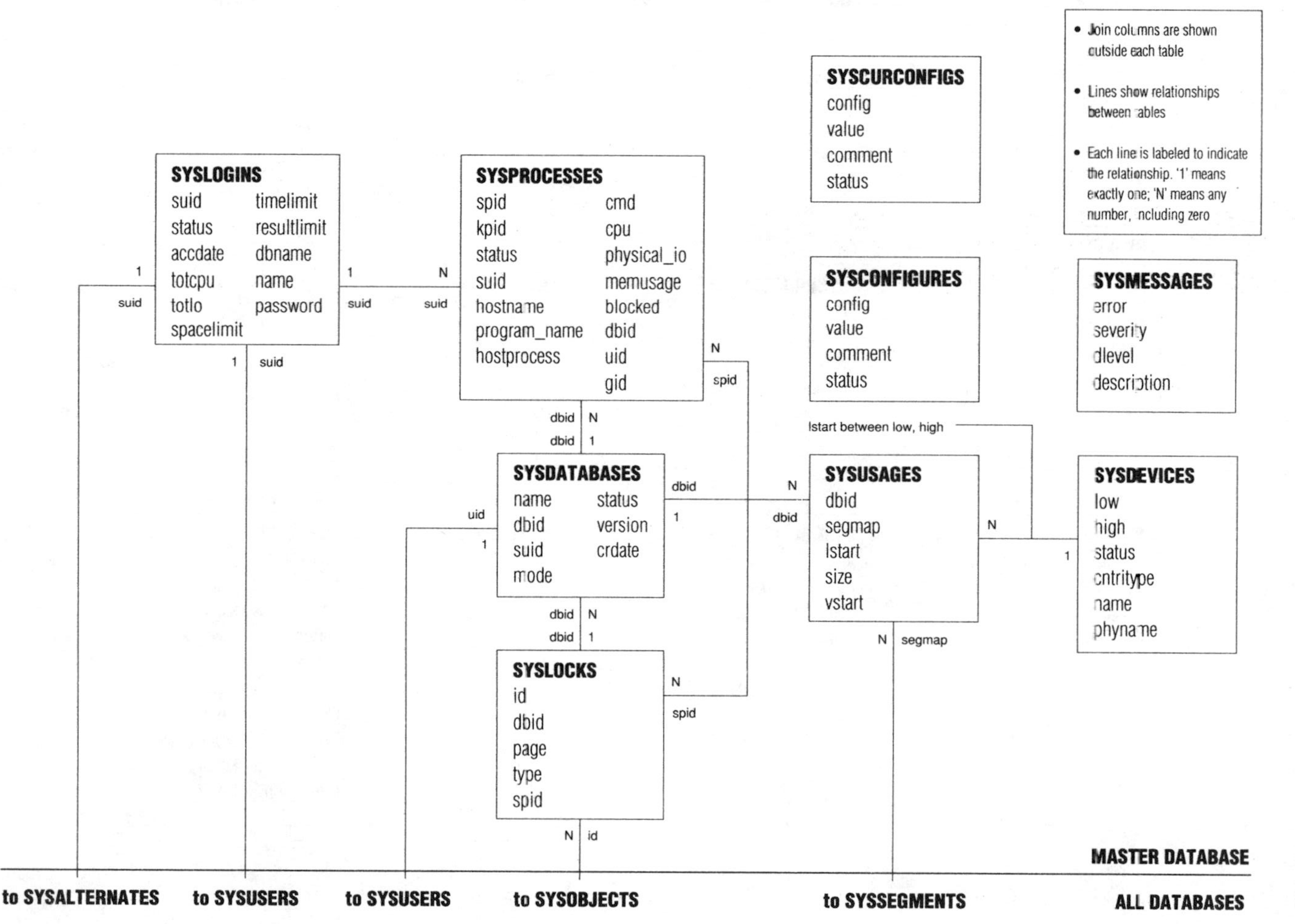
SYSLOGINS
suid timelimit
status resultlimit
accdate dbname
totcpu name
totio password
spacelimit
SYSPROCESSES
spid cmd
kpid cpu
status physical_io
suid memusage
hostname blocked
program_name dbid
hostprocess uid
gid
SYSCURCONFIGS
config
value
comment
status
SYSCONFIGURES
config
value
comment
status
SYSMESSAGES
error
severity
dlevel
description
SYSDATABASES
name status
dbid version
suid crdate
mode
SYSUSAGES
dbid
segmap
lstart
size
vstart
SYSDEVICES
low
high
status
cntrltype
name
phyname
SYSLOCKS
id
dbid
page
type
spid
lstart between low, high
Join columns are shown outside each table
Lines show relationships between tables
Each line is labeled to indicate the relationship. '1' means exactly one; 'N' means any number, including zero
MASTER DATABASE
to SYSALTERNATES
to SYSUSERS
to SYSUSERS
to SYSOBJECTS
to SYSSEGMENTS
ALL DATABASES

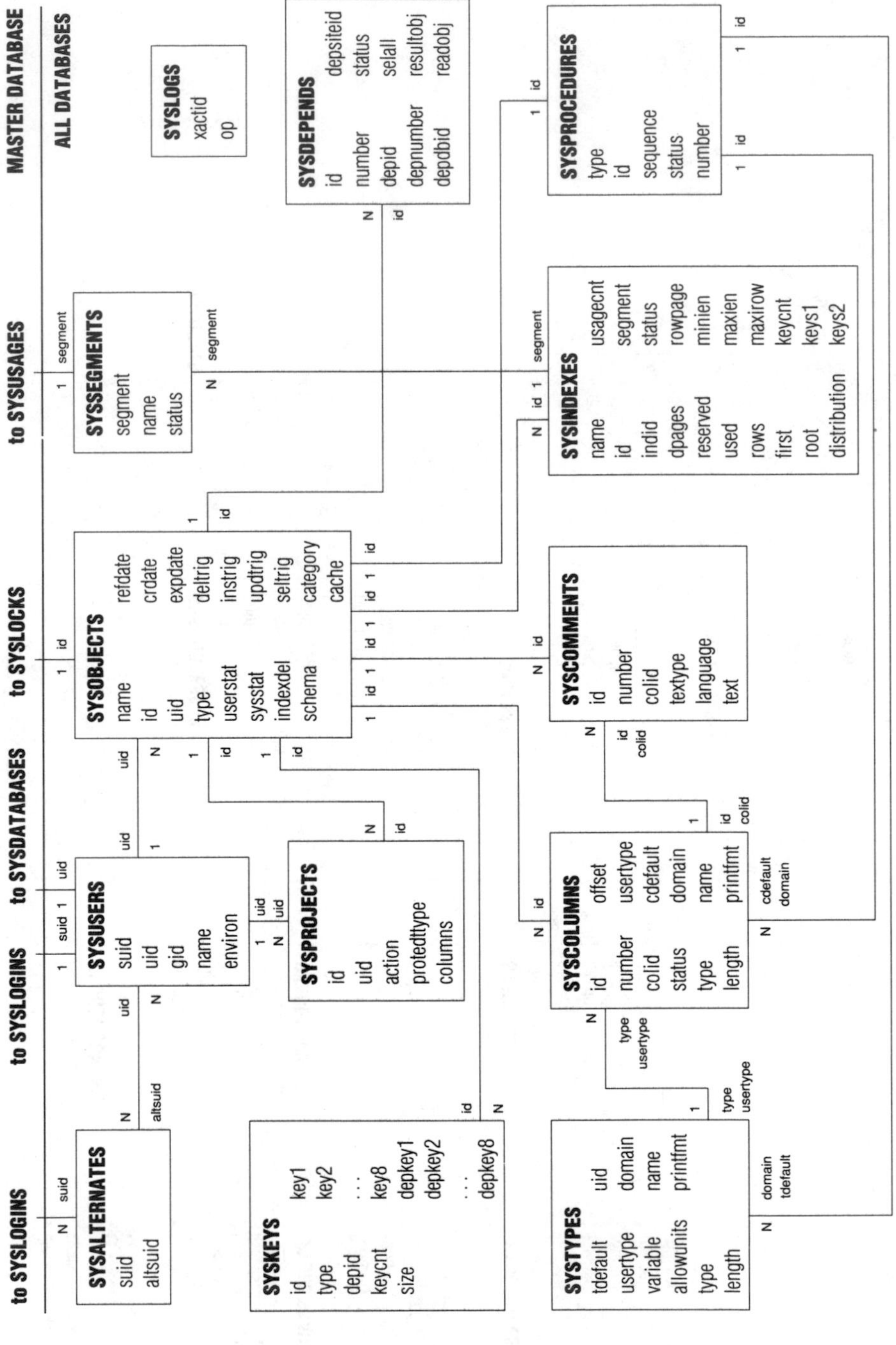

MASTER DATABASE
ALL DATABASES
to SYSLOGINS
to SYSLOGINS
to SYSDATABASES
to SYSLOCKS
to SYSUSAGES
SYSLOGS
xactid
op
SYSDEPENDS
id
number
depid
depnumber
depdbid
depsiteid
status
selall
resultobj
readobj
SYSPROCEDURES
type
id
sequence
status
number
SYSSEGMENTS
segment
name
status
SYSINDEXES
name
id
indid
dpages
reserved
used
rows
first
root
distribution
usagecnt
segment
status
rowpage
minlen
maxlen
maxirow
keycnt
keys1
keys2
SYSOBJECTS
name
id
uid
type
userstat
sysstat
indexdel
schema
refdate
crdate
expdate
deltrig
instrig
updtrig
seltrig
category
cache
SYSCOMMENTS
id
number
colid
textype
language
text
SYSUSERS
suid
uid
gid
name
environ
SYSPROJECTS
id
uid
action
protecttype
columns
SYSCOLUMNS
id
number
colid
status
type
length
offset
usertype
cdefault
domain
name
printfmt
SYSALTERNATES
suid
altsuid
SYSKEYS
id
type
depid
keycnt
size
key1
key2
. . .
key8
depkey1
depkey2
. . .
depkey8
SYSTYPES
tdefault
usertype
variable
allowunits
type
length
uid
domain
name
printfmt

Glossary of Terms

Aggregate functions Functions that generate summary values from a set of values. They are SUM, MIN, MAX, COUNT and AVG, and can be used to generate summary rows or columns.
Alias A mechanism to allow a Server login id to assume the identity of a database user, if the login id is not already defined as a user in the database. The purpose of aliasing is to allow temporary access to databases.
Allocation Page The first page of an allocation unit that describes how the remaining pages within the allocation unit are used. Allocation pages have logical page numbers that are multiples of 256, that is 0, 256, 512, and so on.
Allocation unit The basic unit of disk space allocation for databases. An allocation unit is 256 contiguous pages of disk space (each 2Kb in size), that is, each unit is 0.5Mb in size.
ANSI American National Standards Institute. An organization, based in New York, that is responsible for developing standards for the US.

Applications Programming Interface (API) A programming language interface provided by DBMSs to develop applications programs. See also *Host Language Interface.*
Attributes The properties of entities that identify or describe the entity.
Automatic recovery Recovery from system failures that is performed automatically by the Server as part of starting up. This recovery rolls back all incomplete transactions, and rolls forward all transactions that are complete but not guaranteed to be reflected in the database.
Base Tables The underlying tables on which a view is based.
Batch A sequence of TRANSACT-SQL statements submitted to the Server for execution at one time.
Bridges A network product that enables communication between dissimilar LANs. Bridges usually operate at the network or data link layer.
Browse mode A capability provided by DB-LIBRARY that allows users to retrieve rows derived from several tables, and selectively update columns within it a row at a time.
Cardinality The number of associated entities in a relationship.
Carrier Sense Multiple Access/Collision Detect A LAN protocol in which any node can transmit if it senses that the medium is clear (no transmission is occurring). If any transmitting node senses a collision has occurred (it began transmitting before a previous transmission completed), it immediately stops transmitting and retries a random interval.
Cartesian Product Also called product. A relational operator that operates on two tables and returns all possible combinations of rows from the two tables, i.e., it concatenates the first row from the first table with every row in the second table, the second row in the first table with every row in the second, and so on. If the two tables contain *m* and *n* rows respectively, the product will have *m* x *n* rows.
Cascading deletes Deletes that must be performed on related rows in one table as a result of deletes in another table in order to maintain referential integrity. Implemented in SQL Server through the use of triggers.
Cascading updates Updates that must be performed on related rows in one table as a result of updates in another table in order

to maintain referential integrity. Implemented in SQL Server through the use of triggers.

Checkpointing The process of draining the cache, i.e., causing the database and the log to be synchronized by writing out all the dirty pages to be written to disk.

Client The front-end application that uses the services provided by Server applications.

Client based computing A form of computing on a LAN where most of the application processing is done at the workstation; the server is merely used to handle file requests.

Client server computing A form of LAN computing with a more intelligent division of application processing functions—the server handles all data management and access, whereas the workstation handles all the user interface and application logic.

Clustered indexes An index in which the logical (indexed) order of the key values is the same as the physical order in which the corresponding rows (that contain the key values) exist in the table.

Collision A situation in a CSMA network where two separate messages collide, and neither message is transmitted reliably. A collision occurs when one node begins transmission prior to another node's previously transmitted message reaching its destination.

Compiler The component responsible for generating the executable form of a query.

Complex business integrity The complex integrity rules that stem from regulatory or business policy. Few RDBMSs provide support for enforcing such rules.

Conceptual level The level in a DBMS that is concerned with presenting a logical view of a database for the entire user community.

Control-of-flow language The collective set of TRANSACT-SQL extensions that provide programming language like constructs to control the flow of TRANSACT-SQL statements (IF..ELSE, GOTO, WHILE, etc.), display data (PRINT, RAISERROR), and provide event based processing (WAITFOR).

Controlled access protocols Protocols that use some scheme or algorithm to decide when and for how long a node has access to the transmission medium. Examples are token bus and token ring.

Correlated subqueries A subquery that refers to a table in the outer query and hence cannot be processed independently of the outer query. A correlated subquery is evaluated once for each row in the referenced outer table.

Cursor A language construct that defines the current position within a set of result rows.

Data Facts about places, individuals, objects, events, concepts and so on.

Data sublanguage The set of language constructs within a programming language used to provide database access.

Data type Specifies the kind of data, and the amount of storage required to hold such a column value.

Database A shared, integrated collection of data organized for a specific purpose.

Database catalog The set of system tables in each user database.

Database language The language provided by a DBMS at the external and conceptual levels, for defining and manipulating the objects within a database.

Database model The logical structure used to represent the data at the conceptual or external level of a DBMS.

Database server A DBMS that is based on the client/server architecture, and forms the back end component of the solution.

Database user The name by which a user is known within a particular database. The user name can be different in different databases. The owner of the database is known by the special user name of *dbo.*

DB-LIBRARY The Host Language Interface provided by SQL Server.

DBMS Database Management System. The software that manages the storage and access to the data in the databases.

DBO Database Owner. Database owners have responsibility for all of the objects in their databases.

DDL Data Definition Language. The component of a database language that allows for definition of the database and its objects. It includes statements that allow for the creation, modification and removal of databases and their objects.

Deadlock A situation where two concurrent processes each are waiting for locks on resources held by the other; thus they end up waiting indefinitely. Usually, DBMSs detect and resolve this situation.

Decision support A term used to describe retrieval oriented applications that are used to support decision making.
Default database The database users are connected to when they first log on to the server.
Defaults A database object that bound to a column, causes SQL Server to automatically supply a specified value, if one is not provided explicitly by the user. Defaults, like rules, can be bound to both columns and user-defined data types.
Demand lock A lock request that is granted immediately after all existing shared locks have been released. An exclusive lock is converted to a demand lock after four later shared lock requests have been granted.
Dense indexes An index in which there is an entry for each data row that exists in the table.
Device fragment A contiguous area of a database device that is allocated to a database. Device fragments are tracked in the *master..sysusages* system table. Also referred to as disk pieces.
Dirty Page A page that has been modified since the last checkpoint.
Distributed processing A form of processing that utilizes more than one independent computer system.
DML Data Manipulation Language. The component of the database language allows for manipulation of the data within database objects. It includes statements for insertion, deletion, and update of the data within database objects.
Domain integrity Integrity that enforces column values to adhere to the underlying domain definitions.
Dump device Special devices defined on the Server to which databases and transaction logs can be backed up.
Dumps The process of backing up a database or transaction log onto another device on the same or other media. Dumps are used to recover from media failures.
Embedded Approach An approach to providing a host language interface where the database language statements are embedded in the source program, and indicated by a special character. The source program is processed by a pre-compiler, which translates the statements into appropriate calls to the DBMS run-time interface, and the modified source program is compiled and linked normally.

Entities Any identifiable object or thing of interest. Entities are things about which data are recorded.
Entity integrity An integrity rule that states all primary key columns should not allow null values. Required by the relational model, but not enforced by all RDBMSs.
Equijoin A join that is based on the equality comparison operator.
Errors A term used to refer to errors or messages generated by DB-LIBRARY, the OS, or the network software.
Explicit transaction A sequence of operations that is explicitly defined as a transaction by bracketing it with special statements (to indicate the beginning and end of a transaction).
Extent lock A lock that is acquired for allocation and deallocation of extents (8 contiguous pages) at database or database object creation and destruction, and on the insertion of new data.
External level The level in a DBMS responsible for presenting a subset of the complete conceptual view for an individual user.
File server A type of server whose primary function is to provide shared file storage on a LAN.
Force write The act of causing a dirty page (modified pages) in cache to be written to disk immediately.
Foreign key A column, or set of columns in one table whose values refer to the primary key values of some other table. Foreign keys represent relationships in a relational database, and may be wholly null.
Gateways A network product that allows computers or networks running dissimilar protocols to communicate. Communication is enabled by translating up one protocol stack and down the other. Gateways usually operate at the session layer.
Global variable Pre-defined, system supplied variable that is used to store global server information. Some global variables are maintained by the server on an on-going basis; others can be set by the user to affect server operation. They have names beginning with two @ characters, e.g., @@error.
Groups A mechanism to which a set of database users can be assigned. Every database user belongs to a group (by default, the group PUBLIC). Groups ease the task of assigning permissions to many users.

Groupware Software that is intended for a group of users that share a common task or objective.

Heap A form of physically organizing data, where there is no logical order to the rows (based on some column), rather they are stored in the order they are added to the table. Also termed serial organization.

Hierarchical model A database model wherein entities and relationships are organized into hierarchies. Thus some entities are subordinate to others, e.g., a company has departments, departments have employees, and so on.

Horizontal scalability The ability to add additional servers to the environment to satisfy increased performance or storage requirements, with minimal impact on client applications.

Host Language Interface (HLI) The interface provided for host languages by database management systems. See *Applications Programming Interface.*

Implicit transaction A sequence of operations that is treated as a transaction automatically by the server.

Inconsistent Analysis An update anomaly in multi-user concurrent environments where one user's analysis is based on data retrieved prior to another user's commit.

Indexes A database object that provides efficient access to data in the rows of a table, based on key values. The index is ordered based on key values, and a key can consist of one or more columns.

Integrity constraint A constraint that needs to be enforced to ensure the integrity of the data in the database.

Intent lock A lock that is acquired with the intent of updating a page. The lock can be shared with other shared locks, until it is converted to an exclusive lock for updating the page.

Internal level The level in the DBMS that is concerned with physical storage and access details of a database.

Interprocess communication A high-level mechanism to allow processes on the same or different computers to communicate.

ISO (International Standards Organization) An international body based in Paris that is responsible for developing national and international data communication standards.

Isql A command line, client application provided with SQL Server that allows users to execute TRANSACT-SQL statements

or batches, and view the results returned. isql can also accept input from and direct output to OS files.
Join A relational operator that produces a single table from two tables, based on a comparison of particular column values (join columns) in each of the tables. The result is a table containing rows formed by the concatenation of the rows in the two tables wherever the values of the join columns compare.
Kernel The essential, core component of the Server that handles several functions such as task scheduling, disk caching, locking, and executing of compiled queries.
Key attributes An attribute (or set of attributes) that uniquely identifies the entity.
Library Approach An approach to providing a host language interface where the database interface consists of a special library of functions or procedures. The source program includes calls to these functions and procedures directly, and is compiled and linked just like any other program.
Livelock A situation in which the granting of new shared locks prevents a request for an exclusive lock from being granted. Also known as write starvation.
Loading The process of restoring a database using backups of the database and transaction log. Loading is the complementary process to dumping.
Local Area Network (LAN) A network that enables data communication within a small geographical area.
Local variable A variable declared with the DECLARE statement and assigned a value with the SELECT statement. Local variables have names that begin with the single @ character, e.g., @count.
Locking A mechanism to prevent multiple concurrent user updates from interfering with one another, i.e., of avoiding any of the update anomalies.
Logical database device A contiguous area of disk that is preallocated and known to the Server by a logical name. All space for data and transaction logs in databases is allocated from database devices.
Logical topology Describes how messages flow within the network, i.e., what scheme is used to get the messages from one node

to another. Some logical topologies include token passing, time slots or carrier sense multiple access.

Lost Update A update anomaly in multi-user concurrent environments where one user's update overwrites another user's update, thus causing it to be lost.

Messages A term used to refer to errors or messages generated by SQL Server.

Metadata Data about data. Typically used to describe data that is contained in the data dictionary of a system.

Metadatabase A database of metadata. Synonymous with data dictionary.

Modified comparison operators Comparison operators used to introduce subqueries that are modified by the keywords ANY or ALL, e.g., > ALL.

Natural join An equijoin in which one of the two columns used in the join is deleted from the result table.

Nested Query See *subquery.*

Network Operating System (NOS) Software that resides on one or more servers that provides network services such as file and peripheral sharing, security, inter-process communication, and so on.

Non-clustered indexes An index in which the logical order of the key values is different from the physical order in which the corresponding rows (that contain the key values) exist in the table.

Non-dense indexes An index that has an entry for each data page that exists in the table. Only clustered indexes can be non-dense, since the physical rows are in the same order as the index.

Null An inapplicable or unknown value, that is distinct from any value in a domain. Null values are indicated by the keyword NULL.

Object owner The owner of the object; normally the creator of the object is its owner.

Object permission Defines the operations a database user can perform on the data within a database object. This typically means which DML statements are allowed on the object—INSERT, UPDATE or DELETE for tables and views, and EXECUTE for stored procedures.

On-line transaction processing (OLTP) An environment characterized by multiple on-line concurrent and update intensive applications. This is different from decision support environments, where applications mostly retrieve database information.

Open Systems Interconnect (OSI) A model developed by the International Standards Organization to describe how two different heterogenous systems can communicate over a network.

Optimizer The component in the DBMS responsible for generating the optimum execution plan for a query.

Outer join A join that includes all non-matching rows from one of the join tables in the result table.

Outer Query A DML statement (including a subquery) that contains a subquery.

Owner See *Object owner.*

Ownership chain The chain of database object owners in a dependent object hierarchy.

Page A logical, contiguous area of disk or memory that is read from or written to disk. Pages are two kilobytes (2K) in size, and hold data, log, or code pages.

Parser The component of a DBMS that is responsible for verifying the syntactic and semantic correctness of a query, and generating a processed form of the query that is decomposed into simpler functions.

Password The password associated with a login id.

Permanent table A table that exists on the Server until it is explicitly dropped by a user.

Physical data independence When a change in physical structure or access methods does not affect the logical structure of the data.

Physical locking Locking that is performed at the level of pages (a physical unit), rather than at the level of rows (a logical unit).

Physical topology Describes the physical configuration of the connected devices, i.e., the how the actual wires or cables are connected. Common physical topologies include bus, star, and ring.

Primary key A column or set of columns in a table, whose values uniquely identify the rows in a table. Primary keys must not allow null values.

Procedure groups A group of related procedures. The procedures within the group follow a naming convention: they all have the same group name prefix, followed by a semicolon, followed by a unique integer within the group name, e.g., sales;1, sales;2 and so on. All the procedures in a group can be dropped with a single DROP PROCEDURE statement.

Project A relational operator which returns the specified subset of columns of a table, but all of its rows.

Protocol A specification that describes the rules and procedures that two heterogenous devices should follow in order to communicate with one another, or perform network related tasks. Protocols exist at many different layers of the OSI model.

Protocol software The actual implementation of a specific protocol in software. Depending on the layer at which the protocol is defined, the software may embody several OSI layers. Hence, it is often referred to as a protocol stack.

Qualification The optional process of making object name references unique by prefixing it the object owner name or the database name. For example, if we were referring to the sales table owned by joe in the empdb database, we could qualify the table name as joe.sales or empdb.joe.sales.

Query language A stand-alone language provided by the DBMS for definition and manipulation of database objects. The term query language comes from the fact that it is often used for ad-hoc querying of databases.

Query optimizer See *optimizer.*

Query variable A basic construct in relational calculus. It is a variable that ranges over the rows in a table.

Random access protocols Protocols in which nodes attempt to access the transmission medium randomly whenever they wish to transmit, i.e., there is no scheme to decide when and if the node should access the medium. An example is Carrier Sense Multiple Access with Collision Detect (Ethernet).

RDBMS Relational Database Management System. A DBMS that is based on the relational model.

Recovery interval The maximum time (in minutes) that it will take to recover a Server database at system startup.

Referential integrity An integrity rule that states that all foreign key values must either refer to a matching primary key value, or be wholly null.

Relation The formal term for a *table.*

Relational completeness A term used to describe expressive power of a relational database language. A language is relationally complete if it is at least as powerful as relational calculus. Intuitively it means that if information is derivable from the tables, a query can be formulated to retrieve the information.

Relationships An association between two or more entities.

Remote procedure call The invocation of a stored procedure on a remote server from a procedure on another server.

Repeatable read consistency When a column value retrieved multiple times within a transaction yields the same value every time.

Restrict A relational operator which returns a subset of the rows of a table that match a specified condition.

Rules A database object that bound to a column, serves to further constrain (beyond its data type) the legal values a column can assume. Rules can be bound to either columns or user-defined types. If bound to a user-defined data type, all columns of the user-defined data type inherit the rule.

SA System Administrator. The individual(s) responsible for administration of the entire server environment. The SA inherits special privileges in order to carry out his responsibility, and is the owner of the Master database.

Savepoint An intermediate point within a user-defined transaction to which a transaction can be rolled back. Useful for lengthy transactions.

Scalability The ability to smoothly migrate a solution to additional or different operating environments as needed, primarily for performance reasons. See also *horizontal scalability* and *vertical scalability.*

Segment A named collection of disk pieces. Storage for indexes and tables can be assigned to specific segments.

Self-join A join of a table with itself. In a self join, column values in the same table are compared with one another. The different instances of the same table involved in the self-join have to be aliased to distinguish them, and the column references in the table have to be qualified with the appropriate aliases.

Serial consistency When a sequence of data page reads yields a consistent set of data values. This may be important for certain aggregate operations where the data pages are read in sequence.

Server A computer that makes file, print or communication services available to other computers on a LAN.

Server Administration Facility (SAF) A window-oriented, menu driven client application provided with SQL Server, that is intended primarily for Server administration.

Server login ID A name assigned to a user for identification when logging on to a server. The special login id of sa identifies the System Administrator.

Shared processing A form of processing in which several users share the same CPU. User processes are allocated CPU time slices, thus allowing multiple users to be supported.

Single process, multi-threaded A database architecture which consists of a single process, with internal threads (or tasks) to manage multiple concurrent users. This is different from multi-process architectures which use a separate process to manage users.

SQL Structured Query Language, a data sublanguage for relational database management systems that was originally developed by IBM. SQL includes data definition, data manipulation, and data control statements. There have been several commercial implementations of SQL, and most vendors comply with one or the other standard SQL specification–ANSI and IBM SAA.

Statement block A sequence of TRANSACT-SQL statements enclosed within a BEGIN and END statement that is treated as a single unit.

Statement permission Defines which TRANSACT-SQL statements a database user can execute within the database. They are typically data definition statements, e.g., the CREATE TABLE statement.

Stored procedures A named, pre-compiled sequence of TRANSACT-SQL statements. Once defined, the stored procedure can be executed by name. Stored procedures can also take parameters and invoke other stored procedures.

Subquery A query that is nested within another SELECT, INSERT, UPDATE, or DELETE statement, or another subquery. Also referred to as a nested query.

System catalog The set of system tables in the Master database.

System data types The set of data types that are predefined and supplied by SQL Server. There are fourteen data types supported by SQL Server: char, varchar, binary, varbinary, tinyint, smallint, int, float, bit, datetime, money, text, image, and timestamp.

System databases Databases that are created as part of installing the server. They include the Master, Model, and Tempdb.
System procedures Stored procedures that are predefined and created as part of installation. They provide several functions—data definition, data administration, and retrieval of information from the catalogs.
System tables Special, pre-defined tables in each database used to track information about the server as a whole, and user data within the databases.
Target The list of columns returned in a relational calculus based query.
Temporary table A table that exists only for the life of the current session. Temporary tables are created in *tempdb*.
Tick A unit for counting time. In OS/2, a tick is 31.25 milliseconds.
Token Bus A LAN protocol in which access to the medium is regulated by passing a token between all the connected nodes in some logical sequence. While a node possesses the token, it can transmit or receive messages for a pre-established time period.
Token Ring A LAN protocol in which nodes are connected in a ring, and a token (in a free state) circulates around the ring to control access to the medium. When a node wishes to transmit, it seizes the token, marks it as busy, and begins transmission. When the transmission is complete, the token is returned to its free state, and any other node can transmit.
Topology The configuration in which the communicating devices of a network are connected.
TRANSACT-SQL The enhanced version of SQL provided by SQL Server. TRANSACT-SQL is a superset of ANSI SQL, and provides both additional and enhanced SQL statements. All communication between client applications and SQL Server are in TRANSACT-SQL.
Transaction A sequence of operations (database or otherwise) integral with respect to consistency and recovery, i.e., it is either completed in its entirety or not at all.
Transaction log A reserved area of the database in which a log of all changes to the database is recorded. The transaction log is really a system table; the syslogs table is used to provide recovery.

Transaction processing The means by which consistency and recovery with respect to transactions is provided in a DBMS environment.

Transaction Rollback A process performed during automatic recovery that undoes changes to a database caused by incomplete transactions.

Transaction Rollforward A process performed during automatic recovery that reapplies all transactions that were committed but not guaranteed to be written to the database.

Triggers A special kind of stored procedure that is automatically invoked whenever a specified update event (INSERT, UPDATE, or DELETE) is performed on a table. Triggers are used to enforce referential integrity and complex business integrity rules.

Two-Phase Commit Protocol A protocol used to guarantee the integrity of a distributed transaction (across multiple servers). It has two phases—first, all the servers prepare to commit or rollback, and second, they actually perform the commit or rollback. Hence the name two-phase commit.

Uncommitted dependency A update anomaly in concurrent, multiuser environments where one user bases processing on another user's uncommitted update. Hence the first user's processing has an uncommitted dependency.

User databases Databases created by users using the CREATE DATABASE statement.

User-defined data types Data types defined by the user based on system data types using the sp_addtype system procedure. User-defined data types can include a null specification and have rules and defaults bound to it.

User-defined transaction Same as an explicit transaction. See *explicit transaction.*

Vertical scalability The ability to migrate an existing server environment to a more powerful server environment, with minimal impact on the client applications.

View resolution The process of resolving references to view columns into references to underlying base tables. The process also ensures that the definitions of the underlying tables has not changed.

Views A derived table that is defined on one or more underlying base tables. Views do not actually contain data, but provide a window to a subset of the data in the base tables.

Wide Area Network (WAN) A network that enables data communication over long distances.

Wildcard characters Characters that have special meaning when used in pattern-matching strings with the LIKE keyword. They include the underscore (_) character, the percent (%) character, and the open and close square bracket characters ([,]).

Workstation Any computer on a LAN that uses the services provided by Server computers.

Write-ahead log A transaction logging method in which the log is always written prior to the data.

Bibliography

Codd, E.F., "A relational model of data for large shared data banks", *Comm. of ACM,* 13, 6 (June 1970), pp. 377–397.

"Is Your DBMS Really Relational," *Computerworld,* October 14, 1985, pp. 1–9.

Chamberlain, D.D., Relational Data-Base Management Systems. *ACM Computing Surveys,* Volume 8, Number 1, March 1976, pp. 43–66.

Date, C., *An Introduction to Database System,* Volume I (Fourth Edition). Addison-Wesley Publishing Company, Reading, MA. 1986.

An Introduction to Database System, Volume II. Addison-Wesley Publishing Company, Reading, MA. 1983.

Relational Database: Selected Writings. Addison-Wesley Publishing Company, Reading, MA. 1986.

Emerson, S., Darnovsky, M., and Bowman, J., *The Practical SQL Handbook,* Addison-Wesley Publishing Company, Reading, MA. 1989.

Microsoft SQL Server (Version 1.1) Product Documentation.

SQL Server Getting Started

Learning TRANSACT-SQL

SQL Server Language Reference

SQL Server Administrator's Guide

SQL Server Programmers Reference

Microsoft OS/2 LAN Manager (Version 1.0) Product Documentation.

User's Manual for OS/2 Systems

Administrator's Manual for OS/2 Systems

Programmer's Reference

Microsoft Technical Documentation.

MS OS/2 LAN Manager White Paper, 1989.

Novell Advanced Netware (Version 2.15) Product Documentation.

Advanced Netware System Guide

Advanced Netware User's Guide

Novell Technical Documentation.

Advanced Netware, Theory of Operations (Version 2.1) Technical Document, June 1987.

Communicating in the Netware Environment: An In-depth look at Novell Communication Options.

Stallings, W., *Local Networks: An Introduction,* Macmillan, New York. 1984.

Local Networks, ACM Computing Surveys, Volume 16, Number 1, March 1984, pp. 3–41.

Sybase SQL Server (Release 4.0) Product Documentation.

TRANSACT-SQL User's Guide

Commands Reference

System Administrator's Guide

DB-LIBRARY Reference Manual.

Tanembaum, A., *An Introduction to Computer Networks.* Prentice Hall, Englewood Cliffs, New Jersey.

Van Name, M.L. and Catchings, W., "The LAN Road to OSI," *Byte Magazine,* July 1989, pp. 148–152.

Index